Inventing the Psychological

Inventing the Psychological

Toward a Cultural History of

Emotional Life in America

Edited by **Joel Pfister** and **Nancy Schnog**

Yale University Press   New Haven and London

"Oedipus and America: Historical Perspectives on the Reception of Psychoanalysis in
the United States," by John Demos, was previously published in *Annual of Psychoanalysis* 6 (1978): 23–39. Reprinted by permission
of International Universities Press, Inc.
An earlier version of "Epistemology of the
Bunker," by Catherine Lutz, was published
in *Public Culture* 9:2 (1997), Winter. ©1997
by The University of Chicago. All rights
reserved.

Designed by James J. Johnson and
set in Meridien Roman with Frutiger types
by The Marathon Group, Inc., Durham,
North Carolina.
Printed in the United States of America by
BookCrafters, Inc., Chelsea, Michigan.

*Library of Congress Cataloging-in-
Publication Data*

Inventing the Psychological : toward a cultural history of emotional life in America /
edited by Joel Pfister and Nancy Schnog.
    p. cm.
Includes bibliographical references and index.
ISBN 0-300-06809-3 (cloth : alk. paper)
ISBN 0-300-07006-3 (pbk. : alk. paper)
1. Psychology—United States—History.
2. Social psychology—United States—
History.   3. Psychoanalysis and culture.
4. Psychology and the humanities—United
States.   I. Pfister, Joel.   II. Schnog, Nancy.
BF108.U5I58   1997
150'.973—dc20   96-23275

A catalogue record for this book is available
from the British Library.

The paper in this book meets the guidelines
for permanence and durability of the Committee on Production Guidelines for Book
Longevity of the Council on Library
Resources.

10 9 8 7 6 5 4 3 2 1

For Redmond, Jeremy, and Christopher

&

Eytan and Emily

Contents

Acknowledgments

We thank the many colleagues and friends who gave generously of their time during the years of this volume's creation, especially our contributors, who were as lovely to work with as their writings were provocative to read. We are indebted to Judy Metro, senior editor at Yale University Press, who encouraged this project from the outset, gave us sagacious advice during all of its phases, and brought the manuscript swiftly through production. David Lubin, a true friend, made our diverse challenges more manageable with his enthusiastic support, suggestions, and good humor at just about every stage of the book's development. John Demos was one of the first contributors to sign on, and we're so glad he did. We thank him and his wife, Virginia, the distinguished psychologist, for their hospitality one languid July afternoon outside Boston, when we exchanged thoughts about the possibilities of a cultural history of emotional life. We launched some of our ideas (with Franny Nudelman) at the 1992 American Studies Association convention and were fortunate to have Karen Halttunen there as chair and commentator. She was smart, sympathetic, and funny, and her comments helped give us a flying start.

We are also beholden to a mutual friend and former teacher, Bryan Wolf, who, in addition to igniting our imaginations with his own insights into the history of subjectivity and perception, a decade ago formally introduced us and advised us to investigate one another's work. Richard Brodhead's subtle thoughts on the literary and cultural history of domestic discourse and his unswerving interest in our collaboration have always been a boon. Laura Wexler and Thomas J. Ferraro shared their ideas with us about the book in its formative phase. We are delighted that Leonard Tennenhouse intervened at an early moment of our planning to persuade us to take on the more ambitious scope of a cultural history of psychological and emotional life in America. Noreen O'Connor, our manuscript editor at Yale University Press, was both rigorous and creative.

JP: More individuals than I can thank here are responsible for my commitment to co-inventing *Inventing*. I am especially fortunate to have worked with Alan Trachtenberg, not only in his capacity as my teacher, years ago, but as series editor of my most recent book. From Alan I learned much about editing and about how one might grasp historically the ideological uses to which psychological discourses were put in forming class identities in the twentieth century. I trace my fascination with situating emotional life in American history, not only to my experiences studying and then teaching at Yale, but even before, to my early graduate work in American studies with the late Eric Mottram at the University of London. And the year before that I had received my first glimmer of what a cultural studies history of interiority might look like from Peter Stallybrass at the University of Sussex. I remain grateful to Fredric Jameson for his intellectually adventurous teaching at Yale and for his magnanimous encouragement of my early historical work on Sigmund Freud and Wilhelm Reich in Vienna and on the formation of nineteenth-century American personal life. Four old friends—Sarah Winter, Richard Lowry, Reva Siegel, and Nancy Schnog—read and improved drafts of my chapters for this book. Sarah Winter was especially considerate in sharing her knowledge of the work of Pierre Bourdieu with me. I have gained critical perspective as well as great enjoyment from delivering talks and fielding questions on some of this material at the University of Sussex, the University of London, the University of York, the 1992 American Studies Association convention, Middlebury College, Columbia University, the College of William and Mary, the 1994 MLA Hawthorne Society conference, Yale University, and Willamette University.

Wesleyan colleagues Indira Karamcheti, Jill Morawski, Rishona Zimring, and Henry Abelove gave me bibliographic information and/or ideas that were useful. My debt to three other Wesleyan colleagues is more general but very deep for their smart critical feedback and steady support of this book—Richard Slotkin, Richard Ohmann, and Khachig Tölölyan. The Wesleyan administration did much to make my role in this project possible by allowing me to take a leave that followed my sabbatical, by allocating research funds, and for underwriting some of the final publication expenses. The skilled librarians at Yale and Wesleyan made my life a lot easier. In particular I should like to thank Patricia Willis, curator of American literature and photographs at the Beinecke Rare Book and Manuscript Library at Yale.

Several former Wesleyan students who were also my talented teaching assistants were exceedingly gracious in listening to and commenting on my interminable talk about the project: Claire Weinraub, Polly Meyers, Samera Syeda, Jonathan Fineman, Kate Gordon, and Adrienne Truscott. I'm lucky that two other friends, Wes alums from an earlier group, also chimed in: Joseph Entin offered some bibliographic recommendations as well as a spirited dialogue, and Laurie Woods's conversations with me influenced the critical slant I took in key parts of both of my chapters. Yet again my authorial load has been lightened by the love of my family, and it gives me terrific pleasure to single out in the dedication my vivacious and precocious nephews—Redmond (eight), Jeremy (five), and Christopher (one week) Hill.

NS: I am indebted to many scholars for supporting my work on literature and the history of emotional life. Many years ago the excellent teaching and guidance of Alfred Bendixen at Barnard College helped get me started in this area, while the work of another distinguished teacher, Barbara Sicherman, taught me to pay attention to the historical dimensions of psychological ideas. In 1985 my graduate education was catalyzed by the dynamic teaching of Jane Tompkins. Her compelling readings of texts by nineteenth-century American women and her commitment to research on emotional life have provided an ongoing stimulus for my work. For ten years now Joel Pfister has been a steadfast friend and valued intellectual companion. My work here and elsewhere has profited from his wide-ranging knowledge and editorial acumen. Another longtime friend, Franny Nudelman, eased my labors on this volume considerably by commenting on an early draft of my chapter and by acting as a sounding board for various concerns.

I also owe thanks to the Department of American Literature and Civilization at Middlebury College for providing a supportive (and beautiful) workplace during the period when much of this book was researched and written. This department's climate of intellectual challenge was established in great measure by John McWilliams, and I feel privileged to have benefited so consistently from his strong encouragement of my work in this field. Tim Spears offered important counsel in the book's early stages, shared his editorial skills later on, and gave support in between through his keen interest and ready humor. My colleague Michael Newbury tolerated with abundant kindness my frequent incursions into his office for ideas about relevant scholarship and for conversation at large. During this period two other friends, Holly Allen and Brigitte Szymanek, took a lively interest in the project and its progress.

Much appreciated assistance also came from other quarters of the Middlebury community. Psychologists Marc Riess and Susan Campbell provided me with valuable information concerning methods of psychiatric classification and the development of American academic psychology. Bob Buckeye, the director of Special Collections at Starr Library, aided my research by making available and sharing my interest in the works of Elizabeth Stuart Phelps and Elizabeth Stuart Phelps Ward. Fleur Laslocky made the process of securing primary material through interlibrary loans swift and painless. This book also received generous support from the Middlebury College Faculty Development Fund.

In closing, I want to thank the members of my family, who enlivened my days during this long and demanding project. My husband, Yossi Shain, supported the book through one especially hot summer with his fund of practical advice and his patience for things familial. And it is wonderful to be able to acknowledge in the dedication my two children—Eytan (seven) and Emily (two)—who bring me unaccountable joys.

Contributors

John Demos, Samuel Knight Professor of History at Yale University, is a founder
of the field of American history of family life and has written widely on
colonial America. His books include *A Little Commonwealth: Family Life in
Plymouth Colony* (1970), *Entertaining Satan: Witchcraft and the Culture of Early
New England* (1982), *Past, Present, and Personal: The Family and the Life Course
in American History* (1986), and *The Unredeemed Captive: A Family Story from
Early America* (1994). He is a fellow of the American Academy of Arts and
Sciences.

Richard S. Lowry is associate professor of English and American studies at the
College of William and Mary. He is the author of *"Littery Man": Mark Twain
and Modern Authorship* (1996) and essays on nineteenth-century tourism,
the photography of A. J. Russell, and the culture of boyhood.

David M. Lubin, Gillespie Professor of Art and American Studies at Colby College,
has published *Act of Portrayal: Eakins, Sargent, James* (1985), *Picturing a
Nation: Art and Social Change in Nineteenth-Century America* (1994), and
numerous articles on American art and culture.

Catherine Lutz is professor of anthropology at the University of North Carolina,
Chapel Hill. She is author of *Unnatural Emotions: Everyday Sentiments
on a Micronesian Atoll and Their Challenge to Western Theory* (1988), co-author
(with Jane L. Collins) of *Reading National Geographic* (1993), and co-editor
(with Lila Abu-Lughod) of *Language and the Politics of Emotion* (1990). She
has published many essays on cross-cultural approaches to emotional life.

Jill G. Morawski is professor of psychology and director of women's studies at

Wesleyan University. She has written *Practicing Feminisms, Reconstructing Psychology: Notes on a Liminal Science* (1994) and is the editor of *The Rise of Experimentation in American Psychology* (1988). She has published many articles on the history of American psychology and is a fellow of the American Psychological Association.

Franny Nudelman is assistant professor of English and American studies at Yale University. She has published articles on Harriet Jacobs, Nathaniel Hawthorne, and Toni Morrison and is currently writing a book entitled "'John Brown's Body': The Martyred Soldier and Civil War Nationalism."

Joel Pfister is associate professor of American studies and English at Wesleyan University. He has published *The Production of Personal Life: Class, Gender, and the Psychological in Hawthorne's Fiction* (1991) and *Staging Depth: Eugene O'Neill and the Politics of Psychological Discourse* (1995), as well as articles on British cultural studies and American studies, material culture, and American literature.

Nancy Schnog has taught American literature and civilization at Middlebury College and is a visiting lecturer in the department of English at Tel Aviv University. She has published studies of nineteenth-century literary culture and is revising a book manuscript entitled "Inside the Sentimental: The Psychological Work of Nineteenth-Century American Women's Writing." She is also a book critic for the *Jerusalem Post*.

Robert Walser is associate professor of musicology at the University of California at Los Angeles. He is the author of *Running with the Devil: Power, Gender, and Madness in Heavy Metal Music* (1993) as well as articles on Miles Davis, Prince, Public Enemy, and issues of musical interpretation.

PART I

Introduction

CHAPTER ONE

On Inventing the Psychological

NANCY SCHNOG

What does it mean to invent the psychological? To suggest that the "psychological" is "invented" through cultural history is to reorient the ways that many twentieth-century Americans have been taught to conceive of the self and its interior. The contributors to this volume do not examine psychological theories and ideas for the purpose of extracting insights into timeless human nature. Rather they seek to better understand the reasons why psychological self-definitions ("I'm neurotic"; "I'm suffering from deficiencies in mother-love") and psychological concepts (nervousness, ambivalence, the unconscious, the Oedipus complex) gain cultural authority and lose explanatory power at particular historical moments. In order to address these concerns, *Inventing the Psychological* gathers together multidisciplinary perspectives on the formation of psychological belief and inner experience in nineteenth- and twentieth-century America.

In a departure from many studies of America's therapeutic culture, our project investigates how areas of cultural life not typically associated with the production of psychological knowledge—economics, politics, mass media, and the arts—play key roles in helping to create and disseminate professional and popular languages of interior life. Moreover, this book extends the meaning of the "psychological" in ways that may seem unfamiliar to readers. Here the term is used to encompass the public life of the psychological disciplines (in research institutions, intellectual traditions, social policy, and popular culture), as well as changing cultural visions of the psychological interior (as the soul, as the primitive underside of selfhood, as the nesting ground for the inner child) that come to be felt by people as self-created. Contributors examine psychology's myriad shapes as an academic discipline, a healing industry, a repository of variable ideas about and metaphors of the emotions, a class ideology, and a form of popular entertainment (movies, books, and dramas about the psychological character of people and relationships). Just as important, they approach the "psychological" as an intrapsychic experience that takes on meaning for the self through the cultural practices which endow it with form, value, and significance.

In highlighting the power of culture not simply to discover emotional truths but to create them, our contributors challenge conceptions of innerness that have prevailed in academic circles and popular culture for much of the twentieth century. Since at least the 1920s middle-class Americans have been educated into understandings of self and psyche shaped by mainstream concepts of psychoanalytic thought. While several contributors elaborate the potentially unsettling meanings of this tradition for American minority groups, it is important to clarify the settled meanings—the popular ideas and assumptions—that have informed visions of the psychological interior over the past fifty years. Although multifaceted and perennially rescripted, the mid- to late twentieth-century common language of selfhood can be said to rest on a foundation of accepted "truths" and practices that include the following: an arsenal of basic terms for the inner self and its dysfunctions (ego, unconscious, repression, Oedipus complex, neurosis); a structure of the mind imagined in terms of rational "conscious" processes and irrational "unconscious" desires; a developmental model of the self which posits the self's growth as a progressive movement through psychosocial stages; and a method of cure which depends on a patient's talks with a trained analyst, assumes the primary importance of a patient's family in the etiology of his or her symptoms, and presumes the possibility of a patient's self-improvement.

In *The Rise and Crisis of Psychoanalysis in the United States* (1995), Nathan Hale examines this "psychologization" of the American public and poses the interesting question of whether or not this country's melting-pot of psychotherapeutic ideas and practices can legitimately be tied to Freudian origins.[1] "Are the American modifications [of psychotherapy], even the mainstream orthodox ones, still Freud's psychoanalysis?" Hale asks. His response is that, while Freud may not have recognized the current panoply of clinical practices as his own, many of today's psychoanalysts would: for them, "the core of Freud's psychoanalysis remains intact," while "the emphases have shifted."[2] Hale's formulation resonates, I believe, with the way many social scientists and humanists understand psychodynamic theories of the self and their clinical applications in "depth" or "insight" therapy. These theories may no longer be purely Freudian, but they have descended from the founder of psychoanalysis.

From World War II through the early 1970s, these core ideas—repression, resistance, the centrality of sexuality, the Oedipus complex, transference—wielded a tremendous amount of power within the academy while gradually filtering into and becoming part of the psychological common sense of the American middle and upper classes. One should remember that in institutions of higher education during these years, in just about every humanistic discipline, one was likely to encounter psychoanalysis as a major topic of interest. As a student of American studies, I began my own education with the classic studies of Frederick Crews's *Sins of the Fathers* (1966) and Quentin Anderson's *Imperial Self* (1971), works on American authors grounded in psychoanalytic observations.[3] In psychology, Freud's ideas about parent-child interactions comprised foundational knowledge for researchers including the Harvard educator John Bowlby, who reworked them within the contexts of cognitive and experimental psychology.[4] During this time, Freud's theories entered the social sciences with the publication of studies on the personality types of the world's "great" men.[5] And in 1984 Peter Gay further boosted the visibility of Freud within the historical profession with his account of the European and American middle classes in *The Bourgeois Experience,* a richly documented example of psychohistory.[6]

At the same time, popular cultural forms in America have helped to stir widespread interest in psychoanalysis and its therapeutic offspring. In November 1993, *Time* magazine featured Freud on its cover with the bold headline "Is Freud Dead?" The resounding answer was no, for the article showed how Freud's theory of repression gave impetus to a contemporary cult of therapies in search of the difficult-to-substantiate repressed memories of child sexual abuse.[7] From the 1940s to the present, films such as Alfred Hitchcock's *Spellbound* (1945), Joseph L. Mankiewicz's *All About Eve* (1950), Elia Kazan's *Splendor in the Grass* (1961), Woody Allen's *Annie Hall* (1977), and Barbra Streisand's *Prince of Tides* (1992) have portrayed psychiatrist figures as powerful and intriguing, while imbuing their character-patients with any number of psychoanalytically derived complexes. Writers and journalists have done their part to keep Freud alive by debating his status as scientist, humanist, fraud, corrupter, or liberator of American sexual mores. Almost fifty years before *Time* asked "Is Freud Dead?" the same magazine placed American psychiatry in the spotlight by devoting its cover story to the explanation and clarification of this "relatively new scientific whatsis."[8] Although acknowledging some public skepticism toward psychoanalysis, the article reminded readers that psychiatry's "clinical lingo has been snatched up, misused, and overused by the man in the street. Parents and teachers speak knowingly of 'inferiority complexes.' The comic strips and movies refer familiarly to 'frustrations' and 'repressions.'"[9] These brief examples only begin to suggest what recent scholarship has documented much more fully: the century-long presence of Freud in the media, intellectual life and artistic movements, education, pediatric advice and family counseling, mental health policy, legal processes, and military decision making.[10]

As Ellen Herman has shown, the Cold War era represents a watershed in the history of the exposure of Americans to psychological practice: during this period Americans outside elite circles learned about psychotherapies not only through education, newspapers, and film, but also through one form or another of direct experience.[11] The popularization and democratization of the clinical situation—the trend historians call "therapy for the normal"—can be seen as one important route through which post-Freudian commonsensical notions of the self traveled. Although more research needs to be done on the transmission, and especially reception, of psychoanalytic ideas across social groups in America, one can speculate that the Freudian legacy has contributed to broadly shared skeletal understandings of the nature of the self and its psychodynamic processes. Since Freud, many well-known developmental theorists—including the nation's best-known pediatrician, Dr. Benjamin Spock—have bolstered the idea that self-formation is both uniquely individual and universally patterned.[12] In their views the (transhistorically) conceived "child" develops his or her distinct personality through psychodynamic processes of (mainly) parent-child interaction. This schema envisions biopsychosocial development as unfolding through inner confrontations, or stages, that remain stable across social groups, cultures, and time. If sexuality and the unconscious have remained central to contemporary thought about the self, so, I would argue, has this fundamental assumption about individual psychodynamic growth—one which lies at the core of much contemporary therapeutic practice and organizes the community of expectations among its participants.

To suggest the durability of basic Freudian terms, approaches to development, and practices of cure is neither to deny the variety of psychotherapeutic options that have displaced depth therapy in recent years, nor to overlook the tradition of psychoanalytic criticism that is as old as the theory itself. As the numerous reports and cover stories in national magazines make clear, it is now the age of Prozac, an era in which psychotropic drugs produce the mental changes previously left to the less effectual methods of psychotherapists.[13] In 1990 Daniel Goleman wrote in the *New York Times* that the attraction of orthodox psychoanalysis was finally expiring under the weight of increased competition from professional and lay psychologists and the economic pressures created for patients facing slashed insurance benefits. According to this and many similar articles, post–Vietnam era Americans were in the market for shorter, less expensive, and sometimes less privatized methods of cure.[14] Along these lines we must acknowledge the relatively recent boom in Americans' group-healing forums and new-age spiritualisms—the numerous twelve-step programs, meetings for "survivors" of abuse, and support groups for the emotionally disabled—many of them united under the wider rubric of the recovery movements.[15] Finally, for several decades self-help literature has lined bookstore shelves, bursting with do-it-yourself solutions to daily unhappiness.

Although feminist, Marxist, and cultural critics have challenged the liberatory possibilities of a therapeutic practice marked by racial stigmas, class privilege, gender bias, and social myopia, such critiques and movements have not always succeeded in extirpating Freudian concepts from their own theories of group empowerment. This is particularly evident in the case of women's consciousness-raising groups, which rejected Freud's domestic reading of female nature (and his ever-loathed theory of "penis envy"), while incorporating his method of talk and self-confession as their baseline tactic for their remaking of the social order.[16] Likewise, the antipsychiatry or radical therapy movements of the late 1960s, spearheaded by Thomas Szasz and R. D. Laing, show that, while some intellectuals on the political left rejected psychiatry, others held tight to some of its most basic assumptions. To remodel psychotherapy as "radical therapy" is still to envision radical politics within the conceptual frame of therapeutic talking cures.[17]

The contributors to *Inventing the Psychological* develop the concerns of these earlier critics by focusing on the power of the psychological professions to naturalize oppressive standards of social adjustment, to perpetuate social inequities, to legitimate dangerously personalized visions of pain, and to speak, for better or for worse, to widespread needs for self-disclosure and solace. Unlike their predecessors, however, their critiques are posed less as attacks on the psychiatric establishment and its theories than as issues for consideration within historical and ideological contexts. Some of our questions include: how have the professional psychologies, from the time of their creation in the late nineteenth century to the present, envisioned selfhood and interiority for men and for women of various racial, class, and ethnic backgrounds? What models of the self, of the emotions, and of development existed prior to the cultural ascendancy of medical and psychological authorities, and through what channels did these models find their way into public life? How can we account for the tremendous *variability* of emotional lexicons and developmental paradigms produced within American national history, not to mention across other cultures?

Our ability to pose such questions was enabled by a number of recent developments within historical and literary studies. First, research in American cultural history began to locate subjectivity within its purview, thus highlighting the links between large social transformations and personal life. Research on industrialization and the family, on the transformation of the marketplace and nineteenth-century domestic ideologies, and on the emergence of consumer culture and the rise of a therapeutic ethos has demonstrated the historical *contingency* of concepts of self, personality types, gendered roles, emotional standards, and sexual values. Second, poststructuralist theory has enabled this work through its emphasis on the power of discourse (textual, visual, and auditory) not simply to reflect some given reality, but to constitute it from within ideologically interested "subject positions." Drawing on discourse theory as well as allied research in literary studies, psychology, and anthropology, contributors to this volume have tried to grasp the social and political implications of America's psychological society and its power to naturalize hierarchies of social identity through its labels and formulas of emotional life.

The following chapters thus move *toward* a cultural history of emotional life in America by illustrating the complex interdependency between social change—in political systems, economic practices, social rituals, and family structures—and peoples' means of speaking the languages of emotions and of living out, in their self-understandings and relationships, dramas of the emotions. Our chapters approach the relationship between society and the emotions in different ways: they range across disciplinary borders (connecting emotional life to history, politics, mass media, literature, painting, and music); they develop different perspectives on the historical processes and cultural traditions that shape the emotions; and they pay attention to varying aspects of the psychological, such as its formation as an academic discipline, its role as a self-help industry, and its less obvious functions as an experiential category that confers special kinds of identity, interiority, and insight upon various groups and individuals. What the contributors to this book share, however, are working assumptions about the emotions as historically contingent, socially specific, and politically situated. If today's therapeutic common sense tells us that the "psychological" is the deepest part of ourselves—the most intricate and individual aspect of our personhood—the contributors to *Inventing the Psychological* bring historical perspective to this assumption by identifying the vast public resources—institutional, financial, and cultural—that have gone into the making of this distinctively twentieth-century idea.

Chapter 3 contains historian John Demos's "Oedipus and America: Historical Perspectives on the Reception of Psychoanalysis in the United States" (first published in the *Annual of Psychoanalysis* in 1978) and an afterword written especially for this volume. As Demos explains, "Oedipus and America" evolved from a lecture he presented before a group of psychoanalysts and, after its publication, the essay appears to have come to the attention of mainly the psychoanalytic community. The volume editors stumbled across this work in the mid-1980s, during one of many searches for scholarship that considered psychological experience within historical frameworks (something different from psychohistory, the study of the past through Freudian theory). We found what we were looking for in "Oedipus and America," an essay which appealed to us because of its effort to bring the social history of the family (and the cultural history of a period more generally) to the center of discussions of psychoanalytic concepts and patterns. By including this essay we hope to give greater visibility to a work of scholarship that helped fuel our interest in the cultural history of emotional life.

Demos's "Oedipus and America" asks why Americans in the early decades of the twentieth century received psychoanalytic ideas as their preferred method of self-explanation. Nathan Hale's *Freud and the Americans* (1971) provided one answer to this question in the form of a national "cultural readiness" that derived from two intellectual crises: a "crisis of the somatic style," in which Americans rejected mechanistic views of mental life as physiological and organic in origin, and a "crisis of civilized morality," in which Americans rejected Victorian sexual standards in favor of more liberal styles of conduct. "Oedipus and America" broadens Hale's equation of "cultural readiness" by arguing that changes within American families—and, specifically, the creation of a middle-class "hothouse" or "oedipal" family—prepared the ground for the American acceptance of Freud and his triangulated model (son-mother-father) of family affections. The nineteenth-century privatization of the middle-class family, Demos contends, led to an unprecedented intensification of emotional relationships within the family and set the stage for the psychodynamic patterns that Freud would later call "oedipal"—mothers in increasingly "heated-up" relations with their sons and sons in increasingly distant and competitive relations with their fathers. In "History and the Psychosocial," Demos looks back on the "hothouse family" and explores the durability of this idea in light of more recent work on the psychological and social dimensions of private life. At the same time, Demos elaborates his current theoretical approach to the history of the family.

Chapters 4 and 5 share interests in cultural conceptions of emotion in post–Civil War America and look specifically at the role of literatures—classic American texts, popular mass fiction, and domestic advice manuals—in producing and publicizing them. Nancy Schnog's "Changing Emotions: Moods and the Nineteenth-Century American Woman Writer" enters into dialogue with the title of Louisa May Alcott's *Moods* (1864) and asks what propelled Alcott—the author of so many well-known novels of social reform—to locate the interest of one of her first adult novels in this set of emotions. Schnog reveals that Alcott was one among a larger group of nineteenth-century white middle-class women writers who brought to life the literary figure of the moody woman, while ascribing strongly divergent meanings to her character. Whereas sentimental writers denounced the moody woman as a reckless agent of marital destruction and promoted the ideal of the habitually "cheerful" woman, postbellum women writers drew on masculine traditions of Anglo-American romanticism in order to reclaim the moods of their protagonists as the inner signature of female creativity and individualism. This chapter argues that moods are not merely feelings that, as the dictionary tells us, *change* over time; more accurately, they are feelings whose meanings have been *changed* by the literary and cultural traditions that have encoded and re-encoded their potentials and values.

Richard S. Lowry's "Domestic Interiors: Boyhood Nostalgia and Affective Labor in the Gilded Age" foregrounds Mark Twain's unruly, instinct-driven Tom Sawyer in order to study a difficult "border-crossing" in popular boys' fictions—and boys' lives—in the Gilded Age: the making of fun-loving boys into self-disciplined, socially responsible men. Lowry identifies two key narrative structures of post–Civil War mass fiction for boys—the resistance of male authors to narrating the emergence of boys into men and the insistence of male authors on narrating the boy's antebellum past as the story of pastoral freedom and unregulated play—and considers the kind of cultural and emotional work these textual features performed. In a departure from Daniel Rodgers's interpretation of boyhood fiction as "regressive fantasies" shaped by concerns over the increasingly industrial and bureaucratic nature of work, Lowry reads these stories as participating in middle-class strategies of "affective management" and social reproduction. For Lowry, nostalgia for boyhood is less of an imaginative escape from economic realities than an *entryway into* Victorian ideals of "manly character" and the middle-class marketplace. Revising the historical work of Peter Stearns, Lowry links the textual gap between boys' and men's "emotional cultures" (unruly boys/self-disciplined men) to the social and economic aims of the middle class. Despite the boys' "harum-scarum" antics and wild "savageries," fictional celebrations of lost boyhoods, Lowry argues, lent ideological support to boys' prolonged socialization within the domestic sphere, which suited middle-class parents' interests in molding their sons' characters and promoting their economic success. In another direction, Lowry's chapter challenges the reader to rethink not readily apparent commonalities between romantic stories of antebellum boyhood and sentimental stories of pre–Civil War girlhood, such as Susan Warner's *Wide Wide World* (1850). Whereas women writers used sentimental conventions to depict the work of conscience-making, male writers used tropes of boyhood fantasy and play to perform the less visible but still powerful *labor* of instilling domestic interiors—what the historian Mary Ryan calls a "portable parent"—in boys and men.

Chapters 6 and 7 focus on the modern emergence of a more patently "psychological" culture. David M. Lubin's "Modern Psychological Selfhood in the Art of Thomas Eakins" examines a crucial shift in Eakins's paintings from his early portrayals of subjects involved in specific physical actions or behaviors (boxers, hunters, rowers) to his late subjects, who were more likely to be involved in unspecifically interior forms of meditation, often inflected with a look of sadness, tension, or dejection (for example, pensive women gazing sadly into the beyond, or men poised in private moments of reflection). Lubin asks how we are to account for Eakins's adoption of a "psychological" style in the later days of his career, as well as for Eakins's notably uneven reputation as a psychological portraitist from the 1910s to the present. Lubin argues that, "Like other late nineteenth- and early twentieth-century pioneers of the psychological, Eakins did much to invent the very category by which his work was then retroactively understood and valued." Rather than viewing Eakins as an artist who drew on the prepackaged psychological truths of his era, Lubin shows how Eakins refashioned pre-existing discourses of religious suffering, medical interrogation, and the social defeat of marginalized Americans (Native Americans and African Americans) into a distinctively modern "psychological" rhetoric of middle- and upper-middle-class nervous interiority and class superiority. This chapter highlights Eakins's pivotal role in breaking away from the portrait tradition as the presentation of an eminently public self, while helping to invent through his painting the modern "psychological" individual whose privileged social place is asserted through his inward gaze and self-preoccupied pose.

In "Glamorizing the Psychological: The Politics of the Performances of Modern Psychological Identities," Joel Pfister shows that the early decades of the twentieth century spawned not only the creation of the category of "the psychological" but also the creation of distinctively "psychological" identities and "performances." Pfister asks why, during the 1910s and 1920s, it became *chic* to be neurotic and finds part of the answer in the first and now largely forgotten generation of popular psychology advocates, the cohort of writers who glamorized views of psychoanalysis, of depth-psychology language (repression, the unconscious, inhibitions), and of the inner self as sexually voracious or "primitive." Books including Dr. Louis Bisch's *Be Glad You're Neurotic* (1936) and William J. Fielding's *Caveman Within Us* (1922) taught American readers to believe in the existence of their "primitive" depth (a primitiveness connected to racial ideologies) and to prize the "transgressive sexiness" that comes from probing it. According to Pfister, white middle-class women often stood at the center of these glamorization efforts, as pop psychologists revisioned the female mental interior as sexual and aggressive and persuaded readers that status and fun could be achieved by talking about these "psychological" depths. Although this development contributed to the liberation of white middle-class women from the role of "sentimental angel," this "primitivizing" of femininity, Pfister argues, did little to glamorize and much to abate the more socially engaged collective feminist activity of the 1910s. What stands out as remarkable to Pfister is the power of the "pop psychological essence-and-identity industry" to introduce a concept of freedom "as the challenging of [sexual] taboos" that was seen as far more interesting and urgent than undertaking the reform of the liberal corporate order.

Jill G. Morawski's "Educating the Emotions: Academic Psychology, Textbooks, and the Psychology Industry, 1890–1940" (chapter 8) examines the consolidation of the academic field of psychology through an often neglected vehicle of its rising cultural authority and dissemination—university-level psychology textbooks. This chapter charts the contradictory paths that conceptions of emotion took in the early twentieth century. During this period a "bio-mechanical" model of emotion as internal, physiological events came into conflict with a "humanistic" view of the emotions as drives responsive to behavioral modifications and environmental influences. According to Morawski, college textbooks educated the growing numbers of middle-class psychology students into the professionalizing world of experimental psychology, into its mechanistic methods of research, and, more subtly, into what Morawski calls a "double discourse" of human emotions. On the one hand, students were introduced to the theory of emotions proposed by William James and Carl Lange and their followers: the idea that physiological changes within the body—and not the mind—governed mental life with only the slightest opportunity for social adjustments. Likewise, students were taught to appreciate the (white, male) scientist's status as a researcher, his objective methods of inquiry, and his privileged insight into subjects defined as occupying the lower strata of an implied social hierarchy of personhood. On the other hand, textbooks introduced students into the less dominant, but nevertheless still visible set of ideas about the individual's capacity for emotional self-reformation and self-realization, which resonated with the emphasis of America's expanding consumer culture on leisure and gratification. For Morawski, the dual messages of college textbooks—with their countervailing explanations of the emotions as natural and made, biological and social—secured the place of experimental psychology as a much-needed scientific technology of inner life, while leaving a legacy of uncertainty about the emotions as a limiting substrate or a liberating energy within the self.

In "Epistemology of the Bunker: The Brainwashed and Other New Subjects of Permanent War" (chapter 9), Catherine Lutz examines the alliance between psychology and the military during the early Cold War period and charts the relationship between the rise of the national security state and the emergence of new ideas about the unconscious as a stronghold of subversive political activities. Lutz's essay shows that undergirding the development and authority of many mid-twentieth-century psychologies have been their intimate military connections. These ties led to myriad developments: among them, the professionalization of psychological researchers and the filtering of military money into their fields of study; the application of psychological research questions in the expansion of militarily useful knowledge; and the consolidation of the disciplines of industrial psychology, cognitive psychology, learning theory, and the psychology of propaganda and public opinion. According to Lutz, one of the most stunning psychological expressions of the advent of the national security state can be witnessed in the Cold War creation of a doubled or "bunkered" self. Lutz maintains that, as the U.S. government promoted state policy that divided "top secret" information from declassified material and became increasingly concerned with Communist infiltrators and collaborators, the self became re-imagined as a second front of suspicion, while the "inner self" emerged as the likely place for disloyal Americans to hide their treachery. Double agents, spies, lie-detector tests, fictional truth serums, and, most significant, the popular interest in brainwashing during and after the Korean War were some of the popular expressions of a state policy that supported the division between elite information and public disinformation. Yet the doubled state, Lutz reminds the reader, is not only an external condition; she charts its incorporation *within* the American citizen, who is taught to fear his or her hidden "national neurosis" or subversive Communist within.

Like David Lubin's study of Eakins's paintings, Robert Walser's "Deep Jazz: Notes on Interiority, Race, and Criticism" (chapter 10) demonstrates that arts not commonly associated with psychological projects have been central in producing, popularizing, and debating conceptions of interiority. Walser looks back at the commentaries on and studies of African American jazz performance from the 1910s to the 1950s and uncovers a tradition of musical commentary saturated with racial politics over the nature of black "depth" or interiority. A largely white group of jazz critics, Walser argues, heard in jazz the expression of a precultural African essence of the "primitive"—the soul of black folks unhampered by civilized morality and therefore positioned to create the blood-stirring beat of modern culture. Yet, as Walser shows, black jazz musicians envisioned the sources of their music in just the opposite way, rooting its technical features in the acquired characteristics of discipline and skill and its sound in the social contexts of racism and bohemianism. At the core of jazz criticism Walser locates the recurring practice of "deep jazz thinking," the tendency of mainly white music critics to attribute jazz aesthetics to any number of essentialized views (the precultural self, the primitive self, the ineffable self) of African American depth. Through examinations of two famous musical analyses in jazz scholarship, André Hodeir's interpretation of Duke Ellington's "Concerto for Cootie" (1940) and Gunther Schuller's treatment of Sonny Rollins's "Blue 7" (1956), Walser demonstrates how "deep jazz thinking" has obscured the way jazz musicians used technical virtuosity and musical inventions to infuse their music not with the "raw emotions" of universal human nature but with political challenges to their community of listeners.

In "Beyond the Talking Cure: Listening to Female Testimony on *The Oprah Winfrey Show*" (chapter 11), Franny Nudelman reminds us just how far we have traveled as a sexual and psychological culture: if one hundred years ago Freud invented the "talking cure" as a method of recovery based on the private confession of tabooed sexual and aggressive desires, today public confessions in this line are the plain speech of television talk shows. Nudelman investigates what, if anything, comes of the numerous testimonies of female pain, victimization, and abuse which have become the hallmark of television talk shows as well as survivor discourse and self-help manuals. In 1992 Wendy Kaminer's *I'm Dysfunctional, You're Dysfunctional* blasted "self-help fashion" for degrading and misappropriating the feminist meaning of "the personal is political." Challenging Kaminer, Nudelman highlights the inherent *political* importance of women's televised stories of suffering. What Nudelman illuminates is the role of the format of the talk show in diffusing the social implications of women's speech by sidestepping its interpretation. By placing Oprah Winfrey's group discussions in relation to other contemporary "stages" of confession and recovery—such as feminist consciousness-raising groups, recovery and self-help literature, and private psychotherapy—Nudelman shows how an hour with Winfrey divorces female testimony from practicable solutions, thereby distancing female pain from strategies of cure. This practice simply reinforces cultural stereotypes of female victimization and reproduces the female sufferer as an icon of public curiosity and pity.

Although by no means comprehensive, our selective overview of changing forms of psychological expression in America demonstrates how the context of cultural history can enrich one's understanding of self, interiority, and emotion. The chapters include extensive references to related literature, which draw together research in the history of psychology, the history of the family, literary studies, anthropology, and other fields and will help readers to better appreciate the interdisciplinary vision necessary to establish new perspectives on the making of personal and inner life. *Inventing the Psychological* clarifies just how important and challenging a task it is to think historically and politically about the psychological interiors we identify as our own and about those we presume to have dwelled in the generations before us.

Notes

1. See Hale, *The Rise and Crisis of Psychoanalysis in the United States: Freud and the Americans, 1917–1985* (New York: Oxford University Press, 1995).

2. Ibid., 378–79.

3. Literary criticism has a long tradition of psychoanalytically oriented studies, which has been challenged and revised by feminist, Marxist, Lacanian, and deconstructionist critics. For an overview of psychoanalytic thought within English studies, see Terry Eagleton, *Literary Theory: An Introduction* (Minneapolis: University of Minnesota Press, 1983), 151–94; *The Practice of Psychoanalytic Criticism*, ed. Leonard Tennenhouse (Detroit: Wayne State University Press, 1976); Morton Kaplan and Robert Kloss, *The Unspoken Motive: A Guide to Psychoanalytic Literary Criticism* (New York: Free Press, 1973).

4. See John Bowlby's influential *Attachment and Loss* (New York: Basic, 1969). It is also interesting to note the continuation of Bowlby's emphasis upon intra-familial object relations within contemporary "attachment theory." For one example, see Cindy Hazan and Phillip Shaver, "Romantic Love Conceptualized as an Attachment Process," *Journal of Personality and Social Psychology* 52 (1987): 511–52. I want to thank Susan Campbell for calling this research to my attention.

5. See Erik H. Erikson, *Young Man Luther: A Study in Psychoanalysis and History* (New York: Norton, 1958); Bruce Mazlish, *In Search of Nixon: A Psychohistorical Inquiry* (Baltimore: Penguin, 1973); Ann Jardim, *The First Henry Ford: A Study in Personality and Business Leadership* (Cambridge: MIT Press, 1970).

6. See Peter Gay, *The Bourgeois Experience: Victoria to Freud* (New York: Oxford University Press, 1984).

7. See Paul Gray, "The Assault on Freud," *Time* (Nov. 29, 1993): 45–49.

8. See the Medicine section in *Time* (Oct. 25, 1948): 64–67.

9. Ibid., 64.

10. In addition to the works already cited, a number of studies chart the rise of America's therapeutic society and psychological traditions of thought, among them: Ellen Herman, *The Romance of American Psychology: Political Culture in the Age of Experts* (Berkeley: University of California Press, 1995); Elizabeth Lunbeck, *The Psychiatric Persuasion: Knowledge, Gender, and Power in Modern America* (Princeton: Princeton University Press, 1994); Nancy Chodorow, *Femininities, Masculinities, Sexualities: Freud and Beyond* (Lexington: University Press of Kentucky, 1994); Tom Lutz, *American Nervousness, 1903: An Anecdotal History* (Ithaca: Cornell University Press, 1991); Peter L. Rudnytsky, *The Psychoanalytic Vocation: Rank, Winnicott, and the Legacy of Freud* (New Haven: Yale University Press, 1991); T. J. Jackson Lears, *No Place of Grace: Antimodernism and the Transformation of American Culture 1880–1920* (New York: Pantheon, 1981); Nathan Hale, *Freud and the Americans: The Beginnings of Psychoanalysis in the United States, 1876–1917* (New York: Oxford University Press, 1971).

11. See "The Growth Industry," in Herman, *Romance of American Psychology,* 238–75.

12. See Dr. Benjamin Spock, *The Common Sense Book of Baby and Child Care* (New York: Duell, Sloan, and Pearce, 1946).

13. Media coverage on Prozac has been extensive, especially in the wake of the publication of Peter D. Kramer, *Listening to Prozac* (New York: Viking Press, 1993), and Elizabeth Wurtzel, *Prozac Nation: Young and Depressed in America* (Boston: Houghton Mifflin, 1994).

14. See Daniel Goleman, "New Paths to Mental Health Put Strains on Some Healers," *New York Times* (May 17, 1990): 1.

15. The best recent discussion of self-help movements is Wendy Kaminer, *I'm Dys-*

functional, You're Dysfunctional: The Recovery Movement and Other Self-Help Fashions (Reading, Mass.: Addison-Wesley, 1992). Also see Wendy Simonds, *Women and Self-Help Culture: Reading Between the Lines* (New Brunswick, N.J.: Rutgers University Press, 1992).

16. This important point is made by Herman in her discussion of women's consciousness-raising groups. See *Romance of American Psychology,* 276–303.

17. Ibid., 287.

CHAPTER TWO

On Conceptualizing the Cultural History of Emotional and Psychological Life in America

JOEL PFISTER

Inventing the Psychological aims to open valuable interdisciplinary and theoretically expansive perspectives on the historical contexts and cultural formation of psychological and emotional experience in America. My co-editor and I do not envision this volume as a contribution to the field of psychohistory; in fact, we and several of the contributors, if only implicitly, were eager to challenge the insufficiently historical assumptions about "the psychological" that inform the work of many, if not all, psychohistorians. From the outset, we were interested in approaching "the psychological" not so much as a definitely knowable truth of the self that we could reliably transport (or even trace) back in time, but as an intriguing *cultural category* that had been invented in different ways over time, within every historical era, and across cultures.[1] Similarly, we wanted to extend the possibilities of a history that would investigate emotions not as timeless givens which sprout from the soil of an eternal "inner" self, but as culturally structured experiences, interpretations, and performances of the self.

The cultural studies scholar Raymond Williams has characterized "the psychological" as a "great modern ideological system" that, with the advent of industrial capitalism, began to assume prodigious cultural authority to "assemble and generalize"—and to provide forms for the structuring of—"subjectivity."[2] This volume's chapters, which span the antebellum era to the 1990s, explore phases in which this "modern ideological system" operated with considerable complexity through various fields and forms (in psychology, advice literature, fiction, drama, music, art, television talk shows, the military, and

17

educational institutions). The chapters analyze some of the causes, effects, and political implications of the ascendancy of the "psychological" "subjectivity" that Williams viewed as a modern cultural invention. The development of several fields, including American studies, cultural history, the histories of the family, gender roles, and sexuality, the history of psychological discourses and institutions, and cultural studies work on subjectivity, has made the collective invention of an interdisciplinary volume like this desirable at this time. While it is true that contemporary scholarship has offered wide-ranging discussions of the social "construction" of gender, sexual, racial, ethnic, class, and regional identities, too little attention has been paid to the roles played by cultural concepts of psychological selfhood and of emotions in underwriting these identities (making social identities—for example, the stereotype that women are overly "emotional"—seem unquestionably natural or psychological to some). The chapters that follow help to remedy this.

In our first planning sessions with one another my co-editor and I reflected at length on how we had been taught to read—to have "insight" into—ourselves and others. It didn't shock either of us that the patterns of reading we related—the sorts of "insights" we were socialized to value—were so similar, so "psychological." Such conversations enlivened our historical and political curiosity about how and why commonsense notions of psychological selfhood and of inner emotional life became commonsensical and, thus, powerful—even powerfully invisible—in their influence. At stake in expanding our thinking about the dimensions and possibilities of a history of psychological and emotional life, we realized, was nothing less than the clarification of our cultural and political understanding of how Americans have been influenced to imagine our "selves" and our potential, both individually and collectively.[3]

Often our work together has helped us to formulate productive questions and disagreements with one another, not incontrovertible answers. Foundational questions and debates abide for each of us as we have established our respective critical approaches. Early in our collaboration, for instance, we periodically argued about what we labeled the Romeo and Juliet question: what exactly is historical about passion, or, should we say, about the ways in which we have been persuaded to think about passion as a category? Are these questions the same question? The cultural critic John Berger has reasoned that, "in the fields, on the roads, in the workshops, at school, there are continual transformations: in an embrace very little changes. Yet the construction put on passion alters. Not necessarily because emotions are different but because what surrounds the emotions—social attitudes, legal systems, moralities, eschatologies—these change."[4] Berger's socially unmediated passion, he assumes, is in essence my passion and your passion; but the cultural conditions in which this universal human passion is expressed necessarily encode it, organize it, alter the way we see it with any number of meanings. Thus his historical interest is in the contexts that give relatively transhistorical emotions historically specific meanings.

The therapist Leonore Tiefer, whose work has led her to the conclusion that "sex is not a natural act" (she conceives of sexual acts as being saturated with social conventions), takes this stress on the cultural assignment of meaning one dramatic step further. After describing some wildly variant meanings ascribed to kissing in various cultures, she asserts: "A kiss is not a kiss; . . . your orgasm is not the same as George Washington's, premarital sex in Peru is not premarital sex in Peoria, abortion in Rome at the time of Caesar is not abortion in Rome at the time of John Paul II."[5] For Tiefer, culture doesn't just surround or act on a bedrock of psychobiological "emotions"; it defines, produces, and has us enact in our behavior what we are told and tell ourselves are emotions. Here she is popularizing the assumptions of Michel Foucault, who argued that sexuality—and by implication emotion—is not just shaped; it is complexly *constituted* by culture.[6]

This postmodern emphasis on the cultural making of the self is both illustrated and complicated by Barbara Kruger's richly ambiguous untitled picture, which exhibits the words "You are not yourself" (1984) (fig. 2.1). Kruger takes the conventional, often sexist artistic and advertising image of a woman gazing at herself in the mirror (the figure of Vanity)[7] and shatters it—perhaps with a bullet or a hammer. The circular site of impact is the reflection of the woman's forehead. On first glance the split-up figure seems to be putting the shards back in place; but she may be pulling them apart. The hole and the jagged surfaces of the mirror appear dangerous to touch—and the woman's eye is closed. Is she suffering or just meditative? Is this a scene of crisis or enlightenment or both? On the bright side, the hole resembles the sun—an intense, glaring Cyclops eyeball shooting electric rays, like lightning, everywhere. In this restructured, unpretty self-reflection, the mirrored woman potentially has greater vision with three right eyes. If we can't tell exactly what she would look like reassembled, neither can she, and maybe this is how she learns to see herself and her potential anew.

The meanings of "You are not yourself" vary according to one's perspective—which Kruger overtly splinters and proliferates. I certainly have had unsettling experiences of suddenly seeing my reflection unposed (Ah, I know that guy—or do I?). What is it about the self that one doesn't know? Instincts? Unconscious? What Kruger dramatizes is an image, not of a conventionally spatial "psychological" self who has "inner depth," but of an ambiguous mirrored self composed of surfaces, pieces, printing. We see partial reflections of what we are taught to call "self"; but our attention is also drawn to the surfaces and words that make particular kinds of self-reflections, perspectives, and

2.1 Barbara Kruger, untitled image, from: text by Kate Linker, *Love for Sale: The Words and Pictures of Barbara Kruger* (1990). Reprinted with the permission of Barbara Kruger.

meanings available to our vision. Kruger, like several cultural studies theorists of the 1970s and 1980s, wants us to be intrigued by the possibility that reflecting surfaces and words are not fixed; they can be fractured and re-arranged (one's eye—or "I"—can be multiplied).[8] Her image implies that what our culture has trained many viewers to look for—to assume—to yearn for—is the existence of a coherent, readable representation of "yourself" that will seem to make the pieces fall into place and "reflect" the "whole" self. Kruger may be asking us to resist the magnetic pull of ideologies of yourself-hood and individuality.[9]

If a more traditional psychoanalytic or humanist notion of universality has had us try to "discover" a bedrock of "human nature" (the emotions that Berger says changing historical forces surround), the postmodern universality suggested here is that you are never *your* "self" (the smooth-surfaced cultural illusion of an "individual" self) because "yourself" is made up of alterable frag-ments of culture, seemingly realistic cultural self-reflections, styles of seeing, fashions of reading, and conventions of meaning.[10] Do cultural forces (diverse sorts of mirrors, writing, aesthetics) have the kind of constitutive power that this postmodern shattering of the psychological portrait seems to attribute to them? If so, we must consider the history, politics, and cultural machinery of "selfing": why and how are particular sorts of "selves" sold as real or desirable or stable or normal or fashionably transgressive in American culture, and who benefits from the proliferation of these "psychological" ideologies?[11] The vari-ous reflections of Berger, Tiefer, Foucault, and Kruger make one thing clear: a fundamental challenge one must face in conceptualizing a cultural history of the category of "the psychological" and of concepts of emotions is working out a stance on the difficult question of how transformative is the cultural power of meaning in shaping—or constituting—the self, and how do various cultural industries of "yourselfing" relate to the structures and dynamics of domination and potential liberation in America? Below I outline some concerns that have influenced my own responses to these questions.

Inventing the Psychological in the Context of Inventing Social Meaning

When considering this question it is critical not to take the popular Amer-ican meanings, significance, and mystique usually ascribed to psychological discourses for granted. Because experiences that many of us interpret as emo-tional—having orgasms, giving birth, struggling with anxieties about one's own or a loved one's impending death—can be intense, their gripping reality does not therefore automatically make these experiences universally or authen-tically "human." Not only can the meanings of such experiences differ over

time, within a culture, and across cultures, the historical, material, and ideological conditions that operate as forces in the making of such meanings can
also differ remarkably.

Numerous anthropologists have recognized that Western cultures tend to
be far more preoccupied with distinctly "psychological" notions of selfhood
than many non-Western cultures.[12] Not all cultures have spawned whole industries consecrated to the exploration and advertising of "inner" space. For these
cultures, the "psychological"—at least as many Americans generally understand the term—simply isn't meaningful. Not everyone everywhere would be
able to make sense of J. George Frederick's *What Is Your Emotional Age?* (1928),
when he assures us that "emotions rule us" and then strives to convince us—
sounding like an overinflated ad man—that "Halitosis [bad breath] is a mild
ailment indeed compared with seven or ten years lagging behind in your emotional age."[13] One might surmise that America has distinguished itself over
many non-Western cultures in the inner space race to discover the self; or one
might begin to view the mass marketing of psychological and emotional advice
as itself a curious phenomenon in need of historical inquiry.

Neither the history of categories of emotions nor cross-cultural studies of
conceptions of emotions permit one to assert confidently that humans have
always instinctively understood, defined, or cared about emotions the same
way. Some Western emotions, once deemed vital to human essence, are now
obsolete (the medieval emotion of "accidie" or losing one's zeal for praying, the
Renaissance emotion of melancholy).[14] The cross-cultural scholar Paul Heelas
observes that different cultures house the emotions in different organs (for
example, the heart, liver, stomach), that it isn't unusual for non-Western cultures to see emotions as "external agencies which invade or possess people"
(not as internal forces), and that many non-Western cultures assign little or no
importance to imagining "emotions of the private self."[15] After pointing out
that "the sheer numbers of words and phrases by which languages denote
[inner] states are amazingly variable," the anthropologist Rodney Needham
concludes skeptically: "To the extent that inner states may be discriminable as
universal natural resemblances, they are in the province of physiology. If inner
states are inferred from social expressions, they are social facts like other
facts."[16]

It is enlightening to gain some sense of the degree to which other cultures
have produced variant hierarchies of concerns regarding the self. The Ifaluk of
Micronesia, studied by the anthropologist Catherine Lutz, for example, are
uncertain "about the accessibility of 'the insides'" of others, cannot see their
own "insides," and hence just do not worry much about "insides." Lutz goes on
to state the powerful insight that insight itself is by no means a cultural constant: "The American [therapist's] 'psychological insight,'" she writes, having

narrated an inefficacious cross-cultural encounter, "is the Chinese person's 'self-absorption.'"[17]

Along the same lines, the Marxist psychoanalyst Joel Kovel stresses that "within our culture, introspection signifies participation in a particular class and social relation. . . . I am not saying that working-class people do not develop insight, but for them to do so in analysis means pursuing an activity foreign to their experience of the world."[18] The corollary would be that the cultural *practice* (to borrow Lutz's term)[19] and *performance* of psychoanalytic styles of "introspection" and "insight" help confer middle- and upper-class status— and "emotions"—on one. Kovel understands that particular modes of defining emotions and rituals of reading the self have contributed to the constitution and presentation of middle- and upper-class identity. The studies of sociologist Philip Rieff, of historian Christopher Lasch, of historians Richard Fox and Jackson Lears, among others, have shown that the rise of what they term "therapeutic culture" is allied historically and ideologically to the ascendancy of the white middle class.[20] This class's invention of a therapeutic culture has also been tied to its strategy to establish its "inner" ("human") value over the working class and over subordinate ethnic and racial groups.[21]

The working-class "primitive" in Tennessee Williams's *Streetcar Named Desire* (1947), Stanley Kowalski, has no doubt that the display of a "therapeutic" self is a marker of class status—a display he does not welcome on what he considers his domestic stage. Stanley—listening to his (formerly) aristocratic sister-in-law, Blanche DuBois, complain that she feels worn out—utters a startlingly unpsychological retort: "Well, take it easy." This blunt prescription is an affront to Blanche's romantic concept of her class "depth" and potency, which assigns almost poetic value to her emotional sensitivity and fragility. From the get-go, Stanley (who will later insist that she "cut the re-bop!") is aware that he and Blanche are entangled in a warfare of class—not just gendered—subjectivities.[22] What is needed, really, is not only a cultural history of "psychological" discourses in America but also a companion history of *antipsychological* discourses—novels, plays, poetry, paintings, sculptures, songs, comic books, and advice columns—that refuse to echo and validate white middle- and upperclass representations of human emotions and psychological depth.

Working-class heavy metal and punk rock bands of the late 1970s and 1980s, for instance, produced a self-consciously jarring music that at least implicitly contested the early and mid-1970s therapeutic white middle-class angst-filled reveries of James Taylor and Joni Mitchell.[23] Taylor's lilting plaints of therapeutic zoos (psychiatric hospitals), anxiety-attack blues, chilly dreams, and gray mornings, and Mitchell's coy baring of her nature-sprite bottom, as well as her seemingly eternally love-wracked "inner nature," on her artful album *For the Roses* (1972), are enticing enactments of the post-Romantic artist whose forever misunderstood "depth" is gauged by his or her ability to endow psychological fragility with fascination, charm, and ideological value. During the last years of the Vietnam debacle, in a climate of racial strife, and in the aftermath of Watergate, their easy listening, rhythmic, sweet-harmonied lyrics of self-involvement were commercially lucrative therapeutic poses that their occasional humor seemed to parody. Their catchy songs made and still make certain privatizing and individualizing narratives and conventions of "inner" life seem gut-wrenchingly real, compellingly exposable, and ideologically progressive to the youth of the white middle class and upper class and to the youth of other groups who aspired to move into these classes. Much therapeutic folk-rock served as cultural soundtracks that helped "sell" the romance of white "psychological" individualism to many.

Social groups that invent the "psychological" are engaged in the production of social meanings that are made to appear natural and self-evident through a great range of cultural practices and performances (as I have suggested, not simply through therapy). Psychologist James Averill, sociologist Arlie Hochschild, historians Peter Stearns and Carol Stearns, and historian John Kasson, in their respective work, have argued for the usefulness of some concept of "emotion rules"—broadly based cultural rules, standards, or expectations that inscribe meanings, values, and controls on emotions. Consequently, Hochschild studies how female flight attendants are trained to perform in a mode of service-industry femininity by smiling (always)—an emotional labor that is enforced by corporate "feeling rules." These social rules or conventions can also structure seemingly involuntary responses. Victorian middle-class women, Averill points out, were accustomed to "(implicit) rules for fainting" in particular circumstances, "even though this is presumably an involuntary, largely physiological, response."[24] Fainting was not only "emotional"; it was a historically rooted "involuntary" practice or performance that staged a class-specific femininity. In his work on the rise of industrial capitalism and the concomitant privatization of the European bourgeoisie, sociologist Richard Sennett has also focused on how conventions of "involuntary" or "unconscious" self-disclosure (signs that ostensibly disclosed sexual behavior) factored into the composition of a class semiotics of "individuality."[25]

The cultural history of inventions of the "psychological" must in certain respects take into account how and why cultural significance and cultural hierarchies of problems have been invented. The corporate sponsors of American culture—through the media (news, advertising), educational institutions (preschool to graduate school), leisure industries (professional sports, sex industry), workplaces, the arts (museums, rock music videos, best-selling novels, movies)—invent and disseminate commonsensical notions of what Americans are supposed to get emotional about, to get excited about, to be worried about.[26] It may well be, for example, that many well-housed members of the middle and upper classes are in various ways educated and privatized to get more emotional about subjective concerns promoted by therapeutic culture and the psychology industry than about what and who make homeless persons homeless. This "yourselfing" (as in "hey, gotta look out for yourself") is made to appear more immediate, defensible, and satisfying when, as feminist critic Wendy Kaminer suggests, therapeutic movements make compelling the idea that just about everyone has suffered emotionally in his or her youth and thus qualifies as a mistreated "homeless" person in need of recovery (as if we're all affectively "homeless").[27] The Marxist literary theorist Terry Eagleton quite rightly conceptualizes ideology as "less a question of ideas than of feelings, images, gut reactions."[28] And Foucault, long tuned into this, has pushed us to shed common sense and to reevaluate what a culture succeeds in getting us to invest in emotionally and to preoccupy ourselves with as "problems."[29]

As my co-editor and I debated how and why dominant forces within American culture hook us on particular meanings of selfhood and hierarchies of "problems," we found ourselves continually confronting the basic problem of analytical vocabulary (aware that the language you use also uses you).[30] On the fairly new end of the theoretical spectrum emotions can be viewed as "constructed," "acquired," "inscribed," and "made meaningful" by culture. Over the last ten or fifteen years words on this end of the spectrum have been given critical glamour and perhaps too much explanatory authority (as if to see that something seems to be "constructed" instantly resolves one's historical investigation of the matter).[31] On the other more familiar end, emotions can be seen as "biologically inherent," "discoverable," "expressed," and as "intrinsically meaningful" (as forces that naturally govern the self), quite apart from the contingent ways in which a particular culture encodes them as meaningful. The issue of the terms that one uses (emotions "constructed" versus "discovered") is important, not simply because analytical categories guide our assumptions and our interpretation (even our perception) of evidence, but also because it is remarkably easy to employ theoretical words that have become so commonplace that they seem merely descriptive of a self-evident "psychological" self.

Psychological Vocabulary: The Control of Human Nature

To illustrate the lure of the commonsensical and some of the potential problems or limitations associated with it, I want to examine some of the "psychological" premises allied to the word *control*—as in the control of one's emotions, self-control, controlling "human nature." In 1939 Norbert Elias, an innovative historical sociologist (whose work in German was translated only in the late 1970s), wrote a two-volume history of what he called the "civilizing process" (an ethnocentric term) that focused on the transition from medieval social interactions to the new relations of courtiers in the more centralized power structure of the Renaissance court. He made much of the aspiring courtiers' political needs (unlike their feudal predecessors) to control their behavior, manners, appearance, and emotions. Elias suggested that their efforts to "civilize" or control themselves (partly through the acceptance of new thresholds of shame) produced what we might now term psychological "depth," an inner space defined by repressed "drives" and a restraining "superego." His model of the Renaissance self that was suppressed and deepened by controls was recognizably Freudian—a self that monitored and contained classifiable precultural drives.[32] For Elias the idea of control developed over time and must therefore be situated in the historical process—a valuable theoretical advance. Yet his use of the term *control* automatically evokes a latent self naturally in need of control. It is this evocation, which so shapes his analysis, that requires more exacting historical and theoretical reflection.

John Kasson's *Rudeness and Civility: Manners in Nineteenth-Century Urban America* (1990) builds on Elias's model with rich historical detail (for example, his account of the increasing significance the middle class placed on etiquette). His book demonstrates how important the critical emphasis on "emotional control" can be in analyzing the shaping of the middle class's psychological life, affective needs, and ideological strategies in the nineteenth century. Kasson, like Carroll Smith-Rosenberg and Stephen Nissenbaum in earlier studies (that—taken together—focus on mid-century anxieties about masturbation, menstruation, perceiving character, meat eating, and alcoholism), asks *why* the emerging middle class placed so much stress on controlling the body, sexuality, and emotions, and situates this urge for personal order within the explanatory context of an uncertain marketplace world (steadily populated with immigrants) experienced as disordered or alien. Kasson, like other historians, has drawn on the work of the anthropologist Mary Douglas, who argues that the female body subjected to pollution rituals in various cultures should be read as a displaced "image of society," and that this gendered control of the body is actually a symbolic or displaced attempt to establish social control (that is, bodies are controlled ritually when society at large cannot be). Almost a decade before Douglas published her influential ideas, the historian David Brion Davis, in his study of the antebellum literature of jealousy, proposed that narratives of men obsessed with "ordering" women and their emotions be interpreted historically as symbolic of more encompassing socioeconomic pressures: "Popular writers expressed their fear of change in specifically sexual terms." The meaningfulness assigned to control and the needs for control, Davis and others recognized, are historically structured, not just inherently personal or "psychological."[33]

On one level these historians are inverting the typical psychoanalytic assumption that social activity is simply symbolic of (can be translated into) underlying, often unconscious, desires: they contend that historically specific emotions and sexuality—and the urge to control them in oneself or in others—can become symbolic of (a displacement of) anxieties rooted in encompassing socioeconomic contradictions, transformations, and pressures. If "change and chaos assumed a sexual form," as Smith-Rosenberg put it, the socially symbolic processes that demand historical explanation and *decoding* are the sexualization, biologization, and psychologization of bodies and of relationships in which control is perceived as an extreme emotional need. These historians are somewhat less prone than Elias to regard the very idea of control as a progressive given (the "civilizing" of "drives," the cultural evolution of the "superego," the narrative of the Freudian self coming to know itself as it unfolds in the past) and are even more disposed to examine the symbolism and meanings invested in control as historically contingent and inflected by structures of power (for example, the ideological production of gender, sexual, racial, ethnic, and class differences).[34] Their historical analyses as well as the work in several disciplines I describe below may complicate—more than Elias's—commonsensical uses of the word *control* and assumptions about the emotional self-naturally-in-need-of-control that the word *control* often conjures.

The anthropologist Michelle Rosaldo argues that many cultures have not devised models of the self that highlight the premise of controls and that control paradigms are more likely to emerge within particular sociopolitical or socioeconomic conditions. "For Ilongots—and, I suggest, for many of the relatively egalitarian peoples in the world—there is no social basis for a problematic that assumes need for controls, nor do individuals experience themselves as having boundaries to protect or possessing drives and lusts that must be held in check if they are to maintain their status or engage in everyday cooperation."[35] Contesting the commonsensical view that "rules of emotion are almost exclusively regulative," psychologist Averill—like Rosaldo—broaches the idea that social *regulations* of self (which promote the idea of self as naturally in need of regulation) are social *fabrications* of self: "If we admit that some of the rules of emotion are also constitutive, then the role of society becomes constructive as well as regulative."[36]

Rosaldo contests the very assumption that there is a precultural inner space within which external cultural controls—once taken "inside" in various forms, like mechanisms of guilt and shame—do their managerial work. "The error of the classic 'guilt and shame' account is that it tends to universalize *our* culture's view of a desiring inner self without realizing that such selves—and so, the things they feel—are, in important ways, social creations" (emphasis supplied).[37] To conceptualize the "inner," not as universal, but as a social representation that comes to be experienced as natural—in large part through the formidable and persuasive ideology of controls enforced by social institutions—is to challenge the premise underlying the term *internalization*.[38]

Kovel, a psychoanalyst, thought self-critically about those who possess the cultural power to make "psychological" categories of interiority seem natural and self-evident in America, and arrived at the conclusion "that psychology does not study nature so much as things created by naming . . . [which] itself [is] a very potent, highly rewarded form of labor."[39] This is the case in part because the production of the notion of an "inner" self necessitating control coincides—in the United States—with the popularization of the idea of a "deeper" uncontrolled or unconscious self whose "discovery" is invested with great meaningfulness and value. Thus anthropologists Lila Abu-Lughod and Catherine Lutz ask us to consider how the emotions that "came to be constituted" through cultural representations and institutions as "physiological forces" have acquired seemingly sacred—it should be added, often sexual—significance as the "inner truth about the self."[40]

The dissemination of the ideas that the self is in need of control and that the (frequently sexual) "truth" of the self resides "beneath" culturally imposed controls are two ideological conditions that make possible the operation of what Foucault calls the mechanism of *incitement*. Incitement is the cultural "implantation" (Foucault's word) of "sexualities" in persons.[41] The interesting paradox is in the very word *incitement* (which means to stir up): Foucault maintains that that which has been "implanted" gets stirred up because controls make what was implanted seem natural—an energy, a desire that was there from the start. The literary historians Nancy Armstrong and Leonard Tennenhouse clarify this concept of incitement by suggesting that the *prohibitive* power of culture's categories and institutions be understood as *generative* power: "In placing prohibitions on human nature, culture calls a whole new form of nature into existence, a nature that requires precisely such regulations."[42]

Carol Stearns and Peter Stearns's *Anger: The Struggle for Emotional Control in America's History* (1986) subscribes thoroughly to the psychological "control" model (as the subtitle attests). This interpretive framework sponsors some curious historical and political analyses that may benefit from reconsideration along the lines that Foucault suggests. In their discussion of the early twentieth century the Stearns ask "if the decline of interest in female 'causes' such as temperance and feminism after the 1920s had something to do with a relaxation of the rules for anger expression and therefore a declining need for sublimation," and later "speculate" that "the decline in women's causes after 1920 may have had something to do with an increased ease with expressing anger at home, though the evidence thus far is at best suggestive."[43] Might one infer from this "control" reasoning that if women had been able to "express" anger at home all along, why, there never would have been a nineteenth-century women's rights movement nor a feminist movement during the 1910s and 1920s? Can the trenchant and wide-ranging feminist critiques of the 1910s be explained (away) by the concept of sublimation? Would the mass distribution of punching bags or dartboards to women have satiated their "aggressive" urges and thus exhausted their eagerness to engage in social critique and protest altogether? Here the explanatory value invested in the psychological language of "controls" empties feminist politics of its social specificity, relevance, and validity.

The Stearns employ a psychoanalysis-inspired "hydraulic" model of psychological selfhood that is explicit in their contention that the New Women of the 1920s were permitted "to get in touch with their *true selves,* with anger as well as sexuality" (emphasis supplied).[44] Could the 1920s mass-cultural promotion of this pop psychological rendition of the "true self"—the *incitement* of a self popularly glamorized as "true," as "inner," as being driven by specific desires—have, as the Stearns like to say, "something to do" with the apparent decline of political activity? (See chapter 7, "Glamorizing the Psychological," for more on this.) The Stearns' historical approach seems grounded in the same notions of control, drives, and sublimation that guided Norbert Elias's 1939 work on the "civilizing process." In paying less attention to the politics of the historical production of ideologies that influenced Americans (including themselves) to believe that they "control" and "express" themselves in particular "psychological" ways, they ignore the historical possibility that a powerful mass-cultural machinery of "yourselfing"—based on implantation/incitement—was emerging.

The isolated, uncontextualized idea of "implantation" can sound too conspiratorial and the human beings who are "incited" can seem too passive (not containers of determining instincts, but containers of determining discourses that make them think they have specific kinds of instincts). There is no Board of Conspirators in charge of foolproof strategies to implant/incite. The more subtle, contextual value of the concept is that it asks us to imagine a new kind of multidimensional history that is more suspicious of how human beings have come to read themselves, their innerness, their needs, their desires, and their sense of liberation. The concept's skepticism suggests that some ideologies— which are produced in relation to specific material, political, and cultural conditions—don't simply *act on* "human nature," but they succeed in part by *defining* what it is. I would suggest that such historical considerations are critical, whether or not one chooses to invoke the term *incitement* or to accept its full implications.

The cultural critic, philosopher, and theologian Cornel West did not use the term *incitement,* but I would guess that something like it must have been on his mind after he lectured at a high school in Brooklyn in the mid-1980s. West had faced the despair of inner-city youth who sought solutions to their social predicament in sex and suicide and found himself wondering "whether commercialized sexuality—the stimulation of sexual appetites for pecuniary and personal aims—was but a strategy of power elites in mass media aimed at keeping a lid on such potentially nihilistic explosions" as violence and suicide. Transcendence had been marketed for them—by "Prince in his music and his performance style" and by other artists—as something "incarnate in the lived experience of sexual stimulation." West had no inclination to subscribe to the church's and society's "glib conservative" calls for "chastity and repression."[45] But he could see that the corporate packaging of sexuality—an ideological production of significance, a commodified reduction and refocusing of need and desire—was a questionable emotional or political solution to the gaping contradictions of racism, poverty, disenfranchisement, and disillusionment. The cultural meanings built into sexuality—therapeutic associations of liberation, of transgressiveness, and of expressing one's "inner" essence—were being capitalized on by corporate powers (the music industry, the fashion industry, and so on), not only to "emotionalize" youth as eager consumers, but to channel their desperation into individualized expressions of discontent.

If on one level West regarded a concern with sexuality as an emotional given, as natural, as human (he had no wish to seem "repressive"), yet on another level he saw that the glamorized sexuality in question had been restyled by economic, political, and cultural forces (sex means inner-city "transcendence"). The mechanism of power that West observed was incitement. Incitement could work, not only because of the troubled desire and yearning inflamed by the conditions of poverty and racism, but also because cultural voices—such as the more conservative voices in church and society—prescribed chastity and repression as responses to this situation. Both mechanisms of power—efforts to "control" teen sexuality and the incitement of teen sexuality as transcendence—were reliant on one another. These twin mechanisms of *control* (a mechanism usually more prominent in the nineteenth century's "producer culture") and *incitement* (typically more pervasive in the twentieth century's consumer culture)—in some ways at odds with one another—were more subtly working *in partnership*.[46] West viewed this development not as an overall collective liberation—however much some individuals may have felt enabled by it or have profited from it—but as a politically significant consumer culture creation and restriction of subjectivities, hopes, and dreams.

Hochschild found it necessary to develop a notion of something like what Foucault called incitement, but her approach to emotions differs from Foucault's in significant ways. Hochschild, like Foucault, rejects the "control" model implication that drives or feelings are "stored 'inside' us." Her work with flight attendants who were trained to perform smiling femininity suggested to her that "both the act of 'getting in touch' with feeling and the act of 'trying to' feel may become part of the process that makes the things we get in touch with or the things we manage, *into* a feeling or emotion." But while she thinks it fallacious to conceptualize "acts of emotion as private acts" or emotion itself "as a sealed biological event," she also recoils from interactionist theories that see emotion as wholly socially scripted and humans as only file cabinets of discourses. "From no other authors," she writes about sociologist Erving Goffman, "do we get such an appreciation of the imperialism of rules and such a hazy glimpse of an internally developed self." She concludes that emotion is "a biologically given sense," but also that it is oriented "toward action" and "cognition" and is thus malleable and social.[47]

Poststructuralists (often influenced by Foucault) whose notions of the self almost exclusively focus on the social inscription of meanings might think about Hochschild's challenging criticism of Goffman. Even those historians who are interested in the poststructuralist critical project may find that the conception of subjectivity as "the sites of discursive struggle"[48] (a site dramatized in Kruger's postmodern antiportrait bearing the words "You are not yourself") lacks a certain "individual" (yes, a historical discourse) and "psychological" (yes, another historical discourse) *specificity* when trying to account for persons who somehow, against all odds, manage to resist dominant forces — when others would yield — and thus change the world. When conceptualizing agency and resistance, poststructuralists sometimes refer to "gaps"[49] in ideologies or norms (like the spaces between the fragments of mirror in Kruger's image) that can be perceived and acted on. But it might be argued that this vision of agency tells us little about the "I" or the force or whatever one wants to call that which sees and subverts received meanings and discourses in hitherto unimaginable ways to originate new emancipatory possibilities.[50] In contrast to the Foucaultians and poststructuralists Elias offers us a historical (and Freudian) vision of an "internally developed" agent whose development is modified by social change. But he does so at the cost of failing to reckon with, historically, the social transformations and forces that made his basic model of development (the "control" paradigm) seem (to him) transportable through history as essentially human (essentially "civilized").

Pierre Bourdieu, like Elias, is a sociologist who has long been interested in studying matters of taste, bodily deportment, and the establishment of values, and he has extreme confidence in the power of sociology to reconceptualize radically both agency and "internal development." For Bourdieu, etiquette exemplifies not the social imposition of "civilized" controls on precultural (Freudian) drives, but rather the cultural acquisition of structured and (actively) structuring dispositions that constitute a profoundly social and historical self taught to (mis)read its dispositions as nature. Bourdieu's "socio-analysis"—which, unlike psychoanalysis, makes visible the "social uncon-scious"—jettisons much of the language and assumptions attached to the psy-chological self ("subjectivism"). Even Foucault's notion of incitement may appear to have a subjectivist residue in comparison with Bourdieu's perception of socialization. Bourdieu's analysis of internal development is wholly social and historical. The body is embodied history; the unconscious is nothing more than "the forgetting of history which history itself produces"; the most "unthinkable thought"—that psychological common sense imagines as lurk-ing in one's individual "depth"—is "inscribed in the objectivity and in the his-tory of the social positions that we have held in the past and that we presently occupy"; the "uncreated creator" (Jean-Paul Sartre's term) is a romantic indi-vidualist fantasy. By exposing "externality at the heart of internality, banality behind the illusion of rarity, the common in the search for the unique," Bour-dieu's politically conscious "socioanalysis" of the hypersocialized self would equip us to carry out a sociologically self-reflexive "self-reappropriation." The premise: that which is grasped as social—and not mistaken as natural and unique—can be changed.

Bourdieu's concept of *habitus* (used where one would expect to see refer-ences to "the self")—which I can sketch here only in broad strokes—aims to supplant modern notions of the psychological self and debunk false dichotomies such as individual versus society (the individual, itself a mystified notion, could never stand apart from society in Bourdieu's view). The historically situated habitus is comprised of inculcated and durable, yet "open" and alterable, social systems of dispositions (dating from early childhood—an influential phase) that are structuring structures, that orient rather than determine us, that give one a tacit "feel for the [social] game" and can also change the game, that gen-erate ("free production") thoughts, perceptions, appreciations, meaningfulness, preferences, anticipations. This generative capacity ("conditioned and condi-tional freedoms") is often predictable, as when members of a habitus group reach consensus without being conscious that they are adhering to any "rules of the game" or to the "regularities" that condition them. But this generative power can be "relatively unpredictable" and "infinite" only within limits ("set by the historically and socially situated conditions of its production")—it is not what Bourdieu would classify as "creative" (for him, a mystification). Agency (always grounded in social practices, positions, structures) is worked out in the reciprocally conditioning relationships between the habitus and the "field" (for example, education, economics, culture).[51]

This structure-as-structuring logic—like some poststructuralist theories— still may not completely satisfy those historians who persist in wondering why individuals in similar material and ideological circumstances (the same habitus group) don't all recognize and resist oppression in the same "original" (which is never wholly individual) or critical way. And Bourdieu's representation of agency may not persuade those historians who see that the cultural power of psychological discourse in the modern era is such that it does partly socially transform individuals into "psychological" individuals (who can be partially described, if not fully explained, in "psychological" terms). Curiously, Bourdieu characterizes his distinctly antipsychological "socioanalysis" as "self-therapy" and employs an idiom of purification to describe his intent that recalls—as it must, to him—psychoanalytic studies of handwashing compulsion (symbolic caricatures of the will to *control* one's unconscious and/or forbidden drives). He tries, he says, in praise of his vigilant sociological self-reflexivity, "to cleanse my work of the social determinants that necessarily bear on sociologists."[52] More obviously, and daringly, he has "cleansed" his sociological rendition of "internal" agency of psychological determinants. Bourdieu's challenging work invites the question: if we mean to devise a rigorously historical and cultural understanding of an "internally" developed agent (that the culture labels and popularly represents as "psychological" and "emotional"), must we credit *any* assumptions about psychological human nature and about the need to control it?

Wilhelm Reich and some members of the Frankfurt School—who endeavored to synthesize Marxist and psychoanalytic theories—would probably have criticized Bourdieu's invention of habitus for its erasure of what they conceptualized as a *dialectic* between the social and the body or psychological "human nature."[53] Terry Eagleton, a Marxist theorist heavily influenced by both poststructuralist and historicist criticism, upheld this social-human nature dialectic, but with great theoretical circumspection. Anticipating the objection that "human nature" has often been cited by dominant groups to sanction their oppression of others, he reminds us of the French Revolution to emphasize that the invocation of the category of "human nature" is not "inherently reactionary." To acknowledge that the human being, somewhat constrained by the basic needs and powers of the body, is not infinitely plastic, he insists, is not tantamount to asserting that the self is unchangeable. Both culture and aspects of human nature, he affirms, can be transformed.

Eagleton does specify certain fundamental needs as fairly constant: "Human societies, by virtue of the biological structure of [the] body, all need to engage in some form of labour and some kind of sexual reproduction; all human beings require warmth, rest, nourishment and shelter, and are inevitably implicated by the necessities of labour and sexuality in various forms of social association, the regulation of which we name the political. . . . The fact that these transhistorical truths are always culturally specific, always variably instantiated, is no argument against their transhistoricality."[54] For Eagleton, to accept such corporeal needs as essentially human is to think as a *dialectical materialist:* the body's nature is never outside of culture, but it does have its own properties; culture interacts with the body's always encoded nature and is affected by its properties. Yet, as Eagleton well knows, the socialized individual on which a cultural history of emotional and psychological life might help to shed critical light is far more ideologically complex than this profile of simple human needs suggests—or explains.

The question of the internally developed psychobiological self remains (for me and my co-editor, at any rate) debatable and open. How do the "biological givens" ascertained by psychobiologists explain the extraordinary variations in cultural representations and experiences of the self studied by Needham, Rosaldo, Lutz, Abu-Lughod, and Heelas? Tiefer, as one would expect, has her Foucaultian doubts about psychobiological authority, yet she doesn't efface biology. She was originally trained in physiological psychology (her dissertation was on hormones and mating behavior in golden hamsters), but her experience as a feminist therapist motivated her to criticize the "bio-medical model" and its determinism and to embrace instead a "contextualized" (historical and cross-cultural) perspective. Biology remains in her picture of self, however, not as a given that one can pin down and delimit, but as a set of never wholly knowable potentials "that may or may not be developed by a given culture." She sees the self as "a psychobiosocial unity" whose "biological potentials [are] expressed and constructed very differently in different sociohistorical situations."[55]

It may be that psychobiology will make contributions to the historical comprehension of a "psychobiosocial" self. But these contributions should be weighed cautiously in reference to the historical study of how and why social transformations brought with them quite diverse ideologies of "psychological" selfhood (and "control") that all came to be understood as natural. Whatever position one adopts on matters like biological causality and poststructuralist discursive causality, it is crucial to appreciate why more theoretically self-reflexive histories of psychological and emotional life are needed: not only will they tend to complicate our knowledge of how humans have come to define themselves, they may help us to picture more strategically the social possibilities of more tolerantly redefining—or, perhaps more wisely, *not defining*—ourselves.[56]

The Psychological as Symptom of Vaster Historical Transformations

When many of us in the academic middle class read Hochschild's phrase "internally developed [psychological] self"—or others like it, such as "psychodynamics"—we readily, maybe automatically, think of psychoanalysis, a representation of the self, the family (and its history), and the body that has been popularized for the past eighty years as therapeutic common sense. There is much to say about how psychoanalysis—both as subject and as theory—fits into a cultural history of psychological and emotional life in America. But here I can offer only a few focused remarks that will begin with Fredric Jameson's hint that psychoanalysis and its establishment of cultural authority might be reconsidered historically as an ideological *symptom*. In 1974 this Marxist dialectician wondered: "What if the Freudian raw material (. . . dreams, slips of the tongue, fixations, traumas, the Oedipal situation, the death wish) were itself but a sign or symptom of some vaster historical transformation?" The related historical question here is: Why have many members of the middle and upper classes so enthusiastically preoccupied themselves with—assigned such meaningfulness and fascination to—notions of the self, the family, and the body that center on dreams, childhood conflicts, familial tensions, and ambivalence? In 1980 Jameson gave a bit more historical concreteness to the character of this historical transformation. The "symbolic possibilities" of psychoanalysis, he proposed in passing, historically rely on "the preliminary isolation of sexual experience" and the "autonomization of the family as a private space in the nascent sphere of bourgeois society."[57] In linking the "symbolic possibilities" of psychoanalysis to the complex emotional relations spawned within the privatization of bourgeois families, Jameson was moving in the direction of suggesting that psychoanalysis made sense to—easily became familiar to—members of the middle and upper classes for underlying historical, not just intellectual, reasons.

Several years before Jameson made these comments, the historian John Demos posited more specific linkages of this sort in "Oedipus and America" (1978) (see chapter 3). Without disclosing the details of his argument, I shall note that Demos found the American nineteenth-century white privatized middle-class family heating up emotionally and looking exceedingly psychoanalytic (oedipal) for historical and ideological reasons (not because of eternal "human nature") long before psychoanalysis arrived on these shores.[58] Shortly before Demos sketched these connections, the sociologist Eli Zaretsky argued that the "expansion of inner life" within the nineteenth-century white American middle-class privatized family was symbiotic with "capitalist expansion." In brief, he interpreted the cultivation of (white) "inner life" as a complex emotional and ideological response to the rise of industrial America and thus concluded that psychoanalysis "speaks" to psychological and emotional "needs that have risen historically." Since the mid-1970s historians of the family like Mary Ryan, Stuart Blumin, and Stephanie Coontz have provided more detailed insights into the privatizing tendency of nineteenth-century white middle-class families (and their intensification of affection, guilt, and ambivalence), some of whose early twentieth-century offspring, not surprisingly, recognized and embraced psychoanalysis as universal truth.[59]

Broadly, what begins to fall into place if we reevaluate psychoanalysis more as a revealing historical symptom than as an excavation of "human nature" is a picture of the nineteenth- and twentieth-century production of "psychological" individuals, "psychological" families, and "psychological" bodies—joined ideologically to the rise of and to the identity-formation of the white middle class. What still needs to be investigated historically is the degree to which and the ways in which modern "therapeutic" discourses, while often presuming to fathom and repair universal "human nature," have in fact contributed ideologically to the normative racial construction of *whiteness*. Therapeutic discourses, for example, have made available a "psychological individuality" and a "psychological depth" that, once identified with and enacted, enabled some members of the white middle and upper classes to envision their conflicted, sometimes naughty, and vastly absorbing "human nature" as more human, more universal, yet more individual, and more complex (deeper) than that of Americans of color.

Another key historical condition for the development of the "symbolic possibilities" of psychoanalysis is the alienation the middle class experienced as a result of the rapid reorganization of work and bureaucratic power—an alienation that intensified the needs and expectations of workers who sought therapeutic meaningfulness in the sentimentalized family. "Turned inward by alienation," Kovel observes, American "subjectivity flowers like orchids in a greenhouse. The greenhouse is the bourgeois psyche." Americans are used to the much-publicized and highly acceptable common sense that capitalism's workplaces, technology, and mass culture attempt to standardize humanity into robots (a mechanization of self satirized in films like Charlie Chaplin's *Modern Times* [1936]), but in general we seem to think less critically about the fact that these social forces actively transform us into highly emotional "psychological" subjects. In fact, the culture of capitalism, Kovel maintains, profits enormously from the alienation it creates by mass marketing "curiosity about the individual" as well as "an awareness of neurosis": "psychology is but the formal science of this curiosity."[60] Taking a cue from Jameson, Demos, Zaretsky, and Kovel, if one is truly interested in a cultural history that explores the possibilities that the rise of "psychological" common sense and that the preoccupation with this common sense are symptoms of vaster historical transformations, then one's investigations must go well beyond a disciplinary history of psychology, an intellectual history of psychoanalysis, or an institutional history of psychiatry—although these histories of course remain crucial dimensions of this larger concept of history and causality.[61]

Inventions of the Psychological within the Cultural History of Power

Reading the narratives of his career as a Marxist psychoanalyst, one cannot help but draw the conclusion that Joel Kovel aided a great many persons, even as he saw himself enmeshed in a therapeutic industry that profited from further psychologizing and (as he says) mystifying the self-understanding of individuals already made "psychological" ("inflated and crippled" with "twisted" desire) by material and ideological pressures.[62] Therapeutic rescue efforts such as those undertaken by Kovel are important parts of a history of "the psychological" that chronicles emerging cultural forms of healing in America. The critical emphasis in this volume, however, tends to be more on the fact that rescue efforts were thought to be necessary (in particular ideological forms in literature, art, drama, music, television, psychology, and so on) and on how these efforts—often well intended—have participated in both the reproduction and the contestation of a range of social contradictions. I contend that the history of psychological and emotional life in America demands that we think in more sophisticated and creative ways about the formation and exercise of cultural power draped in "psychological" authority— power that has assumed shapes that are sometimes fairly obvious, sometimes revealingly subtle.

Much more research needs to be done on the connection between the history of psychological institutions and ideologies and the history of racialization in America. From the segregation of African Americans and whites in nineteenth-century asylums, to the "psychological" stereotyping of slaves as mad (who thus benefit from enslavement) and of emancipated blacks as emotionally uncontrollable (possessors of overdeveloped emotions intensified by "freedom"), to the "psychological" screening that (color) barred so many Native Americans and African Americans from the armed services in World War II, to the postwar period's "psychological" reduction of the social contradictions of inner-city poverty and racism to a problem of African American self-esteem— the history we know is at the beginning stages.[63] Those who oversimplify and decontextualize sexuality as an unambiguously fun-filled drive might take note, not only of Cornel West's observations about the Brooklyn high school, but also of the history of late nineteenth-century asylums in which the diagnosis of "hypersexual activity" in white middle-class women was categorized as psychopathic and frowned upon, while female African American inmates who were diagnosed in the same manner were seen as expressing the "ingrained natural immorality of [their] race."[64] African American sexuality was encoded to support ideologies of racial hierarchy and difference which excluded blacks from middle-class "humanity."

The "psychological" stereotyping of nineteenth- and twentieth-century ethnic groups—in psychiatric discourse, literature (high literature, dime novels), art (paintings, cartoons), and popular songs—contributed to ideological efforts to produce a cheap labor pool whose exploitation (like the exploitation of African Americans) would seem only natural. Some nineteenth-century psychiatrists, for example, characterized the working-class Irish as lacking "insight" into their problems, as possessing "imperfectly developed brains," and as taking to drink and going "insane" because of an unaccountably "strong love of their native land."[65] In the twentieth century Eugene O'Neill strategically re-encoded stock (often theatrical) representations of the Irish as mad: the Irish he staged had psychological conflicts, for certain, but now this meant that they were "deep" and possessed a "psychological" capital that non-Irish members of his middle- and upper-class audiences might even covet.[66] The story of efforts to Americanize "ethnic" emotions in schools and other institutions still needs to be recovered. Such a history might prompt some of us to revise or relativize middle-class notions of what constitutes psychological "depth," value, and normality and to better scrutinize how and why such therapeutic concepts took on self-evident meaning (and meaningfulness) so successfully within a social structure of inequality.

The feminizing of women as hyperpsychological humans who are "naturally" saturated with and determined by emotions in need of control and interpretation also has a complex history that requires more refined theorizing and more expansive historical research.[67] The historical rise of mass-cultural sentimental and later officially "psychological" discourses that stereotyped women as overwhelmingly "emotional" should be situated in the history of the emergence of industrial and corporate capitalism. Some of the most fruitful thinking about the causes and politics of the feminization of women has been done by historians and critics—like Hazel Carby, Mary Ryan, Nancy Cott, Carroll Smith-Rosenberg, Karen Halttunen, Christine Stansell, Stephanie Coontz, Catherine Hall, Nancy Armstrong, Mary Poovey, and Joan Scott—who examine the interconnectedness of developments like feminization, capitalist class formations, and racialization.[68] Scott suggests that "the concept of class in the nineteenth century relied on gender for its articulation," and that when the maintenance of the "binary opposition" of genders becomes "part of the meaning of power itself," then "to question or alter any aspect"—say, to question the "psychological" naturalness of femininity or masculinity—"threatens the entire system."[69]

Recent historical and theoretical work, as I have been suggesting, has enabled scholars to contemplate the possibility that "sexuality," "emotions," and "psychology" are not lodged *in* the body in some unmediated natural way but are often inscribed in particular forms *on* the body—as in the case of the

African American female asylum inmates whose ostensibly inherent sexuality of a particular sort enabled white medical authorities to degrade them as morally, intellectually, socially, and emotionally inferior objects. The sexualization of white female middle-class bodies (especially in medical discourse) actually accompanied their sentimental feminization, and operating in alliance, these ideological developments produced a "psychologically" feminine woman who might simultaneously dread and be drawn to her tabooed sexuality (resulting perhaps in "hysteria") or might become more easily convinced that the expression of her "repressed" sexuality is tantamount to expressing her inner truth and liberation.[70] It may be politically advantageous for more reasons than I can go into here for those who hold power to assign bodies "psychological" characteristics if the subordinated occupants of those social bodies (women in various groups, African Americans, immigrants) come to accept ideological ascriptions of "psychological" determinism as naturally emerging from within them. To borrow Scott's phrasing, they can be taught to read their prescribed "psychological" essence as "sure and fixed, outside of human construction."[71]

The power of psychological discourse to transform bodies is particularly evident in the making of the homosexual body, which up to the nineteenth century was only identified as a body that had engaged in illicit acts. As Foucault explains, the meaning of this body was resignified with new kinds of "psychological" histories: "The nineteenth-century homosexual became a personage, a past, a case history, a childhood, in addition to being a type of life . . . with an indiscreet anatomy. Nothing that went into his total composition was unaffected by his sexuality." In short, the homosexual offender's newly implanted "psychology" rendered him (and later her) "sick" and in need of "psychological" analysis. The form this normalizing (aversion) therapy took in 1950s and 1960s America was sometimes shock treatment and the injection of chemicals.[72]

The history of class relations and the production of psychological identities is enormously complex.[73] My few remarks will only address how psychological discourses might be seen as crucial to the formation of American middle-class and upper-class identities (cultural distinctions between the two are not always clear). There are edifying older and newer ways of considering "the psychological" as a dimension of middle-class *affirmation*. The older way is articulated concisely by the literary historian Frederick Hoffman. The "inner drama" that modern psychological discourse offered members of the middle and upper classes, Hoffman observes, performed as "an excellent substitute for social and economic motives in explaining social behavior." Their "inner drama" promised members of these classes a new sense of individualized meaningfulness with which they could busy themselves. Yet these classes were not monolithic. In his study of constructions of intimacy and sexual morality in the American Protestant bourgeoisie of the 1860s and 1870s (the focus is on the famous Beecher-Tilden trial), Richard Fox counsels, "we have to see bourgeois culture as deeply divided against itself."[74] This holds true of bourgeois culture during later periods as well.

Fox's admonition moves us closer to Foucault's way of considering psychological/sexual discourse as a multidimensional tactic of bourgeois affirmation, an idea that I shall elaborate and extend. Many members of the nineteenth- and twentieth-century middle and upper classes have been invested in the internecine conflict of imposing taboos and in breaking taboos. Both sides (members can back one side on some issues and the other side on others, or change sides) have given the taboo wars heightened significance. Observing the keen interest invested in taboos, Foucault notes, in his supremely suspicious manner, that "there can exist different and even contradictory discourses within the same [bourgeois] strategy."[75] The intraclass taboo wars (ceaselessly imposing them—breaking them, defining morality and/or liberation in reference to them) become fascinating and meaningful enough to members of the middle and upper classes that they need not fret overmuch about what Hoffman termed their other "social and economic motives." Taboo battles, viewed as a self-contradictory *unit*, might be considered as the same strategy to deflect or displace the bourgeois gaze from economic and social interests and motives as central to their identity and to their positions within a power structure that maintains inequality.[76]

But what members of the middle and upper classes have done for and *to* themselves with therapeutic culture is even more complex, odd, and intriguing. The nineteenth-century middle class produced sentiment and "angels in the house" partly to affirm itself in its own eyes—and ideally in the eyes of "others," too—as more "human" and more "decent" than other groups. However, members of the twentieth-century middle and upper classes, having adopted psychological and therapeutic discourses (which had nineteenth-century literary and domestic origins), affirmed their social superiority or potency by elevating the cultural value of anxiety, sexual conflicts, and familial tensions. Put differently, an increasing number of persons who belonged to these classes resignified *anxiety as affirmation, emotional turmoil as subjective potency,* and *familial ambivalence as psychological capital.* Curiously, class identity often came to entail not only a "psychological" preoccupation with oneself and with others, but also a measure of suffering.[77]

Members of these classes who represented themselves as "moral" or conservative or commonsensical might still dismiss this psychologization and sexualization of subjective potency. Nevertheless, the battles between these "taboo" groups over how personal life should be conducted would help restrict their collective sense of what was worth struggling over and worrying about to an ideological field dominated by issues like psychology, family life, sexuality, and individualism (the ever-marketable concerns of best-selling novels, movies, pop songs, and pop psychology). Members of the American middle and upper classes profited from reproducing their passions, their consciences, and their rebellions within these favored terms and categories. Modern middle- and upper-class power works in one of its most *subtle* ways not by uniformly imposing taboos (still a force, but so blatant), or by insisting on the preeminence of its "decent," well-mannered, sentimental character over the character of other groups (still a tactic, though too embarrassingly sanctimonious and hypocritical for some), but by getting large numbers of class members to emotionally invest in and fight over identities and notions of resistance and liberation that are informed by a fairly focused register of key concerns (concerns that play a role in what has been termed the "culture wars"). "The psychological" is a key category in this register.[78]

Strategic Openness

Though it is my conviction that the creation of what Raymond Williams termed the "great modern ideological system" of "the psychological" has to be grasped in part as a complex narrative woven into the larger history of the sometimes subtle, sometimes brazen inventions of social power in America, I would not presume to prescribe how one should focus on this history (by drawing on Marxist theories, feminist theories, poststructuralism, Foucaultian theories, Bourdieuian sociology, psychoanalysis, anthropological studies, or other approaches). I shall plead that, whatever theoretical frames one devises, it is exigent to foreground considerations of power precisely because the history of psychological and emotional life is still very much a field in formation. This newly developing cultural history of psychological "yourselfing," which since the 1970s has in sundry forms reached a readership beyond the academy, must not—like much pop psychology—become a pop history or pop criticism that will simply bank on readers' culturally excited curiosity about psychological, emotional, familial, and sexual relations. Instead such intensified curiosity—which is often also the curiosity of historians and critics who do this research—must be self-critically historicized in one's analysis of how cultural power works (and frequently *fascinates* and *gratifies* as it works).[79]

Susan Sontag has lamented the relative lack of informed protest in print and elsewhere about the atrocities in Bosnia (concentration/death camps, mass slaughter, tens of thousands of military-sanctioned rapes), and blasted the we're-here-not-there isolationism of American intellectuals bribed into emotional closure by their positions within a corporate consumer culture whose influence runs deep into the home and the "heart": "All that makes sense is private life. Individualism, and the cultivation of the self and private well-being—featuring, above all, the ideal of 'health'—are the values to which intellectuals are most likely to subscribe." Sontag's moral rebuke is by no means new: similar criticisms were being launched even in the mid-nineteenth century as the middle-class privatization of emotional commitments was gearing up. In mid-century Stephen Pearl Andrews, an American anarchist, was already attempting to pierce the middle class's emotional armor: "The intense concentration of all the affections upon the little circles of immediate family relations and connections, instead of being a positive virtue, as has been assumed, is in fact only a virtue relatively to the existing falseness and antagonism of all the relations outside of the family. It is a secret and contraband hoarding of the affections."[80] If a history of psychological and emotional life can help explicate how it is that many Americans (for all their angst and ambivalence) are basically *emotionally cozy* with the perpetuation of systemic social, economic, and political contradictions—often "legal" contradictions that crush lives on our beleaguered, but potentially magnificent-for-all planet—then it will be worth the effort to read and write this sort of history.

Scholars who have taken on this demanding historical project have already learned—and unlearned—from one another's advances and difficulties, and will no doubt continue to do so in constructive ways.[81] My co-editor and I hope that *Inventing the Psychological* will help promote what the cultural theorist Stuart Hall desires for cultural studies in America generally—a *strategic openness*.[82] We want to meet the interdisciplinary challenge of this historical and critical work head on and raise questions, experiment with theories, and open eyes, not only to better conceptualize the possibilities of a new, less bounded scholarship, but to imagine more freely, responsibly, and compassionately what we might make of ourselves and our world.

Notes

1. The historian Jean-Pierre Vernant has articulated why it is important for historians to be open-minded and to reassess the (unhistorical) premise (subscribed to by many historians, he says) that the psychological is a universal, a "fixed principle of intelligibility," a basis—established by psychologists—for the explanation of motivation, character, and behavior. Vernant urges historians to scrutinize and contextualize "the psychological" itself as a historical category, a phenomenon whose cultural meanings and social significance have altered over time and thus require *explanation*—in short, a "problem that needs to be accounted for in the same way as all the rest of the data" ("History and Psychology" in his *Mortals and Immortals: Collected Essays*, ed. Froma I. Zeitlen [Princeton: Princeton University Press, 1991], 262). Readers who are interested might compare the chapters in *Inventing the Psychological* to those in one of the most

sophisticated, imaginative, self-critical, and socially concerned contributions to psychohistory, which featured the work of Erik H. Erikson, Philip Rieff, Norman Birnbaum, Kenneth Keniston, and Robert Coles, among others: *Explorations in Psychohistory: The Wellfleet Papers*, ed. Robert Jay Lifton with Eric Olsen (New York: Simon and Schuster, 1974). While our volume moves even further away from the "great man" psychohistorical emphasis than Lifton's, my co-editor and I share Lifton's open-ended and highly receptive approach to future critical possibilities: "No one knows what will happen in the future, but one can be sure that things will change" (41). Our volume is one example of how the conceptualization of the history of psychological and emotional life has opened up in America since 1974.

2. Raymond Williams, *Marxism and Literature* (New York: Oxford University Press, 1978), 128–29. Two theorists whose work has had a longstanding influence on my thinking about the history of emotional life are Williams and Jean-Paul Sartre. Williams's emphasis on studying the hegemonic forms, conventions, narratives, and figures (e.g., in literature and art) that materially make up "*structures* of feeling" is crucial: "We are . . . defining a social experience which is still in *process*, often indeed not yet recognized as social [and as having structures] but taken to be private, idiosyncratic, and even isolating, but which in analysis . . . has its [historically] emergent, connecting, and dominant characteristics, indeed its specific hierarchies" (132; see 128–35). He places great stress on the way literary and dramatic *forms* have both shaped subjectivities and contributed to making subjective concerns of certain kinds seem compelling (e.g., the transformation of the forms of Greek tragedy into modern privatized bourgeois "subjective expressionism") (*The Sociology of Culture* [New York: Schocken, 1981], 148–80). Williams has also shown the importance of situating words that represent emotional experience in the context of the historical transformations that have shaped their meanings (e.g., in the twentieth century the word *psychological* narrowed in scope to signify a personal, often unconscious, realm of the self and was used to make the ideological dichotomy between society and individual seem convincing). See Williams's essays on psychological, subjective, individual, sensibility, and art in *Keywords: A Vocabulary of Culture and Society* (New York: Oxford University Press, 1976), 207–09, 259–64, 133–36, 235–38, 32–35. Williams's writing has had a powerful effect on the development of cultural studies in Britain and America. As an example of Williams's influence, the historian Richard Johnson represents cultural studies as the study of forms through which subjectivities have been produced. He has suggested that literary critics' concerns about literary value might be expanded and reconceived: critics might engage in the historical and ideological evaluation of how and why some "textual embodiments of subjective forms come to be valued over others" ("What Is Cultural Studies Anyway?" *Social Text* 16 [1986]: 38–80, see 62). In *Search for a Method*, trans. Hazel Barnes (New York: Vintage, 1968), Sartre outlines why and how subjectivity, family life, and emotional relations (too personalized and individualized in many biographies) must be understood dialectically as complexly historical subjects. In particular see his discussion of what dimensions of history should be considered if one were to write a truly historical biography of Gustave Flaubert. Sartre's outline of 1960 was the basis for his magisterial cultural biography, *The Family Idiot: Gustave Flaubert, 1821–1857* (recently translated and published in five volumes by the University of Chicago Press).

3. The making of the self into a "psychological" self has indeed been a subtle dimen-

sion of political and social change—for example, the making of a class. For a lucid analysis of the ideological relationships between the antebellum formation of the middle class and the shift from the middle class's corporal punishment of children to psychological and emotional disciplining through "love" (i.e., the "implantation" of a guilty conscience made effective by the child's intensified love for sentimentalized parents), see Richard H. Brodhead, "Sparing the Rod: Discipline and Fiction in Antebellum America" (13–47), in his *Cultures of Letters: Scenes of Reading and Writing in Nineteenth-Century America* (Chicago: University of Chicago Press, 1993). For a theoretically provocative study of twentieth-century American culture that situates the production of subjectivities as forms of ideological power see Michael Leja, *Reframing Abstract Expressionism: Subjectivity and Painting in the 1940s* (New Haven: Yale University Press, 1993). An earlier and very influential study of the complex relationships between literature, social power, and the cultural encoding and production of "inwardness" is Stephen Greenblatt, *Renaissance Self-Fashioning: From More to Shakespeare* (Chicago: University of Chicago Press, 1980).

4. Berger, *And Our Faces, My Heart, Brief as Photos* (New York: Pantheon, 1984), 66. Also see *Passion and Power: Sexuality in History*, ed. Kathy Peiss and Christina Simmons with Robert A. Padgug (Philadelphia: Temple University Press, 1989), and three important books by the philosopher Robert C. Solomon: *The Passions* (New York: Doubleday, 1976), *About Love* (New York: Simon and Schuster, 1988), and *A Passion for Justice: Emotions and the Origin of the Social Contract* (Reading, Mass.: Addison-Wesley, 1990).

5. Tiefer, *Sex Is Not a Natural Act and Other Essays* (Boulder, Colo.: Westview Press, 1995), 7. Ludwig Wittgenstein would have found merit in Tiefer's Foucaultian argument: in his ruminations on "psychological language" he suggested that "love" is inseparable from the conventions, narratives, roles, and performances that cultures concoct to represent it. Wittgenstein is quoted in Paul Heelas, "The Model Applied: Anthropology and Indigenous Psychologies," in *Indigenous Psychologies: The Anthropology of the Self,* ed. Paul Heelas and Andrew Lock (London: Academic Press, 1981), 49.

6. See Foucault, *The History of Sexuality, Volume 1: An Introduction,* trans. Robert Hurley (New York: Vintage, 1980).

7. See: text by Kate Linker, *Love for Sale: The Words and Pictures of Barbara Kruger* (New York: Harry N. Abrams, 1990), 31. On the figure of Vanity see John Berger, Sven Blomberg, Chris Fox, Michael Dibb, Richard Hollis, *Ways of Seeing* (Harmondsworth, England: Penguin, 1979): "The mirror was often used as a symbol of the vanity of woman. The moralizing, however, was mostly hypocritical. You painted a naked woman because you enjoyed looking at her, you put a mirror in her hand and you called the painting *Vanity,* thus morally condemning the woman whose nakedness you had depicted for your own pleasure. The real function of the mirror was otherwise. It was to make the woman connive in treating herself as, first and foremost, a sight" (51).

8. What Kruger's postmodern image may be disrupting is a process that the French Marxist theorist Louis Althusser termed *interpellation* or "hailing": the hailed individual ("Hey, you there!" shouts the policeman) "will turn around" and become "a *subject*. . . . The existence of ideology and the hailing or interpellation of individuals as subjects are one and the same thing" (*Lenin and Philosophy, and Other Essays,* trans. Ben Brewster [New York: Monthly Review Press, 1971], 174–75). Influenced by Althusser, the British cultural studies theorist Stuart Hall aimed to move beyond Raymond Williams's concept of "structures of feeling" and to argue that theorists must reconceive the "I" not as "the

seat of consciousness and the foundation of ideological discourses" or as the "integral Cartesian centre of thought" but as "a contradictory discursive category constituted by ideological discourse itself." See Hall's "Cultural Studies and the Centre: Some Problematics and Problems," in *Culture, Media, Language: Working Papers in Cultural Studies, 1972–79* (London: Hutchinson and CCCS, 1980), 33. For Hall's critique of Williams's concept of "structures of feeling," see his chapter "Politics and Letters," in *Raymond Williams: Critical Perspectives*, ed. Terry Eagleton (Boston: Northeastern University Press, 1989), 62. Another foundational British cultural studies text that focused on the cultural and semiotic constitution of the "I" is Rosalind Coward and John Ellis, *Language and Materialism: Developments in Semiology and the Theory of the Subject* (London: Routledge & Kegan Paul, 1977). Peter Stallybrass has brought a more concrete historical awareness of capitalism and individualism to Althusser's notion that interpellation transforms the individual into a subject and has reversed the terms. According to Stallybrass, Althusser is mistaken that "the individual" who is "subjected" or "interpellated" is—prior to this "subjection"— the "center of free consciousness and independent judgment"; rather, the concept of the "free" "individual" is itself the most subtle "interpellation" that has gathered ideological strength over the past few hundred years: "within a capitalist mode of production, ideology interpellated, not the individual as a subject, but the *subject* as an *individual*." See Stallybrass, "Shakespeare, the Individual, and the Text," in *Cultural Studies*, ed. Lawrence Grossberg, Cary Nelson, and Paula Treichler (New York: Routledge, 1992), 593.

9. I thank Richard Lowry for suggesting the elaboration of the argument developed in the previous two sentences.

10. For interdisciplinary scholarship (mainly by anthropologists) that illuminates ideologies of "self-making" and of what I have termed "yourselfing," see *Rhetorics of Self-Making*, ed. Debbora Battaglia (Berkeley: University of California Press, 1995).

11. Again I am indebted to Richard Lowry for his phrase—a politics of "selfing"—and for suggesting that I expand on this.

12. See Paul Heelas, "Emotion Talk Across Cultures," in *The Social Construction of Emotions*, ed. Rom Harré (Oxford: Basil Blackwell, 1986), 255.

13. Frederick also wrote books on sales management and advertising. See his *What Is Your Emotional Age? And 65 Other Mental Tests* (New York: Bourse, 1928), 1, 2.

14. On accidie and melancholy see Rom Harré, "An Outline of the Social Constructionist Viewpoint," 2–14, and Rom Harré and Robert Finlay-Jones, "Emotion Talk Across Time," 220–33, in *Social Construction of Emotions*.

15. See Heelas, "Emotion Talk Across Cultures," 244–45, 247, 260. On melancholy also see Jennifer Radden, "Melancholy and Melancholia," in *Pathologies of the Modern Self: Postmodern Studies on Narcissism, Schizophrenia, and Depression*, ed. David Michael Levin (New York: New York University Press, 1987), 231–50.

16. Needham, "Inner States as Universals: Sceptical Reflections on Human Nature," in *Indigenous Psychologies*, 68. Also see Richard A. Shweder with Edmund J. Bourne, "Does the Concept of the Person Vary Cross-Culturally?" in Shweder's *Thinking Through Cultures: Expeditions in Cultural Psychology* (Cambridge: Harvard University Press, 1991), 113–55. Shweder and Bourne's answer is that it does.

17. Lutz, "Depression and the Translation of Emotional Worlds," in *Culture and Depression: Studies in Anthropology and Cross-Cultural Psychiatry of Affect and Disorder*, ed. Arthur Kleinman and Byron Good (Berkeley: University of California Press, 1985), 72, 70. On

the anthropology of constructs of emotions also see Benedicte Grima, *The Performance of Emotion Among Paxtun Women: "The Misfortunes Which Have Befallen Me"* (Austin: University of Texas Press, 1992), Unni Wikan, *Managing Turbulent Hearts: A Balinese Formula for Living* (Chicago: University of Chicago Press, 1990), and Robert R. Desjarlais, *Body and Emotion: The Aesthetics of Illness and Healing in the Nepal Himalayas* (Philadelphia: University of Pennsylvania Press, 1992).

18. Kovel, *The Radical Spirit: Essays on Psychoanalysis and Society* (London: Free Association Books, 1988), 152–53.

19. See Lutz's fascinating study *Unnatural Emotions: Everyday Sentiments on a Micronesian Atoll and Their Challenge to Western Theory* (Chicago: University of Chicago Press, 1988), in which she explains that her aim is "to treat emotion as an ideological practice rather than as a thing to be discovered or an essence to be distilled" (4).

20. See Rieff, *The Triumph of the Therapeutic: Uses of Faith after Freud* (New York: Harper & Row, 1966). Lasch has written several relevant books in this area including *The Culture of Narcissism: American Life in an Age of Diminishing Expectations* (New York: Warner, 1979), *Haven in a Heartless World: The Family Besieged* (New York: Basic, 1977), *The Minimal Self: Psychic Life in Troubled Times* (New York: Norton, 1984). For critical perspectives on Lasch's work see Christopher Lasch, Michael Fischer, Larry Nachman, Janice Doane, and D. L. Hodges, "A Symposium: Christopher Lasch and the Culture of Narcissism," *Salmagundi* 46 (Fall 1979): 167–202, and Fred Siegel, "The Agony of Christopher Lasch," *Reviews in American History* (Sept. 1980): 285–95. See Richard Wightman Fox, *So Far Disordered in Mind: Insanity in California, 1870–1930* (Berkeley: University of California Press, 1978), T. J. Jackson Lears, *No Place of Grace: Antimodernism and the Transformation of American Culture 1880–1920* (New York: Pantheon, 1981), Lears, *Fables of Abundance: A Cultural History of Advertising in America* (New York: Basic, 1994), and the two collections of essays edited by Fox and Lears: *The Culture of Consumption: Critical Essays in American History, 1880–1980* (New York: Pantheon, 1983), and *The Power of Culture: Critical Essays in American History* (Chicago: University of Chicago Press, 1993). Also see one other sociological classic that makes use of historical perspective to criticize therapeutic culture: Robert N. Bellah, Richard Madsen, William M. Sullivan, Ann Swidler, and Steven M. Tipton, *Habits of the Heart: Individualism and Commitment in American Life* (New York: Harper & Row, 1985). Critiques of therapies and of aspects of the therapeutic ethos include Joel Kovel, *A Complete Guide to Therapy: From Psychoanalysis to Behavior Modification* (New York: Pantheon, 1976), Edwin Schur, *The Awareness Trap: Self-Absorption Instead of Social Change* (New York: Quadrangle/New York Times Book Co., 1976), and Philip Cushman, *Constructing the Self, Constructing America: A Cultural History of Psychotherapy* (Reading, Mass.: Addison-Wesley, 1995). Lawrence Birken, however, argues that political gains (e.g., the challenging of ideologies of sexual difference) have been made because "sexual science" has developed into such a strong force in consumer culture (*Consuming Desire: Sexual Science and the Emergence of a Culture of Abundance, 1871–1914* [Ithaca: Cornell University Press, 1988]).

21. On the ideological uses of the "unconscious," "depth," "innerness," and "the primitive" in aesthetic practices that contributed to the formation of modern middle- and upper-class white identity, see Leja, *Reframing Abstract Expressionism*, and Joel Pfister, *Staging Depth: Eugene O'Neill and the Politics of Psychological Discourse* (Chapel Hill: University of North Carolina Press, 1995).

22. Tennessee Williams, *A Streetcar Named Desire* (New York: New American Library, 1984), 31, 40.

23. For an astute discussion of heavy metal see Robert Walser, *Running with the Devil: Power, Gender, and Madness in Heavy Metal Music* (Hanover, N.H.: University Press of New England, 1993). Nancy Schnog and I are grateful to David Lubin, with whom we developed the idea of *antipsychological* art forms and cultural practices (the term may very well have been his). I do not wish to suggest that Mitchell wrote only angst-filled reveries. Some of her songs of the late 1960s and early 1970s clearly were indebted to the folk tradition of direct social critique.

24. See Hochschild, *The Managed Heart: Commercialization of Human Feeling* (Berkeley: University of California Press, 1983), 18. Averill, "The Acquisition of Emotions during Adulthood," in *The Social Construction of Emotions*, 109, 113, and 107 (on fainting). Stearns and Stearns, "Emotionology: Clarifying the History of Emotions and Emotional Standards," in *Psycho/history: Readings in the Method of Psychology, Psychoanalysis, and History*, ed. Geoffrey Cocks and Travis L. Crosby (New Haven: Yale University Press, 1987), 284. Kasson, *Rudeness and Civility: Manners in Nineteenth-Century Urban America* (New York: Hill and Wang, 1990), 147–81.

25. See Sennett's *The Fall of Public Man: On the Social Psychology of Capitalism* (New York: Vintage, 1978), especially 177–83, and his essay "Destructive Gemeinschaft," in *An Introduction to Sociology*, ed. Robert Bocock, Peter Hamilton, Kenneth Thompson, and Alan Walton (Brighton, England: Harvester, 1980). Also see Michel Foucault and Richard Sennett, "Sexuality and Solitude," *Humanities in Review* 1 (1982): 3–21.

26. See Herbert I. Schiller, *Culture, Inc.: The Corporate Takeover of Public Expression* (New York: Oxford University Press, 1989) and Tom Frank, "Hip Is Dead," *Nation* 262 (April 1, 1996): 16, 18–19. Frank examines individualistic "hip" (as in being hip) as a business style of the corporate "Culture Trust": Hip "holds that the problem with capitalism is that it oppresses us through puritanism, homogeneity and conformity, and that we resist by being ourselves, by pushing the envelope of uninhibition, by breaking all the rules in pursuit of the most apocalyptic orgasm of them all. . . . The problem isn't that hip has been co-opted but that it isn't adversarial in the first place" (18). He concludes that we must "rediscover the language of class, the non-market-friendly concept of industrial democracy. Leave hip to the M.B.A.s." (19).

27. Kaminer, *I'm Dysfunctional, You're Dysfunctional: The Recovery Movement and Other Self-Help Fashions* (New York: Vintage, 1993), 155.

28. Eagleton, *Ideology: An Introduction* (Minneapolis: University of Minnesota Press, 1991), 149.

29. Foucault, *The History of Sexuality, Volume 2: The Use of Pleasure*, trans. Robert Hurley (New York: Vintage, 1986), 10. For an elaboration of Foucault's discussion of this matter also see Elspeth Probyn, *Sexing the Self: Gendered Positions in Cultural Studies* (New York: Routledge, 1993), 108–37, especially 128.

30. Here I am paraphrasing a passage from Adrienne Rich's essay "Power and Danger," in *On Lies, Secrets, and Silences: Selected Prose, 1966–1978* (New York: W. W. Norton, 1979), 247.

31. For critical reflections on "social construction" theories see George Levine's introduction to *Constructions of the Self*, ed. George Levine (New Brunswick, N.J.: Rutgers University Press, 1992), 1–13, especially 2–4.

32. Elias, *Power and Civility,* vol. 2 of *The Civilizing Process,* trans. Edmund Jephcott (New York: Pantheon, 1982), see 229–319, and *The History of Manners,* vol. 1 of *The Civilizing Process,* trans. Edmund Jephcott (New York: Pantheon, 1978). Also see two related theoretical works by Elias: "Sociology and Psychiatry," in *Psychiatry in a Changing Society,* ed. Siegmund Heinz Foulkes and Gordon Stewart Prince (London: Tavistock, 1969), and *What Is Sociology?* trans. Stephen Mennell and Grace Morrissey (New York: Columbia University Press, 1978). For a brief assessment of Elias's contribution see Peter Burke, *History and Social Theory* (Ithaca: Cornell University Press, 1993), 148–50. Patrick H. Hutton reviews Elias's work in connection with that of the *Annales* school, of Philippe Ariès, and of (the pre-*History of Sexuality*) Michel Foucault in "The History of Mentalities: The New Map of Cultural History," *History and Theory* 20 (1981): 237–59. As codes and restraints on the self pile up during the evolution of "civilization," Hutton writes about Elias's theory of depth, "the instinctual needs they were designed to tame [do not disappear]. But the conflict between them is joined to the deep structures of the psyche, from which they surface only in dreams. The price of civilization, Elias contends, is not only higher barriers of social restraint, but deeper degrees of psychological stress. The rise of civilization, in effect, is matched by a descent into self" (250).

33. Kasson, *Rudeness and Civility;* on the socially symbolic significance of control see especially 124, 195–201, 208–11, 257–60. See Smith-Rosenberg's "Sex as Symbol in Victorian Purity: An Ethnohistorical Analysis of Jacksonian America," *American Journal of Sociology* 84 (Special Summer Supplement, 1978): 212–47, especially 218, 220, 228, 244, and "Davey Crockett as Trickster: Pornography, Liminality, and Symbolic Inversion in Victorian America," 90–108, in her *Disorderly Conduct: Visions of Gender in Victorian America* (New York: Oxford University Press, 1985), particularly 90, Nissenbaum, *Sex, Diet, and Debility in Jacksonian America: Sylvester Graham and Health Reform* (Westport, Conn.: Greenwood, 1980), 129, Douglas, *Purity and Danger: An Analysis of Concepts of Pollution and Taboo* (London: Routledge and Kegan Paul, 1979), 98–99, Davis, *Homicide in American Fiction, 1798–1860* (Ithaca: Cornell University Press, 1957), 209, G. J. Barker-Benfield, *Horrors of the Half-Known Life: Male Attitudes Toward Women and Sexuality in Nineteenth-Century America* (New York: Harper Colophon, 1977), 290, Louis Kern, *An Ordered Love: Sex Roles and Sexuality in Victorian Utopias—The Shakers, the Mormons, and the Oneida Community* (Chapel Hill: University of North Carolina Press, 1981), 38–39, and Joel Pfister, *The Production of Personal Life: Class, Gender, and the Psychological in Hawthorne's Fiction* (Stanford: Stanford University Press, 1991), 29–37, 59–79. Thomas Laqueur, in his work on late eighteenth-century and early nineteenth-century Europe, also rooted the scientific urge to recategorize female bodies and sexuality as dangerous, defective, and disordered in anxieties about political and social transformations: see "Orgasm, Generation, and the Politics of Reproductive Biology," in *The Making of the Modern Body: Sexuality and Society in the Nineteenth Century,* ed. Catherine Gallagher and Thomas Laqueur (Berkeley: University of California Press, 1987). In addition consult Laqueur's *Making Sex: Body and Gender from the Greeks to Freud* (Cambridge: Harvard University Press, 1990).

34. Smith-Rosenberg, "Sex as Symbol in Victorian Purity," 220; also see 244. Hutton observes of Elias: "Elias relies heavily upon Marxian categories of social classification. He identifies the development of the cultural traits of Western civilization with a succession of social elites which displace one another as legislators of the codes of social behavior: the feudal nobility of the thirteenth century; the court aristocracy of the sev-

enteenth century; and the bourgeoisie of the eighteenth century. . . . Although he employs Marxian terminology, his is less a model of social conflict than it is of social integration. The history of Western civilization in Elias's view is a vast process of democratization, in which civilized behavior, originally the preserve of the social elite, is adopted by society as a whole" ("History of Mentalities," 249).

35. Rosaldo, "Toward an Anthropology of Self and Feeling," in *Culture Theory: Essays in Mind, Self, and Emotion,* ed. Richard A. Shweder and Robert A. LeVine (Cambridge: Cambridge University Press, 1984), 148. Also see Rosaldo, *Knowledge and Passion: Ilongot Notions of Self and Social Life* (Cambridge: Cambridge University Press, 1980).

36. Averill, "Acquisition," 113.

37. Rosaldo, "Toward an Anthropology," 149.

38. As the feminist theorist and poststructuralist philosopher Judith Butler explains: "The critical question is not how did that identity become *internalized?* as if internalization were a process or a mechanism that might be descriptively reconstructed. Rather, the question is: From what strategic position in public discourse and for what reason has the trope of interiority and the disjunctive binary of inner/outer taken hold?" (*Gender Trouble: Feminism and the Subversion of Identity* [New York: Routledge, 1990], 134).

39. Kovel, *The Age of Desire: Reflections of a Radical Psychoanalyst* (New York: Pantheon, 1981), 33.

40. Abu-Lughod and Lutz, "Introduction: Emotion, Discourse, and the Politics of Everyday Life," in *Language and the Politics of Emotion,* ed. Catherine Lutz and Lila Abu-Lughod (Cambridge: Cambridge University Press; Paris: Editions de la Maison des Sciences de l'Homme, 1990), 6.

41. Foucault, *History of Sexuality,* 1:12–13.

42. Armstrong and Tennenhouse, *The Imaginary Puritan: Literature, Intellectual Labor, and the Origins of Personal Life* (Berkeley: University of California Press, 1992), 166.

43. Stearns and Stearns, *Anger: The Struggle for Emotional Control in America's History* (Chicago: University of Chicago Press, 1986), 97, 109. Also see Peter N. Stearns, *American Cool: Constructing a Twentieth-Century Emotional Style* (New York: New York University Press, 1994), whose chapters seek to provide contexts for the "ventilating" of emotions and the "dampening" of passions in the modern era.

44. Stearns and Stearns, *Anger,* 97.

45. West, "Sex and Suicide," in *Prophetic Fragments* (Grand Rapids, Mich.: Eerdman's; Trenton, N.J.: Africa World Press, 1988), 155–56.

46. See *Culture of Consumption,* ed. Fox and Lears, Berger et al., *Ways of Seeing,* Stuart Ewen and Elizabeth Ewen, *Channels of Desire: Mass Images and the Shaping of American Consciousness* (New York: McGraw-Hill, 1982), Stuart Ewen, *All Consuming Images: The Politics of Style in Contemporary Culture* (New York: Basic, 1988), Stuart Ewen, *Captains of Consciousness: Advertising and the Social Roots of the Consumer Culture* (New York: McGraw-Hill, 1976), Guy Debord, *Society of the Spectacle* (Detroit: Black & Red, 1977).

47. Hochschild, *The Managed Heart,* 17–18, 27, 217. For some discussions of how ideology has shaped biological research (the managed psychobiology?) see R. C. Lewontin, Steven Rose, and Leon Kamin, *Not in Our Genes: Biology, Ideology, and Human Nature* (New York: Pantheon, 1984), and Anne Fausto Sterling, "Society Writes Biology/Biology Constructs Gender," 61–75, in *Learning About Women: Gender, Politics, and Power,* ed. Jill K. Conway, Susan C. Bourque, and Joan W. Scott (Ann Arbor: University of Michigan Press, 1989).

48. Consult the important work of Chris Weedon, *Feminist Practice and Poststructuralist Theory* (Oxford: Basil Blackwell, 1987), 106. Also see the perceptive criticism of Craig Owens (whose theorizing of subjectivities, sexualities, and gender was conceptually linked with and sometimes explicated Barbara Kruger's art), collected posthumously in *Beyond Recognition: Representation, Power, and Culture,* ed. Scott Bryson, Barbara Kruger, Lynne Tillman, and Jane Weinstock (Berkeley: University of California Press, 1994).

49. See Judith Butler, "Critically Queer," *GLQ: A Journal of Lesbian and Gay Studies* 1 (1993): 22. I thank Henry Abelove for recommending that I read this article, which discusses Butler's notion of "performativity."

50. Mette Hjort develops an impressive critique of the poststructuralist representations of both agency and humanism in *The Strategy of Letters* (Cambridge: Harvard University Press, 1993). For a superb defense and critique of (mainly Foucaultian) poststructuralism that places it in historical relation to the writings of Marx, the Frankfurt School, Sartre, and Foucault, see Mark Poster, *Critical Theory and Poststructuralism: In Search of a Context* (Ithaca: Cornell University Press, 1989). See discussions of how poststructuralism can contribute to and expand our comprehension of the comprehensiveness of historicity in *Post-structuralism and the Question of History,* ed. Derek Attridge, Geoff Bennington, and Robert Young (Cambridge: Cambridge University Press, 1987).

51. For my sketch of Bourdieu's ideas I have primarily drawn on and quoted freely from Bourdieu's chapter "Structures, Habitus, Practices" in his *The Logic of Practice,* trans. Richard Nice (Stanford: Stanford University Press, 1990), 52–65, Bourdieu's discussion of habitus in Bourdieu and Loïc J. D. Wacquant, *An Invitation to Reflexive Sociology* (Chicago: University of Chicago Press, 1992), 115–40, and Bourdieu, *Distinction: A Social Critique of the Judgement of Taste,* trans. Richard Nice (Cambridge: Harvard University Press, 1984), 169–75. Also see useful overviews of the concept of habitus in John B. Thompson, editor's introduction, in Pierre Bourdieu, *Language and Symbolic Power,* ed. John B. Thompson, trans. Gino Raymond and Matthew Adamson (Cambridge: Harvard University Press, 1991), 11–14, and Randal Johnson, editor's introduction, in Pierre Bourdieu, *The Field of Cultural Production,* ed. Randal Johnson (New York: Columbia University Press, 1993), 3–7. Bourdieu is in several ways indebted to the work of Norbert Elias. As a matter of fact, Elias employed the term *habitus* (many years before Bourdieu) in *The Court Society* (written in 1930) (trans. Edmund Jephcott [New York: Pantheon, 1983]). The historian Roger Chartier writes of Elias's thesis: "When life at court located distinction in proximity, reality in appearance and superiority in dependence, it required of those who participated in it specific psychological gifts that are not common to all, such as the art of observing others and oneself, the censorship of sentiments and the mastery of passions and the internalization of the disciplines that govern *civilité.* A transformation of this sort modified not only ways of thinking but the entire structure of personality and the psychic economy of the individual to which Elias gives an old name: the *Habitus.* The process of 'courtization' was also a remodeling of affectivity (*Affektmodellierung*) that subjected the courtier to a tight network of automatic self-controls reining in all spontaneous impulses and movements" (*Cultural History: Between Practices and Representations,* trans. Lydia C. Cochrane [Ithaca: Cornell University Press, 1988]), 88, see chapter 3, "Social Figuration and Habitus: Reading Elias," 71–94. Bourdieu writes that what links his work with that of Elias is their common theoretical emphasis: *"the real is relational: what exist in the social world are relations—not interactions between agents or inter-*

subjective ties between individuals, but objective relations which exist 'independently of individual consciousness and will,' as Marx said" (*Invitation*, 97). But there are also differences in their respective approaches. As Bourdieu notes: "Just like [Max] Weber before him, Elias always fails to ask who benefits and who suffers from the monopoly of the state over legitimate violence, and to raise the question . . . of the domination wielded *through* the state" (*Invitation*, 93). Bourdieu also recognizes certain critical affinities with Foucault, such as their "anti-institutional disposition" (*Invitation*, 64). However, Bourdieu, unlike Foucault, has faith both in reason and science—the result of rigorous and rigorously self-reflexive sociology: "Scientific knowledge allows us to locate real points of application for responsible action; it enables us to avoid struggling where there is no freedom [e.g., unrigorously conceptualized resistances to power] . . . in such a manner as to dodge sites of genuine responsibility" (*Invitation*, 196). Moreover, Bourdieu argues that "Foucault refuses to look anywhere except in the 'discursive field' for the principle that will elucidate each of the discourses inserted in it" ("The Peculiar History of Scientific Reason," *Sociological Forum* 6 [1991]: 11).

52. See Bourdieu and Wacquant, *Invitation*, 211. In the sentence that follows the two from which I quoted, Bourdieu represents himself as a sociological Pandora, again using psychological language: "At every moment I would like to be able to see what I do not see and I am endlessly, *obsessively* wondering: 'Now, what is the next black box that you have not opened?'" (emphasis supplied, 211). I would love to know how Bourdieu, in the light of his choice of what has become psychoanalytic vocabulary, theorizes and historicizes psychoanalytic writings on obsession, including Sigmund Freud's "Obsessive Acts and Religious Practices" (1907) in his *Character and Culture*, ed. Philip Rieff, trans. James Strachey (New York: Collier, 1963), 23–24, Otto Fenichel, *The Psychoanalytic Theory of the Neurosis* (New York: Norton, 1945), 289, and Sandor Ferenczi, *Further Contributions to the Theory and Technique of Psycho-Analysis* (London: Hogarth, 1950), 311. It is intriguing that Bourdieu has selected culturally prevalent psychological terms to support his description of his "socioanalysis" (perhaps with the intent of radically resignifying such terms). Socioanalysis, as Loïc J. D. Wacquant portrays the project, aims to reveal the social "unconscious": "Socioanalysis may be seen as a collective counterpart to psychoanalysis: just as the logotherapy of the latter may free us from the individual unconscious that drives or constricts our practices, the former can help us unearth the social unconscious embedded into institutions as well as lodged deep inside us. Whereas Bourdieu's work shares with all (post-)structuralisms a rejection of the Cartesian *cogito* . . . it differs from them in that it attempts to make possible the historical emergence of something *like* a rational subject via a reflexive application of social-scientific knowledge" (*Invitation*, 49). Yet Bourdieu's discussions of socioanalysis, determinism, and the unconscious may lead one to infer that he would have socioanalysis replace psychoanalysis (as a theoretical approach to conceptualizing individual agency): "Social agents will *actively* determine, on the basis of these socially and historically constituted categories of perception and appreciation, the situation that determines them. One can even say that *social agents are determined only to the extent that they determine themselves.* But the categories of perception and appreciation which provide the principle of this (self-)determination are themselves largely determined by the social and economic conditions of their constitution. . . . At bottom, determinisms operate to their full only by the help of unconsciousness, with the complicity of the unconscious" (*Invitation*, 136). Here Bourdieu

employs the category of the unconscious. It must be underscored, however, that Bourdieu associates the idea of the "unconscious" with socially produced "unthought categories of thought which delimit the thinkable and predetermine the thought" and with "the forgetting of history which history itself produces" (*Invitation*, 40, 136). The conceptual problem, then, might be to work out how the cultural machinery of and cultural fascination with "the psychological" operates as a powerful cultural determinism that helps produce as private and individual a modern "unconscious" that Bourdieu argues is rather a social-historical "unconscious"—more specifically, a "forgetting of history" that is culturally encoded, explained, and experienced subjectively as internally "psychological." Bourdieu criticizes psychoanalytic theory for the subtle ideological role it plays in making historical forgetting (the "unthought" cultural and institutional history of selfing) seem inherently natural: "Psychoanalysis . . . forgets and causes to be forgotten that one's own body and other people's bodies are only ever perceived through [culturally produced] categories of perception which it would be naive to treat as sexual, even if . . . these categories [e.g., leading to a perception of some pottery as phallic] always relate back, sometimes very concretely, to the opposition between the biologically defined properties of the two sexes" (*Outline of a Theory of Practice*, trans. Richard Nice [Cambridge: Cambridge University Press, 1977], 92). He then offers an example of how the perceived "opposition" between the sexes—bodies encoded in different sexual ways to appear "opposite"—must be understood historically and sociologically as being produced in relation to "socially defined vision[s] of the sexual division of labour" (93). For an impressive example of self-socioanalysis (that looks radically different from psychoanalytic therapy), see Bourdieu's socioanalysis of himself—delivered in the form of his inaugural lecture at the Collège de France—his "Lecture on the Lecture," in his *In Other Words: Essays Toward a Reflexive Sociology*, trans. Matthew Adamson (Stanford: Stanford University Press, 1990), 177–98.

53. See Reich, "Dialectical Materialism and Psychoanalysis" (1929, 1934), reprinted in the collection of Reich's early writings, *Sex-Pol Essays, 1929–1934*, ed. Lee Baxandall, trans. Anna Bostock, Tom DuBose, and Lee Baxandall (New York: Vintage, 1972), 3–74, Martin Jay, "The Integration of Psychoanalysis," in *The Dialectical Imagination: A History of the Frankfurt School and the Institute of Social Research, 1923–1950* (Boston: Little, Brown, 1973), 86–112, and David Held's discussion of Erich Fromm, Reich, Theodor Adorno, and Herbert Marcuse and their uses of psychoanalysis in *Introduction to Critical Theory: Horkheimer to Habermas* (Berkeley: University of California Press, 1980), 10–47.

54. Eagleton, *The Ideology of the Aesthetic* (Oxford: Basil Blackwell, 1990), 409–10.

55. Tiefer, *Sex Is Not a Natural Act*, 2, 1, 3, 37, 195, 185. On the subject of imagining human potential, Eagleton clarifies that potential is sometimes difficult to envision because our socially inflected notion of potential is so often circumscribed as that which is classified as "repressed" (repressed "human nature") by oppressive forces. It is imperative, he writes, to demand "an equal right with others to discover what one might become [and not assume that one possesses] some already fully fashioned identity which is merely repressed. All 'oppositional identities' are in part the function of repression, as well as of resistance to that oppression; and in this sense what one might become cannot be simply read off from what one is now. The privilege of the oppressor is his privilege to decide what he [*sic*] shall be; it is this right which the oppressed must demand too, which must be universalized" (*Ideology of the Aesthetic*, 414).

56. It is rare for any one scholar to acquire the historical knowledge requisite to write wide-ranging accounts of the American history of emotional life that encompass critiques of the ideologies, individuals, and institutions that have shaped popular understandings and misunderstandings of human potential. See two ambitious projects whose scope ranges from the colonial era to the twentieth century: Merle Curti, *Human Nature in American Thought: A History* (Madison: University of Wisconsin Press, 1980), and John Owen King III, *The Iron of Melancholy: Structures of Spiritual Conversion in America from the Purtian Conscience to Victorian Neurosis* (Middletown, Conn.: Wesleyan University Press, 1983). Also consult Curti's brief but expansive study *Human Nature in American Historical Thought* (Columbia: University of Missouri Press, 1968).

57. The first quotation is from Jameson, *Marxism and Form: Twentieth-Century Dialectical Theories of Literature* (Princeton: Princeton University Press, 1974), 27. The second quotation is from Jameson, *The Political Unconscious: Narrative As a Socially Symbolic Act* (Ithaca: Cornell University Press, 1980), 64.

58. Demos, "Oedipus and America: Historical Perspectives on the Reception of Psychoanalysis in the United States," *Annual of Psychoanalysis* 6 (1978): 23–39. For more of his reflections on the nineteenth-century family, privatization, and the shaping of emotions, see Demos, *Past, Present, and Personal: The Family and the Life Course in American History* (New York: Oxford University Press, 1986). In the 1920s the Russian Marxist semiotician V. N. Vološinov endeavored to locate psychoanalysis within dominant currents of bourgeois philosophical and scientific thought (*Freudianism: A Critical Sketch*, trans. I. R. Titunik [Bloomington: Indiana University Press, 1976], 7–15). Several decades later Jerome Bruner reviewed some of the major intellectual trends that influenced Freud ("Freud and the Image of Man," *Partisan Review* 3 [Summer 1956]: 340–47). Both Vološinov and Bruner help one infer why psychoanalysis would have been welcomed by segments of the American bourgeoisie. But neither Vološinov nor Bruner examined the relationship between psychoanalysis and a *history* of family life—as Demos did—to explain in part the American reception of psychoanalysis. Vološinov, however, offered much insight into the privatizing psychology favored by the modern bourgeois family: psychoanalysis, in line with other bourgeois philosophies, attempted "to create a [private familial and individual] world [imagined as] beyond the social and historical." And within this project the significance of the bourgeois family—economically, the "castle and keep of capitalism"—is reencoded as mainly sexual and is mystified as the "oedipal" family: "The father is not the entrepreneur and the son is not his heir—the father is only the mother's lover, and his son his rival!" (90–91). In 1960 Philippe Ariès published his groundbreaking history of the family from the medieval to the modern and demonstrated that the family, childhood, and discourses of feelings were historically variable (*Centuries of Childhood: A Social History of Family Life*, trans. Robert Baldick [New York: Vintage, 1962]). Ariès's work and the far-reaching outline of how to situate subjectivity and the family in history that Sartre proposed in 1960—in *Search for a Method* (see page 61, where he moves from psychoanalysis to a history of family life)—established the intellectual framework for approaches such as the one that Demos helped develop in the mid-1970s.

59. Zaretsky, *Capitalism, the Family, and Personal Life* (New York: Harper Colophon, 1979), 76, 120. See Ryan's *The Cradle of the Middle Class: The Family in Oneida County, New York, 1790–1865* (Cambridge: Cambridge University Press, 1981), and *The Empire of the*

Mother: American Writing About Domesticity, 1830–1869 (New York: Harrington Park Press, 1985), Blumin, *The Emergence of the Middle Class: Social Experience in the American City, 1760–1900* (Cambridge: Cambridge University Press, 1989), and Coontz's *The Social Origins of Private Life: A History of American Families, 1600–1900* (London: Verso, 1988) and *The Way We Never Were: American Families and the Nostalgia Trap* (New York: Basic, 1992). Arthur Calhoun's three-volume *Social History of the American Family* (1917–19) made the American family its object of study, and this in itself was a significant theoretical step. But Calhoun, unlike Philippe Ariès in the 1960s, or Demos and Zaretsky and other historians that followed them, was less sophisticated conceptually in linking changes in the family to a history of feelings. One of Ariès's most ambitious and invaluable projects is the five-volume *History of Private Life*, which he co-edited with Georges Duby (Cambridge: Harvard University Press, 1987–1991). Also consult Philippe Ariès and André Béjin, *Western Sexuality: Practice and Precept in Past and Present Times*, trans. Anthony Forster (New York: Basil Blackwell, 1985), and Ariès's *Western Attitudes Toward Death: From the Middle Ages to the Present*, trans. Patricia M. Ranum (Baltimore: Johns Hopkins University Press, 1974). See David Brion Davis's general comments on the field as it was emerging in the late 1970s, "The American Family and Boundaries in Historical Perspective," in *The American Family: Dying or Developing*, ed. David Reiss, M.D., and Howard Hoffman, M.D. (New York: Plenum Press, 1979), 13–33. For an excellent critique of some major twentieth-century theoretical readings of the family (e.g., Sigmund Freud, Wilhelm Reich, Frankfurt School), including readings by historians (Peter Laslett, Ariès, Edward Shorter, Lloyd de Mause), see Mark Poster, *Critical Theory of the Family* (New York: Seabury Press, 1980).

60. Kovel, *Age of Desire*, 202, 61, 128, 61. Also see Michael Lerner, *Surplus Powerlessness: The Psychodynamics of Everyday Life . . . and the Psychology of Individual and Social Transformation* (Atlantic Highlands, N.J.: Humanities Press International, 1994). On pertinent theoretical matters see Bertell Ollmann, *Alienation: Marx's Concept of Man in Capitalist Society* (Cambridge: Cambridge University Press, 1971). For some key developments of the mechanization of self theme see Lewis Mumford, *Technics and Civilization* (New York: Harcourt, Brace & World, 1962), Siegfried Giedion, *Mechanization Takes Command: A Contribution to Anonymous History* (New York: Norton, 1948), Mark Seltzer, *Bodies and Machines* (New York: Routledge, 1992), Anson Rabinbach, *The Human Motor: Energy, Fatigue, and the Origins of Modernity* (Berkeley: University of California Press, 1990), and Martha Banta, *Taylored Lives: Narrative Productions in the Age of Taylor, Veblen, and Ford* (Chicago: University of Chicago Press, 1993). The therapy industry feeds on the production not just of alienated but of *anxious* individuals. See Louis Uchitelle, "The Rise of the Losing Class," *New York Times* (Nov. 20, 1994), section 4, Week in Review, 1, 5. Observing that joblessness is now afflicting both the poor and $200,000-a-year Ivy League MBAs, Uchitelle writes: "A class consciousness may be emerging from this shared anxiety—an awareness among millions of Americans that they occupy the same unsteady boat. . . . But the growing sense that people of different levels of salary, education and skill may be victims of the same economic forces lacks two crucial elements of class consciousness as the term has historically been used: a class vocabulary and a class enemy. The traditional adversaries—big business, owners of capital, managers—are no longer viewed that way. Instead, business is seen as also a victim, caught in a global competition that forces cost-cutting and lay-offs" (1). One may hope that the study Uchitelle cites as evidence of this trend is not as representative as its authors make out and that workers—at various lev-

els—are not quite so naive (in thinking "we're all victims") in their assessment of who and what is to blame. In any event, it is imperative to grasp how the therapy industry and therapeutic culture more generally teach workers how to think about the sources and causes of their feelings of anxiety and alienation, and how this teaching affects the potential formation of a critical class consciousness capable of discriminating between victims and victimizers.

61. On the disciplinary history of psychology see *The Rise of Experimentation in American Psychology,* ed. Jill Morawski (New Haven: Yale University Press, 1988), and Kurt Danziger, *Constructing the Subject: Historical Origins of Psychological Research* (New York: Cambridge University Press, 1990). On the history of psychoanalysis in America see Nathan Hale, *Freud and the Americans: The Beginnings of Psychoanalysis in the United States, 1876–1917* (1971; rprt., New York: Oxford University Press, 1995), and Hale, *The Rise and Crisis of Psychoanalysis in the United States: Freud and the Americans, 1917–1985* (New York: Oxford University Press, 1995), and also Russell Jacoby, *Social Amnesia: A Critique of Contemporary Psychology from Adler to Laing* (Boston: Beacon Press, 1975). Also see John C. Burnham's work on the rise and popularization of psychology and psychoanalysis, including *How Superstition Won and Science Lost: Popularizing Science and Health in the United States* (New Brunswick, N.J.: Rutgers University Press, 1987), *Psychoanalysis and American Medicine, 1894–1918: Medicine, Science, and Culture* (New York: International Universities Press, 1967), and his classic essay "The New Psychology: From Narcissism to Social Control," in *Change and Continuity in Twentieth Century America: The 1920s,* ed. John Braeman, Robert H. Bremmer, and David Brody (Columbus: Ohio State University Press, 1968). And on the institutionalization of psychiatry see the books published by Gerald N. Grob, who synthesizes some of his historical work in his overview, *The Mad Among Us: A History of the Care of America's Mentally Ill* (New York: Free Press, 1994). Arthur Kleinman, M.D., offers a discussion of psychiatry based on his cross-cultural research in *Rethinking Psychiatry: From Cultural Category to Personal Experience* (New York: Free Press, 1988). An important cultural history of psychiatry (which focuses on the Boston Psychopathic Hospital) and its encoding of women is Elizabeth Lunbeck, *The Psychiatric Persuasion: Knowledge, Gender, and Power in Modern America* (Princeton: Princeton University Press, 1994). The most daring book-length critique of the production of psychological discourses in America is a study written by two French scholars and an American: Robert Castel, Françoise Castel, Anne Lovell, *The Psychiatric Society,* trans. Arthur Goldhammer (New York: Columbia University Press, 1982). And the finest radical essay on the ideological ascendancy of psychological discourses and institutions is Joel Kovel's "The American Mental Health Industry," in *Critical Psychiatry: The Politics of Mental Health,* ed. David Ingleby (New York: Pantheon, 1980), 73–101. Tom Lutz illuminates the cultural history of neurasthenia in *American Nervousness, 1903: An Anecdotal History* (Ithaca: Cornell University Press, 1993). On the sexology industry see Janice M. Irvine, *Disorders of Desire: Sex and Gender in Modern American Society* (Philadelphia: Temple University Press, 1990).

62. Kovel, *Age of Desire,* 128, 72.

63. On segregation in asylums see Grob, *Mad Among Us,* 88. On the "psychological" stereotyping of slaves as "mad" and emancipated blacks as emotionally unstable see Sander L. Gilman, *Difference and Pathology: Stereotypes of Sexuality, Race, and Madness* (Ithaca: Cornell University Press, 1985), 147, 137, 140. For discussions of World War II screening and racism (89) and of the representation of African American social problems as mainly

psychological ones, such as "self-esteem" (199, 205), see Ellen Herman, *The Romance of American Psychology: Political Culture in the Age of Experts* (Berkeley: University of California Press, 1995). Also see *Racism and Mental Health*, ed. Charles V. Willie, Bernard M. Kramer, and Bertram S. Brown (Pittsburgh: University of Pittsburgh Press, 1973). On the African American family see E. Franklin Frazier, *The Negro Family in the United States* (New York: Dryden, 1948), Herbert G. Gutman, *The Black Family in Slavery and Freedom, 1750–1925* (New York: Pantheon, 1976), and Jacqueline Jones, *Labor of Love, Labor of Sorrow: Black Women, Work, and the Family from Slavery to the Present* (New York: Vintage, 1985) (see Jones's extensive bibliography). Consult Franz Fanon's analyses of the psychological damage wrought by racism and imperialism in *The Wretched of the Earth* (New York: Grove Press, 1963) and *Black Skin, White Masks* (New York: Grove Press, 1967). Three recent sophisticated discussions of the cultural formation of racialized subjectivities are Eric Lott, *Love and Theft: Blackface Minstrelsy and the American Working Class* (New York: Oxford University Press, 1993), Glenn Jordan and Chris Weedon, *Cultural Politics: Class, Gender, Race and the Postmodern World* (Oxford: Blackwell, 1995), and Anne McClintock, *Imperial Leather: Race, Gender, and Sexuality in the Colonial Context* (New York: Routledge, 1995).

64. Grob, *Mad Among Us*, 151.

65. The first quotation is from Dr. Issac Ray and the second is from Dr. Ralph L. Parsons (Grob, *Mad Among Us*, 87). The third quotation is from a director of the Worcester asylum and is cited in Castel, Castel, and Lovell, *Psychiatric Society*, 18.

66. See Pfister, *Staging Depth*, 26–32, 123–24, 137.

67. See a useful sociological study (with sketchy historical perspective) on this ideological development: Francesca M. Cancian, *Love in America: Gender and Self-Development* (Cambridge: Cambridge University Press, 1987). Consult Nancy Schnog's "Inside the Sentimental: The Psychological Work of *The Wide Wide World*," *Genders* 4 (Mar. 1989): 11–25, and "'The Comfort of My Fancying': Loss and Recuperation in *The Gates Ajar*," *Arizona Quarterly* 49 (Spring 1993): 21–47. Also see David M. Lubin's insights into nineteenth-century American painting and the construction and contestation of "feminine" emotions in *Picturing a Nation: Art and Social Change in Nineteenth-Century America* (New Haven: Yale University Press, 1994), 159–271. I discuss some of the historical research on the production of feminine emotions and its relation to the rise of the middle class in *Production of Personal Life*. It is important, however, to be aware that middle-class women—even when the cult of domesticity attained great cultural power in the mid-nineteenth century—were not just emotionally privatized; their concerns could be both public and reformist. See Nina Baym, *American Women Writers and the Work of History, 1790–1860* (New Brunswick, N.J.: Rutgers University Press, 1995).

68. I have already cited some of Ryan's and Coontz's contributions. See Carby's *Reconstructing Womanhood: The Emergence of the Afro-American Woman Novelist* (New York: Oxford University Press, 1987), and "Policing the Black Woman's Body in an Urban Context," *Critical Inquiry* 18 (Summer 1992): 738–55; Cott's *The Bonds of Womanhood: "Woman's Sphere" in New England, 1780–1835* (New Haven: Yale University Press, 1977), and *The Grounding of Modern Feminism* (New Haven: Yale University Press, 1987); Smith-Rosenberg's *Disorderly Conduct* and "Sex As Symbol in Victorian Purity"; Halttunen's *Confidence Men and Painted Women: A Study of Middle-Class Culture in America, 1830–1870* (New Haven: Yale University Press, 1982), "From Parlor to Living Room: Domestic Space, Interior Decorating, and the Culture of Personality," in *Consuming Visions: Accumulation and*

Display of Goods in America, 1880–1920, ed. Simon J. Bronner (New York: Norton, 1989), and "Early American Murder Narratives: The Birth of Horror," in *Power of Culture*; Stansell, *City of Women: Sex and Class in New York, 1789–1860* (Urbana: University of Illinois Press, 1987); Leonore Davidoff and Catherine Hall, *Family Fortunes: Men and Women of the English Middle Class, 1780–1850* (Chicago: University of Chicago Press, 1987), and Hall, "Missionary Stories: Gender and Ethnicity in England in the 1830s and 1840s," in *Cultural Studies*, ed. Grossberg, Nelson, and Treichler; Armstrong, *Desire and Domestic Fiction: A Political History of the Novel* (New York: Oxford University Press, 1987), and Armstrong and Tennenhouse, *Imaginary Puritan*; Poovey, *Uneven Developments: The Ideological Work of Gender in Mid-Victorian England* (Chicago: University of Chicago Press, 1988); Scott, "Gender: A Useful Category of Historical Analysis," *American Historical Review* 91 (Dec. 1986): 1053–75.

69. Scott, "Gender," 1072–73.

70. On some of these issues see Barker-Benfield, *Horrors of the Half-Known Life*, and Lunbeck, *Psychiatric Persuasion*, 185–228.

71. See Armstrong, *Desire and Domestic Fiction*. Also see Sander L. Gilman's *Difference and Pathology*, and *Disease and Representation: Images of Illness from Madness to AIDS* (Ithaca: Cornell University Press, 1988). Consult Pfister, *Staging Depth*, especially 108–39. Scott, "Gender," 1073.

72. Foucault, *History of Sexuality*, 1:43. On therapy for homosexuals see Castel, Castel, Lovell, *Psychiatric Society*, 241. See *The Lesbian and Gay Studies Reader*, ed. Henry Abelove, Michèle Aina Barale, and David M. Halperin (New York: Routledge, 1993), and its fine bibliography section. Also see John D'Emilio and Estelle B. Freedman, *Intimate Matters: A History of Sexuality in America* (New York: Harper & Row, 1988), John D'Emilio, *Sexual Politics, Sexual Communities: The Making of a Homosexual Minority in the United States, 1940–1970* (Chicago: University of Chicago Press, 1983), and Ken Plummer, *The Making of the Modern Homosexual* (London: Hutchinson, 1981). Although psychoanalysis helped transform homosexuals into "psychological" case studies, it must also be emphasized that many psychoanalytic and pop psychological texts encouraged ostensibly nonjudgmental "psychological" (rather than conventionally "moral") responses to homosexual behavior. On the popularization of a therapeutic nonjudgmental ethos see Hale, *Rise and Crisis of Psychoanalysis*, 83, 87, 95.

73. On American working-class identities and emotional relations see, for example, Tamera K. Hareven, *Family Time and Industrial Time: The Relationship between the Family and Work in a New England Industrial Community* (New York: Cambridge University Press, 1982), Kathy Peiss, *Cheap Amusements: Working Women and Leisure in Turn-of-the-Century New York* (Philadelphia: Temple University Press, 1986), Lillian Breslow Rubin, *Worlds of Pain: Life in the Working-Class Family* (New York: Basic, 1976), Mirra Komarovsky, *Blue-Collar Marriage* (New York: Vintage, 1962), Richard Sennett and Jonathan Cobb, *The Hidden Injuries of Class* (New York: Vintage, 1973), Stanley Aronowitz, *False Promises: The Shaping of American Working-Class Consciousness* (New York: McGraw-Hill, 1973). For useful reflections on British working-class subjectivities see Carolyn Kay Steedman, *Landscape for a Good Woman: A Story of Two Lives* (New Brunswick, N.J.: Rutgers University Press, 1987), and Reginia Gagnier, *Subjectivities: A History of Self-Representation in Britain, 1832–1920* (Chicago: University of Chicago Press, 1991).

74. Hoffman, *The Twenties: American Writing in the Postwar Decades* (New York: Viking,

1953), 198–99. Also see Hoffman's invaluable historical study *Freudianism and the Literary Mind* (Baton Rouge: Louisiana State University Press, 1945). Fox, "Intimacy on Trial: Cultural Meanings of the Beecher-Tilton Affair," in *Power of Culture,* 120.

75. Foucault, *History of Sexuality,* 1:102.

76. The politics of taboo-breaking that is focused on "pleasure" as liberation has been and will no doubt continue to be much debated on the Left. Recent works that contribute to this debate include: *The Left and the Erotic,* ed. Eileen Phillips (London: Lawrence and Wishart, 1983), *Powers of Desire: The Politics of Sexuality,* ed. Ann Snitow, Christine Stansell, and Sharon Thompson (New York: Monthly Review Press, 1983), *Pleasure and Danger: Exploring Female Sexuality,* ed. Carol S. Vance (London: Routledge & Kegan Paul, 1984), Barbara Ehrenreich, Elizabeth Hess, and Gloria Jacobs, *Re-Making Love: The Feminization of Sex* (Garden City, N.Y.: Anchor, 1986), Sheila Jeffreys, *Anticlimax: A Feminist Perspective on the Sexual Revolution* (London: The Women's Press, 1990), *The Erotic Impulse: Honoring the Sensual Self,* ed. David Steinberg (New York: Jeremy P. Tarcher/Perigree, 1992), Linda Singer, *Erotic Welfare: Sexual Theory and Politics in the Age of Epidemic,* ed. Judith Butler and Maureen MacGrogan (New York: Routledge, 1993), Lynne Segal, *Straight Sex: Rethinking the Politics of Pleasure* (Berkeley: University of California Press, 1994), Jonathan Dollimore, *Sexual Dissidence: Augustine to Wilde to Foucault* (Oxford: Clarendon Press, 1991), *Caught Looking: Feminism, Pornography and Censorship,* ed. Kate Ellis, Beth Jaker, Nan D. Hunter, Barbara O'Dair, and Abby Tallmer (East Haven, Conn.: Long River Books, 1992), *Debating Sexual Correctness: Pornography, Sexual Harassment, Date Rape, and the Politics of Sexual Equality,* ed. Adele M. Stan (New York: Delta, 1995), Lisa Duggan and Nan D. Hunter, *Sex Wars: Dissent and Political Culture* (New York: Routledge, 1995). Also see Michel Foucault, "A Preface to Transgression," in his book *Language, Counter-Memory, Practice: Selected Essays and Interviews,* ed. Donald F. Bouchard, trans. Donald F. Bouchard and Sherry Simon (Ithaca: Cornell University Press, 1977), 29–52. For complex historical and theoretical analyses of transgression that develop the work of Mikhail Bakhtin (focusing on the seventeenth to the early twentieth centuries in Europe), see Peter Stallybrass and Allon White, *The Politics and Poetics of Transgression* (Ithaca: Cornell University Press, 1986). On the history of censorship see Paul S. Boyer, *Purity in Print: The Vice-Society Movement and Book Censorship in America* (New York: Scribner, 1968).

77. See Susan Sontag, "The Artist As Exemplary Sufferer" (1962), in *Against Interpretation and Other Essays* (New York: Octagon, 1978), 39–48.

78. On the culture wars consult James Davison Hunter, *Culture Wars: The Struggle to Define America* (New York: Basic, 1991), Todd Gitlin, *The Twilight of Common Dreams: Why America Is Wracked by Culture Wars* (New York: Holt, 1995), and Duggan and Hunter, *Sex Wars.* See Pfister, *Staging Depth,* 63–104, for comments on the role of the psychological in the taboo wars of the 1910s and 1920s.

79. As Terry Eagleton points out, the operations of power in corporate capitalism prefer to convince or seduce people to be complicit in their own domination and/or the domination of others rather than resort to naked coercion (which is more expensive and frequently more risky), and that ideologies of the "free" "inner self" contribute to the *subtlety* and *elasticity* of this domination. This ideologically created "transcendent" "'inner space' is," Eagleton writes, "actually where we are least free. If we were simply hedged round with oppressive powers, we would no doubt have a reasonable chance of putting up some active resistance to them. But no dominant political order is likely to survive if

it does not intensively colonize the space of subjectivity itself. No oppressive power which does not succeed in entwining itself with people's real needs and desires . . . is likely to be very effective. Power succeeds by persuading us to desire and collude with it" (*The Significance of Theory* [Oxford: Blackwell, 1990], 36–37).

80. Sontag, "A Lament for Bosnia," *Nation* 261 (Dec. 25, 1995): 818–20, see 820. I thank my brother Jordan for insisting that I read Sontag's piece immediately. Andrews, *Love, Marriage, and Divorce, and the Sovereignty of the Individual; A Discussion between Henry James, Horace Greeley, and Stephen Pearl Andrews and a Hitherto Unpublished Manuscript: Love, Marriage, and the Condition of Women,* ed. Charles Shively (Weston, Mass.: M & S Press, 1975), 49, 50. On the same wavelength in 1992, Ann Cvetkovich proposes: "If the transformation of capitalism requires the redistribution of property, then the transformation of the family might involve a redistribution of affect, so that desire and affective relations would not be so narrowly confined to the individual bonds between family members" (*Mixed Feelings: Feminism, Mass Culture, and Victorian Sensationalism* [New Brunswick, N.J.: Rutgers University Press, 1992], 2).

81. Difficulties that have been pointed out include misdating transformations in the experience and perception of emotional life, generalizing on the basis of evidence that is too vague or insufficiently representative of what or who one wants to generalize about, interpreting demographic evidence too narrowly (e.g., inferring only one kind of parent-child affective bond from a high infant mortality rate), the problem of specifying causality, relying on psychoanalysis as the truth of the transhistorical self that can be transported into the past (exemplified by some examples of psychohistory). On some of the pitfalls of writing the history of emotional life see John Demos, "Introduction: Family History's Past Achievements and Future Prospects," in *The American Family: Historical Perspectives,* ed. Jean E. Hunter and Paul T. Mason (Pittsburgh: Duquesne University Press, 1991), and Stearns and Stearns, "Emotionology." Also see Stearns and Stearns, introduction, in *Emotion and Social Change: Toward a New Psychohistory,* ed. Carol Z. Stearns and Peter N. Stearns (New York: Holmes & Meier, 1988), and Peter N. Stearns, *Jealousy: The Evolution of an Emotion in American History* (New York: New York University Press, 1989). For a discussion of European cultural studies contributions and American studies contributions to the theorizing and historicizing of subjectivities, and for some suggestions on how to synthesize these contributions, see Joel Pfister, "The Americanization of Cultural Studies," *Yale Journal of Criticism* 4 (Spring 1991): 199–229.

82. Stuart Hall, "Cultural Studies and Its Theoretical Legacies," in *Cultural Studies,* ed. Grossberg, Nelson, and Treichler, 277–86. Also see Stuart Hall, *Critical Dialogues in Cultural Studies,* ed. David Morley and Kuan-Hsing Chen (New York: Routledge, 1996), especially Hall, "The Problem of Ideology: Marxism Without Guarantees," 25–46, and Colin Sparks, "Stuart Hall, Cultural Studies and Marxism," 71–101. Hall's work—his thinking and rethinking—is characterized by strategic dialogue rather than dogmatism.

PART II

Family, Literature, and the Nineteenth-Century Emotional Revolution

Oedipus and America: Historical Perspectives on the Reception of Psychoanalysis in the United States

JOHN DEMOS

There is a famous remark attributed to Freud by Ernest Jones: "America is a mistake: a gigantic mistake, it is true, but nonetheless a mistake" (Jones, 1955, p. 60). Jones does not say when the remark was made, or in what specific context; however, Freud's skepticism about most things American is well known. It is tempting to think that the founder of psychoanalysis referred, perhaps just half-consciously, to the reception accorded his ideas in the early decades of this century. The issue, in that case, was the very success achieved by psychoanalysis in the United States—a success which seemed to Freud surprising, ill-founded, and in some ways quite unwelcome. Eager as he clearly was to associate himself with the finest traditions of scientific and humanitarian concern in Europe, he saw his ideas criticized or (worse) ignored by the great majority of his cultural peers. And yet, an ocean away, psychoanalysis was taking firm root in the shallow cultural soil of upstart, bourgeois America. There was indeed a "mistake" here—and of quite unsettling proportions.[1]

In fact, the passage of psychoanalysis from Europe to the United States has long intrigued intellectual historians (Hale, 1971; Burnham, 1960, 1967; Matthews, 1967). It presents a singularly vivid instance of the transmission of ideas from one cultural setting to another. Viewed from the American side these ideas were indisputably "foreign" in origin; though American psychologists and psychiatrists had, like their European counterparts, previously reconnoitred some parts of the same intellectual territory, no one questioned Freud's primacy as its true "discoverer." Moreover, the arrival of the Freudian system in the United States was carefully planned and highly visible. The famous conference at Clark University in 1909, the founding of the American Psychoanalytic Association a few years later, the translation and publication of Freud's early writings: all this was stage-managed by a small circle of psychoanalytic pioneers, both here and abroad; and the master himself, despite his ambivalence in relation to America, lent a hand at various critical junctures. Indeed the history of this process has acquired some of the trappings of legend: picture, for example, the great William James moving solemnly down the aisle after the Clark conference to announce to the lecturer, "Yours is the psychology of the future"—or asking Freud, on a walking trip a few days later, to carry his briefcase for a while (Jones, 1955, p. 57; Freud, 1925, p. 52).

But such anecdotal flourishes aside, there is no doubting the impression made by psychoanalysis in the United States beginning about 1910. Freud himself wrote, looking back years later on the Clark conference: "In Europe I felt as though I were despised; but over there I found myself received by the foremost men as an equal. . . . [Furthermore] psychoanalysis has not lost ground since our visit; it is extremely popular among the lay public and is recognized by a number of psychiatrists as an important element in medical training" (Freud, 1925, p. 52). Paul Roazen (1968) expresses the common verdict of scholars, in affirming "the extraordinary nature of the success of Freud's doctrines in one country in particular—the United States. This is true medically as well as among the general public" (p. 96). And Nathan G. Hale, Jr. (1971), author of the almost-definitive study *Freud and the Americans,* measures this success through detailed analysis of press and magazine coverage:

Within six years of the Clark conference psychoanalysis had eclipsed all other psychotherapies in the nation's magazines. . . . Psychoanalysis received three-fifths as much attention as birth control, more attention than divorce, and nearly four times more than mental hygiene between 1915 and 1918. The figures are impressive: between 1910 and 1914 eleven articles about Freud and psychoanalysis were published, most of them favorable; between 1915 and 1918, about thirty-one, of which twenty-five were favorable. Perhaps one-fourth reviewed psychoanalytic books, more than another fourth were full-dress popularizations; the rest were serious short expositions or criticisms, sometimes summarized from medical journals. In 1915 psychoanalysis reached the mass circulation women's magazines, and the first American psychoanalytic novel, *Mrs. Marden's Ordeal,* was published two years later. (p. 397)

Of course, there was opposition—indeed bitter hostility—in some quarters, and those early years marked the beginning of a long and arduous struggle.[2] But, whether as converts or antagonists, Americans *engaged themselves* with psychoanalysis on a scale unparalleled elsewhere in the world. And is it not true even now that there are more analysts, and presumably more analysands, in the United States than in all other countries combined?

So here is the nub of a genuine historiographic problem: psychoanalysis has won its widest and most favorable hearing where least expected to do so by its creator.[3] And the question, of course, is *why*? Professor Hale has explored, and perhaps exhausted, a broad range of possible answers from the standpoint of intellectual history. Briefly, he has focused on a pair of professional and cultural "crises" confronting Americans just after the turn of the century. The first was specific to psychiatric medicine: the so-called "crisis of the somatic style." There was, Hale argues, growing disaffection with the organic theory on which treatment of mental and nervous disorders had rested heretofore. The second crisis was much broader in scope; it involved nothing less than a wholesale revision of accepted mores and customs—what Hale terms the "crisis of civilized morality." This was, of course, the twilight—if not the late evening—of Victorian culture, the time when the great "sexual hush" began finally to lift. Hale contends that psychoanalysis fell right into line as these trends unfolded, replacing the somatic style with a new, radically different *psycho*therapy, and confronting civilized morality with a franker, freer view of human sexuality. In addition, he argues the importance of other psychotherapies (just beginning to hatch after 1900) in paving the way for Freud, and finds certain points of congeniality between psychoanalytic ideas and the social ethos of American progressivism. In short, there was in this country a *readiness* for psychoanalysis, which Freud and his followers skillfully exploited (Hale, 1971, chaps. 1–9).

Now this interpretation is persuasive up to a point—but it does not settle all questions. For even by Hale's own account there were significant counter-tendencies—trends and influences that would seem to have qualified American "readiness" for psychoanalysis. The somatic style, for example, was still the dominant force in American neurology and psychiatry at large; its critics were only a small, albeit resourceful, band until at least 1910 (Hale, 1971, pp. 17, 172, 277ff). And civilized morality was less attacked than readjusted during the same period; the cutting edge here was a new frankness about sex, in the service of suppressing its least attractive manifestations. So-called "purity campaigns" were organized by leading progressives to oppose prostitution and reduce venereal disease, and increasingly their spokesmen deplored the polite façade of reticence that had veiled such problems from public scrutiny (Lubove, 1961; Feldman, 1967). However, the larger point is that candor in sexual matters was advocated in the service of ever-greater "purity"; except for a tiny minority of cultural radicals, American progressives reaffirmed the central core of traditional mores.

But there is no reason to argue at length with Hale's work—which remains a signal contribution overall. It permits us to follow some enormously complex and elusive lines of intellectual transmission; indeed it constitutes a historical map which helps considerably to locate the development of psychoanalysis in time and space. More, the specific arguments for "cultural readiness" retain at least some of their importance, even after allowance has been made for the various caveats and qualifications. The aim of this paper is to propose an alternative line of explanation for the "mistake" of psychoanalytic success in America. Perhaps it should not even be called an alternative, but simply a complement. After all, as historians no less than psychoanalysts will agree, "mistakes" are notoriously overdetermined.

I

It is necessary in what follows to redirect the focus toward certain different areas of American life and culture, during the period preceding the arrival of psychoanalysis. This will mean a shift, broadly speaking, from intellectual to social history. More specifically, it will entail some extended consideration of the subject of family life in the American past. We should recognize at the outset that this subject has been "legitimated" for historians only during the past decade or so. Previous generations of scholars avoided such seemingly mundane and personal matters—preferring instead to concentrate on politics, diplomacy, commerce, and other manifestly "public" themes. Thus the field of "family history," as we are coming to call it, is quite new and in some respects unexplored. Still, many historians are now busily at work in this and related areas, and the sum-total of results so far is quite substantial. Certain of these results seem fairly surprising, others may well be completely *un*surprising; but in any case they do bear on the question from which this paper began.[4]

To summarize the central point in a couple of anticipatory sentences: it will be argued that a family system developed in these United States, during the last several decades of the nineteenth century, which involved significant departures from the dominant modes of family life in still earlier historical periods. In fact, these changes were *so* significant and encompassing that it is reasonable to speak of a "critical period" in the history of the American family. The result was the flowering of a kind of "hothouse family," which did indeed lay the cultural and psychological ground in which Freudian ideas would subsequently take root. To some extent, the themes that we will emphasize could be explored in terms of other Western countries as well; to that same extent, therefore, this discussion will embrace the historical context of Freud's life and work in the very broadest sense. However, it appears that the family system described in what follows was more widely and deeply normative in this country than anywhere else. If so, perhaps it supplies that additional element of "cultural readiness" which finally escaped Professor Hale.

Let us proceed now with an overview of central conclusions in recent historical scholarship on nineteenth-century American family life. These conclusions will be presented in summary form and virtually without documentation. Considerations of space preclude any systematic effort to sample the voluminous evidence which might otherwise flesh out our rough and skeletal outline.

In the first place: by at least 1850 (perhaps earlier) Americans had developed a view of the family that assumed its radical disjunction from all other aspects of their culture. The individual household, and the world at large, were pictured as contrasting "spheres," and the relation between them was that of adversaries. Community life—epitomized by the growth of the modern city—seemed agitated, disordered, unpredictable, and insidiously conducive to the expression of the worst of human instincts (Sennett, 1969, 1970; Jeffrey, 1972). To all this, family life stood as a deeply necessary foil. The evocative significance of home—the word itself became highly sentimentalized—is manifest through an enormous range of literary and personal artifacts of the period. Home became the abiding source of all the tender virtues in life. Love, kindliness, altruism, peace, harmony, good order: these were among the leading qualities attributed exclusively to the domestic environment.[5] It should be emphasized that there was something very new here. In the colonial period of American history, family and community had been experienced as complementary to one another; indeed the household unit was typically viewed as the "little commonwealth" which prepared the individual in a wholly natural way for social and political roles in the wider world (Demos, 1970; Morgan, 1966; Bailyn, 1960). In sum: we can view the changes of the nineteenth century as involving the establishment of a sharp social boundary, where previously things had been open, and free, and relatively undivided. The effects of this dichotomy were profound, for many aspects of popular culture, but one that deserves special emphasis here is the equation of home life with the development of individual character. Whereas, in a still earlier period, responsibility for character training was shared among a variety of people and institutions (parents, other kin, neighbors; churches, courts, and local government), from henceforth this responsibility belonged to the family alone.

Even as the family was progressively marked off from other networks of human interaction, it underwent a process of *internal* subdivision as well. There developed, for example, a massive system of sex-role stereotyping, whereby maleness and femaleness were set apart as never before. Men and women were thought to occupy entirely different "spheres"—indeed they were presumed to have essentially different *characters* (Welter, 1966; Barker-Benfield, 1976). Women were charged with maintaining the sanctity of the home, while men became the representatives of individual families in the wide and dangerous world at-large. This contrast was explicitly pejorative: women were supposed to be "pure" in all things, while men, alas, were necessarily tainted by their contact with life outside the home. Once again we must recognize the historical novelty of these trends. In the colonial era men and women had shared a broad range of everyday experience, easily and informally; and within the household the roles of husband and wife had overlapped at many points (Demos, 1970, chap. 5).

As the nineteenth century progressed, a further splitting of roles and statuses within the family developed along *generational* lines. This was the era of what has been called "the discovery of childhood."[6] For the first time in Western history children emerged from the larger social backdrop as distinctive creatures with their own needs and tendencies; no longer were they viewed simply as "miniature adults." From here on children would have their own patterns of work and play; or rather, to put it more accurately, some children would have no meaningful work at all, while others would be steered into very special work. (Consider, for example, the phenomenon of child labor in the factories.)[7]

Now this is a very large and complex historical process, impossible to discuss in a few sentences, but clearly the main engine of change was the movement from a local, rural, agrarian culture to the increasingly urban, industrial, "mass society" of modern times. It is easy enough to see that in a farm household work and recreation are everywhere joined—and *shared* by men and women, young and old, pretty much alike. But take that same household and transplant it in the city—and experience is so profoundly divided that *people* come perforce to occupy a range of distinct positions. (The formal term for this process, in the language of academic sociology, is *structural differentiation*.) There were, moreover, demographic trends which reinforced the process of differentiation. Throughout the nineteenth century the birth rate was falling steadily, so that by 1900 the number of children born to an average couple had been reduced almost by half.[8] For the first time large numbers of parents were attempting to control their own fertility, and this meant not only fewer children, but also the compression of reproductive activity into a much shorter time span. Whereas in colonial America a household might contain as many as ten children, ranging from one or two who were virtually adult down to toddlers and even a babe at the breast, a typical middle-class family of the late nineteenth century would consist of parents and two, three, or four children relatively close to one another in age. In a sense, therefore, families were becoming more visibly two-generational; in the parlance of our own time, there was the basis here for a "generation gap" (Demos and Demos, 1969).

These powerful long-term trends, both the narrowly demographic ones and the broader transformations of economic and social structure, converged in their effects on family life—and particularly on the lives of children. What seems most important is the way the whole process of individual maturation became disjunctive and problematic. No longer could growth and development be taken for granted—that is, assumed as a natural concomitant of universal social processes. Instead, it became increasingly difficult to believe that the experience of the older generation would directly prefigure the life of the younger one.

As one result of these altered circumstances, there sprang into being a new genre of popular literature—the literature of child-rearing advice. Since the care of children had become a self-conscious activity, full of unexpected risks and dangers, a variety of self-appointed "experts" busied themselves with the production of books and essays designed to resolve the questions of increasingly troubled parents. The line of these authors descends, in virtually unbroken continuity, from a nucleus of Protestant clergymen and "scribbling ladies" (writing in the 1820s and 1830s) to our own Dr. Spock (Wishy, 1968; Sunley, 1963). We will undertake in the next few pages to focus more sharply on the question of child-rearing, and in doing so will be obliged to rely heavily on these early advice books. The use of such materials is open to question—the gap between advice and behavior being, in many instances, quite substantial— but there is, on balance, enough supporting and confirming evidence from other sources to make this a worthwhile inquiry. From all we can tell about nineteenth-century America, children were raised in new and different settings, according to altered goals and precepts, and with distinctive effects on their adult lives later on. So, herewith some brief observations about the dominant strain of child-rearing advice:

1. All authorities agreed on the extreme urgency of careful, responsible parenting. In the brave new world of nineteenth-century America there was no alternative to home life for the proper rearing of children. If parents did not perform effectively, no one else would do the job for them. Furthermore, the stakes were so high and initial trends so hard to reverse, that the rearing process should begin when children were very young. The Rev. Horace Bushnell, a Congregational minister whose enormously influential book *Christian Nurture* was published in 1843, declared flatly: "Let every Christian father and mother understand, when the child is three years old, that they have done more than half of what they will do for his character" (p. 248). The resonance between this particular statement and views which would subsequently be derived from psychoanalysis is so obvious as hardly to need mentioning.

2. In speaking of parental responsibility for raising children, Americans of the nineteenth century actually meant *maternal* responsibility. Father simply vanished from the domestic stage, and mother's role was correspondingly enlarged. Her influence would be absolutely decisive for the character of her children—especially her *male* children, for these issues were formulated most

conspicuously in terms of mothers of sons. In the words of a favorite period cliché: "All that I am, I owe to my angel mother." This relationship, as typically described, had literal qualities of symbiosis. "Every look, every movement, every expression"—wrote one authority—"does something toward forming the character of the little heir to immortal life" (Child, 1832, p. 8). And the same pattern prevailed even in embryo; thus, for example, a mother is supposed to have spent leisure hours during her pregnancy gazing at engravings of handsome buildings, in order to destine her child to greatness as an architect. (In some cases, it appears, this strategy was fully vindicated by the results; the instance cited here involved the mother of Frank Lloyd Wright! [Wright, 1932, p. 8].)

3. The *goals* of child-rearing, as expressed in the advice literature, were somewhat divided and confused. On the one hand, there was much emphasis on encouraging qualities of independence, resourcefulness, initiative—a whole expressive mode. Only thus would a young person be prepared to seize the main chance and "get ahead" in the open society of modern America. On the other hand, the same authorities also stressed the development of inner discipline and self-control. For, without a moral compass—and that was a favorite metaphor—a child might go wildly astray as soon as he ventured beyond the threshold of home. These twin goals, of expressiveness and control, seem to have constituted a kind of double message from parents; and one wonders how the balance was struck in the day-to-day experience of average households.

4. The authorities spoke with a clearer voice on the subject of methods and procedures. Discipline, they agreed, must be based on the good example of parents—and on repeated appeals to *conscience* in the child. Important values and standards must be *in*ternalized, as early and as fully as possible. Just as the American nation was founded on a principle of "self-government" in its public affairs, so the young person must develop a similar capacity to guide his private life.[9] In our own terms, the touchstone of this disciplinary regime was guilt; the child's inner feelings became the chief agency of punishment. It is in the materials from this era, incidentally, that one first encounters that remarkable bit of domestic sophistry—the parent who says, as he bends a whimpering child over his knee, "It hurts me to spank you, more than it hurts you to be spanked." But this notion, that the wrong one does causes distress and dismay for others, is the inner foundation of a "guilty" orientation to the world. And here, once again, is a sharp contrast with the norms of an earlier time. In colonial America, child-rearing (and social control, more generally) had been based on a principle of *shame*—that is, the exposure of wrong doing to the ridicule and contempt of others.[10]

5. These different themes join at one important point: together they imply

a massive intensification of the parent-child bond. I have already underscored the burden of responsibility which the culture assigned to parents for the welfare and future prospects of the young, but sometimes the case was turned the other way around: children, for *their* part, had the power to blight the happiness of parents by falling into paths of wickedness. Nineteenth-century fiction plays endless variations on this theme. A virtuous couple anxiously rears their beloved son for a life of decent respectability (if not of greatness); the son grows up and goes out into the world, is exposed to the influence of "evil companions," takes to drink and gambling or whatever; his misdeeds are reported back to his parents, who in turn are so literally "heart-broken" that they may sicken and die. Seen in this light, domestic bonding had become a matter of life-and-death.[11]

So much for the child-rearing literature; we must now try to integrate certain additional considerations reflecting the shape and substance of the culture at large. It is well known that sexual behavior in this "Victorian" era was hedged about with uniquely restrictive ideas and values. There is no point in attempting to cover this familiar ground in detail; we should, however, notice one aspect of nineteenth-century sexual conventions for its specific relevance in the present context. For the first time in Western history the idea was propounded, and widely accepted, that women are passionless—not merely chaste, but literally devoid of sexual feelings (Cott, 1974, chap. 6; Barker-Benfield, 1976, pp. 113–116, 275). Sometimes this was presented as a prescribed standard, and sometimes as an experiential reality; and where reality diverged from the standard, women (literally by the thousands) resorted to a drastic remedy—the surgical procedure of clitoridectomy (Barker-Benfield, 1976, p. 120 ff.). One way or another, feminine "purity" would be sustained and "sensual wishes" repudiated. What, then, may we infer about the role of such women as mothers? Recall that the advice literature was essentially a body of morality tales about mothers and sons. Is it too much to suppose that many nineteenth-century women—faced with overbearing cultural constraints on their sexuality in relation to sweethearts and husbands—proved to be rather "seductive" in their maternal function? This was, after all, the period when the great American tradition of "Mom-ism" began to flourish (Erikson, 1950, pp. 288–297); an early and extraordinary manifestation was the vast corpus of folksongs and ballads spawned by the experience of the country in fighting a terrible Civil War (Moore, 1889). The pre-eminent figure in this Civil War music is Mother—Mother for whose sake the war must be won, Mother whose influence keeps her soldier-son from yielding to various forms of battlefield temptation, Mother whose past self-sacrifices justify the supreme sacrifice of life itself, and so forth. There is, of course, no overtly sexual reference in all this;

Mother is sentimentalized, not erotized; but perhaps in the world of unconscious process the distance from sentiment to Eros was not so great after all.

And what about fathers, in this same framework of psycho-cultural circumstance? Fred Weinstein and Gerald Platt have developed an ingenious argument around this question in their book *The Wish to Be Free* (1969, chap. 5). The success of psychoanalytic theory, they contend, was made possible by long-term changes in the role of *paterfamilias*. The traditional father of pre-modern times was able to assert a variety of "patriarchal" claims, because of the many immediate and personal services he performed for other members of his household. Beginning with the Industrial Revolution, however, he was increasingly drawn out of the home (especially by his work), and his relation to his children became less nurturant and more instrumental. In a sense this amounted to a loss of legitimacy; at any rate, in Weinstein and Platt's own words, "the father had become available at last for conscious examination" (1969, p. 147). This argument seems substantially persuasive; perhaps, though, we may add to it one element deriving from specifically American circumstances. The "success creed" that took hold in this country during the nineteenth century strongly urged that young men should aspire to continual improvement of their social and economic rank—and, more, that the position of their own fathers should serve as their chief criterion of measurement. In short, success in America meant surpassing one's father. Here was a covert inducement to competition in the relation of fathers and sons; and it was one of the truly new things that blossomed under the American sun (Rischin, 1965; Cawelti, 1965; Lynn, 1955; Tebbel, 1963; Wyllie, 1954).

Certainly, too, these ideological tendencies were reinforced from the direction of life experience and life history. Mobility of two sorts—social and geographic—was notoriously characteristic of American society in the nineteenth century. Immigrants from the Old World poured into the country in a gathering tide after about 1840. Meanwhile another *internal* migration brought vast numbers of the native-born from farms and villages in the rural countryside to the burgeoning life of Metropolis. Americans of this period were truly "men in motion"—to borrow an apt phrase from a recent study of migration (Thernstrom and Knights, 1971). Presumably this quality of motion reorganized the inner—no less than the outward—frame of their experience.

The immigrants who left the blighted heaths of Ireland, or the mountain sheepfolds of Greece, or the teeming ghettos of central Europe, were fellow-travelers in a long existential journey. Wrenched from the encasing web of traditional culture, they sought a highly individualized fulfillment in a new and volatile setting. Irrevocably, they were parted from "the land of their fathers"—not to mention *the living presence* of those same fathers. Uprooted, they were also liberated; anxious and sometimes guilt-ridden, they tasted as well the rewards of *self*-improvement (Handlin, 1973). And the farm boys who made good in the city traced a similar, if less dramatic, course. They, too, exchanged one world for another, and emerged profoundly transformed.

The central myths and metaphors of American experience conveyed, at least by implication, the *filial* meaning of all this. The "man in motion" was physically separated from his father's influence. The "self-made man" declared that he owed his father nothing. The "successful man" demonstrated, in his very success, a superiority over his father. These natural and adopted "sons" of America had not, of course, done away with fathers altogether; indeed, in some respects they had only complicated their entanglement. But from henceforth the relation of father and son was on a substantially new footing. Much that had been taken for granted hitherto was now open to question. Bonds of blood and tuition that seemed wholly "natural" in traditional settings became problematic, self-conscious, and infused with chronic tension.

II

That completes our panoramic survey of the history of American family life; it is necessary now to pull these ideas more closely together, so as to rejoin the issue from which our inquiry began. And let us adopt the metaphor of *theater* as a way of epitomizing the changes that transformed the family during the period under consideration. Note, in the first place, that the domestic stage itself has been more sharply articulated; lifted whole from out of the general cultural backdrop, it now encompasses a distinct and consciously realized portion of social space. The cast of characters has been reduced in number; declining birth rates have meant fewer children among whom to divide (and diffuse) the action of this familial drama. Moreover, the roles themselves have been more sharply differentiated than was ever true before. The Husband-Father, the Wife-Mother, and the Child: here was a central, structural triangle around which all else revolved. Within the triangle, culture prescribed a delicate balance of exchange. The Child—we might as well say, the Son—derived from the Mother both everyday nurturance and the shape of his character in years to come; all this was framed in lavish hues of sentiment—which may perhaps have covered "earthly" feelings as well. The relation of the Father and the Son was quite different. There was affection, to be sure, but there was also distance; there was modeling, but also rivalry. Each of the actors and actresses aspired to "self-government," and the Parents tried especially hard to stimulate the Child's capacity to experience inner guilt. At the same time, each one was made to feel responsible for all the others. Last but not least, a mood of urgency and intensity, of ultimate (and potentially dire) consequence, suffused the entire script. Each scene led on to the next with inexorable certainty; missed cues and bungled lines would be lasting in their effects.[12]

At some point much earlier we spoke of the group which typically played out this drama as the "hothouse family." But let us change the frame of reference a bit, and adopt a psychoanalytic terminology; and the hothouse family may also be called the "oedipal family." If the Oedipus complex was indeed a *sine qua non* of the theoretical system devised by Freud, then we may surmise that its importance—and the response it evoked in others—was rooted in historically specific patterns of domestic relationship. People accepted and endorsed the Freudian system, or alternatively they resisted and denounced it, because at some level they *recognized* its correspondence to basic aspects of their own experience. This kind of implicit recognition is, in fact, an underlying dynamic of social response to all significant intellectual and scientific "discoveries."

Now at this point we can anticipate a possible source of misunderstanding. We need not argue that fresh intrapsychic patterns were created *de novo* by the historical process itself, or that at some point in the nineteenth century large numbers of people suddenly began to have Oedipus complexes where before there was nothing of the kind. It is, of course, sometimes maintained that Freudian theory applies only to modern Western society; but that is another issue, substantially at variance with what is proposed here. Almost by definition, the Oedipus complex has *multiple* points of origin—which presumably encompass biology, psychology, sociology, and history, in intricate combination. To put it another way, the Oedipus complex is a significant developmental potential in all persons, no matter what their location in time and space. However, particular patterns of historical and cultural circumstance have much to do with the way this potential is realized—whether it is highlighted, or muted, or neutralized, or whatever. Now the main line of historical change in the nineteenth century did, we suggest, create a situation in which oedipal issues become highly charged for many people. And among all the Western countries, this situation was most fully elaborated in the United States.

Which brings us back to the starting line—namely, the tricks played, and the "mistakes" made, by the historical process. The mistake is not that Freud created psychoanalysis; nor is it that America responded to psychoanalysis so fully and on the whole so favorably. Instead, as we can now clearly see, the mistake is that Freud himself was not an American! He should by all rights have been born and raised in some bustling new metropolis, surrounded by "hothouse families," egged on by the peculiarly American and patricidal cult of success. But, then, there are some mistakes which even historians cannot account for.

Notes

1. In his "Autobiographical Study," Freud (1925) complained that in America psychoanalysis "has suffered a great deal from being watered down. Moreover, many abuses which have no relation to it find a cover under its name" (p. 52). For additional comment on Freud's skepticism about the reception accorded his work in the United States, see Hale (1971, p. 331). On Freud's general disenchantment with American life and culture, see Jones (1955, pp. 59–60).

2. On early opposition to psychoanalysis among Americans, see Jones (1955, pp. 110ff.) and Hale (1971, chap. 11). Some of this opposition itself implies the growing strength of the movement; for example, the psychologist Boris Sidis, speaking at a meeting of the American Psychological Association in 1909, attacked "the mad epidemic of Freudism now invading America."

3. Admittedly, this broad formulation glosses over certain important historical questions: e.g., by *what groups*, in particular, were psychoanalytic ideas so well received? And *which* psychoanalytic ideas? And *how* were these ideas understood, and perhaps transformed, in the course of their passage into American culture? For the purposes of this essay the significant reception is that associated with the educated middle class (not the literary and/or intellectual leadership). Furthermore, psychoanalysis is considered primarily as a belief system (not as a form of therapeutic treatment). And, finally, some modification of the system, under the influence of American norms and values, is simply assumed. (On this issue, see Hale, 1971, passim.) Each of these points deserves extended treatment in itself, but none is directly germane to the argument presented here. Another matter that lies beyond the scope of this essay is the cultural readiness for psychoanalysis of the various countries of Europe. Ideally, the trends examined here should be tested on a comparative basis, i.e., alongside parallel materials from European history. But detailed investigations of such materials will have to await another time and a different hand.

4. For a summary of recent historical scholarship on American family life, see Demos (1974). See also Demos (1973). A number of valuable essays appear in two collections: Laslett (1973) and Gordon (1973). The seminal work that began the current vogue of family history is Ariès (1960). A major and very recent contribution (though touching only slightly on American materials) is Shorter (1975).

5. Popular fiction from the mid-nineteenth century displays this viewpoint most forcibly. See, for example, Sedgwick (1854).

6. The classic study of "the discovery of childhood" is Ariès (1960). Ariès traces the beginnings of this development to the experience of elite groups in sixteenth- and seventeenth-century Europe. For average people, both in Europe and in the United States, the sequence seems to have occurred considerably later. See, for example, Wishy (1968), Kett (1971), and Demos and Demos (1969).

7. For instances of child labor in nineteenth-century America see Bremmer et al. (1970).

8. The timing and steepness of this trend are reflected in a demographic measure which compares the number of children less than five years old in a given population, with the number of women of childbearing age (16–44 years). The figures for the United States in the nineteenth century are as follows: *1800*—976 per 1,000; *1850*—699 per 1,000; *1900*—541 per 1,000. Interestingly enough, from the standpoint of the present

argument, the process of declining fertility seems to have begun much earlier, and to have been substantially more dramatic overall, in this country than in Europe. (The starting point, however, was a higher American level of fertility.) On these points the standard works are Yasuba (1962) and Okun (1958).

9. Note, for example, this comment from one of the earliest of the advice books: "The child must be his own chief disciplinarian through life, and the art of self-government must be taught him, as a regular point of his education, and that both by precept and example" (Dwight, 1834, p. 113).

10. Two brief quotations may serve to exemplify this change. For the earlier period, consider the following advice attributed to Rev. John Ward (a New England minister of the seventeenth century): "Whatever you do, be sure to maintain shame in [children]; for if that be gone, there is no hope that they'll ever come to good" (Mather, 1853, 1:522). For the nineteenth century, note the opinion of Mrs. Child: "Punishments which make a child ashamed should be avoided. A sense of degradation is not healthy for the character" (Child, 1832, p. 37). (For a similar vein of comment, see Bushnell [1843, pp. 300, 332].) For a brief discussion of the colonial pattern see Demos (1970, pp. 138–39).

11. See, for example, the plot line in Sedgwick (1854)—one of the most popular works of fiction in the mid-nineteenth century. The child-rearing literature displayed a similar viewpoint, e.g., this comment from Abbott (1833): "How entirely is your earthly happiness at the disposal of your child. His character is now in your hands, and you are to form it for good or evil. If you are consistent in your government, and faithful in the discharge of your duties, your child will probably, through life, revere you—to be the stay and solace of your declining years. If, on the other hand, you cannot summon resolution to punish your child when disobedient; if you do not curb his passions; if you do not bring him to entire and willing subjection to your authority, you must expect that he will be your curse" (p. 25).

12. Although it has been impossible to give any systematic consideration to the same issues in European history, some brief speculations may prove useful. In certain respects European and American trends seem to have been roughly similar: e.g., the bounded quality of nineteenth-century family life; the sharpened definition of sex roles; the "Victorian" culture of sexual repressiveness; and the "discovery" of childhood. In other respects European developments had the same direction as American ones, but not the same intensity: e.g., the cult of motherhood; the shift to a child-rearing regime based on guilt more than shame; the declining birth rate; the sense of exclusive responsibility among the family members for one another. In still other ways the American pattern found no significant parallel in Europe whatsoever: e.g., the "cult of success," and the transforming effects of vast in-migration. Europe, in short, experienced some, but not all, of these influences which created the "hothouse" (or "oedipal") family in America. Thus, from a cumulative standpoint, her "readiness" for psychoanalysis was less— though hardly nil.

Works Cited

Abbott, J. S. C. (1833). *The Mother at Home.* Boston.

Ariès, P. (1960). *Centuries of Childhood,* trans. R. Baldick. New York: Knopf.

Bailyn, B. (1960). *Education in the Forming of American Society.* Chapel Hill: University of North Carolina Press.

Barker-Benfield, G. J. (1976). *The Horrors of the Half-Known Life: Male Attitudes Toward Women and Sexuality in Nineteenth-Century America*. New York: Harper & Row.

Bremmer, R., Barnard, J., Hareven, T. K., and Mennell, R. M. (1970). *Children and Youth in America: A Documentary History,* vol. 1. Cambridge, Mass.: Harvard University Press.

Burnham, J. C. (1960). Psychology, psychoanalysis, and the progressive movement. *Amer. Quart.,* 12:457–65.

———. (1967). *Psychoanalysis and American Medicine, 1894–1918: Medicine, Science, and Culture*. New York: International Universities Press.

Bushnell, H. (1843). *Christian Nurture*. New York.

Cawelti, J. G. (1965). *Apostles of the Self-Made Man*. Chicago: University of Chicago Press.

Child, L. M. (1832). *The Mother's Book*. Boston.

Cott, N. F. (1974). In the bonds of womanhood: Perspectives on female experience and consciousness in New England, 1780–1840. Ph.D. diss., Brandeis University.

Demos, J. (1970). *A Little Commonwealth: Family Life in Plymouth Colony*. New York: Basic Books.

———. (1973). Reflections on the history of the family: A review essay. *Comparative Studies in Society and History,* 15:493–503.

———. (1974). The American family in past time. *Amer. Scholar,* 43:422–46.

Demos, J., and Demos, V. (1969). Adolescence in historical perspective. *J. Marriage and Family,* 31:632–38.

Dwight, T. (1834). *The Father's Book*. Springfield.

Erikson, E. (1950). *Childhood and Society*. New York: Norton.

Feldman, E. (1967). Prostitution, the alien woman, and the progressive imagination. *Amer. Quart.,* 19:29–51.

Freud, S. (1925). An autobiographical study. *Standard Edition,* 20:3–70. London: Hogarth Press, 1959.

Gordon, M., ed. (1973). *The American Family in Social Historical Perspective*. New York: St. Martin's Press.

Hale, N. G., Jr. (1971). *Freud and the Americans*. New York: Oxford University Press.

Handlin, O. (1970). *The Uprooted*. Boston: Little, Brown, 1973.

Jeffrey, K. (1972). The family as utopian retreat from the city: The nineteenth-century contribution. *Soundings,* 55:21–41.

Jones, E. (1955). *The Life and Work of Sigmund Freud,* vol. 2. New York: Basic Books.

Kett, J. (1971). Growing up in rural New England, 1800–1840. In: *Anonymous Americans: Explorations in Nineteenth-Century Social History,* ed. T. Hareven. Englewood Cliffs, N.J.: Prentice-Hall, pp. 1–16.

Laslett, P., ed. (1973). *Household and Family in Past Time*. Cambridge: Cambridge University Press.

Lubove, R. (1961). The progressive and the prostitute. *The Historian,* 24:308–25.

Lynn, K. (1955). *The Dream of Success: A Study of the Modern American Literary Imagination*. Boston: Little, Brown.

Mather, C. (1853). *Magnalia Christi Americana*. Hartford.

Matthews, F. (1967). The Americanization of Sigmund Freud. *J. Amer. Studies,* 1:39–62.

Moore, F., ed. (1889). *The Civil War in Song and Story*. New York.

Morgan, E. (1966). *The Puritan Family*. New York: Harper & Row.

Okun, B. (1958). *Trends in Birth Rates in the United States since 1870*. Baltimore: Johns Hopkins University Press.

Rischin, M., ed. (1965). *The American Gospel of Success*. Chicago: Quadrangle.

Roazen, P. (1968). *Freud: Political and Social Thought*. New York: Knopf.

Sedgwick, C. M. (1854). *Home*. Boston.

Sennett, R. (1969). Middle-class families and urban violence: The experience of a Chicago community in the nineteenth century. In: *Nineteenth-Century Cities: Essays in the New Urban History*, ed. S. Thernstrom and R. Sennett. New Haven: Yale University Press, pp. 386–420.

———. (1970). *Families Against the City: Middle-Class Homes of Industrial Chicago, 1872–1890*. Cambridge, Mass.: Harvard University Press.

Shorter, E. (1975). *The Making of the Modern Family*. New York: Basic Books.

Sunley, R. (1963). Early nineteenth-century American literature on child rearing. In: *Childhood in Contemporary Cultures*, ed. M. Mead and M. Wolfenstein. Chicago: University of Chicago Press, pp. 150–67.

Tebbel, J. (1963). *From Rags to Riches: Horatio Alger, Jr., and the American Dream*. New York: Macmillan.

Thernstrom, S., and Knights, P. (1971). Men in motion: Some data and speculations about urban population mobility in nineteenth-century America. In: *Anonymous Americans: Explorations in Nineteenth-Century Social History*, ed. T. Hareven. Englewood Cliffs, N.J.: Prentice-Hall, pp. 17–47.

Weinstein, F., and Platt, G. (1969). *The Wish To Be Free: Society, Psyche, and Value Change*. Berkeley: University of California Press.

Welter, B. (1966). The cult of true womanhood: 1820–1860. *Amer. Quart.*, 18:151–74.

Wishy, B. (1968). *The Child and the Republic*. Philadelphia: University of Pennsylvania Press.

Wright, F. L. (1932). *An Autobiography*. New York: Longmans Green.

Wyllie, I. G. (1954). *The Self-Made Man in America: The Myth of Rags to Riches*. New Brunswick, N.J.: Rutgers University Press.

Yasuba, Y. (1962). *Birth Rates of the White Population in the United States, 1800 1860*. Baltimore: Johns Hopkins University Press.

History and the Psychosocial: Reflections on "Oedipus and America"

JOHN DEMOS

Rereading, and reflecting on, my twenty-year-old article, "Oedipus and America: Historical Perspectives on the Reception of Psychoanalysis in the United States," feels a bit like revisiting a former life. How much has changed, how much remains the same!

In substance, form, and tone, "Oedipus and America" shows the circumstances of its creation. I was, in those days, acting director of the Center for Psychosocial Studies in Chicago and a special student at the nearby Institute for Psychoanalysis. The lecture from which the article emerged was an invited presentation to the institute. The audience—for both lecture and published article—consisted mainly of practicing psychoanalysts.

I hoped that the theme would appeal to this audience, since psychoanalysts are endlessly fascinated with the growth of their discipline. And I wanted to nudge them toward a fully *historical* view of the growth process—one that would acknowledge the shaping role of cultural conditions. Psychoanalysis, I aimed to demonstrate, cannot simply be described as the step-by-step discovery of Timeless Truth; instead, like every other theoretical system, it bears the impress of its surrounding environment.

Since my own expertise was American history and culture, I proposed to explore its specifically American manifestations. Somewhat fortuitously, I found an obvious and excellent entry point for this investigation: the longstanding enigma of the "success" of psychoanalysis in the twentieth-century United States. Why, in short, did Americans receive this cultural import from overseas with such warm and widespread interest? Were there underlying ele-

ments of correspondence—or affinity, or even a kind of emotional reciprocity—
to explain the nature (and extent) of the response? Was American society, in
effect, prepared for the arrival of psychoanalysis by specific parts of its own
history?

The context for the article included another piece as well. I had, by this
time, been plying my trade as a social historian for a good dozen years, and I
wished to make a point with certain of my fellow scholars. Those who studied
"intellectual history" seemed, not unlike the psychoanalysts, strangely inat-
tentive to social developments. In their hands, ideas were made to form,
change, and disappear through a process of cognitive transmission—from
place to place and time to time, from person to person, from brain to brain.
Again, I wondered: were there not broader (and deeper) questions of "receptivity" to consider here? And should this not, in turn, implicate affective, as
much as cognitive, factors?

Against the backdrop of these different, but intersecting, considerations,
my argument would slowly take shape. My previous work on the colonial-era
family was its immediate stimulus—and crucible. Those first generations of
Americans had experienced one pattern of family relations (largely inherited
from their European countries-of-origin). But postcolonial Americans knew
quite another pattern: more bounded, internally tighter, altogether more
intense, and (in a sense) "hotter." From this I sought to (re-)construct a prevalent social type: the "hothouse family" of the nineteenth century—which
might equally be called the "oedipal family." Here, I argued, lay the social and
cultural "soil" in which psychoanalysis would subsequently take root.

Brief as it was, and broad as it was, the argument could hardly achieve
conclusiveness. It was sketchy in several senses—long on speculation and
short on evidence, schematic, spotty, oversimplified. Indeed, in retrospect its
deficiencies seem painfully clear. American *versus* European contrasts are tossed
around almost offhandedly. And "American" is itself presented as virtually a
single thing—without the sort of refinements that might reflect class, race, and
ethnic difference. Gender lies close to the heart of the argument; but effects are
traced much more fully for men than for women (especially daughters). Moreover, no attempt is made to examine the details of American receptivity to psychoanalysis—to learn whether, in fact, family experience loomed more strongly
in professional and popular commentary than other themes (such as sexuality,
repression, or the unconscious).

To be sure, in 1978 much of this historical terrain was unexplored; hence,
sketchy formulations seemed more excusable then than they would be now. In
the interim, the edifice of family history has been building apace. And now
there is much new material to support, modify, or refute my original argument
(some of it included or referenced in the present volume). I will not attempt

specific reassessments here, but I do think the broad paradigm of the "hot-house family" has been sustained.

And yet, as noted above, much has changed within the past twenty years. The "historicity" of culture is now widely assumed. Intellectual historians have become far more closely attuned to the social matrix of influential ideas. And institutions like the family are no longer represented as transhistorical constants.

Indeed, the balance could well shift too far in the opposite direction; hence we should remind ourselves that "historicity" also has its limits. Family history shows us both a vast spectrum of specific forms and the remarkable endurance of underlying structures. In particular, the "nuclear" household—a domestic core of man, woman, and their "natural" children—has been central to virtually every phase of Euro-American history since at least the Middle Ages. And even in those non-Western societies where "extended family" patterns seem prevalent, nuclear subgroups can often be found embedded somewhere within. When one considers, in the abstract, the possible range of family forms, the actual range does not loom so large.

Emotional experience, as well, is not unbounded. Whereas, in 1978, it seemed necessary to assert the social channeling of oedipal themes, now I would give a different emphasis. One sentence from my original article may bear repeating: "The Oedipus complex is a significant developmental potential in all persons, no matter what their location in time and space." Admittedly, its specific shapes (and intensity) are determined by all manner of environmental factors. But its potential is always present.

A claim like this one expresses the double-sided thrust of a truly psychosocial perspective.[1] The "social" piece weighs heavily on the side of variance, but the "psycho" reflects a deep bedrock behind all human experience. To change the metaphor: individual humans draw on a common fund of intrinsic "potentials." To change it yet again: we share a finite number of intrapsychic "building blocks" from which our separate lives (and cultures) fashion unique permutations and combinations.[2]

In fact, the "psycho" is rooted in the still deeper substrate of anatomy and neurology; hence the appropriate terminology should finally be "bio-psycho-social." Recent and ongoing neurological research leaves traditional mind-body distinctions in tatters, by showing that the mind itself is very much "embodied." This research, in turn, is closely linked to a revived interest in evolutionary process—the human organism, in *all* its aspects, changing and developing as an integrated "system." And just as the physical elements of that system are limited by the terms of their adaptation to each other (and to the wider environment), so, too, are their psychological counterparts.[3]

Recent advances in the theory of emotion have made this particularly evident. Most psychologists agree on the importance—and omnipresence—of certain "primary affects." Genetically programmed, biologically grounded, and phenomenologically distinct, these include such familiar states as fear, anger, joy, interest, distress, disgust, surprise, and contempt. Researchers are still exploring (and arguing about) the details of the list; but the need for *some* list seems clear.[4]

Indeed, there is mounting evidence of inter-cultural universality in emotional life. The same "affect constellations"—as expressed in facial patterns and their autonomic accompaniments (e.g., heart rate, skin conductance)— have been found in widely different settings around the world. Moreover, the meaning attached to such constellations is also broadly similar (irrespective of culture). A sad face is a sad face—and is recognized as such—here, there, everywhere.[5] And, it seems safe to assume, what is demonstrably true across cultural space must also have been true across historical time. To argue thus is not to deny the enormous variety of actual emotional experience. From the "building blocks" come many, and widely different, mansions.

Something can be said, finally, about the reception accorded "Oedipus and America" in the 1970s. The operative word would be *silence*. The psychoanalysts who heard my lecture were politely indifferent and/or disbelieving. And historians—because the article was buried (from their standpoint) in a psychiatric journal—were simply unaware. Nothing else I've written has elicited such limited, and disappointing, response.

Imagine my surprise, then, when the editors of this volume approached me with a plan to republish the article. In truth, the times do seem more propitious now. Emotion history has begun to emerge as a distinct scholarly subfield, and prospects for its further growth seem bright. (The current volume should be a major stimulus.) Psychologists themselves have only recently acknowledged the centrality of emotion in their own research terrain. Historians, as usual, are a bit further back, but seem ready to make up for lost time. And if, as the psychologists contend, affects are "primary motives in man [read: humans]," then scholarship in several adjacent disciplines may need to be realigned.

I began this afterword by mentioning my author's sense of "Oedipus and America" as part of a former life. But from another perspective—that of the article itself—its re-publication signals a kind of *second* life. Perhaps it will fare better this time around.

Notes

1. The term *psychosocial* was invented by Erik H. Erikson. See the essays included in his landmark work *Childhood and Society* (New York: Norton, 1950).

2. This viewpoint on individual (and cultural) psychological differences is beautifully developed in Peter Gay, *Freud for Historians* (New York: Oxford University Press, 1985). I have borrowed the metaphor of "building blocks" from Gay's discussion of "The Social Share," 156–71.

3. See, for example, Gerald M. Edelman, *Bright Air, Brilliant Fire: On the Matter of the Mind* (New York: Basic Books, 1992).

4. The most important contributor to recent work on the psychology of emotion was the late Silvan S. Tomkins. For a very helpful introduction to the main elements of his theoretical system, see *Exploring Affect: The Selected Writings of Silvan S. Tomkins*, ed. E. Virginia Demos (New York: Cambridge University Press, 1995).

5. See ibid., 217–90.

CHAPTER FOUR

Changing Emotions: Moods and the Nineteenth-Century American Woman Writer

NANCY SCHNOG

Sometimes it may seem as if there were nothing more natural or inherent to emotional life than a mood. Moods, common knowledge tells us, are those subtle emotional influences which color perception, shape behavior, and yield sustained, if not durable, moments of happiness, sadness, nostalgia, and regret, among other feelings. Everyday experience confirms that moods are emotional states which are labile, sometimes volatile, and seemingly inexplicable in origin, while a psychological common sense about emotional life teaches us that moods always have been an inextricable part of human emotional experience. It is an open question whether or not moods, as described by contemporary usage, comprise what the historian John Demos has called a fundamental "building block" in human nature; what is more certain, however, is that moods, as a category for locating the nature of emotion, have shifted in meaning and ideological significance across cultures and centuries. The diagnostic manual of psychiatry DSM-IV defines mood as "a pervasive and sustained emotion that colors the perception of the world. Common examples of mood include depression, elation, anger, and anxiety." However, if people of all generations have felt moods, they have conceived of them, and thus interpreted their meaning, in very different ways.[1]

Historically, the term *mood* has varied in meaning and in the avenues of authority construing that meaning.[2] Through the eighteenth century, mood designated thought or emotion of a particular stripe: "mind, heart, thought, feeling" with "specific colouring" (of courage, spirit, stoutness, pride, or anger). Although early use of mood included the idea that mood changes one's state of mind, only during the nineteenth century did mood connote something more uncontrollable and less desirable than that: during the mid-1800s mood accrues the meaning of "Fits of variable or unaccountable temper; especially melancholy, gloomy, or bad-tempered fits." In the twentieth century the term *mood* entered scientific discourse as part of the classificatory systems of psychiatry: what was once thought of as "fits of variable temper" was re-imagined in the 1940s as the clinically unhealthful "mood swing." In 1987 psychiatrists further tightened the relationship between mood and pathology by re-classifying the major syndromes of depression and manic-depression as "mood disorders."[3] As this brief genealogy suggests, it is a specifically twentieth-century invention of the psychological that assumes "mood" to be a basic unit and diagnostic measure of psychological normality and abnormality.

Moreover, recent scholarship suggests that to equate moods with the vagaries of merely personal feeling is to forget that moods enter the social world as a gendered concept and a weapon of cultural politics. Moved to action by the linkage between women and moods in the premenstrual syndrome controversies of the 1970s, contemporary feminists have been among the first to analyze the politics implicit in widely accepted essentialized notions of female moodiness. Eerily reminiscent of late nineteenth-century contentions that the womb controls the female mind and disposes it toward irrationality and debility, today's diagnosticians and promoters of PMS argue that hormones control the woman and ineluctably dispose her to monthly occurrences of irritability, moodiness, and anger. Feminists responding to such theories, while never denying the possible biological basis for PMS, have become sophisticated deconstructors of the cultural messages embodied in this rhetoric of cyclic female moodiness. Anthropologist Emily Martin has shown, for example, how popular concerns with women's moods vary according to the market interests of late industrial capitalism.[4] Martin argues that when women are needed in the workforce, as in wartime, they are deemed sufficiently rational as people and as workers; on the other hand, when the workforce contracts and women's services are no longer required, as in postwar years, the culture rationalizes their exclusion with a doctrine of physical weakness and emotional volatility. For Martin the PMS controversy of the 1970s—a national debate about women's emotional nature and trustworthiness as citizens and as workers—functioned as part of what Susan Faludi has called "the backlash myth"; it was there to remind Americans that, even as women make their most significant economic and professional inroads into public life, they are, by nature, physically handicapped and emotionally unstable.[5]

If various groups can use a rhetoric of moods as a tool of social conservation, women, feminist anthropologists argue, can use moody self-expression as a vehicle of social protest. During the first wave of feminist writing on men-

struation, feminists told women that the time had come to put an end to culturally entrenched negative visions of "the curse" and to celebrate the potential creativity and good stemming from this biological fact.[6] Moving beyond a
politics of reversal and celebration, feminist scholars have provided compelling
new readings of menstruation and its avowed symptomology. Of a piece with
her writing on moods and work attitudes, Emily Martin views women's assertion of moodiness through PMS as a subversive challenge to an industrial system that places women in lower ranks of the service economy and demands of
them bodily and emotional "work discipline."[7] For Martin, mood symptoms
provide women with a valve for intermittent shutdowns, a protest against the
dehumanizing organization of labor. In a different vein, anthropologist Alma
Gottlieb argues that PMS discourse actively socializes women into a two-sided
view of female personality: twenty-one days a month, they feel beholden to the
traditional script of sweet-tempered and altruistic femininity, yet they can use
the period surrounding the menses to enact its opposite.[8] Gottlieb suggests
that, from the moment adolescent girls learn about their periods, they are
taught by teachers, parents, and doctors "about anticipated mood shifts from
'nice' to 'irritable,'" which are then viewed as "a natural occurrence." Far from
a subversive transition in emotional demeanor, the moody PMS sufferer gives
voice to anger and complaints when she knows that "those complaints will be
rejected as illegitimate," while enacting a script intrinsic to Western culture's
dualistic and ambivalent views of women.[9]

In this chapter I use this historically and politically constituted category of
moods as a guide for exploring the meaning of the many nineteenth-century
writings by American women writers that take "moods" as a central term and
subject. I was cued to the importance of this topic by the title of Louisa May
Alcott's early novel, *Moods* (1864), and this chapter builds on the curiosity it
sparked. In a time when so many literary sentimentalists wrote novels dealing
with matters of social reform, why did Alcott choose a title so resonant with
emotional implications? Critics know that Alcott's *Moods* was largely autobiographical: what might this tell us about the ways moods were shaped—or generated—by nineteenth-century social structures and tolerated as part of the
course of female development? And, finally, how did nineteenth-century middle-
class Americans think about moods—as good or bad, as empowering or dangerous—in a time when, as Warren Susman has argued, both male and female temperament was defined by a concept of "character" that subordinated the self to
the higher moral claims of duty, self-denial, citizenship, and integrity?[10]

In this chapter I show how, in the second half of the nineteenth century,
white middle-class women writers used the category of moods to stage a public conversation about their inner potential to assume roles beyond the prover-
bial angel in the house—in particular, those of the romantic individual and the

inspired artist. Part one of this chapter focuses on mid-nineteenth-century sentimental attitudes toward women's moods and the large prescriptive literature
that sought to control them through the social performance of female cheerfulness. Part two goes on to examine three works of women's fiction—Louisa
May Alcott's *Moods* (1864), Elizabeth Stuart Phelps Ward's *Story of Avis* (1877),
and Kate Chopin's *Awakening* (1899)—that challenge the domestic standard of
constructed serenity through their thematization of their female protagonist's
moods.[11] In contrast to scholarship in nineteenth-century American literature
that posits an opposition between the genres of female sentimentality and male
romanticism, this chapter studies the importance of masculine romantic ideologies to postbellum women writers who sought to reconfigure their literary
work as aesthetically complex and their literary personae as emotionally
"real."[12] The novels of Alcott, Phelps, and Chopin reveal that the transition in
women's writing from sentimentality to literary realism—from the conceptual
world of the "true woman" to that of the "new woman"—involved a major
shift in the scripting of female emotion and especially in the encoding of
women's moods. Whereas mid-century women writers tended to erase moods
from their female heroines in conformity with domestic principles, women
writers of the late nineteenth century reclaimed them in conjunction with a
masculine romantic philosophy that, for at least a century, had equated moods
with individualism, creativity, and emotional depth.

The Moody Woman

The sentimental literature of the antebellum era—the form that, according to the historian Mary Ryan, peaked in its popularity in the 1850s—constituted moodiness as a major problem and flaw in female temperament.[13] Literary scholars have shown how sentimental novels such as Catharine Maria
Sedgwick's *New-England Tale* (1822) and Susan Warner's *Wide Wide World* (1851)
functioned as spiritual training narratives, teaching young women how to control intense emotion, especially anger, and how to deny self-fulfilling wishes in
the service of what Anna Freud called "altruistic other-direction." A related
genre of women's sentimental writing has received less attention: the stories of
prenuptial and marital relations that continued women's emotional education
by placing strong taboos on the acknowledgment and display of the married
woman's moods. Authors of sentimental fictions and domestic advice manuals
employed two literary figures as a mode of organizing the proper emotional
expressions of married women. They introduced the figure of the moody
woman who instructed readers to censure a whole arsenal of negative feelings
(anxiousness, sadness, nervousness, and irritability) and to ward off their display through the outward demeanors of self-absorption, sulkiness, standoff-

ishness, and coldness. Emerging in tandem with this image and helping to render it unacceptable was an alternative portrait of the habitually cheerful woman, unshakable in her pose of contentment and a symbol of perfect emotional adjustment to the roles of spouse and homemaker.

In 1833 Emma Willard, the founder of Troy Female Seminary, explained that in her era the label of moodiness was often used to stigmatize women who consorted too closely with political feminism. In *The Advancement of Female Education*, Willard commented that women's rights advocates are often accused of losing their feminine characters and "often when such women are found moody and are thought capricious it is this which is the cause of their ill-humor and dejection."[14] Early sentimental fiction writers instructed their women readers to sidestep such epithets—and the progressive politics that provoked them—by suppressing "moody" behavior and by assuming the visibly "domestic" look of cheerfulness. In sentimental literature these messages were articulated with particular force in the writing of Elizabeth Stuart Phelps, one of the most popular early nineteenth-century women writers and the mother of the well-known postbellum writer Elizabeth Stuart Phelps Ward.[15] Like many authors of her generation, Phelps used her stories to establish middle-class standards of female deportment and home management. What makes Phelps's stories unusual, however, is the explicit way in which they tie domestic practices—housekeeping, childrearing, dress, and personal cleanliness—to emotional conduct. One witnesses this extension of domestic ideology into the realm of the emotions in what is, today, Phelps's most often anthologized tale, "The Angel over the Right Shoulder: Or, The Beginning of the New Year" (1852), as well as in her lesser-known collection of stories, *The Tell-Tale: Or, Home Secrets Told by Old Travellers* (1853).[16]

The conventional happy ending of Phelps's "Angel over the Right Shoulder" provides one index of the importance the author attributed not simply to the role of divine motherhood but to the "angelic" wife's and mother's emotional self-presentation. This story's protagonist, Mrs. James, at her husband's prodding commits herself to a long-desired course of study and, when faced with constant interruptions from her family, must ultimately come to grips with the futility of her program. Within this framework the story's main line of interest is Mrs. James's journey out of the depression caused by her daily routine of self-sacrifice and her emergence into a state of happiness with her limited domestic role. What makes this story's happy ending different from hundreds of other sentimental tales is that it literalizes and personalizes the meaning of a "happy" outcome: this story's act of closure spotlights not the positive resolution of a family problem, but the specific duty of Mrs. James to become a happy person. Thus in the closing paragraph we learn that, through the agency of a dream (recounting Mrs. James's future salvation through

maternal benevolence), the protagonist leaves behind "Sad thoughts and sad-
der misgivings—undefined yearnings and ungratified longings" in order to
approach a "*Glad* New Year" with "fresh resolution and cheerful hope, and a
happy heart" (215). Phelps's triple reiteration of adjectives of glee in the penul-
timate sentence of her story is neither an empty cliché nor a meaningless
pattern of repetition.[17] Rather, in this case Phelps's underlined and capitalized
"*Glad*" and its synonyms are used to underscore the specifically emotional
responsibility of the middle-class mother to maintain and express a "happy
heart."

The marriage stories in Phelps's *Tell-Tale* repeat and expand on these ideas.
These tales picture properly and improperly domesticated homes and associate
them with their female housekeepers' either rightly or wrongly conceived
notions of bodily care and emotional carriage. In these stories Phelps links her
properly domesticated homes—places which feature disciplined children,
arranged parlors, neat dinner tables, and well-dressed family members—to the
presence of happy wives and mothers. The women in these homes fill "cheerful parlors" with "cheerful chat" (114); they are "full of affection" and "kind
and genial" (104); they nurture "sweetness of character" (25) and exude "a
calm and steady light" (123). Oppositionally, Phelps attaches her improperly
domesticated homes—places defined by messy parlors, unruly children in
shabby clothes, and disorderly family meals—to the stewardship of housekeepers who are physically unkempt and emotionally uncontrolled. These stories identify an expansive list of emotional demeanors that are disruptive to the
goal of domestic cheerfulness. At different times, the tales censure women who
adopt "a distressed tone of voice" (18), wear "a doleful expression" (18), sport
a carriage both "glum" and "mum" (50), fall into "the sulks" (103), act "off-
ish" or "blue" (104), exude "chilliness" as opposed to "sunshine" (106), become
"irritable and nervous" (125), or exhibit "moody ill-humour" (43) or "moody
silence" (118). Altogether, the marriage stories in *The Tell-Tale* offer a veritable
compendium of negative demeanors and, by extension, negative feelings not to
be tolerated in middle-class women.

There is, however, one story in *The Tell-Tale* that significantly disrupts the
volume's otherwise consistent perspective of disdain toward the moody
woman. This tale, "The Husband of a Blue," points to a current of ambivalence
within Phelps's writing on self-enforced cheerfulness—an uncertainty that has
important implications for the way we ultimately understand the ideological
functions of the literature of female emotional comportment. In "The Husband
of a Blue," Phelps gingerly concedes that, due to variations in temper and interest, not every woman can or should assume the duties of matrimony and its
related work of emotional uplift. This story records the marital history of a
woman who is "blue" in two senses of the word: she is a bluestocking, an eru-

dite woman who "cared for little but her books" (98), and blue by temperament, a woman with tendencies for the "sulks" (103). As in "The Angel over
the Right Shoulder," the moral lesson this story teaches is the harm done to
family life through a wife's and mother's "selfish" devotion to her own intellectual interests. Yet in a more direct fashion than the earlier story, "The Husband of a Blue" links the anti-domestic nature of its protagonist, Marion Gray,
to her proclivity for changing emotions and their expression. Marion's Aunt
Clara, the story's narrative voice and embodiment of true womanhood, underscores this fact in the following analysis of her niece's character:

> She [Marion] seemed to feel it her right to call upon Mr. Ashton [her
> husband] to accommodate himself to her hours and plans. . . . If he failed to
> do so, she was sufficiently offended to be moody. Did he urge her leaving
> her study at an inconvenient time, to receive and entertain callers, her brow
> was clouded; in short, whenever his wishes crossed hers, and he did not read-
> ily yield them, she fell into what must, even in a learned woman, be called
> the *sulks*. She was unsociable and reserved: she read almost constantly, and
> there was an indescribable chill and constraint about her, which sensibly
> affected one's spirit like going into a damp cellar. Aunt Clara saw that
> Marion was never *genial*, excepting when she had her own way. (103)

As this passage suggests, Marion has got her lessons in domesticity upside-
down: instead of caring for and serving her husband in accordance with the
tenets of true womanhood, she expects her husband to perform this role for
her. Indeed, Marion's freewheeling expression of negative sentiment—the
clouded brows, sulks, and chilliness mentioned here, as well as the standoff-
ish and irritable behavior described later in the story—marks her failure in
domestic rectitude as much as her ill-conceived notion of women's labor. At the
end of the story the narrator establishes her negative assessment of this
"moody and exacting wife" (104) with the following words: "little did Marion
think . . . that, in the final summing up of the results of her life, its most important item would be the effect which her character as an *affliction* had upon the
work and influence of her husband" (134).

One fact in this story, however, dramatically modifies the narrator's indictment of Marion's character: that is, the ethical dilemma that Phelps builds
around the conditions of Marion's marriage. As the story opens, Marion is presented as being fully aware of and perfectly open about her indisposition to
things domestic. Marion, we are informed, had "told him [her suitor] frankly,
with look and voice, which spoke more even than her words, 'that she loved
him, but she hated house-keeping, and that next to his society, she cared for little but her books'" (99). In the face of this confession, Ashton Gray overrides
his beloved's anxieties toward marriage with a guarantee to "so adjust the cares
of his new home that his wife's studies should not be broken in upon" (100).

The story's ethical dilemma is established when Ashton retreats from his side of this bargain. As a husband and father, Ashton yearns for a more complete domesticity, and expects, increasingly, that Marion play her part. Carefully, then, Phelps divides the responsibility for this couple's disastrous marriage between the wife's bookishness and the husband's deceit. As Marion says in response to one of her husband's many postmarital reproofs: "I am wholly unfitted for domestic employments; and you are unhappy because I do not give them my thoughts and time. You do expect from me a degree of attention to them which you gave me to understand that you should not expect. You have deceived me in this matter" (107).

This aspect of the plot should be noted with care for two reasons. On the one hand, by pinpointing the external forces that drive Marion toward moodiness, Phelps mitigates the blame that the story otherwise places on her reputation as an "affliction." Here, in other words, Phelps seems to show an understanding that the moodiness she vilifies in women is not always of their own making. Most intriguingly, however, readers of the work of Elizabeth Stuart Phelps Ward will note that her mother's story of a broken marital compact in "The Husband of a Blue" apparently served as the prototype for her own novel of derailed female talent in *The Story of Avis*.[18] In rewriting her mother's tale, Ward rescripts its moral content and its negative vision of female moods. In the daughter's story, sympathy, not judgment, is brought to the career-oriented woman, whose individuality and creativity are equated with the positive value of her moods.

The Cheerful Woman

In her day Phelps was not alone in marketing the image of the ever-cheerful housewife. One of the most forceful articulations of cheerfulness as the middle-class woman's normative emotional pose can be found in Catharine Beecher and Harriet Beecher Stowe's *American Woman's Home* (1869), in a chapter entitled "The Preservation of Good Temper in the Housekeeper."[19] According to these authors, the key to family happiness lies with the temper of the housewife, with the woman who is, specifically, "gentle, sympathizing, forbearing, and cheerful" (212). Although a composite portrait of female character, the essay most often repeats the quality of cheerfulness, which thus surfaces as its dominant term. The Beecher sisters' ideal housewife maintains a "cheerful temper," possesses a "cheerful and vivifying power," sustains others through her "cheerful kindness and sympathy," and works hard to preserve a "cheerful frame of mind." If, on the one hand, the device of repetition helps Beecher and Stowe communicate their belief in the power of cheerfulness, the use of contrast aids them on the other. The authors' picture of the cheerful woman is situated against a portrait of her opposite: the woman who "jars the spirits" of her family by wearing "a sorrowful, a discontented, or an angry face" or by indulging "in the frequent use of sharp and reprehensive tones" (212). In their attempt to present cheerfulness as a singular ideal of female temperament, these writers clearly delimit the states of feeling that have the potential to disrupt it: the feelings, specified here, of sorrow, discontent, and anger.

In Beecher and Stowe's understanding of it, cheerfulness is neither a transitory state nor a static ideal of character; for them, cheerfulness amounts to a specifically female strategy of social control within middle-class family life. The Beecher sisters perceive cheerfulness as a disposition with *agency*, one that, when enacted, sheds a positive "influence" over family life. For, as the authors contend, the sphere "illuminated by her [the mother's] smile, and sustained by her cheering kindness and sympathy," exerts "a peaceful and invigorating influence" that "everyone, without thinking of it, or knowing why it was so, experienced" (212). In order to ensure the proper expression of cheerfulness, the authors provide specific directions for its staging, instructions focused mainly on a woman's regulation of voice and face. The woman who wears "a countenance of anxiety and dissatisfaction" and indulges "in tones of anger or complaint" destroys the comfort of her family, while the mother who wears a smile and speaks in "kind and gentle tones" sheds "a cheering and vivifying power" (212) over her household. Working from a premise akin to modern-day behaviorism, Stowe and Beecher suggest that the "habitual" performance of this role will facilitate a woman's successful adjustment to the stance of cheerfulness.

Antebellum guides to marriage also identified female cheerfulness as an emotional and economic asset within middle-class family life. In his advice manual *The Young Wife; Or, Duties of Women in the Marriage Relation* (1837), William A. Alcott opens his fourth chapter, "Cheerfulness," with the admonition that the young wife "owes it to her husband and to the world to be cheerful."[20] Alcott designs his chapter around family histories of failure and success. The home governed by a cheerless housewife invites disaster: children in these families grow up to be "peevish," "gloomy," "discontented," and "unhappy" (44), while their fathers head for the companionship of the "tavern-keeper" (45). Alternatively, the cheerful wife "warms his [her husband's] heart, and inspires hope" while leading her partner to "habits of industry . . . to other virtues and to happiness" (46). While many domestic writers envisioned middle-class women as providing therapeutic relief to husbands drained of energy by commercial life, Alcott imagines female cheerfulness as the specific agent of relief. As the author notes, the domestic woman performs the work of helping her husband to recuperate: "Above all . . . by the reception she gives him in the evening. When he comes home . . . after dark . . . he finds not only the lighted window and the blazing hearth, but the still more cheering light of his wife's countenance, to welcome him" (47).

Like Stowe and Beecher, Alcott instructs his female readership on the correct means of performing cheerfulness. In Alcott's conception, a woman properly sustains her husband, "Not by wise words, in the form of direct instruction—not by her sage counsels—not even by her example, alone. It is by her never-tiring cheerfulness; or at least chiefly so. . . . I need only say that her countenance always wears a smile, an unaffected one, too, when she meets him; and that her every word or action corresponds to the feelings indicated by her countenance. Everything she says or does in his presence warms his heart and inspires his hope" (47). Here the wife's role is most effectively performed not through her intellectual or rational self—the self capable of offering "instruction" or "counsels"—but through her uplifted and uplifting emotional self. This self must enlist both her "countenance" and "feelings" in her enactment of cheerfulness: the look of cheerfulness must correspond with and reflect the feeling of happiness it refers to. Even more, this performance must be "never-tiring" or perpetual: as Alcott states in a related passage, "maternal kindness" must operate "not through the medium of occasional smiles or acts of kindness but by an uninterrupted series of those looks and acts that make their impression on the heart" (44). As this passage spells it out, the proper administration of female cheerfulness depends on its saturation of a woman's whole being: it must be displayed physically, felt inwardly, and enacted permanently.

The Politics of Cheerfulness

The cheerful woman of nineteenth-century domestic fiction and advice manuals appears as the not too distant ancestor of the "happy housewife heroine" that Betty Friedan finds at the heart of the mass women's magazine fiction of the 1950s: a woman perfectly "happy" in her private, domestically defined role, "existing only for and through her husband and children."[21] "Staring uneasily at this image," Friedan writes, "I wonder if a few problems are not somehow better than this smiling, empty passivity. If they are happy, these young women who live the feminine mystique, then is this the end of the road? Or are the seeds of something worse than frustration inherent in this image?"[22] Friedan's questions are important for understanding why early nineteenth-century women writers not only held to but helped produce the image of the cheerful woman. Did the ideology of cheerfulness reflect an ideal, a reality, a veiled frustration, a dishonest charade, or some combination of all of the above?

At the most basic level, the literature of cheerfulness appears to have worked in tandem with and assisted the creation of the image of the "true woman." It is now a truism of women's history that the cult of domesticity constructed the white middle-class woman as pietistic, pure, submissive, and selfless: examining this construct, one wants to note that these traits locate the nature of exemplary behavior while saying little about the inner states that attach to them.[23] The writing on cheerfulness filled this gap: it helped secure women's secondary status by refusing any sustained analysis of feelings potentially threatening to the perception of women's perfect social adjustment. In this sense the cultural arbiters of cheer reveal an implicit understanding of just how easily sadness and sulkiness, anger and offishness, resentment and clouded brows can translate into "female complaints" and marital quarrels, the seedbed of potentially larger protests. Working from expression to feeling, the rhetoric of cheerfulness sought to harmonize women's outward display of cheerfulness with its emotional referent, happiness, and, in so doing, to diffuse the emotional seeds of women's personal and social discontent.

However, behind the scenes of women's idealized depictions of cheerful housewives lay a more complicated reality. As Mary Kelley has shown in a related context, the popular women writers who came of age in the 1850s faced painful psychological contradictions—what Kelley calls "a crisis of being"—as they tried to merge their private identities as mothers with their public identities as authors.[24] As a first generation of women striving for a professional literary role, writers like Phelps and Stowe widened their sphere of public activity, while never straying too far from their domestic compass; the woman writer, who won a public self through her authorship, made significant retreats from it by hiding her name through a pseudonym, by clinging to a moral and domestic rather than an artistic definition of her work, and by feeling guilt, self-doubt, and ambivalence connected with her disassociation from her traditional role. If we return to the case of Elizabeth Stuart Phelps, we can see that her career mirrored these patterns of professional development and emotional conflict: she wrote under the name H. Trusta; she understood her writing in terms of domestic instruction; and, as memorials of the author show, she experienced a "crisis of being" that was intimately connected to both her authorship and her fictional insistence on habitual maternal happiness.

In her autobiography Elizabeth Stuart Phelps Ward speaks this way of the mother she lost as an eight-year-old: "The author . . . lived before women had careers and public sympathy in them. Her nature was drawn against the grain of her times and of her circumstances: and where our feet find easy walking, hers were hedged."[25] She was "one of those rare women of the elder time whose gifts forced her out, but whose heart held her in."[26] Both Ward and her father, Austin Phelps, recorded their memories of Elizabeth Stuart Phelps, and their memoirs provide fascinating, if sometimes opposing, insights into the way

Phelps managed her family, her work, and her emotions as she stepped into an early version of the role of "new woman." The daughter claims that her mother obtained "a strong and lovely symmetry" between the roles of writer and mother, but she also insists, to the contrary, that "her last book and her last baby came together and killed her."[27] In Austin Phelps's recollections, his wife emerges as a woman desperately struggling to obtain "symmetry" in a context that refused it. Austin Phelps's memoir highlights the autobiographical content of Phelps's stories of married intellectual women: it suggests that Phelps herself actively guarded against the consuming interest of her intellectual labors in order to avoid becoming like Marion Gray, and that she did so by consciously placing her home duties before her work like the reformed Mrs. James. As Austin Phelps says, "The Angel over the Right Shoulder" illustrates "the sincerity of the religious convictions which she [Elizabeth Stuart Phelps] carried into these [her own] household plans," while "The Husband of a Blue" reflects "her jealous vigilance over her own tastes, lest they should encroach on the comfort of those who were dependent upon her."[28]

Even more to the point, Austin Phelps offers the following description of the emotional struggle undergone by his wife:

It was the "struggle of her life" to control the fickleness of her physical temperament, and rise above despondency. "Nobody knows," she would often say, "how I do struggle for it." It was her habitual fear that her family might suffer for the want of a cheerful, sunny home. This is a disclosure, however, which will surprise the majority of her friends—so vigilant was she in watching her various moods, and so successful in breathing the spirit of joy around her. Her presence in any group was almost invariably a guarantee of vivacious and genial conversation. She often concealed physical infirmity, that she might come to her little home circle with a cheerful look. (66–67)

This passage shows that, for Phelps, the cheerful woman was neither an accomplished ideal nor present reality; it was, instead, a laboriously and painfully sought-after goal, one struggled toward through vigilance, concealment, and what the literary critic Alfred Habegger has called "a methodical sort of buoyancy."[29] From the vantage point described by Austin Phelps, it appears that Elizabeth Stuart Phelps used the figure of the cheerful woman as a psychological life-line to a domestic self-image that, in her own life, was under siege. Seeking the goal of cheer through a script of vivacity and geniality (recall that Marion Gray was never "genial") seems to have enabled Phelps to invest herself in her new authorial position, while retaining an emotional bridge to a role she was, in fact, distancing herself from (at least for the two hours a day that, like Mrs. James, she permitted herself to write). Put another way, the performance of cheerfulness seems to have acted for Phelps as a solvent for the guilt produced by her dual careers as well as a strategy for negotiating the transition between domestic woman and professional writer. Although Austin Phelps frames the major struggle of his wife's life as a matter of her "physical temperament," drawing a line between his wife's constitutional weakness and the social pressures upon her, it seems likely that both the physical and the social contributed to the inner drama Phelps enacted between her "various moods" and "cheerful look."

This examination of Phelps's life enables us to see that her fictional depictions of moody women were multivalent in meaning. Biographical documents suggest that physical problems, in combination with the legacies of her upbringing, did indeed complicate Phelps's search for an evenly experienced cheerfulness. As a young woman Phelps suffered from illness, invalidism, and what appears to have been an episode of "hysteria." At the same time, Phelps was afraid of perpetuating within her own family her father's severe Calvinism and morbid attunement to death.[30] Moreover, as Phelps's first popular novel, *The Sunny Side; Or, The Country Minister's Wife* (1851), suggests, Phelps experienced her own role as the minister's wife as an exhausting performance—yet always one to be represented as "sunny"—in other-directedness. Joel Pfister has argued that "the heated-up" psychological relations of middle-class families in mid-nineteenth-century America led to literary expressions by Poe, Hawthorne, and Melville of marital aggressivity and murder.[31] In the case of Phelps, moods appear to have been the problematic emotional upshot not simply of a frail body but of social arrangements in which the minister's sermons came before the wife's fictions, in which children had to be cared for while publishers waited for more copy, in which private conscience contended with public aspirations, and in which personal troubles had to be harnessed to the demeanor of cheerfulness.

Reconsiderations and Challenges

In the post–Civil War years, a number of "second-generation" middle-class women writers—writers whose careers peaked in the last three decades of the nineteenth century—used their fiction to rethink and challenge the domestic construction of female character as uniformly cheerful. At the head of this list stands Louisa May Alcott, whose 1864 novel *Moods* explored the emotional roles available to middle-class girls and women of her time. Although many of Alcott's critics regarded her book as a "divorce novel" and condemned the young author for approving of divorce, Alcott always maintained that her intent with her early novel was to study not marriage but girls' emotional preparedness for it. *Moods,* Alcott wrote, was "meant to show a life affected by *moods,* not a discussion of marriage which I knew little about, except observing that very few were happy ones."[32] In a letter to one disgruntled reader, disturbed by what he took to be the novel's endorsement of sexual attraction as the foundation for marriage, Alcott tried to set the record straight by telling him: "The design of Moods was to show the effect of a moody person's moods upon their life, & Sylvia, being a mixed and peculiar character, makes peculiar blunders & tries to remedy them in an uncommon manner."[33]

Whereas Phelps typically places her moody women within the context of marriage, Alcott focuses her point of interest on the "naturally" moody girl and her prospects for entering into a happily conceived marriage. Alcott's protagonist, the seventeen-year-old Sylvia Yule, represents a significant departure from Phelps's negatively characterized moody woman, yet a markedly ambivalent one. *Moods* deals with its avowed subject matter—the moods of girls and women—in a contradictory fashion. On the one hand, the novel strives for a positive characterization of its female protagonist by showing how her inborn moodiness fulfills a male transcendental ideal of emotional spontaneity and individualism. On the other hand, the novel imagines a dark future for the girl who carries this ideal into her marriage and adulthood. As this novel sees it, it is lovely and charming to be a moody tomboyish girl, but it is dangerous, even deadly, to enter womanhood lacking emotional stability, constancy, and self-control.

In *Moods* Alcott traces Sylvia Yule's development from transcendental girl to genteel woman and highlights, thereby, the oppositional ways that Emersonian transcendentalists and Stowian domestics construct male and female emotion. In the opening chapters Alcott establishes Sylvia Yule as the novel's emotionally tempestuous heroine and scripts her moodiness as a positive attribute by linking it to an Emersonian philosophy of emotional spontaneity. Alcott ties Sylvia's character to a masculine transcendentalism in a number of ways. She opens the novel by sending Sylvia, along with three male companions, on a boating expedition reminiscent of Henry David Thoreau's journey down the Concord and Merrimack rivers. Later, she again likens Sylvia's character to Thoreau's by presenting her as a witness to "a battle between black ants and red" and as a chronicler of nature who learns "the landscape by heart." But Alcott associates her heroine with transcendental philosophy in an even more important way: in *Moods* she takes pains to show that Sylvia's inborn moodiness fulfills Emerson's transcendental injunction to emotional self-contradiction and freedom.

In "Self-Reliance" (1841) Emerson presents his exemplary individual as the nonconforming man who heeds the call of what Emerson refers to variously as Spontaneity, Instinct, and Whim. Describing his own creative method, Emerson proudly declares: "I shun father and mother and wife and brother when my genius calls me. I would write on the lintels of the door-post, Whim."[34] Alcott situates her protagonist within this discourse of creative individualism by introducing the reader to Sylvia Yule in a chapter that, following Emerson, is entitled "Whims." Like Jo March of Alcott's *Little Women* (1869), Sylvia Yule is a tomboy: she dresses like a "lad," befriends insects and animals, insists that she can "walk, run, and climb like any boy" (51), and manipulates events in order to get herself invited on her brother's river boat trip. Yet in this novel, Sylvia's tomboyism is defined as much by her volatile emotional life as by her physical skills. What draws the two male protagonists and every other character to Sylvia is her tumultuous emotional self, described as "whimsical and hard to please" (24), "always in extremes" (24), "many-sided" (22), "capricious" (57), and subject to "perverse fits" (17) and the performance of "wild things" (25). Drawing on a theory of inherited personality, Alcott casts Sylvia as the offspring of an unhappy marriage, a "regretful husband" and "sad wife," who conferred upon their daughter "conflicting temperaments, with all their aspirations, attributes, and inconsistencies" (84). In a deliberate echo of the language in Emerson's essay "Experience" (1844), the narrator tells us, "These two masters ruled her soul and body, making Sylvia an enigma to herself and her life a train of moods" (84).

As Barbara Sicherman has noted, in the 1860s tomboy characters were "not only tolerated but even admired—up to a point, the point at which they were expected to become women."[35] This is precisely the case for Sylvia Yule: when she is a seventeen-year-old "child," Sylvia's moods function positively and mark her as a female individual distinct from the conventional girls "all made on the same pattern" who "all said, did, thought, and wore about the same things" (24). Yet once she becomes an eighteen-year-old "woman" enveloped in the rituals of courtship, Alcott's moody female is doomed to unhappiness and untimely death. Similar to Emily Dickinson, who described marriage as "the soft Eclipse" of a "Girl's life,"[36] Alcott portrays Sylvia's eighteenth birthday as the dividing line between the past and future, the time when Sylvia "looked backward to the girlhood just ended, and forward to the womanhood just beginning" (28). Consequently, the sections that follow Sylvia's "fateful" river trip—fateful because it is there that she becomes entwined in a love triangle that disappoints its three participants—move her swiftly toward an unhappy fate. Enviable in youth, moods, according to Alcott, do not mix with marriage. They lead Sylvia down the path of divorce and early death.

As was the case for Phelps, Alcott's choice of moods as the subject of her early novel reaches back to her personal life and, in particular, to contradictions she herself experienced in relation to cultural scripts of domestic and romantic emotion. Those scripts shaped Louisa's young life in unusually intimate ways: her father strictly adhered to domestic ideals of female emotional self-regulation, while her adolescent hero and close family friend, Ralph Waldo

Emerson, exuberantly endorsed the exceptionalism of male emotional freedom. The Alcott family letters show that Amos Bronson Alcott, in compliance with these gendered ideals, interpreted the emotionally volatile temperaments of his wife, Abigail, and his second daughter, Louisa, as dangerous and unnatural. In his journal he characterizes these family members as "Two devils—the mother fiend and her daughter." He describes Louisa as "impulsive and moody" and calls her the "Possessed One."[37] Growing up in a family governed by Bronson's vision of a celestial home "where peace and joy, and gentleness and quiet, abide always, and from which sounds of content and voices of confiding love, alone ascend," Louisa had little option but to construe her "moody" nature as a problem of temperament, an abnormal deviation from her father's and her culture's dominant ideals of femininity.[38]

Ironically, Alcott's *Moods* appropriates Emerson's romantic rhetoric of moods as the authority through which to challenge and revise her father's (and broader culture's) demonic conception of them. Alcott links her subject directly to Emerson by opening her novel with an epigraph drawn from "Experience": "Life is a train of moods like a string of beads; and as we pass through them they prove to be many colored lenses, which paint the world their own hue, and each shows us only what lies in its own focus."[39] Written in the aftermath of the death of Emerson's young son, "Experience" uses what Stanley Cavell has called "the logic of moods" to locate a new pessimism in Emerson's thought, his strongly reduced faith in the self's power to apprehend the world objectively, and his increased sense of life as "a succession of moods or objects" where "gladly we would anchor, but the anchorage is quicksand."[40] Here it is important to note that Emerson's invocation of moods as a critique of objectivity retains a strain of the romanticism that marks his earlier essays. Moods, one must remember, give "color" to experience even as they block a synthesizing vision of it. Most important for Alcott, however, Emerson's meditation on life as a "train of moods" registers an idea of emotional flux as a natural and universal component of human experience—an idea, it appears, that spoke powerfully to the "moody" girl stigmatized by her father as "the Possessed One." In 1864, when Alcott published the first edition of *Moods*, she left the work of formulating a woman's inner life as a "train of moods" as wishful, unfinished business. Eighteen years later, she finished it. In 1882 Alcott rewrote her novel's ending and allowed her moody heroine to live.

In *The Story of Avis*, one of the first major studies of female artistic development in American women's writing, Elizabeth Stuart Phelps Ward moves the representation of women's moods further along the trajectory of creative individualism. Ward endows her artist-protagonist with a proclivity toward moods not only to signify her singularity but also to reference her potential to develop as a great "high cultural" artist of her time. In a major departure from the representational technique of her mother, Ward endows her protagonist with moods as one of her primary means of establishing Avis's artistic temperament and extraordinary nature. Whereas Alcott connects her heroine's moods to a concept of female individualism derived from transcendental philosophy, Ward links her heroine's moods to a concept of inspired artistry derived from nineteenth-century ideas of romantic genius. In *The Story of Avis* Ward scripts Avis's moods as the foundation of her anointed identity as an artist and as the source of the prophetic visions which inspire her best work.

Literary historians have shown that the writing of Johann Wolfgang von Goethe, Jean-Jacques Rousseau, and William Wordsworth, among others, bequeathed to nineteenth-century Euro-Americans romantic ideas of the artist as an elevated being more sensitive, passionate, and introspective than others, as a solitary self alienated from society, and as a person disposed to imaginative reverie and spiritual insight.[41] As Eli Zaretsky has written, "Beginning with romanticism, artists declared that art was the product less of a particular craft of discipline than of the artist's inner life."[42] When that "inner life" was characterized, it was typically imaged as tempestuous, unstable, and, in some cases, mad. Romantic poets, in particular, appear to have favored the term "mood" as a vehicle for locating this kind of extra-sensitive and emotionally fluid interiority. In his autobiographical poem *The Prelude* (1850), Wordsworth links his younger self's communion with nature to his capacity for "fleeting moods" which confer "visionary power."[43] Later in the poem Wordsworth discloses that, as a young man, he experimented with gestures of poetic temperament by indulging in "Moods melancholy, fits of spleen, that loved / A pensive sky, sad days, and piping winds" (VI, 170–75). In this regard it is of note that Emerson begins his essay "The Poet" (1844) with a poem that echoes Wordsworth's vision of the artistic power of moods. Emerson's verse epigraph speaks of "A moody child and wildly wise" who becomes the poet who communicates "musical order, and pairing rhymes."[44]

In *The Story of Avis*, Avis's moods are affiliated with these romantic meanings. Ward presents Avis—whose name derives from the Latin for bird—as more capable of transcendence than the typical woman of Harmouth by virtue of her aesthetic gifts, her physical beauty, and her visionary moods. The book opens just after Avis's return from Europe on an evening when she makes her homecoming debut at the Harmouth Poetry Club, a small-town literary affair in which male faculty readers and their female students have gathered to read Edmund Spenser's *Faerie Queen*. In order to emphasize the gifted nature of her protagonist, Ward presents Avis to the reader as the charmed subject of a tableau vivant. Surrounded by her peers, Avis cuts an imperial image by sitting in front of carmine drapery which accentuates her "solitary look," emphasizes "the aloofness in her very beauty" (7), and draws the attention of the group like a "magnet" (4). On this evening Avis's re-entry into Harmouth society is brought to completion when she agrees to exhibit her sketch of Spenser's Una, an occasion of textual importance insofar as it calls forth Avis's romantic conception of the artist's calling. When Philip Ostrander, in a foreboding of Avis's later subjection to him, says that her sketch of Una reveals "Truth . . . subject to Love, omnipotently subject" (10), Avis responds with the following denial: "I am not responsible for Spenser's theology . . . and an artist has such gloriously lawless moods! Why should I trouble myself to think about Una every day? I had a pretty girl to draw so I drew her. But I put the lion in, so people shouldn't make a mistake" (10).

In speaking of the artist as one who possesses "such gloriously lawless moods," Ward places her heroine within a specifically Wordsworthian and, more broadly, romantic interpretation of the artist's interiority. This is not surprising, as Ward herself was an avid reader of Wordsworth and tied her intellectual awakening at the age of sixteen to her father's readings of De Quincey and Wordsworth, which "opened for me, as distinctly as if I had never heard of it before, the world of letters as a Paradise from which no flaming sword could ever exile me."[45] Like the opium eater and poet portrayed by these writers, Avis's creativity is tied to the romantic trope of intense inner experience; her "fertile moods" serve as the occasion for prophetic vision. For example, the night before Avis is to exhibit her first American portrait, one of Ostrander, she lies sleepless, "seeing the souls of unwrought pictures, like disembodied spirits, sweep by, vision upon vision, electrotyped upon the darkness with the substance of wine or opium fantasies; an experience which chanced to her only in her most fertile moods" (61). A far cry from her mother's view of moods as afflicting, Ward endows Avis with moods as the extrasensory power which stirs "the souls" of pictures from the artist's unconscious. In a related scene, Avis's mood provides the impetus for her discovery of the idea of her sole masterpiece, a painting of the Sphinx. This scene opens with Avis locking herself in her room, trying to block out the voices of college boys singing Civil War songs, while her own civil war takes place over her wish to find the inner resources to work and live as an artist. On this night, "Avis shut and locked the door of her bare, old-fashioned room, looking about it with a kind of triumphant rebellion. These four walls shut out the world from the refined license of her mood. She wanted nothing of it,—the great unholy world, in which seers struggled and sinned for their visions. Let them go fighting and erring on" (79).

In this scene Avis courts the "refined license of her mood" not by partaking in "opium fantasies" but by doing something related to it (and unprecedented in nineteenth-century middle-class women's fiction): she *elects* to imbibe a "cautious dose" of "*liqueur*" (80). Avis nurtures her feelings of moody rebelliousness by drinking French wine and laying down to experience "a self-

articulate hour" (88) of drunken revery. It is in this state of mind that a parade
of portrait subjects appears to Avis—an earthen vase, a mid-ocean wave, a med-
ley of faces grown old with toil—and, finally, the mystery of womanhood as
embodied in the Sphinx. Through this experiment with a mind-altering substance, Avis attempts to empower her own artist-psyche by claiming the traditionally male privileges of "high stimulant, rough virtues, strong vices, all the
great peril and power of exuberant, exposed life" (79). Through this scene
Ward suggests that to be an artist is not simply to be a highly skilled painter,
but also to harbor a particular kind of "inner life"—one marked by potent and
prophetic moods. As the narrator says after Avis's night of intoxication, "there
had been nothing unprecedented in the character of these fantasies, excepting
in their number and variety. Her [Avis's] creative moods were always those of
tense vision, amounting to optical illusion, failing of it only where the element
of deception begins" (83).

It is important to acknowledge, however, that, for all the inner power
assigned to Avis through her "fertile" and "creative" moods, and for all the distance this encoding marks from the moral position of her mother, Ward's
scripting of this emotionally "deep" female protagonist does nothing to save
her from a fate akin to Marion Gray's and Sylvia Yule's. Similar to her predecessors', Avis's careers, both artistic and marital, end in failure. In Ward's novel
romantic identity is thus divorced from social empowerment: there is never a
suggestion that Avis's visionary moods will help her navigate her way out of a
situation of unforeseen marital demands and domestic entrapment. When, in
1899, Kate Chopin brought the theme of the moody woman to life again in the
character of Edna Pontellier, the aspiring artist-protagonist of *The Awakening*,
she mapped more carefully than Ward the liabilities of this romantic inscription of female moods. In *The Awakening* Chopin shows how readily romantic
tropes of interiority can slide into a disabling form of emotional self-absorption,
at the same time inviting pejorative labels of female irrationality and emotional
disorder.

One finds all the signs in Chopin's novel that Edna's character should be
interpreted within an idiom of emergent romantic individualism: Edna seeks
liberation from her bourgeois marriage, rebels against convention, prefers solitude to sociability, longs for an impossible fusion with men and nature, and
identifies herself with the artistic worlds of music and painting. Read in relation to the literary traditions outlined above, Edna Pontellier's propensity for
moods figures as one more convention through which Chopin marks her protagonist's capacity for romantic subjectivity. The overt romanticism of the
book's lyrical refrain—"The voice of the sea is seductive; never ceasing, whispering, clamoring, murmuring, inviting the soul to wander for a spell in abysses
of solitude; to lose itself in mazes of inward contemplation" (57)—finds a psy-

chological correlative in the book's description of Edna's susceptibility to moods—feelings that also lose the protagonist in "mazes of inward contemplation." This discourse of the emotions surfaces early in the text in a scene that depicts one summer's night of marital discord between the Pontelliers and that recounts in some detail Edna's response to it. The reader's introduction to Edna's emotional character reads this way: "An indescribable oppression, which seemed to generate in some unfamiliar part of her consciousness, filled her whole being with vague anguish. It was like a shadow, like a mist passing over her soul's summer day. It was strange and unfamiliar; it was a mood. She did not sit there inwardly upbraiding her husband, lamenting at the Fate, which had directed her footsteps to the path which they had taken. She was just having a good cry all to herself. The mosquitos made merry over her. . . . The little stinging imps succeeded in dispelling a mood which might have held her there in the darkness half the night longer" (49).

Here, as in *The Story of Avis,* the female protagonist's potential to experience complex and deep emotion is translated into a rhetoric of mood saturated with romantic overtones: Edna's mood emerges from some hidden and "unfamiliar" part of her consciousness and possesses an intensity that is overwhelming and enchanting. Yet in a departure from her precursor, Chopin also suggests how romantic conventions of mood can steep the self in paralyzing forms of self-preoccupation and emotional self-mystification. The description above begins to point to such meanings by having Edna construe her "indescribable oppression" in a register of the emotions provided by romanticism; that is, as a set of overpowering feelings that are inwardly generated, undefinable, and spellbinding. The novel's omniscient narration suggests, however, that to define the self's emotions this way is to separate them from a specific causality—in this case from the anger and spousal resentment that inspired Edna's "mood" in the first place—and to estrange them from those origins. Indeed, Edna's mood becomes knowable to her precisely because it is constituted by "vague anguish" and *not* by the affective processes of "inwardly upbraiding her husband" and "lamenting" at "Fate." Thus this first account of Edna's discovery of her mood points subtly to the ways in which a romantic vocabulary of interiority can foster a belief in privatized, generalized, and ultimately enigmatic forms of psychological suffering. Divorced from a social context and concrete origins, Edna's mood indeed functions like the novel's "voice of the sea": it "invites the soul to wander for a spell in abysses of solitude."

Later sections of the novel reveal that, once ensconced in the explanatory mechanism of mood, Edna can process only the outcomes but never the causes of her feelings. In Chopin's novel, in other words, mood describes a condition of emotional confusion that Edna is unable to move beyond. During Edna's period of apprenticeship to her art she wavers between "the days when she was very happy without knowing why . . . happy to be alive and breathing" and "the days when she was unhappy, she did not know why—when it did not seem worthwhile to be glad or sorry, to be alive or dead" (109).[46] In a similar vein the narrator speaks of the many periods when "Edna stayed indoors and nursed a mood with which she was becoming too familiar for her own comfort and peace of mind. It was not despair; but it seemed to her as if life were passing by, leaving its promise broken and unfulfilled" (127). Through such descriptions Chopin exhibits the limits of a discourse of mood as romantic agony: the terminology of mood enables Edna to comprehend her situation in terms of some sketchy apprehension of romantic desire and longing, but it stalls her ability to search for these feelings' concrete origins and social meanings.

The discourse of moods in *The Awakening* brings with it another variety of disablement: Edna's romantic enactment of female selfhood is construed by the men around her as a sign not of emergent individualism, but of innate female weakness. Alcée Arobin, Edna's high-society lover, harnesses Edna's moods to his self-interest by using them in the service of his love-making. As the narrator says, Alcée makes himself attractive to Edna by displaying "good-humored subservience," "tacit adoration," and by remaining "ready at all times to submit to her moods, which were as often kind as they were cold" (133). When Léonce Pontellier becomes concerned that his wife is "growing a little unbalanced mentally," he procures the advice of the family physician, Dr. Mandelet, who offers the following diagnosis of Edna's condition: "Woman, my dear friend, is a very peculiar and delicate organism—a sensitive and highly organized woman, such as I know Mrs. Pontellier to be, is especially peculiar. . . . Most women are moody and whimsical. This is some whim of your wife, due to some cause or causes which you and I needn't try to fathom" (119). In the thought of Dr. Mandelet, women's moods should not be taken too seriously, nor should their "causes" be plumbed, because they are an innate characteristic and evanescent expression of, it is implied, the inferior sex. Thus it is with perspicacity and irony that Chopin uncovers the fundamental likeness between the book's romantic and patriarchal readings of Edna's moods: Edna's reverential attention to her feelings and the doctor's dismissive stance toward them share common ground in their disregard of and disinterest in their socially specific origins.

Conclusion

In conclusion, I want to return to my earlier question about the title of Louisa May Alcott's novel and summarize my response to the set of interests Alcott and other women writers explored through their discussions of mood. Alcott, it seems, chose the title *Moods* because she sensed that culturally created ideas about emotion played a key role in underwriting and naturalizing gendered social roles and their accompanying modes of interiority. In taking on moods as her subject, Alcott tried to revise a tradition of domestic emotional ideals by injecting it with a powerful dose of American romantic ideology, notably Ralph Waldo Emerson's. If middle-class women were going to be freed from the prescriptive mandates of smiles and cheer, they had to learn first, Alcott's novel suggests, that their "whims" contained signifying purposes that transcended the evangelical and moral interpretations of antebellum domestic writers. What this chapter has shown is that Alcott was far from alone in her efforts.

In the post–Civil War period middle-class women writers, who, in many cases, were themselves choosing literary lives over maternal careers, moved to rescript the habitually smiling face of domestic emotion by reaching out to romantic ideas of artistic selfhood that had been in circulation for nearly a century. To continue Mary Kelley's observation about women's transforming professional identities, when middle-class women writers sought to reinvent themselves as individuals and artists and to put behind them the legacy of the woman writer as domestic moralist or professional hack, they gravitated toward romantic concepts of genius that posited a "deep" inner life and one, more often than not, traversed by vacillating and "fertile" moods. In their time Ward and Chopin were criticized for portraying these emotional tendencies in their heroines. One contemporary reviewer of *The Story of Avis* called the book "morbid through and through" and added, "the author represents unhealthy and abnormal moods of mind and emotions as being normal and typical."[47] *The Awakening* called forth similar diatribes: it was referred to as a "picture of soul-dissection" that was "morbid" and "unhealthily introspective."[48] For many twentieth-century critics influenced by post-Freudian concepts of inner conflict and sexual desire, it is precisely these features of the texts—the characters' various "moods of mind and emotions"—that qualify them for reconsideration as important if not unforgettable works of women's psychological realism.

In this chapter I have tried to show how the emotional "deepening" of the female subject in mid- to late nineteenth-century women's writing arose not from writers' unprecedented insights into universal conflicts in human nature nor from a changing social climate that, in the post–Civil War era, suddenly enabled women writers to talk about them. Rather this chapter argues that, in a time when middle-class women writers sought to move their representations of female interior life beyond sentimentality, they did so by drawing on romantic literary conventions that had supplied Anglo-American male writers with a language of emotional power, spontaneity, and depth for nearly a century. The white middle-class woman writer who wanted to represent the female self as an artistically inspired and emotionally profound individual took hold of a pre-

Freudian idiom—a romantic language of "moods"—as a means of expressing these previously unrecognized potentials.

Notes

1. See *Diagnostic and Statistical Manual of Mental Disorders, Fourth Edition* (Washington, D.C.: American Psychiatric Association, 1994), 768.

2. For historical usage of the term *mood*, I draw on the *Oxford English Dictionary*.

3. See *Diagnostic and Statistical Manual of Mental Disorders, Third Edition—Revised* (Washington, D.C.: American Psychiatric Association, 1987). Here the category once called "affective disorders" is re-classified as "mood disorders." The label "affective disorders" came to be seen as an inadequate term for mental illnesses which involve "prolonged" changes in emotional states, such as major depression and bipolar disorder. I want to thank Marc Riess for sharing with me his knowledge of psychiatric methods of classification.

4. See Martin, *The Woman in the Body: A Cultural Analysis of Reproduction* (Boston: Beacon Press, 1987), 113–38.

5. The term is from Faludi's wide-ranging discussion of the cultural politics of gender in *Backlash: The Undeclared War Against American Women* (New York: Doubleday, 1991).

6. Some of this politics of reversal is exhibited in Janice Delaney, Mary Jane Lupton, and Emily Toth, *The Curse: A Cultural History of Menstruation* (Urbana: University of Illinois Press, 1976).

7. Martin, *Woman in the Body,* 113–38.

8. Gottlieb, "American Premenstrual Syndrome: A Mute Voice," *Anthropology Today* 4 (1988): 10–13. For another interesting discussion of the cultural symbolism and political uses of women's moods, see Carol Tavris, *The Mismeasure of Woman* (New York: Simon and Schuster, 1992).

9. Gottlieb, "American Premenstrual Syndrome," 13.

10. See Susman, *Culture as History: The Transformation of American Society in the Twentieth Century* (New York: Pantheon, 1984), 271–85.

11. The chapter uses the following editions of these texts: Louisa May Alcott, *Moods,* ed. Sarah Elbert (New Brunswick, N.J.: Rutgers University Press, 1991); Elizabeth Stuart Phelps, *The Story of Avis,* ed. Carol Farley Kessler (New Brunswick, N.J.: Rutgers University Press, 1985); Kate Chopin, *The Awakening,* ed. Sandra M. Gilbert (New York: Penguin Books, 1983). All subsequent references to these editions will appear parenthetically in the text.

12. For two important examples, see Jane Tompkins, *Sensational Designs: The Cultural Work of American Fiction, 1790–1860* (New York: Oxford University Press, 1985), and the introduction in *Provisions: A Reader from Nineteenth-Century American Women,* ed. Judith Fetterley (Bloomington: Indiana University Press, 1985).

13. See Ryan, *The Empire of the Mother: American Writing about Domesticity, 1830–1869* (New York: Harrington Park Press, 1985).

14. As quoted by Anne Firor Scott in "The Ever Widening Circle: The Diffusion of Feminist Values from the Troy Female Seminary," *History of Education Quarterly* (Spring 1979): 21.

15. For the sake of clarity, the mother (1815–1852) will be referred to as Elizabeth Stu-

art Phelps, and the daughter (1844–1911) will be referred to as Elizabeth Stuart Phelps Ward.

16. Elizabeth Stuart Phelps (pseudonym H. Trusta), "The Angel over the Right Shoulder: Or, The Beginning of the New Year," reprinted in Fetterley, *Provisions*, 203–15; and Phelps, *The Tell-Tale: Or, Home Secrets Told By Old Travellers* (Boston: Phillips, Sampson, and Company, 1853). Further references to these editions will be cited parenthetically in the text.

17. Divergent interpretations of the "real" ending of this story can be found in Carol Holly, "Shaming the Self in 'The Angel over the Right Shoulder,'" *American Literature*, 60 (March 1988): 42–60, and in Fetterley, *Provisions*, 203–09.

18. Carol Farley Kessler makes a similar claim in her essay "A Literary Legacy: Elizabeth Stuart Phelps, Mother and Daughter," *Frontiers* 5 (1981): 28–33. Whereas Kessler reads Marion Gray as a woman motivated "by a passion for creative activity," I argue that she is presented as a student and intellectual, a bluestocking. The elder Phelps was still far from defining the creative woman in artistic terms; this shift would be tested in the writing of her daughter.

19. See Catharine Beecher and Harriet Beecher Stowe, *American Women's Home: Or, Principles of Domestic Science* (Hartford, Conn.: Stowe-Day Foundation, 1987). Further references to this edition appear parenthetically in the text.

20. See "Cheerfulness," in William A. Alcott, *The Young Wife; Or, Duties of Women in the Marriage Relation* (Boston: George W. Light, 1837), 4. Subsequent references to this edition appear parenthetically in the text.

21. See Betty Friedan, *The Feminine Mystique* (New York: Bantam Doubleday, 1983), 47.

22. Ibid., 64.

23. There is still much to be discovered about the emotional prescriptions connected to the ideology of "true womanhood." On middle-class women and grief, see Karen Halttunen, *Confidence Men and Painted Women: A Study of Middle-Class Culture in America, 1830–1870* (New Haven: Yale University Press, 1982); on love, see Karen Lystra, *Searching the Heart: Women, Men, and Romantic Love in Nineteenth-Century America* (New York: Oxford University Press, 1989); on emotion and gender roles, see Peter N. Stearns, "Girls, Boys, and Emotions: Redefinitions and Historical Change," *Journal of American History* 80 (June 1993): 36–73.

24. For a densely documented portrayal of the lives and writing of mid-nineteenth-century women, see Kelley, *Private Woman, Public Stage: Literary Domesticity in Nineteenth-Century America* (New York: Oxford University Press, 1984).

25. See Elizabeth Stuart Phelps Ward, *Chapters from a Life* (Boston: Houghton Mifflin, 1896), 12–13.

26. Ibid., 13.

27. Ibid., 12, 14.

28. See Austin Phelps, *A Memorial of the Author*, in Elizabeth Stuart Phelps [H. Trusta], *The Last Leaf from Sunny Side* (Boston: Phillips, Sampson, 1853), 66. Further references to this work appear parenthetically in the text.

29. For a suggestive discussion of Elizabeth Stuart Phelps Ward's literary identifications with her mother, see Alfred Habegger, *Gender, Fantasy, and Realism in American Literature* (New York: Columbia University Press, 1982), 51.

30. Information about Phelps's life must be gleaned from Austin Phelps, *A Memorial of*

the Author, and Elizabeth Stuart Phelps Ward, *Chapters from a Life*. There is some discussion of the Phelps family, albeit not wholly flattering, in Ann Douglas, *The Feminization of American Culture* (New York: Avon, 1977).

31. See Pfister, *The Production of Personal Life: Class, Gender, and the Psychological in Hawthorne's Fiction* (Stanford: Stanford University Press, 1991).

32. *The Journals of Louisa May Alcott*, ed. Madeleine Stern (Boston: Little, Brown, 1989), 147.

33. *The Selected Letters of Louisa May Alcott*, ed. Joel Myerson, Daniel Shealy, and Madeleine Stern (Boston: Little, Brown, 1987), 110.

34. See Emerson, *Selected Essays*, ed. Larzer Ziff (New York: Penguin Books, 1982), 179.

35. See Barbara Sicherman, "Reading *Little Women*: The Many Lives of a Text," in *U.S. History as Women's History: New Feminist Essays*, ed. Linda Kerber, Alice Kessler-Harris, and Kathryn Kish Sklar (Chapel Hill: University of North Carolina Press, 1995), 255.

36. See Emily Dickinson, *Final Harvest*, ed. Thomas H. Johnson (Boston: Little, Brown, 1961), 22.

37. Amos Bronson Alcott, *Journals*, ed. Odell Shepard (Boston: Little, Brown, 1938), 173. See entries for Mar. 16, 1846, and Feb. 7, 1847. Whether Louisa's mother, Abigail Alcott, derived her sense of mother-daughter likeness from her husband's or her own observations, she implicated herself as the source of Louisa's uneven temper, tying it to a depression she suffered when Louisa was in utero: "I was suffering," Abigail writes in her diary, "under one of those periods of mental depression which women are subject to during pregnancy, and I had been unusually so with Louisa—which accounts to me for many of her peculiarities and moods of mind, rather uncommon for a child of her age." Amos Bronson Alcott, *Journals*, 145. See entry for July 26, 1842.

38. As quoted in Karen Halttunen, "The Domestic Drama of Louisa May Alcott," *Feminist Studies* 10 (Summer 1984): 235. An excellent study of the emotional designs of Alcott's *Little Women* can be found in Judith Fetterley, "*Little Women*: Alcott's Civil War," *Feminist Studies* 5 (Summer 1979). Fetterley provides a related analysis of Alcott's *Behind a Mask* in "Impersonating 'Little Women': The Radicalism of Alcott's *Behind a Mask*," *Women's Studies* 10 (1983): 1–14.

39. Emerson, *Selected Essays*, 288–89.

40. Ibid., 292. For philosophical studies which examine Emerson's use of a discourse of moods see Stanley Cavell, *The Senses of Walden* (San Francisco: North Point Press, 1981): 123–60, and Anthony J. Cascardi, "The Logic of Moods: An Essay on Emerson and Rousseau," *Studies in Romanticism* 24 (Summer 1985): 223–37.

41. Helpful discussions of nineteenth-century conceptions of the artist can be found in Maurice Beebe, *Ivory Towers and Sacred Founts* (New York: New York University Press, 1964), and Raymond Williams, *Culture and Society, 1780–1950* (Harmondsworth, England: Penguin, 1963). On women, genius, and artistry, see Christine Battersby, *Gender and Genius: Towards a Feminist Aesthetics* (Bloomington: Indiana University Press, 1989).

42. Zaretsky, *Capitalism, the Family, and Personal Life* (New York: Harper & Row, 1976), 59.

43. See Wordsworth, *The Prelude: A Parallel Text*, ed. J. C. Maxwell (New Haven: Yale University Press, 1981). Subsequent references to this edition (the 1850 version of Wordsworth's poem) appear parenthetically in the text. For the relevant passage, see book II, lines 303–13.

44. Emerson, *Selected Essays*, 259.

45. See Ward, *Chapters from a Life*, 64. In the same passage Ward credits Elizabeth Barrett Browning with the power of having "revealed to me my own nature" (64).

46. The narrator directs the reader's interpretation of this emotional reportage with the additional remark that "It was during such a mood [as the latter] that Edna hunted up [her friend] Mademoiselle Reisz" (109).

47. "New Books," *Philadelphia Inquirer* (Oct. 31, 1877), in Ward, *Story of Avis*, ed. Kessler, 273.

48. See contemporary reviews in Chopin, *The Awakening*, ed. Margaret Culley (New York: Norton, 1976), 145–53.

CHAPTER FIVE

Domestic Interiors: Boyhood Nostalgia and Affective Labor in the Gilded Age

RICHARD S. LOWRY

At the end of *The Adventures of Tom Sawyer* (1875), Mark Twain appends a terse note: "So endeth this chronicle. It being strictly a history of a *boy,* it must stop here; the story could not go much further without becoming the history of a *man.*" The ending is as abrupt as it could be: until its final chapters the text celebrates what Twain calls "the pure unalloyed pleasure" of boyhood, inviting adult readers to immerse themselves once again in the "pattern—restless, noisy, and troublesome" of childhood energy. By the end, however, as Tom's summer adventures draw to a close and he must once again face the socializing injunctions of home, school, and church; as Huckleberry Finn is adopted by the widow Douglas; the boyhood world of St. Petersburg grows increasingly constricted, haunted by the specter of an adult manhood that, as Twain acknowledges in his conclusion, threatens the novel's idyllicism.[1]

I point to the awkward conclusion to emphasize how indelibly linked and yet fundamentally antagonistic are boyhood and manhood in the novel, a tension acknowledged in Twain's prefatorial promise "to pleasantly remind adults of what they once were themselves" even as he insists on "what queer enterprises they sometimes engaged in." In the novel men are judges, teachers, and ministers; together they enforce a moral universe of right and wrong, deferred pleasure, and certain retribution. They ceaselessly rehearse that authority by disciplining boys, who themselves resist with practical jokes and more often escape into fantasy worlds of violence and superstition. Yet boys, as Twain backhandedly acknowledges in his conclusion, must become men—"pretty grave, unromantic men, too, some of them" (254)—men who will either embody the self-controlled lives they once rebelled against, or, like Injun Joe, succumb to their anger, commit murder, and plot to mutilate respected widows. The narrator tells us that Tom "would be a President, yet, if he escaped hanging" (173), and it is this anxiety about the future, the sense that the end of childhood will transform Tom utterly into the embodiment of either authority or criminality, that suffuses Twain's conclusion.

Yet if some mysterious metamorphosis of boy into man marks the border of Twain's fictional imagination, what Twain calls a "rightly constructed boy's life" (175) was built out of—an inverted reflection of—the very adult masculinity the text tries to keep at bay. What Twain would later call his fictional "hymn" to boyhood grew out of a conviction that emerged in middle age that "the romance of life is the only part of it that is overwhelmingly valuable, & romance dies with youth. After that, life is a drudge, & indeed a sham. . . . I should greatly like to re-live my youth, & then get drowned."[2] Given the privation and uncertainty that characterized his youth—particularly after the death of his father when Twain was twelve—a youth that Twain himself recalled elsewhere as "so damned humiliating," it is apparent that the novel's architecture (to borrow a word from Twain's preface) of a boyhood past rests on the foundation of an adult present.[3] The boy may be but father of the man, to paraphrase one of William Wordsworth's best-known poems of the period, but he is also in this case the man of the father, the projection onto boyhood of a specific adult experience of masculinity.

It is precisely this dual gesture of forgetting and projection that defines the core of the novel's nostalgia, and that makes the text such a resonant example of nineteenth-century America's remaking of childhood in general and boyhood in particular. For *Tom Sawyer* is but the most enduring product of an era that invented boyhood in fiction, autobiography, childrearing manuals, and the domestic home itself, as a separate sphere of experience—complete with its own psychic geography—that served both as a therapeutic retreat from the demands of an adult masculinity *and* as a space in which that masculinity could best be formed. As such, Twain's nostalgic splitting of boyhood and manhood—which necessarily acknowledges that boys and men are (opposed) components of a common masculinity—teaches us much about the sheer complexity of the Gilded Age's making of gender. But the ways in which the novel fashions that masculinity suggest that the logic that separated the two seemingly divergent topoi of boy and man itself was the manifestation of a more fundamental form of cultural work. In what follows I shall suggest that *Tom Sawyer* represents the culmination of the century's construction of a sensibility that assigned to boys and men radically different emotional natures, a sensibility that was both the product of, and finally legitimated, what I shall call an affective labor dedicated to building an internal masculine character that appeared most visibly as the middle-class self-controlled man. Beneath the history of Twain's fictional boyhood lies the history of the nineteenth century's ideologies of selfhood.

The social roots of this contradictory history lie in the formation of the middle-class home. Early in the century, Tom Sawyer and his fictional kin were born of a marriage between a sexual division of labor that reconfigured family government as mothering, and Lockean notions of the child as "plaster," to use a common trope of advice writers, susceptible to the impress of environment and awaiting the moral molding of parental care.[4] The environment identified as most conducive to this molding was the domestic home—a private enclave dedicated to the cultural preservation and emotional redemption of values seen as missing in the competitive public sphere. There "the boy" emerged as the product of the middle class's attempt to secure for itself a foothold amid the profound upheavals that were transforming a largely rural nation of republican communities into a nation of industrial capitalism. The most immediate threats to economic and social stability were recognized as the erosion of the apprenticeship system, and the increasing need for young men to leave their homes and communities to find work in what Benjamin Franklin, the century's best-known prodigal son, called "the wide World." No longer able to guarantee their sons' placement in specific trades, families turned to preparing for the future by building character rather than imparting skills. Thus advice writers urged parents to inculcate boys with a conscience, what Mary Ryan has called a "portable parent"—an internal mechanism of control that would in the future allow a man to resist the temptations and vices of the outside world. This character not only would guarantee a safe crossing of the border between the domestic and the economic, it would build a loyalty to the family that would solidify its financial prospects and social status.[5]

No doubt these strategies of privatized consolidation and character building—whether pursued consciously or not—provided families with important resources for successfully negotiating a changing economic world. These material concerns, however, unfolded within a discourse that increasingly seized upon the domestic home as a symbolic domain of class-specific values, attributes, practices, and expectations. Thus to frame nostalgically the play of boys in fictions like Twain's, to isolate them from manhood, was to effect in the naturalized figure of the boy a form of sentimental synecdoche similar to that which invested such components of the home as the kitchen hearth and the easy chair with a cultural aura that affirmed and even perpetuated the domesticity that produced it. Such fictions gave eloquent and coherent expression to what Eli Zaretsky has called the signature fantasy of the middle class: "that humanity can pass beyond a life dominated by relations of production."[6]

The popular success of Twain's nostalgic rendering (it was reviewed as a "realistic" depiction of boys' lives) not only attests to the hegemony of this vision, it suggests the ways in which insisting on the gap between boy and man helped justify the middle-class family's retreat into self-protective privacy.[7] Certainly this was clear early in the century, when the growing characterization of children as infinitely susceptible to the influence of environment coincided with the reorganization of the home into a reproductive sphere: just as motherhood was charged with the full weight of femininity, boyhood emerged as the legitimating object for its fulfillment.[8] By the 1870s such a developmental gap helped transform that retreat into another source of capital: the longer a son was held out of productive life, the more he was prepared for a career, the greater his value as a marker of class status. Thus boyhood served as an important component in what Stephanie Coontz has described as the production of "the class-specific values so necessary for the social reproduction of capitalism. . . . Men's economic and political patterns determined the class status of the family; women's socialization reproduced the values and behaviors necessary for the male child to step into and maximize his position in the social order."[9]

With this in mind, I would like to situate Twain's novelistic entree into the late-Victorian construction of boyhood as an active constituent in this complex process of class reproduction. Twain's boy naturalizes and finally legitimates, even as it obscures (indeed because it obscures), a subtle yet assiduous form of affective labor that refocused social anxieties onto the building of character — a labor that, according to the century's childrearing and educational experts, was best pursued in the socially isolated family. Thus *Tom Sawyer* makes visible both those forms of work that created a separate boyhood in the service of a middle-class masculinity, and the necessity for hiding, or evading, the constructedness of that separation.

Indeed, to momentarily exceed the limits of this chapter, I would argue that in the conventions of boy-making underwriting Twain's fiction lay the nascent formation of a code of *internal* character development that prepared the ideological ground for the emergence of the twentieth century's middle-class therapeutic culture. To be sure, a vast gulf separates Tom's fictive life from the popular contemporary construction of an "inner child" at the core of a psychological self. Orphan that he is, in his robust energy Tom bears none of the fragility that would presumably make him vulnerable to the wounds of family dysfunction. Nor would Twain and his contemporaries have recognized any such "wounds" as relevant to their own emotional health. Nevertheless, the conditions and discourses which for the middle class made possible, and finally compelling, both the split between boy and man, and the assumptions that the preparation of one shaped the destiny of the other, at the very least anticipate our culture's assumption that childhood survives as a distinct emotional sphere within our adult experience of gender and class. In suggesting that there is a little Tom Sawyer in all of us, I urge a historical, rather than a psychological, argument.[10]

The dynamics of this boy-making labor emerge in the opening pages of Twain's novel, when Tom's half-brother Sid betrays to Aunt Polly Tom's lie that he had gone to school instead of swimming. Instantly Tom rushes from the house vowing revenge, only to find, "within two minutes, or even less," that his troubles have vanished. "Not," the narrator tells us, because they were "one whit less heavy and bitter to him than a man's are to a man, but because a new and powerful interest bore them down and drove them out of his mind for the time—just as men's misfortunes are forgotten in the excitement of new enterprises" (5). Tom, then, suffers no less than a man, and he responds to that suffering no differently than does a man. Thus when he immerses himself in the "new enterprise" of learning to whistle, Tom's delight in his skill leaves him feeling "much as an astronomer feels who has discovered a new planet." With this joy, however, emerges a difference: "No doubt, as far as strong, deep, unalloyed pleasure is concerned, the advantage was with the boy, not the astronomer."

At the heart of this comparison lies a language of emotional investment. The relationship between boys and men is marked not so much in physiological terms—the book is remarkable for, with few exceptions, its utter lack of attention to its characters' physical appearances—as it is in their relative capacities for apparently unmediated emotion. A whistling boy striding "down the street with his mouth full of harmony and his soul full of gratitude" may prefigure the more mature triumphs of science, but only by underscoring the astronomer's emotional diminution.

Or rather, the astronomer's emotional focus: for whistling is not Tom's only form of unadulterated pleasure. Twain marks boyhood's "pattern" with the sheer energy of Tom's naive capacity for emotional investment both in physical objects—dollops of jam, bits of brass, fruit, a dead cat, or gold—and fantasies of mystery and power that lead Tom beyond the purlieus of St. Petersburg to haunted houses, Jackson's Island, and McDougall's Cave. Once in the grip of love, dejection, terror, remorse, "a raging desire" (175) for hidden treasure, Tom cannot resist his impulses; he must follow them until they run their course. Men, on the other hand, extend to their charges the same modes of restraint and control they demand of themselves: it takes a Sunday school superintendent dressed in a collar so stiff it "compelled a straight lookout ahead, and a turning of the whole body when a side view was required," to understand the importance of asking his students to "sit up just as straight and pretty as you can," eyes forward in the classroom (32).

These distinctions of emotional control both offer an imaginative vocabulary with which to constitute a sex-based field of identity, and allow Twain to endow adult masculinity with an authority associated directly with institutions of social discipline: the school, the church, the courts. As such, this implied developmental narrative—whose trajectory carries boys from the margins to the center of social power—unfolds squarely within what Peter Stearns has described as the "emotional culture" of late Victorian America, "a complex of interrelated norms, standards, and ideals that govern[ed] the endorsement, the expression, and ultimately, even the acknowledgment of emotions." In his formulation, such culture performed primarily a regulatory and legitimating function by identifying and refining appropriate modes, spaces, and times for both the expression and the repression of certain emotions. This process of "emotional differentiation" was particularly important in the construction of gender, as boys and girls were taught to embrace and control emotions appropriate for what were perceived as their separate adult destinies. Alongside this, however, emotional culture also served a constitutive function by gendering such emotions as anger (masculine) and jealousy (feminine) as markers of identity, thus "convinc[ing] men and women that gender labels were secure."[11] In this light Twain's text naturalizes an affective cultural vocabulary of bodily control and emotional channeling underwriting authoritative adult masculinity.

Yet surely this overstates the case about the novel. After all, St. Petersburg boys bubble with "adventurous, troublesome ways" (3) that overrun the discipline of men: Tom and his friends play hooky from school, run away from home, and find any diversion at hand to relieve the tedium of discipline. Once free, they visit graveyards at midnight with dead cats, steal from the sugar bowl, lie when they have to, and laugh in church. They follow their passions into a contumacious world of "secret troubles" regulated by superstitions, magical incantations, oaths signed in blood, and dominated by ghosts, devils, pirates, and robbers. At times the energetic naiveté of boys grows so forceful it overwhelms adult self-control. When Tom's prize pinch bug escapes his grasp in the middle of a sermon and leaves the church firmly clamped to the rear end of a yelping dog; when Tom and his friends appear from behind a pew in the church at their own funeral; and finally when he and Becky return to town after being given up for lost in McDougall's Cave, adults break out in a release of laughter and tears—in the latter instance "swarming" the streets "frantic" and "half-clad," "roaring huzzah after huzzah" in their excitement (233–34).

To the extent that such moments of emotional release dramatize the nostalgic pleasure Twain strives to provoke in his readers, they tie the novel to a Wordsworthian tradition which "discovered" in the child new possibilities for spiritual renewal. In this formulation, Twain's novel challenges, rather than reinforces, the disciplined emotional differentiation Stearns describes. But to say this is at once to say too much and far too little: Tom's incitements to release deliver no emotional redemption. As he and his friends discover when they run away to the freedom of Jackson's Island only to find that "swimming's no good . . . when there ain't anybody to say I shan't go in" (121), the transgressive pleasure of boyhood adventure depends on the efforts of unredeemed adults to hold in place rules of behavior. The same holds true for Twain's authorial adventures. Boys are boys, men are men: astronomical success may but dimly reflect a boy's pleasure in learning to whistle, but it is Twain's assumption of that dimness that allows his narrator to suggest that "the reader probably remembers how to do it if he has ever been a boy" (5). The pleasure of Twain's text lies not in any rediscovery of a state of boyishness, but in its managed emotional response to a distant boyhood.

Nor is this boyhood as Wordsworthian as it first appears. For Twain, like Stearns, understands the inherent conventionality of affective discourse. Consider, for instance, Tom's romance with Becky Thatcher. When Tom first spots the "lovely little blue-eyed creature" (19) in the garden of Jeff Thatcher's house he is instantly smitten. It takes only two days to arrange a schoolyard tryst with "the Adored Unknown" and seal their engagement with a kiss; and it takes only a few minutes more, in a dizzying turn of events appropriate only to the highest melodrama of love, to lose her affection. Tom is devastated enough to consider suicide—"it must be very peaceful, he thought, to lie and slumber and dream forever and ever"—but the disadvantages of death outweigh its effectiveness as a vehicle for revenge on the heartless Becky ("She would be sorry some day—maybe when it was too late"). So "the elastic heart of youth" leads Tom to other fantasies: he will run away to become a clown, a soldier, an Indian, or finally, a pirate. "And at the zenith of his fame, how he would suddenly appear at the old village and stalk into church . . . and hear with swelling ecstasy the whisperings, 'It's Tom Sawyer the Pirate!—the Black Avenger of the Spanish Main!'" (64). At a stroke Tom's imagination delivers him from a maudlin indulgence in a Werther-like sentiment for death into a priapic fantasy of revenge.

In one sense, of course, Tom's melodrama of romance evokes yet one more instance of his boundless capacity for emotional investment. Yet Twain narrates Tom's lachrymose wanderings and displaced plots of revenge, and Becky's swerve from coquetry to abjection, in a voice that facilely mimics sentimental euphemism and dime-novel enthusiasm even as it deploys literary conventions of romance (the two lovers, for instance, share an encounter that parodies the balcony scene of *Romeo and Juliet*). The result is a text that insists on the artificiality, even the theatricality, of Tom's emotional adventures. Tom in effect *performs,* rather than embodies, the anguishes and joys of romance; like a child actor he delivers his lines without quite understanding the play. From this standpoint, the novel's representation of the "unalloyed pleasure" of boyhood is nothing more, or nothing less, than an alloy of an adult emotional culture.

From this perspective Twain's tale, far from representing a story of liberatory rediscovery, unfolds most coherently as a narrative of affective management. But even this reading does not tell the whole story. To the extent that Twain assigns appropriate feelings to different levels of maturity (boys pursue passion while adult readers indulge in meditative amusement), his text seems to reinforce Stearns's argument that emotions served as tools to create and finally to adjudicate distinctions between boy and girl, boy and man. But this conjunction also points to where author and historian most clearly part company. For Stearns, manliness was the product of the right management of boyhood excess. For Twain, the need for right management is the product of the split between boyhood and manhood. In other words, in suspending the conventional developmental narrative, Twain locates the genesis both of his novel's representative boyhood *and* the perceived need for the emotional management of that boyhood *within* the affective discourse of manhood. The gendered labor so apparent in the novel itself depends on, as much as it legitimates, the discursive production of a masculine selfhood that needs to be emotionally regulated. In this sense *Tom Sawyer* most powerfully participates *as a novel* in its era's emotional culture by bringing into focus two interanimating discourses—gender differentiation and affective constitution—powerful enough to bring to fictive life an eternal boyhood, and to historical life a far more dynamic story about the history of emotions than that told by Stearns.

The Adventures of Tom Sawyer was but one of a number of books Twain wrote on boyhood. Indeed, Twain wrote about boys so often—in *The Prince and the Pauper* (1882), *Life on the Mississippi* (1883) and *Huckleberry Finn* (1885)—two sequels to *Tom Sawyer*—and *The Mysterious Stranger* (1916)—that by the end of his career the composite childhood constructed in his texts had become for his public, and to some extent for Twain (whose memory was always more creative than accurate), indistinguishable from that of the author himself. Yet as intimate a part of his own literary psyche as it may have been, Twain's investment in youth was but one note in his era's sustained chord of adulation for the child, and boyhood in particular. Twenty years earlier Samuel Goodrich, who spent a lifetime educating and entertaining children (including the young Samuel Clemens) as "Peter Parley," remembered his own youth as "one bright current of enjoyment, flowing amid flowers, and all in the company of companions as happy and jubilant as myself." So powerful were the "exultant emotions" of walking barefoot in summer "that I repeated them a thousand times in happy dreams."[12]

Whether or not such sentimental romanticism was repeated in dreams, it certainly appeared thousands of times in print. *Tom Sawyer* entered a popular reading market for and about children, shaped by pulp fiction, textbooks, instructional works, and pleasure fiction, even magazines like *St. Nicholas* and *The Riverside Youth Magazine*. Eschewing the overt didacticism of earlier writing for children, writers like Twain embraced a mass-market emphasis on entertainment to address an audience primed, in the words of a contemporary reviewer, to "look back to our childhood, as the paradisiacal period of our life, our Eden before we are driven into the world by sin." In their nostalgia, these texts joined painting, popular illustration, verse, and song to capture the period's fascination with childhood and shape what has been called the Golden Age of children's writing. By the second decade of the twentieth century, when the tide began to ebb, the "boy book" genre had attracted the talents of some of the era's most distinguished writers—William Dean Howells, Louisa May Alcott, Henry James, Stephen Crane—and yielded some of the era's most enduring popular fiction.[13]

The two earliest examples of what by the turn of the century became a widely popular convention give a good idea of the cultural tenor of this celebration. In 1869 Thomas Bailey Aldrich published his boyhood reminiscence, humorously entitled *The Story of A Bad Boy*, which celebrated a forever-lost "happy, magical Past" in which even a boyhood enemy is transfigured into a Wordsworthian angel "with a sort of dreamy glory encircling his bright red hair." Several years later Charles Dudley Warner, himself a respected essayist and co-author with Twain of *The Gilded Age* (1873), predicated his widely read fictional memoir, *Being a Boy* (1878), on the simple statement that "one of the best things in the world to be is a boy." Like much of the children's writing emerging during the late nineteenth century, each text returns in fantasy to a childhood that is admittedly lost forever. Just as Tom Sawyer is bound in the pastoral world of St. Petersburg, Aldrich's Tom Bailey lives in the small town of Riverhead, while Warner's youth lives on a working farm where he varies his chores with wandering the fields and fishing. Both boys endure the agonies of youthful romance (Aldrich explicitly compares the sufferings of his pseudonymous hero to Goethe's Werther); while Tom orchestrates with his friends elaborate practical jokes and attempts to run away from home, Warner's protagonist immerses himself in a natural world that recalls Tom Sawyer's excursion to Jackson's Island. And, like *Tom Sawyer*, the conjunction of and distance separating boyhood and manhood bring each narrative to a halt before maturity. This tension is most apparent in Aldrich's narrative, where the narrator makes it clear in the beginning that his account is at least partially autobiographical: "This is the story of a Bad Boy. Well, not such a very bad, but pretty bad boy; and I ought to know for I am, or rather I was, that boy myself." The indeterminacy of Aldrich's "I"—"I am," or "I was" that boy—registers the same discomfort with linking boy and man as Twain's novel.[14]

In its conventionality, such writing seems to reflect what E. Anthony Rotundo has described as the "heady and even liberating experience" of boy culture during the last half of the century: "separate both from the domestic world of women, girls, and small children, and from the public world of men and commerce," boys formed a subculture of rituals and games that both allowed escape from home and school and prepared them for the graver responsibilities of manhood. Marcia Jacobson has recently read these texts as their authors' fictional engagements with biographical crises in fatherhood. Clearly these formulations have the virtue of situating such writing in specific historical contexts, but both miss the extent to which these texts, and all fiction, actively shaped the affective culture of manhood they seemed to reflect.[15]

The historian Daniel Rodgers has offered the grounds for a more dialectical approach by characterizing popular boys' fictions as regressive fantasies shaped by contemporary anxieties about modernization: "Retreating to preserves of the imagination or to rural and child-centered oases of boyhood memory, children's writers tried to carve out a place unviolated by . . . industrial society." In his formulation carefree childhood typified a spontaneous creativity and self-expression denied by modern forms of industrialized or bureaucratized labor and patterns of urban social life. Aligned as it was in a historical narrative extending from rural to modern, the gap between boy and man registered a sense of lost horizons, even a historical inevitability; it helped readers accommodate to an alienating and reified present they did not understand. Like the era's political nostalgia-filled oratory, like the flowering of antiquarian history and regionalist writing, boys' books enacted a "sentimental regression" from a disturbing present. In this light, the fictional child functioned therapeutically, in the words of T. J. Jackson Lears, by offering readers "a vision of psychic wholeness, a 'simple, genuine self' in a world where selfhood had become problematic and sincerity seemed obsolete."[16]

Such readings persuasively suggest that authors produced such escape fantasies for the same reasons they were read: to objectify in a simpler past middle-class yearnings for cultural homogeneity and tradition. As Rodgers outlines the problem (and as Jacobson's readings suggest), the sense of historical disjunction posed a particular difficulty for those men who most endured the modern reorganization of work. One need only compare such texts with, for instance, Susan Warner's *Wide Wide World* (1850) and Alcott's *Little Women* (1869) to see that the dream of idyllic childhood survived in public rhetoric as a male fantasy. Jo March, the central figure in *Little Women*, matures in an environment founded on injunctions to self-discipline and diligent labor, not boundless play. Most strikingly, in both of these novels the authors posit an end to childhood when a girl assumes her mother's role as the authority in her own domestic world, a position for which she prepares throughout the novel. [17]

From this point of view the disjunction between boy and man in boyhood fictions delimits a profound conflict at the heart of their implicit conceptualizations of masculinity. When at the end of *Little Women* Marmee exclaims to her married daughters, "Oh, my girls, however long you may live, I never can wish you a greater happiness than this," she recognizes in her children the perpetuation of the very traditions of labor and character that had formed her, in a way that virtually no fictional father did in his sons. [18] At one level, this fictional discontinuity attests to the profound distance separating boys and men: while the former embodied a psychic wholeness, the restrictive demands of the ideals of manhood led men to register extraordinary concern for evaluating and reaffirming their "manliness." [19] By the 1870s writers of advice literature and etiquette guides, virtually assuming the urban marketplace as the arena for manliness, figured manhood as a precarious balancing act by advising their readers to perform as "athlete[s] of continence" even as they embraced a "battlefield code" of vigor and prowess. Nowhere did these strains appear more clearly than in advice on anger. "The man who is liable to fits of passion," warned one mid-century advice writer, "who cannot control his temper, but is subject to ungovernable excitements of any kind, is always in danger. The first element of a gentlemanly dignity is self-control." And yet, as Stearns has argued, men were also counseled that they "needed anger as an emotional spur for the competitive zeal and righteous indignation desirable in the worlds of business and politics." [20]

In these terms then, "the history of a *man*" unfolded as a strained, self-conscious performance of what John Kasson has called "feeling rules." Boys, on the other hand, followed a very different script. When Aunt Polly yet again forgives Tom Sawyer his trespasses because he is "just giddy and harum-scarum" (116), she echoes the opinions of Jacob Abbott, whose work as an educator and writer of countless children's books qualified him as one of his era's most authoritative childrearing experts. Writing in his *Gentle Measures in the Management and Training of the Young* (1871), he argued that "nine-tenths of the whispering and playing of children in school, and of the noise, the rudeness, and the petty mischief of children at home, is just this hissing and fizzling of an imprisoned power, and nothing more." Let your boy, he would have advised Aunt Polly, be a boy: tolerate rather than extinguish the "rapid succession of bodily movements and of mental ideas, and the emotions mingling and alternating with them" that are necessary to healthy children (193–94). [21]

The gap between these proscriptions of men and boys reflects in shorthand what Carroll Smith-Rosenberg has described as the "structured psychic discontinuity" experienced by middle-class boys. Because of the rapid rational-ization of labor, the traditional pathways to manly occupations of apprenticeship and/or inheritance which in the past had linked generations of artisans, farmers, and merchants were dwindling. No longer able to rely on the guidance of fathers for their entry into the workforce, sons left home to strike out on their own. This discontinuity was registered culturally by expressions of fear of rootless young men in the city, and displaced as deep concerns, even fears, of male sexuality. Young men themselves dealt with this liminal passage by flocking to secret fra-ternal orders like the Odd Fellows and Freemasons, where they participated in elaborate initiation rituals which repeatedly—members spent hours each of sev-eral nights a week in attendance—dramatized a transition of naif into initiate, boy into man. By the end of the century parents and educators had responded by expanding the scope of "man-making" institutions—Boy Scouts, youth organi-zations like the YMCA, fraternities and other activities of college life, boys' schools, organized sports—thereby virtually inventing adolescence as a stage of protracted border-crossing that could extend into a young man's thirties.[22]

Each of these strategies represents a practical response to a perceived prob-lem of rightly constructing, out of the raw material of boyhood, a manhood capable of succeeding in a dangerously fluid economic order. More to the point, they suggest that the "oases" of boyhood most readers knew lay less in the antebellum idyllicism described by Rodgers than in the middle-class home. This is not to argue, however, that such writing represents only a fictional reaction to changing social conditions. For both boyhood and the domestic home which nourished it were most recognizable as social categories not in the myriad households of nineteenth-century America, but in the outpouring of fiction and prescriptive writing—printed sermons, magazines on mothering and home life, didactic fiction of all kinds, publications on medicine, ethics, religion, eti-quette—which comprised what Daniel Walker Howe has called the "commu-nications system" of mid-Victorian America. Seeking to link values with infor-mation, authors of advice manuals for young men, childrearing guides, and children's literature offered practical advice to parents intent on preparing their children for a modernizing world in such a way as to link the day-to-day con-cerns of family life to a rhetoric of social order and class success.[23] In this sense Twain's novel stands as but one of the best-known instances of a discourse that, in celebrating and analyzing boys, finally constructed boyhood as the linchpin in an elaborate middle-class narrative which integrated family practices with broader visions of class reproduction and modern selfhood.

In short, the "boy's life" embodied in fictions like Twain's was "rightly con-structed," as much discursively and ideologically as it was socially, by a middle class that had as much invested in creating, maintaining, and dwelling on gaps of masculine development as it did in bridging them. Whereas working-class boys were expected at an early age to help support the family at least as secondary wage earners, the middle class held its sons out of productive life as long as feasible to educate and prepare them for careers that promised more social mobility and financial security. Such strategies made economic sense— white-collar employers expected formal education at least until the age of fourteen, preferably as late as eighteen, and other professions demanded more. At the same time, they made an extended boyhood an important source of cultural capital, and the resulting momentous transition to manhood a mark of status legitimating the expenditure of that capital.[24]

These same distinctions functioned to separate the white middle class from the majority of African Americans. Newly emancipated black families, finding themselves yoked to the demands of sharecropping and unskilled industrial work, felt the same incentives as European working-class families to bear more children and put them to work at early ages.[25] Moreover, the middle-class creation of a discrete childhood dovetailed well with a century-long propensity to characterize African Americans, Native Americans, and immigrant groups as either children or savages. Just as antebellum Irish workers were, in the words of Ronald Takaki, "denounced for their failure to develop self-restraint—the quality which separated adult from child," black slaves were stigmatized as children in need of the discipline of paternalistic slave ownership. Whatever mixed motives underwrote this projection, such distinctions served to legitimate through the trope of boyhood a white manhood of emotional and sexual restraint.[26]

Yet, if "harum-scarum" middle-class boys were metaphorically akin to African Americans, they were *distinguished* from them by the mere fact that their savageries were performed safely within the confines of the emotionally controlled home. Thus insisting on the distance of boy and man allowed domestic authorities to position the affective labor of women at the center of visions not only of class reproduction, but of the entire social order. If, in Warner's words, "Every boy who is good for anything is a natural savage"; if, with his "primal, vigorous instincts and impulses," he is more akin to "primitive man" than to adults "in this sophisticated age"; then at stake in his developmental genealogy is nothing less than the making of civilization itself. "Your future happiness is in the hands of your children," warned one writer to his mother readers. Otherwise, as Goodrich cautioned in his own childrearing book, if boys were "permitted to grow up ungoverned, when they go forth into society they are likely to surrender themselves [as do, for instance, African Americans] to every species of license."[27] Inherent in such admonitions was the perception that social order was less the result of the institutional regulation of collective life than it was the product of "civilized" character: what men were would determine what men did.

The fit between such fantasies of order and boyhood emerges most clearly in what was probably the most significant book on family government during the century: Horace Bushnell's *Christian Nurture* (1861). With rhetorical mastery the Hartford, Connecticut, minister—an elder member of the city's intellectual circles that included Twain and Warner—links the ways of God with those of the middle-class home, building a vision of social reproduction around an environment of intimate labor that, in its urge to "restore" the tradition "we have well nigh lost," frames an ideological template for the nostalgic regression characteristic of boyhood fictions. Indeed, whatever practical advice Bushnell may have offered families eager to have their sons succeed, it is clear from the text's insistent social fantasy that at root his concern lay in casting the home as the vehicle for "family propagation": a site of reproductive labor that joined biology with culture to produce a "populating force of faith and piety." The key constituent of this ambitious vision was the internally malleable boy: bear more sons, inculcate them from infancy with Christian virtues—a respect for authority, privacy, duty, and self-control, all the behavioral codes of the middle class— and it will come "to pass that a son, grown almost to manhood, will gladly serve the house, and yield to his parents a kind of homage that even anticipates their wishes."[28]

At the heart of this vision lies a metaphor of organicism. Americans, he argues, have lost any sense of the "organic" relations between state, church, and family: "All our modern notions and speculations have taken a bent toward individualism. . . . Instead of being wrought in together and penetrated, to some extent, by historic laws and forces common to all the members, we only seem to lie as seeds piled together, without any terms of connection." Bushnell seeks to supply just those terms by transposing the sexually and generationally prescribed divisions of labor and authority of the Biblical family ("The children gather wood, and the fathers kindle the fire, and the women knead dough") to the physically isolated and affectively autonomous family of the nineteenth century. The result is a hothouse environment fertile enough to spawn "a common character" among its inhabitants: "inclosed within the four walls of the dwellings," family members participate in a "common life . . . so nearly absolute" in its pervasive power that they become "partakers in a common blood, in common interests, wants, feelings, and principles."[29]

The organic unity of the family grows out of the multitudinous and ineffable "transactions and feelings" that incorporate "the whole circle of the house" into a shared culture of privacy. But nowhere are the restorative possibilities of this unity more visible than in the relations between parents and children. The young child (almost universally "he"), after all, is born unformed, impressionistic, "more a candidate for personality than a person." Thus in a manner consistent with much of the century's advice literature, Bushnell urges parents to begin early in shaping their children's characters. He is not, however, interested in how parents "teach, encourage, persuade, and govern"; in short, he is not interested in what he calls the conscious and predetermined exercise of "influence." Such efforts at rational persuasion are important, of course, but what determines a child's personality, and thus what he will become as an adult, comes from what Bushnell calls "the spirit of the house": manifested in "manners, personal views, prejudices, practical motives," it forms "an atmosphere which passes into all and pervades all, as naturally as the air they breathe." Thus character is built most powerfully "unconsciously and undesignedly" in a "bond" between parents and children "so intimate" that parents' "character, feelings, spirit, and principles must propagate themselves, whether they will or not."[30]

In locating the site of affective labor in an arena beyond conscious control, Bushnell proposes a complementary fit between a privatized family and what could be called a psychological pedagogy that takes as its subject an affective unconscious instead of a rational consciousness. The right construction of children entails a manifestly *internal*, even hidden, labor, that depends for its efficacy less on what a parent does than on who a parent is. "Now," he instructs his readers, "there is a perpetual working in the family, by which the wills, both of the parents and the children, are held in exercise, and which, without any design to affect character on one side, or conscious consent on the other, is yet fashioning results of a moral quality, as it were by the joint industry of the house." He must qualify his point with "as it were" because, as his passive verbs imply, the industrial arts he imagines are less applied than they are constitutive: "It is not what you intend for your children so much as what you are, that is to have its effect."[31]

Whether or not such a family would propagate the Christian family state Bushnell envisioned, his text helped to propagate an ideological rationale for linking the perpetuation of a privatized domestic sphere to affective labor. More particularly it made the unformed boy a prism through which the domestic split between public society and private family life was refracted in the distinction between conscious influence and unconscious management. "A wise parent understands that his government is to be crowned by an act of emancipation"; governed rightly, the boy will leave home with the "odor of the house . . . in his garments, and the internal difficulties with which he has to struggle will spring of the family seeds planted in his nature."[32]

Boys may or may not have been prepared for the future as self-consciously as Bushnell and his peers advised, but as they were portrayed in advice literature they provided a rhetorical meeting place for the envisionment of a patently psychological, and finally homogeneous, society perfected by the assiduous application of affective labor. This utopian narrative in turn depended on the creation of a boyhood both open to such attention and in need of the intimate management that only a privatized domesticity could provide. Boys had to be different from men to legitimate the bounded world of the middle-class family. The harum-scarum boy was necessary to the vision of "a rightly constructed boy's life," which in turn was formed in the image of the bourgeois man.

This at least was what the novelist Frank Norris found when just after the turn of the century he surveyed the boy-book genre shaped in part by Aldrich, Warner, and Twain: "The ten year old—who always went in swimmin' and lost his tow. . . . Do you know who he is? He is the average American business man before he grew up. That accounts for his popularity. The average business man had clean forgotten all about all those early phases of primitive growth, and it amuses him immensely to find out that the scribe has been making a study of him and bringing to light the forgotten things that are so tremendously famil-iar when presented to the consideration."[33] If Norris rightly sees the business-man reflected in the ten-year-old, his uncertain pronouns suggest he is less sure about which is image and which subject. Who is it the "scribe" studies, the boy who will naturally grow up to be a man? Or is it the adult, who creates boy-hood precisely as the image of the familiar in things forgotten? And what is it that has been forgotten? Norris's confidence that boys grow into men, that they follow a natural course of development, implies that *he* has forgotten, or is unaware of, how *un*natural, how social, is the separation of boy and man. In this sense his ironic dismissal of the hackneyed conventions of boy narratives recalls nothing more than the pronominal shifting that opens Aldrich's tale. For if the indeterminacy of "I am, or rather I was" bespeaks a gender anxiety, the easy humor with which he accepts this relationship to the "not such a very bad" boy of his youth acknowledges the sanguine confidence of an adult in his unconscious training as a youth—a training that takes place outside of his story even as it makes possible the nostalgia of its reminiscence.

But what of Tom Sawyer? His story, after all, is told by an adult narrator who clearly stands apart from the boy culture he celebrates. But Tom too fol-lows unwritten rules. He may be "full of the Old Scratch," as Aunt Polly says; he may resist with all his heart the socializing injunctions of tyrannous men; he may in short be immune to the power of conscious "influence," but he has been managed. The efficacy of that affectionate construction emerges in the conscience that qualifies the pleasure of transgression on Jackson's Island, and most powerfully drives him to break his oath of silence with Huck—an oath grounded in the preservation of all that is boyish from the prying eyes of adults—and testify in court against Injun Joe, the racial half-breed who never manages to control his emotions. It emerges as well in the care Twain and his peers took in cutting off the developmental narratives that would show the transformation of boys into men, even as they supplied their protagonists with the inner resources for adulthood. Of course, properly managed boys do not know where their consciences come from, and authors of fictional boyhood care not to remember: thus the selective forgetfulness of a nostalgia for "swimmin,'" dead cats, and dollops of jam. But as Bushnell explains, "What they do not remember still remembers them, and now claims a right in them. What was before unconscious, flames out into consciousness."[34] That flame burns most brightly in those fictions like Twain's, Warner's, and Aldrich's, which most insist on forgetting.

Notes

1. Mark Twain, *The Adventures of Tom Sawyer* (Berkeley: University of California Press, 1982), 260, 30. Subsequent citations will appear in the text.

2. Letter to Mrs. Bowen, June 6, 1900, in *Mark Twain's Letters to Will Bowen, "My First, & Oldest & Dearest Friend"* (Austin: University of Texas Press, 1941), 27. See also his unmailed letter of Sept. 9, 1887, where he declares, "Tom Sawyer is simply a hymn, put into prose form to give it a worldly air," in *Mark Twain's Letters,* vol. 2, ed. Albert Bigelow Paine (New York: Harper, 1917), 477.

3. For a brief discussion of Twain's motives for writing the novel, see Marcia Jacobson, *Being a Boy Again: Autobiography and the American Boy Book* (Tuscaloosa: University of Alabama Press, 1994), 44–70; the quotation, taken from William Dean Howells's *My Mark Twain,* appears on 47. I discuss boyhood's place in the novel more fully in *"Littery Man": Mark Twain and Modern Authorship* (New York: Oxford University Press, 1996).

4. Samuel Goodrich wrote in an early advice book for parents that children are "then like plaster, prepared by the moulder, soft and impressible, taking forms and images from everything we may chance to touch." *Fireside Education* (New York: F. J. Huntington, 1838), 62.

5. *The Autobiography of Benjamin Franklin,* ed. Leonard W. Labaree et al. (New Haven: Yale University Press, 1964), 107. Ryan, *Cradle of the Middle Class: The Family in Oneida County, New York, 1790–1865* (Cambridge: Cambridge University Press, 1981), 145–86 passim; the phrase is on 161.

6. Zaretsky, *Capitalism, the Family, and Personal Life* (New York: Harper, 1976), 77. The best-known invocation of the hearth comes in chapter 13 of Harriet Beecher Stowe's *Uncle Tom's Cabin* (1852), where she describes the kitchen of "The Quaker Settlement." See also Henry Russell's popular ballad, "The Old Arm Chair" (Boston: George P. Reed, 1840), the sheet music for which went through dozens of printings. Stuart Blumin cogently discusses the paradoxes of middle-class awareness in "The Hypothesis of Middle-Class Formation in Nineteenth-Century America: A Critique and Some Proposals," *American History Review* 90 (1985): 298–338.

7. In his review of the novel, William Dean Howells praised Twain's presentation of his hero for being marked by "a fidelity to circumstance which loses no charm by being realistic in the highest degree." *Atlantic Monthly* (May 1876), 621, reprinted in *Mark Twain: The Critical Heritage,* ed. Frederick Anderson (London: Routledge & Kegan Paul, 1971), 59.

8. As Carl Degler has written, "It is surely not accidental that the century of the child

is also the century of the Cult of True Womanhood. Exalting the child went hand in hand with exalting the domestic role of woman." *At Odds: Women and the Family in America from the Revolution to the Present* (New York: Oxford University Press, 1980), 74. See also Jan Lewis, "Motherhood and the Construction of the Male Citizen in the United States, 1750–1850," in *Constructions of the Self,* ed. George Levine (New Brunswick, N.J.: Rutgers University Press, 1992), 143–63.

9. Coontz, *The Social Origins of Private Life: A History of American Families, 1600–1900* (New York: Verso, 1988), 269.

10. Christopher Lasch and T. J. Jackson Lears have done the most to suggest a history of "therapeutic culture" in, respectively, *The Culture of Narcissism: American Life in an Age of Diminishing Expectations* (New York: Norton, 1978), and *No Place of Grace: Antimodernism and the Transformation of American Culture, 1880–1920* (New York: Pantheon, 1981). Lasch has succinctly characterized the transformation I allude to here when he describes American society as changing from "seeing the child as an undeveloped adult" to seeing "the adult as an undeveloped child" in *The New Radicalism in America: The Intellectual as Social Type* (New York: Knopf, 1965), 86. Two of the more popular texts on "the inner child," chosen from a veritable cascade of titles, are Kathrin Asper, *The Abandoned Child Within: On Losing and Regaining Self-Worth,* trans. Sharon E. Rooks (New York: Fromm International, 1993), and John Bradshaw, *Homecoming: Reclaiming and Championing Your Inner Child* (New York: Bantam, 1990). On the relationship between what is broadly defined as a "fragile," "vulnerable" masculinity and childhood, see Willard Gaylin, *The Male Ego* (New York: Viking Penguin, 1992), who argues that "the early lessons . . . little boys learn about becoming men may tragically become the spears on which their self-respect will be impaled in modern adult life" (35, 241). Dan Kiley posits a different relationship between boyhood and masculinity in *The Peter Pan Syndrome: Men Who Have Never Grown Up* (New York: Dodd, Mead, 1983). Barbara Ehrenreich, in *The Hearts of Men: American Dreams and the Flight From Commitment* (New York: Doubleday, 1983), describes how class shaped definitions of male maturity during the 1950s.

11. Stearns, "Girls, Boys, and Emotions: Redefinitions and Historical Change," *Journal of American History* 80 (1993): 36, 42. I derive my formulation of gender from Joan Scott, "Gender: A Useful Category of Historical Analysis," *American Historical Review* 91 (1986): 1053–75. For a discussion of the social construction of emotions in contemporary child development, see Claire Armon-Jones, "The Social Functions of Emotions," in *The Social Construction of Emotions,* ed. Rom Harré (New York: Basil Blackwell, 1986), 57–82.

12. Goodrich, *Recollections of a Lifetime, or Men and Things I Have Seen: In a Series of Familiar Letters to a Friend, Historical, Biographical, Anecdotical, and Descriptive,* vol. 1 (New York, 1857), 44–45, 28.

13. W. A. Jones, "Children's Books," *The United States Magazine and Democratic Review* 15 (1844): 544. On boys' fiction see Richard L. Darling, *The Rise of Children's Book Reviewing in America, 1865–1881* (New York: R. R. Bowker, 1968), Albert E. Stone, Jr., *The Innocent Eye: Childhood in Mark Twain's Imagination* (New Haven: Yale University Press, 1961), Daniel T. Rodgers, *The Work Ethic in Industrial America, 1850–1920* (Chicago: University of Chicago Press, 1974), 125–52, and Jerry Griswold, *Audacious Kids: Coming of Age in America's Classic Children's Books* (New York: Oxford University Press, 1992). On painting and illustrations, see Sarah Burns, "Barefoot Boys and Other Country Children: Sentiment and Ideology in Nineteenth-Century American Art," *American Art Journal* 20 (1988): 24–50.

14. Aldrich, *The Story of a Bad Boy, The Little Violinist, and Other Essays,* in *The Writings of Thomas Bailey Aldrich,* vol. 7 (Boston: Houghton Mifflin, 1911), 13, 3. Warner, *Being a Boy* (Boston: James R. Osgood, 1878), 9.

15. Rotundo, *American Manhood: Transformations in Masculinity from the Revolution to the Modern Era* (New York: HarperCollins, 1993), 31–55. The quotation appears on 31. Jacobson, *Being a Boy Again,* 1–24; in *Audacious Kids,* Griswold argues for a more structural, and finally more oedipal reading of the same writing.

16. Rodgers, *Work Ethic,* 134. "Sentimental regression" is from George B. Forgie, *Patricide in the House Divided: A Psychological Interpretation of Lincoln and His Age* (New York: Norton, 1979), see especially 159–200. On the middle class's "escape from history" see Ann Douglas, *The Feminization of American Culture* (New York: Avon, 1977), 197–239. Lears, *No Place of Grace,* 146.

17. For a discussion of the domestic landscape in nineteenth-century women's writing see Nina Baym, *Women's Fiction: A Guide to Novels by and about Women in America, 1820–1870* (Ithaca: Cornell University Press, 1978). On the differing developmental destinies of boys and girls, see John Demos, *Past, Present, and Personal: The Family and the Life Course in American History* (New York: Oxford University Press, 1986).

18. Alcott, *Little Women* (New York: Bantam, 1983), 459.

19. Rotundo, in examining a wide range of correspondence between middle- and upper-class parents and sons, notes that "one of the main topics in nineteenth-century correspondence . . . was ideals of manhood." See his "Learning About Manhood: Gender Ideals and the Middle-Class Family in Nineteenth-Century America," in *Manliness and Morality: Middle-Class Masculinity in Britain and America, 1800–1940,* ed. J. A. Mangan and James Walvin (New York: St. Martin's, 1987), 35–51. The quotation appears on 43. The lifetimes of the three male authors I consider span this half-century; Warner was born in 1829, Twain in 1835, and Aldrich in 1836.

20. Charles E. Rosenberg, "Sexuality, Class, and Role in Nineteenth-Century America," *American Quarterly* 25 (1973): 139; David Leverenz, *Manhood and the American Renaissance* (Ithaca: Cornell University Press, 1989), 73. "Fits of passion" quoted in John F. Kasson, *Rudeness and Civility: Manners in Nineteenth-Century Urban America* (New York: Hill & Wang, 1990), 148. Stearns, "Girls, Boys, and Emotions," 44. See also Carol Zisowitz Stearns and Peter Stearns, *Anger: The Struggle for Emotional Control in America's History* (Chicago: University of Chicago Press, 1986), 36–109.

21. Kasson, *Rudeness and Civility,* 147. Abbott, *Gentle Measures in the Management and Training of the Young* (New York: Harper, 1872), 193–94. While Abbott's mention of schools implies similarly liberal attitudes toward education, most public schools emphasized the rigorous physical and moral discipline of children. At the same time, by the 1870s the influence of the more maternally oriented and play-centered models of the German educator Friedrich Froebel had led to the establishment of a number of urban kindergartens. See Lawrence A. Cremin, *The Transformation of the Public School: Progressivism in American Education, 1876–1957* (New York: Random House, 1964). On kindergartens, see Karen Feinstein, "Kindergartens, Feminism, and the Professionalization of Motherhood," *Journal of Women's Studies* 3 (1980): 28–39.

22. Smith-Rosenberg, "Sex as Symbol in Victorian Purity: An Ethnohistorical Analysis of Jacksonian America," *American Journal of Sociology* (Special Summer Supplement, 1978): 219. On the effects of changing labor patterns on urban youth, see Allan Stanley

Horlick, *Country Boys and Merchant Princes: The Social Control of Young Men in New York* (Lewisburg, Pa.: Bucknell University Press, 1975). On fraternal orders, see Mark C. Carnes, *Secret Ritual and Manhood in Victorian America* (New Haven: Yale University Press, 1989). Of course some man-making institutions were already active by the 1870s, but they were not so explicitly focused on masculinity until later. The essential book on the formation of male adolescence remains Joseph F. Kett, *Rites of Passage: Adolescence in America 1790 to the Present* (New York: Basic Books, 1977). The quotation appears on 139. On the Boy Scouts and similar organizations, see David I. Macleod, *Building Character in the American Boy: The Boy Scouts, YMCA, and Their Forerunners, 1870–1920* (Madison: University of Wisconsin Press, 1983). Ray Raphael has explored contemporary issues stemming from the lack of male initiations into adulthood in *The Men from the Boys: Rites of Passage in Male America* (Lincoln: University of Nebraska Press, 1988).

23. Howe, "Victorian Culture in America," in *Victorian America* (Philadelphia: University of Pennsylvania Press, 1976), 23. On the authority of print, see Burton J. Bledstein, *The Culture of Professionalism: The Middle Class and the Development of Higher Education In America* (New York: Norton, 1976), 65–79.

24. On working-class families, see Coontz, *Social Origins,* 287–324; on young men and careers, see Kett, *Rites of Passage,* 144–72.

25. Coontz, *Social Origins,* argues that African American families followed much the same patterns as those of the working class. While this certainly acknowledges shared demands of labor, it neglects the extent to which racial ideologies and experiences shaped and were in turn shaped by concepts of childhood and gender development. Any adequate attention to this issue would begin with determining how compelling an ideal blacks found white, mainly Northeastern, domesticity. This in turn would depend on exploring how domesticity was used by such institutions as the Freedman's Bureau both as a tool for socialization and a yardstick against which African American family life was measured, and how African Americans practiced their own family strategies both in response to it and independently. In any case, Violet J. Harris's argument that Paul Laurence Dunbar's *Little Brown Baby* (1895) represents the first children's book written by and for African Americans suggests a far different cultural construction. See her "African American Children's Literature: The First One Hundred Years," *Journal of Negro Education* 59 (1990): 540–65. On the postbellum African American family, see Jacqueline Jones, *Labor of Love, Labor of Sorrow: Black Women, Work and the Family, from Slavery to the Present* (New York: Random House, 1985), 58–68, 85–90, and Leon Litwack, *Been in the Storm So Long: The Aftermath of Slavery* (New York: Random House, 1979), 229–47. On domesticity and African Americans, see Elizabeth Fox-Genovese, *Within the Plantation Household: Black and White Women of the Old South* (Chapel Hill: University of North Carolina Press, 1988), 58–70, 297–98; and Hazel Carby, *Reconstructing Womanhood: The Emergence of the Afro-American Woman Novelist* (New York: Oxford University Press, 1987), 22–39.

26. Takaki, *Iron Cages: Race and Culture in Nineteenth-Century America* (Seattle: University of Washington Press, 1979), 108–44, the quotation appears on 116. See also George M. Fredrickson, *The Black Image in the White Mind: The Debate on Afro-American Character and Destiny, 1817–1914* (New York: Harper & Row, 1971), 97–129. On the paternalistic practices of slave masters, see Eugene Genovese, *Roll, Jordan, Roll: The World the Slaves Made* (New York: Random House, 1972). In a similar instance of projection, David Roediger, Alexander Saxton, and Eric Lott have explored the uneasy amalgam of desire, envy, and

disgust that led antebellum working-class audiences to simultaneously embrace and ridicule African American culture in blackface minstrelsy; Roediger, *The Wages of Whiteness: Race and the Making of the American Working Class* (New York: Verso, 1991), 95–131; Saxton, *The Rise and Fall of the White Republic: Class Politics and Mass Culture in Nineteenth-Century America* (New York: Verso, 1990), 165–82; Lott, *Love and Theft: Blackface Minstrelsy and the American Working Class* (New York: Oxford University Press, 1995).

27. Warner, *Being A Boy,* 198–99. Warner echoes Charles Darwin's genealogy of emotions outlined in his *Expression of the Emotions in Man and Animals* (1872). John S. C. Abbott, *The Mother at Home: Or, The Principles of Maternal Duty Familiarly Illustrated,* 2nd ed. (Boston: Crocker Brewster, 1833), 21. Goodrich, *Fireside Education,* 105.

28. Bushnell, *Christian Nurture* (New Haven: Yale University Press, 1947), 165, 280.

29. Ibid., 74, 75, 79.

30. Ibid., 74, 206, 77, 76.

31. Ibid., 88, 97. Richard Brodhead identifies this joint industry as a form of disciplinary intimacy that constrains both children and adults in a bond of love. I emphasize more its constitutive function: as is implied by Bushnell's displacement of what one does by what one is, at stake in his book is the formation of an environment conducive to a particular kind of emotional interiority. See Brodhead's "Sparing the Rod: Discipline and Fiction in Antebellum America," *Representations* 21 (1988): 70–74.

32. Bushnell, *Christian Nurture,* 281, 78.

33. Norris, "Child Stories for Adults" (1902), quoted in Jacobson, *Being a Boy Again,* 2.

34. Bushnell, *Christian Nurture,* 211.

PART III

The Rise of
Psychological Culture

CHAPTER SIX

Modern Psychological Selfhood in the Art of Thomas Eakins

DAVID M. LUBIN

However much the portraiture of the Philadelphia realist Thomas Eakins (1844–1916) may resemble that of Rembrandt, Titian, Velázquez, and other old masters, it is different from theirs because it points toward a paradigm of selfhood qualitatively different from the premodern or early modern one intrinsic to their work. In their world, introspection, whether achieved through prayer or Cartesian self-analysis, provided clear and definite access to the wellsprings of one's identity. At the time Eakins painted, however, and even more so in the decades following his death, educated middle-class Americans came increasingly to view themselves as complex and multifaceted creatures of ultimately unfathomable psychological depth. More than any other visual artist, Eakins provided them with the means not only of "seeing" their elusive interiority—exteriorized through facial expression and bodily posture—but also of considering such interiority to be a mark of moral distinction.[1]

This chapter is an attempt to look for the sources of Eakins's psychological portraiture not simply in the most obvious location, old-master portraiture, but also in contemporary imagery used for depicting the defeated or dejected outsider, a category to which he himself in certain respects belonged. His reputation as an artist only began to take hold at the close of his career, when his rendering of middle-class solemnity and internal depth caught the imagination first of disaffected writers, intellectuals, and artists and then eventually of a broader audience, who found in his poignant late portraits an ennobling mirror in which to see themselves.[2]

Positivist and Postpositivist Psychology

Over the course of the nineteenth century, theories of individual psychology underwent a series of transformations. For Romantics such as the poet and literary critic Samuel Taylor Coleridge, who introduced the neologism *psychological* as an analogue to *physiological,* psychology was the study of the psyche: the mind, the emotions, the unique subjectivity of an individual—in a word, the soul. A psyche was that which inhabited the body and remained contingent upon it but nonetheless possessed an independent or transcendent status. In 1811 Coleridge praised Shakespeare for availing himself "of his psychological genius to develop all the minutiae of the human heart." The Elizabethan's manner of depicting character "makes visible what we should otherwise not have seen: just as after looking at distant objects through a telescope, when we behold them afterwards with the naked eye, we see them with greater distinctness than we should otherwise have done." Although Coleridge's metaphor alludes to the science of astronomy, neither he nor Shakespeare was in any sense scientific in their attempt to examine or represent psychological interiority.[3]

In the second half of the nineteenth century, in a Comtean age of medical positivism that eschewed metaphysics, revelation, and faith as sources of knowledge and in turn invested its own enormous reserves of faith in observable and quantifiable physical facts, psychology came to be seen as an adjunct to physiology. Positivists regarded the so-called psyche as nothing more than an internal appendage to the physique. On both sides of the Atlantic, philosophers of mind as well as physicians now regarded the psychological as a manifestation of the physiological. Previous religious and romantic conceptions of the soul were besieged, and in many cases overwhelmed, by mechanistic views of it as a somatic state generated by electromagnetic charges coursing through the human nervous system. Wrote one turn-of-the-century commentator in a typical formulation: "The human soul is contained in the nerves of the body."[4]

After the Civil War, prominent physicians who were partially attracted to this view included Oliver Wendell Holmes, George M. Beard, and S. Weir Mitchell. For example, Mitchell's book *Fat and Blood* (1877) suggests that nervous illness can be repaired by fattening up the blood cells. Nevertheless, he and the other writer-physicians turned primarily to cultural explanations of illness, as well as to older, residual forms of religious and moral explanation.

In this they differed from such academic psychologists as William James, who initially sided with the mechanistic position. James's magisterial two-volume *Principles of Psychology* (1890) presents human subjectivity as a phenomenon largely accessible to quantification, calibration, and scientific representation. This view was the antecedent of modern behavioral psychology, with its refinement of clinical and technological procedures for investigating mind and emotion. By the end of the century, however, James—like Sigmund Freud in Vienna—became dissatisfied with mechanistic accounts of interiority and, as a result, turned away from an *experimental* to an *experiential* psychology. Here a patient's emotional history, filtered through the proper hermeneutic lens, was thought to offer more accurate information about the psychological process than could be acquired from mere diagnosis and quantification of somatic states.[5]

Despite his enduring fascination with the latest medical, optical, and photographic technologies, Eakins, too, came to reject a strictly mechanistic view of individuality. Although he began his career in the 1860s under the aegis of French positivism, with its empirical zeal for factuality, by the 1890s he was growing disenchanted with the positivist program. Increasingly he sought to produce a form of portrait painting that might compensate, in Fairfield Porter's words, "for a society that did not believe in anything beyond material facts."[6] With its emphasis on interiority and hence inscrutability, his late portraiture puts forth a look of nervous or enigmatic modernity that implicitly challenges self-confident positivism and empirical realism.

"After having proclaimed the omnipotence of scientific observation and deduction for eighty years with childlike enthusiasm, and after asserting that for its lenses and scalpels there did not exist a single mystery," wrote the French antipositivist Albert Aurier, "the nineteenth century at last seems to perceive that its efforts have been in vain, and its boast puerile. Man is still walking about in the midst of the same enigmas, in the same formidable unknown, which has become even more obscure and disconcerting since its habitual neglect."[7] For all the received wisdom about Eakins being a clear-eyed realist and visual scribe of daily life in late nineteenth-century America (painter of rowers, hunters, boxers, ball players, doctors, and musicians), his late portraiture quietly took part in the growing international reaction of advanced thinkers against the certitudes and platitudes of positivism.

Nowhere in Eakins's late portraiture is the dialectic between his long-standing positivist proclivities and his emerging antipositivist doubts more fully played out than in the portrait of Professor Henry A. Rowland (1897, fig. 6.1). The portrait depicts Rowland, a prominent physicist and inventor, seated imperiously in a darkened laboratory with light-measuring devices of his own invention placed conspicuously in his hand and at his side. A smattering of his original mathematical formulae have been inscribed by Eakins on the painting's broad, burnished-gold wooden frame. In the shadowy space beyond Rowland, pressed close to the margin of the painting, an assistant with a workman's smock and rolled-up sleeves bends over his lathe.

In one sense the painting unabashedly celebrates scientific progress, as

6.1. Thomas Eakins, *Professor Henry A. Rowland,* 1897. Oil on canvas, 80 1/4 × 54 in. Addison Gallery of American Art, Phillips Academy, Andover, Massachusetts. Gift of Stephen C. Clark.

embodied by Rowland, his inventions, his formulae, and his industrious assistant. And yet the visual language of the portrait undermines any such blandly triumphal celebration. To the lay viewer, the formulae on the frame are as inscrutable as Egyptian hieroglyphics, and the wide, eye-catching expanse of golden luster harks back to the celestial gold backgrounds of Byzantine icons and early Renaissance depictions of the Madonna enthroned. These visual elements may be understood as redounding to the glorification of modern science, treating it as a religious, even awe-inspiring experience, but they may just as well be understood as proclaiming there to be enveloping mysteries that mere positivism, for all its self-assurance, can never plumb. The chiaroscuro lighting, enlivened not by the stolid and stiff-backed physicist but by the multicolored spectral diffraction grating that he holds in his hand, romanticizes and dramatizes what would otherwise be the most prosaic of settings, the modern scientific laboratory, and it even introduces a note of potential class disharmony between this enthroned scientific manager and the diminutively scaled, drably enshadowed manual laborer who stands at his bidding.

The word *spectral* means divided into bands of color according to the wavelengths of the light spectrum, but it also means ghostly or phantomlike, and both meanings are at play in this portrait. All is not fully rational and accounted for here, and not everything of importance is accessible to the light. Whatever Eakins's conscious intentions may have been, his portrait of Rowland clutching a ghostly magic wand while surrounded by mysterious shadows and hieroglyphics transforms an 1890s champion of contemporary physical science into a latter-day wizard or necromancer, a premodern alchemist not entirely at home in the starched collars and pince-nez glasses of the modern bureaucratic era.[8]

This is not to say that, as in certain realist or naturalist fictions of the era, the portrait reveals its protagonist to be internally tormented, a psychologically complicated member of the modern urban bourgeoisie. But what the portrait does suggest, by means of its technical devices (lighting, composition, framing, and so on), is that there is more to this man than meets the eye, depths of character, whether good or bad, that must remain hidden beneath the surface. Given Rowland's particular scientific achievement—the invention of machines for calibrating invisible or only ambiguously visible electromagnetic forces— the irony here is that Eakins's portrait of him suggests that an individual's mind, emotions, and social relationships can never fully be brought to light. The painting, in effect, is a metaportrait showing that even a substance as transient and ineffable as light is more conducive to scientific measurement than is the human mind and the differential social relationships it devises.

In its insistence upon the doubleness, the always partially hidden identity, of its sitters, Eakins's portraiture pushed against the grain of conventional portraiture, which served chiefly a public function and was in this sense resolutely positivist. A portrait of any given sitter typically enunciated that sitter's public identity or social role: patriarch, statesman, general, gentleman, gentlewoman. Portraitists such as the colonial painter John Singleton Copley or Eakins's cosmopolitan contemporary John Singer Sargent were adept at constructing individuating identities for their sitters, as in Copley's portrait of a handsome young lawyer named Thaddeus Burr (1765, St. Louis Art Museum) or Sargent's full-length portrait of the flamboyant Dr. Pozzi (1881, Armand Hammer Foundation, Los Angeles). In both of these instances, the so-called psychology of the sitter appears to be wholly a matter of postured self-presentation, rather than intimate self-disclosure.[9] These portraits are theatrical and external, not novelistic and internal like Eakins's late portraiture and the psychological fiction of his contemporaries Kate Chopin, Stephen Crane, Theodore Dreiser, Charlotte Perkins Gilman, Henry James, and Edith Wharton.

Whereas at this time a middle-class literary market fell into place for fictional representations of individuals who seemed amazingly lifelike in their psychological complexity, a similar market for the visual representation of real-life individuals with a corresponding degree of inner texture did not and could not come into being. When Eakins portrayed the bourgeois individuals of his generation in such a way as to suggest that the private was being made public, the sitters and their families often expressed disappointment if not displeasure, in some cases refusing to accept the finished portraits or doing so only to hide them from sight. Asked why he did not sit for Eakins, the prominent artist Edwin Austin Abbey replied: "Because he would bring out all the traits of my character that I have been trying to hide from the public for years."[10] Even when the rejection was focused not on the way the portrait appeared to expose a private self but simply on the artist's tendency to make his subjects look haggard and worn, what was at stake was the credibility of the sitter's public persona. By seeming to bare the side of his sitter normally hidden from view, Eakins appeared to offer indiscreet revelations of how within each of them the "other half" lived.

Eakins's first major psychological portrait, *The Artist's Wife and His Setter Dog* (c. 1884–86, fig. 6.2), depicts the thirty-four-year-old Susan MacDowell Eakins, to whom he had been married for about a year.[11] Compare *The Artist's Wife* to *The Muse* (1835–37, fig. 6.3), Samuel Morse's portrait of his daughter, Susan Morse, painted half a century earlier. It would be incorrect to say that the Morse portrait idealizes its subject whereas the Eakins does not, for *The Artist's Wife* embodies a current social type no less than *The Muse* embodies a conventional poetic trope. Still, the Morse portrait, with its formal symmetries, monumental architecture, and theatrical staginess, has all the earmarks of a public presen-

6.2. Thomas Eakins, *The Artist's Wife and His Setter Dog,* c. 1884–86. Oil on canvas,
30 × 23 in. Metropolitan Museum of Art, New York. Fletcher Fund, 1923.

6.3. Samuel F. B. Morse, *The Muse: Susan Walker Morse*, 1835–37. Oil on canvas, 73 3/4 ×
56 5/8 in. Metropolitan Museum of Art, New York. Bequest of Herbert L. Pratt, 1945.

tation, whereas the Eakins portrait, with its individualizing domestic setting,
slouching body posture, and ambiguous if not downright dejected facial expression, seems by contrast meant only for private consumption.

Evidence based on a period photogravure suggests that Eakins later
repainted portions of *The Artist's Wife,* aging the features of the face and compressing the figure, but it is not known when he did this, or which version of the
painting he publicly exhibited in 1887, when critics called it "unfortunate" and
"disastrous." Their complaints were aesthetic in nature, asserting the rendering
of the figure to be overly detailed, but a deeper source of their discomfort may
have been the untoward view that such a rendering provided of the modern
middle-class female personality, generalizing it to be feckless and prematurely
worn. One has only to recall William Dean Howells's influential generalization—"Our novelists . . . concern themselves with the more smiling aspects of
life, which are the more American"—to understand how *The Artist's Wife* would
have set teeth on edge. Serious writers, eventually including Howells himself,

6.4. John Singer Sargent, *Lady Agnew of Lochnaw*, 1892–93. Oil on canvas, 47 × 39 1/4 in. National Galleries of Scotland, Edinburgh.

chose to ignore or reject this dictum, but for the vast majority of portrait painters, dependent upon the goodwill of their patrons, it remained inviolable.[12]

By producing inner-directed, seemingly soul-disclosing works such as *The Artist's Wife,* Eakins departed not only from past traditions in American portraiture but also from the stylistic orientation of his most commercially successful, as well as critically acclaimed, fellow portraitists. Consider, for example, Sargent's dazzling portrait of Lady Agnew (1892–93, fig. 6.4), in which the beautiful young aristocrat coolly addresses the viewer with her direct gaze. This is public portraiture through and through, a spectacularly glamorous surface that eschews any discourse of intimate disclosure or revelation.[13] At a time when international literary naturalism was moving increasingly toward the representation of psychological complexity and interiority, international portraiture tended to pursue the opposite route, in large part, no doubt, because of the particular economic imperatives of commercial patronage to which most portraitists, apart from Eakins, felt themselves bound.

How is it that Eakins took such a different track from his contemporaries when it came to portraiture and its goals? Modestly supported by his father and not ambitious for wealth, he did not depend upon outside patronage. But this in itself does not explain why he so ardently sought a visual language for addressing the private emotion or psychological subjectivity of his sitters when most of his fellow painters remained content to render their sitters in a more traditionally public, exteriorized mode. Before confronting this question, let us first ask where Eakins acquired the visual language that enabled him to depict—that is, produce in the minds of his viewers—the subjective, privatized, psychologized self. If he had neither predecessors nor contemporaries among his fellow American portraitists to whom he might turn when seeking visual inspiration for the depiction of textured interiority, where did he turn?

Discourses of Defeat

In the art of his later years, Eakins drew upon visual rhetorics traditionally employed for the depiction of defeated "others"—outcasts, subalterns, conquered enemies. Many centuries earlier, in the public sculpture of ancient Rome, the expression of anguish was reserved exclusively for conquered barbarians, whose bodies and faces betrayed personal emotions that were not fit or seemly for imperial citizens. From that time forth, Western art perfected its discourses of interiority, but these continued to be used typically for the depiction of failure, not success; defeat, not triumph; suffering, not serenity. Or, to rephrase this, worldly failure, worldly defeat, worldly suffering—for in the Christian era, saints and martyrs were those who sorrowed most profoundly in this world, only to reap joy everlasting in the world to follow.

Biographical details about Eakins do not indicate that he was a religious man, certainly not in any formal sense. Nevertheless his late portraiture bears striking resemblance to various saint, martyr, and prophet paintings from the Renaissance and Baroque periods of Western art. I wish to claim not that Eakins was clinging to or trying to resuscitate a longstanding tradition of picturing spirituality but, to the contrary, that he was appropriating this venerable tradition to contribute to a newly arisen secular and modernist cause, the visualization of anxious personal interiority, or what Freud during the same years was to characterize as "common everyday unhappiness." With his late portraiture, Eakins became the unappreciated painter laureate of bourgeois neurosis.

His rescripting of religious passion into modern psychological tension can best be seen in his 1904 portrait of a middle-aged Englishwoman named Edith Mahon (fig. 6.5). As portrayed by Eakins, Edith Mahon emerges from the depths of a somber background into the narrow space defined by her beaded black evening gown and the heavy carving of a high-backed chair. Eyes moist,

6.5. Thomas Eakins, *Edith Mahon*, 1904. Oil on canvas, 20 × 16 in. Smith College Museum of Art, Northampton, Massachusetts. Purchase, Drayton Hillyer Fund, 1931.

brow contracted, and face ruddy with color, she exudes an undefined yet singularly intense emotion. Since the early Renaissance, artists had shown grief and lamentation in religious art, as in virtually any *Entombment* or *Pietà*. During the Baroque period artists also portrayed religious figures with an emotional intensity not normally allotted to secular subjects. For instance, Bernini's sculptural portrait of the blessed Ludovica Albertoni depicts a dying woman at the moment that the agony of death gives way to the ecstasy of the hereafter (1671–74, fig. 6.6). It is of little importance whether or not Eakins knew of this portrait when he painted *his* modern martyrs (although he may well have examined it when he visited Rome as an art student). What is significant, and undeniable, is that he was well aware of Renaissance and Baroque idioms for depicting religious sufferers as figures of transcendent status, individuals who were envisioned suffering physically and mentally in one world even as they were being born into another world spiritually—that is, psychologically.

The rough equivalence I have made here between *spiritually* and *psycholog-*

6.6. Gianlorenzo Bernini, *The Blessed Ludovica Albertoni* (detail), 1671–74. Marble. Church of San Francesco a Ripa, Rome.

ically is not, of course, my doing, but that of William James. Indeed, it is the secularization and modernization of the former term into the latter that both Eakins and James, as well as many of their contemporaries, helped to bring about. James's widely read *The Varieties of Religious Experience* (1902) talks about the subjective realities of a diverse range of religious believers, especially saints, mystics, and prophets, in terms that go beyond the limits of modern experimental psychology, which by now James had come to view as inadequate. Thus he writes, "To describe the world with all the various feelings . . . all the various spiritual attitudes left out from the description . . . would be something like offering a printed bill of fare as the equivalent for a solid meal. Religion makes no such blunder [and hence] always remains infinitely less hollow and abstract . . . than a science which prides itself on taking no account of anything private at all."[14]

The late portraiture of Eakins similarly rejects the narrow confines of positivism. This is not to say that the late portraiture actually conveys tangible information about the inner lives of its subjects, but only that it conjures for the viewer an *impression* of gaining access to such personal, individualized information. "Individuality is founded in feeling," writes James, "and the recesses of feeling, the darker, blinder strata . . . are the only places in the world in which we catch real fact in the making" (379). As devoted to scientific experimentation as Eakins may have been, the rhetoric of sober introspection permeating much of his late portraiture indicates that he, like other dissatisfied artists and intellectuals, bridled at the epistemological limitations of positivist science. If positivism insists that reality is constituted meaningfully only by that which is measurable, quantifiable, reducible to linguistic or mathematical formula, antipositivism treats this position as fatuous and complacently nearsighted. Like both William James and James's brother Henry, Eakins sought to demonstrate, in a phrase of Henry's, "The power to guess the unseen from the seen, to trace the implication of things, to judge the whole piece by the pattern."[15]

A portrait of Louis Kenton from 1900, entitled *The Thinker*, imparts a sense of its subject's inner, psychological activity, a sense of mental or spiritual drama, the details of which are not and cannot be specified but are palpable to the viewer nonetheless (fig. 6.7). *The Thinker* shows a lanky, dour-faced, middle-aged man dressed in black, his hands thrust into his trouser pockets, his gaze downcast, his eyes screened from sight by a pair of pince-nez glasses perched upon his nose. By denying the viewer access to Kenton's eyes, permitting only a portion of one dark pupil to be seen, the portrait tantalizes the viewer, creating the impression that this is a man who plunges deep into thought in the same way that he plunges his hands into his pockets. This thought—whatever it may be, for it is as inaccessible as the eyes—is of such weight that Kenton's broad shoulders are bowed by it and his suit coat rumpled. The emotional gravity of the idea he confronts is delineated by the physical gravity that seems written across his body, or, to switch metaphors, the wrinkling of Kenton's sleeve mirrors the wrinkling of his brow, both of which suggest a profound wrinkling of his mind.

The Thinker was one of the few portraits by Eakins to achieve recognition during the artist's lifetime. On three separate occasions between 1901 and 1907 Charles H. Caffin, representing a younger, more adventurous generation of art critics, praised it for "the grasp which it suggests of the subject's personality." In Caffin's estimation, this "record of a human individual is extraordinarily arresting and satisfactory," and he marveled at how Eakins had made it seem "as if the gentleman had been caught pacing the room in the solution of some problem and were unconscious of anybody's presence." Although Caffin's admiration for Eakins as a revelator of character is reminiscent of Coleridge's praise for Shakespeare a century earlier, the distinctly psychological language that

6.7. Thomas Eakins, *The Thinker: Portrait of Louis N. Kenton,* 1900. Oil on canvas, 82 × 42 in. Metropolitan Museum of Art, New York. John Stewart Kennedy Fund.

Caffin employs—"the subject's personality," "record of an individual," "unconscious"—was new to Eakins criticism and, indeed, American art criticism in general, marking a shift away from an exclusive emphasis on the formal or publicly biographical properties of a portrait and toward its apparent grasp or revelation of interiority.[16] Whereas viewers previously had been put off by the markers of nervous subjectivity with which the late Eakins portraits abounded, now, as indicated by progressive critics like Caffin, the professional middle class—or at least its nonphilistine faction—was becoming fascinated with this new image of itself as sensitive, complex, and profound.

The Thinker bespeaks a tendency toward asceticism. As an artist, Eakins himself was an ascetic, austere and self-denying in color and style, unlike Sargent, William Merritt Chase, and James McNeill Whistler, who were aesthetes, dedicated to the pursuit of sensuous beauty.[17] William James writes that asceticism "symbolizes . . . the belief that there is an element of real wrongness in this world, which is neither to be ignored nor evaded, but which must be squarely met and overcome by an appeal to the soul's heroic resources, and neutralized and cleansed away by suffering" (281).[18] Hence the attraction for Eakins of saint and martyr painting as he searched for a visual language to convey the psychological dimension—the "spiritual suffering," it would more likely have been termed—of his era, a suffering otherwise militantly repressed by scientific positivism, Gilded Age optimism, and the burgeoning ethos of consumerism, which William James dismisses as "mere syllabub and flattery and sponge-cake" (282). Eakins was not interested in sponge-cake. He had become disenchanted with "the more smiling aspects of life" in modern America. Ironically, during the twentieth century the look of sensitive suffering that was so congruent with Eakins's ascetic and nonconsumerist values became, as suggested above, the badge of cultivated modernity for an educated and often consumerist social elite, yet another means, in the terms of the sociologist Pierre Bourdieu, of marking class distinction.

There are additional visual discourses that may have contributed to the rhetoric of melancholy, rumination, or dejection that paintings like *Edith Mahon* and *The Thinker* so eloquently bespeak. One such discourse was that of nineteenth-century medical illustration of mental alienation, and another was the nineteenth-century convention in American art for the depiction of such defeated subaltern groups as African Americans and Native Americans.

As is well-documented, Eakins studied modern medical science no less avidly than the art of the old masters. Recent writers have noted congruences between his late, psychological portraiture and the theories of S. Weir Mitchell, the Philadelphia novelist and physician who devised a widely practiced "rest-cure" system of therapy for sufferers from nervous exhaustion, known then as neurasthenia. In popular medical treatises such as the frequently reprinted

Wear and Tear, or Hints for the Overworked (1871), Mitchell described modern-day administrators, professionals, and bureaucrats, or "brain-workers," as those who were dangerously prone to working themselves into a state of anxiety or depression from lack of proper rest and relaxation. As for the young middle-class females of the day, wrote Mitchell ruefully, "You will be struck with a certain hardness of line in form and feature . . . and if you have an eye which rejoices in the tints of health, you will too often miss them on the cheeks we are now so daringly criticising."[19]

For such prematurely aged young women, all that remains, tut-tuts Mitchell, "is the shawl and the sofa, neuralgia, weak backs, and the varied forms of hysteria,—that domestic demon which has produced untold discomfort in many a household." If this description seems to fit Eakins's depiction of his wife, this is not to propose that he wished to show her as neuralgic or hysteric, or on her way to becoming so. Nor is it to say that he was self-consciously offering either an endorsement of or attack on the dominant social ideology that relegated middle-class women to the role of listless automatons (a criticism leveled by Mitchell's resentful former patient Charlotte Perkins Gilman in her 1892 short story "The Yellow Wallpaper").[20] In the absence of corroborating documents, Eakins's attitude toward his wife in particular and middle-class women in general can be only a matter of speculation, but what seems clear is that the popularized medical language of the time and place at which he did paint her provided him with a conceptual category—worn and torn middle-class modernity—that appears to have underpinned much of his portraiture from this time forth.

Although Mitchell's descriptions of mental malaise were entirely verbal, there were important photographic representations in circulation as well, especially within the quasi-specialized literature readily available to Eakins. The most widely disseminated of such photographs were those produced by the clinic of the celebrated French doctor and public lecturer Jean-Martin Charcot, who specialized in the treatment of hysteria, which, in the language of the time, referred primarily to female madness. Charcot's audiences, which in the mid-1880s included his young Austrian assistant Freud, were enthralled, if not also titillated, by his artistic skill at externalizing the inner, physiologically defective mind, bringing it forth, as it were, out of its ostensible recesses onto the clinically observed body for all to see.[21] There is virtually no resemblance between the Charcot photographs and Eakins's late portraits of women (or men), except in this: Eakins's portraiture is similarly surveillant in the sense of offering privileged access to supposedly private moments, whether, in Charcot's case, of the hysteric isolated in her manic delusions or, in Eakins's case, of Edith Mahon alone with her thoughts.

Like Charcot, the British physician Hugh W. Diamond extensively pho-

6.8. Thomas Eakins, *Amelia Van Buren*, c. 1891. Oil on canvas, 45 × 32 in. The Phillips Collection, Washington, D.C.

tographed female mental patients for diagnostic purposes, at once borrowing from and contributing to Victorian conventions for conveying soulful interiority.[22] Eakins's portraiture partakes of this imagery, whether advertently or not, as one can see in comparing the hand-to-the-head portrait of *Amelia Van Buren* (c. 1891, fig. 6.8) with Diamond's photograph of a similarly posed young patient tormented by a sense of guilt (c. 1855, fig. 6.9). The claim here is not that Amelia Van Buren was clinically depressed but that Eakins's aesthetic choices in depicting her intersect with those of psychiatric photographers like Diamond who had earlier searched for and settled upon conventional means of making visible the mind's invisibility.

Another possible source of Eakins's visual language of sensitive, suffering interiority may have been sentimental or romantic representations of African Americans and Native Americans. During the Reconstruction era when Eakins began his career, American blacks were commonly caricatured in the visual arts as lazy, sensually exaggerated, childlike creatures. Yet at the same time, African

6.9. Hugh W. Diamond, "A Melancholic Asylum Patient," c. 1855. Photograph. Royal Society of Medicine, London.

American writers, intellectuals, and progressive church leaders such as Charles Chesnutt, Anna Julia Cooper, W. E. B. Du Bois, and Francis W. Harper—fore-runners of what came to be called the New Negro movement—strove to cast off the longstanding stereotype of blacks as all body and brawn, with no brain or depth.

Eakins may well have been unaware of this nascent New Negro movement, although much of its intellectual leadership was headquartered in Philadelphia. Still, his portrait of the expatriate New Negro artist Henry Ossawa Tanner (c. 1902, fig. 6.10), who came from Philadelphia and had studied with him, attributes intellectuality and subjectivity to an American black in distinct contrast to the egregiously racist representations more typical of the period.[23] Whatever Eakins's own sentiments may have been in regard to the racial issues of his time, the newly emerging rhetoric of noble black immiseration and tragic sensibility typified in the writings of Chesnutt, Du Bois, Harper, and other black intellectuals may have provided some of the conceptual groundwork for his

6.10. Thomas Eakins, *Henry O. Tanner,* c. 1902. Oil on canvas, 24 1/16 × 20 1/4 in. The Hyde Collection, Glens Falls, New York.

own depiction of stressful and internalized bourgeois individuality. The concept of "tragic color" that emerged in their literary work and was propagated through serialization in leading national magazines may have helped Eakins to arrive at his unique method of painting portraits redolent with tragic whiteness.

Although the nineteenth century provided few sympathetic visual images of American blacks, depictions of the American Indian as a "noble savage" were plentiful indeed. James Earle Fraser's *End of the Trail,* sculpted for the 1893 World's Columbian Exposition in Chicago and frequently reproduced thereafter, portrayed the defeated, head-bowed Native American as the New World's equivalent to the dejectedly vanquished barbarians embodied on the sarcophagi and triumphal monuments of ancient Rome. Unlike Rome's barbarians, however, who did not cease to be a threat to imperial sovereignty, by 1893 the Native Americans no longer posed an ongoing danger to the adversaries who memorialized them.[24]

Eakins's 1895 portrait of Frank Hamilton Cushing, a brilliant anthropolo-

6.11. Thomas Eakins, *Frank Hamilton Cushing,* 1895. Oil on canvas, 90 × 60 in. Thomas Gilcrease Institute of American History and Art, Tulsa, Oklahoma.

6.12. Edward S. Curtis, "Chief Joseph—Nez Percé," 1903. Photograph. Colby College, Waterville, Maine.

gist who lived for five years among the Zuni and lectured widely on their customs, shows an emaciated, pockmarked, saturnine Anglo-American adorned in Zuni boots and britches, a hoop earring dangling from his ear, and hair cascading over his shoulder (fig. 6.11). The dour expression on Cushing's face is pure late Eakins, but it is pure "dying Indian" as well. Other late portraits by Eakins also bear affinities to what passed then for ethnographic Indian portraiture, as can be seen in a comparison of *Edith Mahon* to the neoromantic Indian photography of Edward S. Curtis (1903, fig. 6.12), whose twenty-volume publication, *The North American Indian* (1907–30), sought to record the physiognomy of the Native American before it was gone forever.[25]

Biographical Sources of Eakins's Late Portrait Style

But why paint turn-of-the-century white middle-class Philadelphians with the gloomy demeanor more commonly reserved for visual representations of dejected or resigned subalterns such as religious martyrs, ascetic prophets, female mental patients, African Americans, and American Indians? If Eakins's late portraiture is based both stylistically and conceptually on these particular visual parlances devoted to the representation of defeat, why would this be so? What motivated him to produce a rhetoric of dejection suited to describing the professional-managerial middle class to which he belonged, albeit as a marginal figure?

Surely biographical factors are relevant though they are not, by any means, wholly explanatory. For instance, upon returning to Philadelphia in 1870 from his three-year sojourn in Europe, Eakins came into close daily contact with the face of mental illness when his mother, Carolyn Cowperthwait Eakins, suffered a psychosis from which she never recovered. For nearly two years, the young artist never dared leave home in the evenings for fear of adding to his mother's anxiety. She was attended at her death by a physician from the Philadelphia Hospital for the Insane, and the city register identified the cause of death as "exhaustion from mania." Whether or not Eakins's mother was literally a madwoman in the attic, the young painter would have had much cause to ponder psychiatric illustration.[26]

Yet this alone would not account for why in later years so many of his portrait subjects seem to be characterized by the look of depressive anxiety. Other events in his life, taken cumulatively, may have been decisive in this regard. Eakins himself suffered a nervous breakdown in 1887, the year after he was forced by scandal to resign as director of instruction at the Pennsylvania Academy of Fine Arts. Earlier, meningitis had taken away his first fiancée and typhus a much beloved sibling. Later, his young niece committed suicide (owing to a sexual molestation by the artist, some family members charged in an unproven allegation). Meanwhile, throughout most of his career he faced critical disapproval or neglect of some of his most ambitious works. Thus it is not difficult to imagine that Eakins would have found any such preexisting imagery of mental desolation and defeat, regardless of its lineage or context, appropriate to a melancholy vision of humanity in general and women in particular as suggested to him by the circumstances of his own life and the lives of those with whom he was close.

Although he was not friends with any African Americans, unless, intermittently, with Tanner, Eakins certainly would have had reason to identify with black Americans of the post-Reconstruction era to the extent that he saw himself, particularly after the debacle at the Academy, as a marginalized individual, blocked by the prejudice and ignorance of his superiors from access to the social privileges they enjoyed. From the Civil War to the early twentieth century, the span of Eakins's career, Philadelphia had the largest African American population of any Northern city, was the headquarters of leading black organizations, and, as noted earlier, was a center of the New Negro movement. Yet it was also America's capital city of black crime and ghetto violence, as well as of white violence toward blacks in the form of police harassment and lynchings.[27] In other words, all around Eakins, whether he gave this his attention or not, blacks were conspicuously demeaned and mistreated, the very situation into which he believed himself to have fallen.

Bearing this in mind, we may plausibly consider Eakins to have been an early instance of a relatively common twentieth-century phenomenon, the disaffected white person (in Norman Mailer's terms, "the white Negro"), who not only discerned in the victimization of blacks or Indians or immigrants a metaphoric equivalent to his or her own sense of victimization and alienation but also entered into an emotional identification with that subaltern class as a means toward therapeutic relief. White, affluent, Harvard-educated political analyst Walter Lippmann was speaking for his own social class when he claimed in 1914 that "All of us are immigrants spiritually. We are all of us immigrants in the industrial world."[28]

For members of the dominant middle class, nervous suffering during this period amounted to a form of secular martyrdom, primarily but by no means exclusively the province of women. For all the "wear and tear" it may have entailed, the refined capacity for emotional suffering provided a means by which disempowered or alienated white middle-class social subjects achieved—or, more specifically, constructed for themselves—a transcendent, hence socially superior, status. When Eakins endowed his late portrait subjects—including himself (1902, fig. 6.13)—with the look of *tedium vitae,* to use William James's term, or neurasthenia, to use that of the physician George M. Beard, he may in fact have been conferring upon them (whether or not they desired this) an honorific, ennobling visual label that characterized them (and him) as more sensitive, more internally alive, than their crude and grasping Gilded Age or fin-de-siècle counterparts. Though certainly not willing to position itself at the lower social levels occupied by African Americans, Native Americans, and uprooted immigrants, the "brain-working" middle class that Eakins represented may nevertheless have appropriated for itself the appearance of noble suffering occasionally associated with these lower classes in sentimental liberal accounts.[29]

Eakins in the Twentieth Century

Historically, this newly arising sensibility not only encouraged Eakins to paint the way that he did in the late phase of his career but also laid the groundwork for the old-master status that came after his death. Although no single date marks the rise of the new sensibility, 1908–09 might symbolically

6.13. Thomas Eakins, *Self-Portrait,* **1902. Oil on canvas, 30 × 25 in. National Academy of Design, New York.**

serve the purpose. In 1909 Freud visited the United States, literally inaugurating America's great boom in psychoanalysis, the therapeutic study of the unconscious that by the 1920s dominated advanced artistic and intellectual circles. But one year earlier, D. W. Griffith began directing films for the Biograph Company. Griffith's most important cinematic invention was not, as is commonly thought, cross-cutting, but rather the introduction of character-oriented, psychologistic narratives and the naturalistic acting styles and filmic techniques suitable for such concerns. The close-up, for example, had entered film language earlier as a shock gimmick (showing, in one celebrated instance, a bandit firing his gun directly at the audience), but Griffith's innovation was to appropriate the technique as a way of directing the viewer's attention to the subjectivity of individual characters.[30]

Also in 1908, the twenty-two-year-old intellectual Van Wyck Brooks, recently graduated from Harvard, published *The Wine of the Puritans,* a wide-ranging attack on modern America that characterized it as a culturally blighted and morally bankrupt civilization that had failed to shrug off its Puritan legacy of crass individualism and pragmatic self-interest. Brooks's thesis, which was widely embraced by a new generation of critics, helped make it possible to look back at Eakins's turn-of-the-century portraits and regard them as a testament to the soul-deforming pressures of the Gilded Age. In another influential essay, "On Creating a Usable Past" (1918), Brooks urged his contemporaries to seek out marginalized and forgotten figures from the past who had struggled against the current of mainstream America, refusing to bend to its conformist pressures or celebrate its banality.[31]

In 1908 Robert Henri, an artist inspired by the realist principles of Eakins, formed the Eight (also known as the Ashcan School), a group of neorealists who painted genre scenes of crowded urban life and portraits that conveyed the isolated inner life of the modern city-dweller. Generally regarded as the most influential art teacher of the early twentieth century, Henri would invoke nineteenth-century dissident figures such as Eakins, or Eakins's friend Walt Whitman, when he wished to launch jeremiads against the materialism of modern America and argue that the purpose of art was to enable viewers to peer beneath the superficialities of daily life and grasp at inner realities.

"Beauty is no material thing," Henri proclaimed. "True art strikes deeper than the surface." He contended that the purpose of art was to bring viewers, through the artist's own self-reflexivity, into direct contact with the ineffable, invisible regions of lived experience: "The American who is useful as an artist is one who studies his own life and records his experiences; in this way he gives evidence." Of Eakins he stated, "I consider him the greatest portrait painter America has produced. . . . You find yourself, through the works, in close contact with a man . . . who was in love with the great mysterious nature as manifested in man and things." The value of Eakins's portraiture, in Henri's estimation, was that it probed the surface reality of the individuals portrayed, and this in turn was important precisely because Americans lived in a world in which "self-acquaintance is a rare condition" and "there are mighty few people who think what they think they think."[32]

Like the fictional portraits of Sherwood Anderson, Willa Cather, and Theodore Dreiser and the dramatic portraits of Eugene O'Neill, Eakins's portraiture must have seemed to the new generation to testify to the psychological devastation wrought on the bourgeois individual by the exigencies of modern American life. Randolph Bourne's influential essay of 1917, "The Puritan's Will to Power," drew a picture of puritanical guilt, sexual repression, and pragmatically motivated self-renunciation that would surely have resonated with viewers of Eakins's late portraits at the New York memorial exhibition of that year, as well as with readers of such striking fictional portraits of nineteenth-century repression as to be found in Anderson's *Winesburg, Ohio* (1919), Cather's

My Ántonia (1918), and Booth Tarkington's *Magnificent Ambersons* (1918; Pulitzer Prize, 1919) and in Henry Adams's autobiographical *Education of Henry Adams* (posthumously published 1918, Pulitzer Prize, 1919). "Insipid prettiness did not appeal to him," wrote the curator of an Eakins memorial exhibition held in Philadelphia: "it was always character, character, character."[33]

In the years following the avant-garde Armory Show exhibition of 1913, the progressive artists and intellectuals associated with Alfred Stieglitz made Henri and his circle of urban realists appear passé. But even if such Stieglitz protégés as Stuart Davis, Charles Demuth, Marsden Hartley, John Marin, and Georgia O'Keeffe turned decisively away from realist representation in favor of cubism, fauvism, and expressionism, they admired Eakins for his dogged rejection of bourgeois America in the pursuit of his own non-utilitarian point of view. That Eakins had been shunned by polite society for his artistic fascination with the naked human body made him all the more a hero to a bohemian vanguard that equated sexual liberation, or what Greenwich Village radical Floyd Dell called "love in the machine age," with political and artistic liberation.

The rediscovery—or perhaps the discovery—of Eakins roughly coincided with the Melville revival of the 1920s. Henry McBride, writing in the literary magazine *The Dial,* believed that "The cases of Herman Melville, writer, and Thomas Eakins, painter, have enough in common to make one at least think about the vagaries of fame." Now that Melville's reputation had been resurrected, predicted McBride, the same would occur with Eakins: "That his time will come is inevitable and because of certain murmurs that may be heard in an ear that is held close to the ground I do not think the time afar off."[34]

In part, the Melville revival resulted from the effort of Brooks and others, including his friend Lewis Mumford, to recover "a usable past" of nineteenth-century writers and artists who were naysayers to materialistic American civilization rather than cheerleaders for it. In words that might well have been applied to the Eakins of the late portraits, Mumford declared that "Melville's work, taken as a whole, expresses that tragic sense of life which has always attended the highest triumphs of the race. . . . Where that sense is lacking, life shrivels into small prudences and weak pleasures and petty gains."[35]

Although Henri and other progressives in the 1910s and 1920s admired Eakins as an artist who exposed the troubled, even anguished private lives of his bourgeois sitters, the earlier view of him as a staunchly objective reporter, a fact-based positivist, returned in full force during the 1930s under the influence of Lloyd Goodrich and his followers. The author of the first scholarly monograph on the painter, Goodrich portrayed him more as a neutral recorder of American daily life than as one of its dark Melvillian critics. This characterization of Eakins as a scientifically rigorous fact-gatherer swiftly came to dominate all future discussions, thereby repressing the alternative understanding of him as a dissenter from bourgeois society, someone more interested in defying mainstream America than in reproducing it with photographic verisimilitude. Thus with the onset of the Depression, Eakins the tragic visionary was suddenly derailed and replaced by Eakins the sunny pragmatist, and instead of being valued as a dour social critic who undermined the status quo, he was now popularly praised, in the title of an essay by one admirer, as "Thomas Eakins—Positivist."[36]

Goodrich himself never entirely dispensed with the progressives' view of Eakins, but he depoliticized it. He was particularly adept at synthesizing his conception of the portraitist as a dedicated scientific investigator with the new therapeutic language of subjectivity, psychological introspection, and the privatized self ("His vision had mordancy like that of a powerful acid, eating away surface graces and leaving only the irreducible nucleus of character"). By far the most influential champion of the artist over the next fifty years, Goodrich made it possible to regard Eakins without self-contradiction as both a pragmatic scientific realist and a modern prophetic seer, the one state of mind no longer considered the antithesis of the other but rather its partner in a largely apolitical humanism.[37]

This in turn licensed the way that the artist was talked about in the therapeutic language of Sylvan Schendler, who in his 1967 book on Eakins saw in the portraits a "continued deepening of psychological analysis . . . [and] a renewed discovery of the tragic," or of John Wilmerding, whose 1979 essay on the late portraits began: "Poignant almost beyond possibility, weighted with age both in the personal as well as period sense, the late portraits of Thomas Eakins are among the supreme works of his career." What vanished along the way was any recognition of the potential of Eakins's dour late portraits to constitute an implicit attack on the American middle class and the social, economic, and political forces that produced it. To the contrary, this same middle class, or, more accurately, its offspring, had finally found a way to love him, precisely because now, in a fully therapeutic age, it was no longer an insult to the middle class but instead a compliment to regard its members as "tragic" and "poignant almost beyond possibility."[38]

During the early 1980s, Eakins's reputation among scholars mostly held to the course laid out by Goodrich, thanks to the publication of Goodrich's long-awaited two-volume critical biography (1982) and Elizabeth Johns's *Thomas Eakins* (1983), which portrayed the artist as a scientifically minded investigator of both external and internal reality whose work sought to affirm "the heroism of modern life." By mid-decade, however, contrary assessments began to appear. Largely influenced by European poststructuralism and critical theory, my *Act of Portrayal* (1985) and Michael Fried's *Writing, Realism, Disfiguration* (1987) proffered a distinctly antipositivist and non-affirmational view of Eakins. This latter, fin-de-siècle conception has increased in appeal, perhaps because it is better suited to the downbeat temper of the post–Cold War era, with its heightened distrust of science and technology as solutions to world disorder. Johns begins a subsequent essay on Eakins's photographs (1994) by stating that "the common description of Thomas Eakins as a 'scientific realist' no longer seems to apply." For the time being, at least, the positive, heroic Eakins is in the process of being re-replaced by the negative, antiheroic one.[39]

Whatever the changing tides of critical reception of Eakins over the course of the twentieth century, his impact on the manner in which middle-class Americans conceive of themselves visually has been great, even if generally unacknowledged. Although the various art movements of the time—modernist abstraction, regionalism, abstract expressionism, minimalism, and so forth—appear to have had little use for Eakins and his psychological realism, he legitimately can be seen as the American originator of the twentieth-century *look* of profound introspection and tormented affect. To compare the face of Greta Garbo in the film version of Eugene O'Neill's *Anna Christie* (1930, fig. 6.14) with Eakins's *Edith Mahon,* or that of the method actor Marlon Brando in *On the Waterfront* (1954) with Eakins's own self-portrait, or even Willem de Kooning's violently expressionist *Woman IV* (1952–53, Nelson-Atkins Museum) with *The Artist's Wife,* is to begin to comprehend how far-reaching has been the physically expressive language of psychological interiority that Eakins was the first American visual artist to summon forth.

Eakins and the Invention of Modern Psychological Subjectivity

The late psychological portraits of Thomas Eakins cannot legitimately be subsumed under the category of scientific positivism, whatever their antecedents may have been in the positivist procedure of grasping reality. This is not to say that his late art amounted to a wholesale rejection of the positivism that had informed his youth and early middle age, but rather that it was a renegotiation of it, proclaiming, in effect, that the psychological individual is something more than the sum of his or her scientifically measurable parts. By insisting upon the immeasurability of modern consciousness, the late portraiture advances the underlying premise of modern antibehaviorist and antipositivist psychology. At the same time, it accords well with modern, or, in the view of some theorists, postmodern conceptions of the psychological self as fragmented, dislocated, and insatiably hungry for fulfillment, whether by social community or by therapeutic consumption.

Like other late nineteenth- and early twentieth-century pioneers of the

6.14. Unknown photographer, "Greta Garbo in *Anna Christie,*" 1930. Photograph. BFI Stills, Posters, and Designs.

psychological, Eakins did much to invent the very category by which his work was then retroactively understood and valued. Drawing from sources as diverse as old-master portraits and depictions of saints, martyrs, and prophets, clinical depictions of mental illness, and rhetorics of alienated and dejected subalternity, his psychological portraits gained currency not in his era but in ours because their look of nervous modernity is one that the twentieth-century, with its burgeoning ethos of the needy, consumption-driven, isolated self, has better prepared us to receive. No matter how the artist himself regarded this newly emergent identity, and regardless of whether he sought to portray it in a spirit of clinical description or critical dissent, over time the portraits he painted became advertisements for a modern bourgeois self that could be admired narcissistically as "deep," "complex," and "universal," and thus largely drained of any political content.

Notes

My thanks to the first readers of this chapter, Martin Berger, Libby Lubin, Joel Pfister, and Nancy Schnog, who helped me to clarify and develop my ideas.

1. Describing the new sense of individualism that arose in Europe on the heels of the Renaissance, Rembrandt scholar H. Perry Chapman claims that "The growth of individualism marked a radical reordering of society that prompted many to turn inward and closely examine their lives, values, and beliefs as they attempted to reorient and reintegrate themselves. From this intense introspection would emerge a fundamentally altered type of personality, governed more by reason than emotion, with a high degree of self-awareness, a personality endowed with inner authority." *Rembrandt's Self-Portraits: A Study in Seventeenth-Century Identity* (Princeton: Princeton University Press, 1990), 5. The historical phase of individualism described in the present chapter is one in which Cartesian reason no longer appeared capable of harnessing wayward emotion, and personality came to seem endowed not with inner authority but perpetual self-doubt.

2. Rembrandt revisionists have contended that the familiar view of Rembrandt as a psychological portraitist preoccupied with the inner life of his sitters is "unacceptable because it is anachronistically founded on modern psychology." See Chapman, *Rembrandt's Self-Portraits*, 140, n. 15, which argues against the revisionist claim, and E. de Jongh, "The Spur of Wit: Rembrandt's Response to an Italian Challenge," *Delta* 12:2 (1969): 49–67, which first made it. Regardless of whether it is anachronistic to describe Rembrandt and other old masters as psychological artists, the conception of human identity embodied in their respective oeuvres is, in any case, different from the new conception that gathered force in Eakins's time.

3. Samuel Taylor Coleridge, from John Payne Collier's report of Lecture 7 of the 1811–12 series of Shakespeare lectures (this one on *Romeo and Juliet*), in *Coleridge's Criticism of Shakespeare*, ed. R. A. Foakes (Detroit: Wayne State University Press, 1989), 137. See also M. M. Badawi, *Coleridge: Critic of Shakespeare* (Cambridge: Cambridge University Press, 1973), esp. ch. 4. As a term denoting the scientific study of mind or soul, *psychology* can be traced as far back as the sixteenth century. See François H. Lapointe, "Who Originated the Term 'Psychology'?" *Journal of the History of the Behavioral Sciences* 8 (1972): 328–35. On the retroactive transformation of Shakespeare into a psychological author, see Terence Hawkes, *That Shakespeherian Rag: Essays on a Critical Process* (New York: Methuen, 1986), and Gary Taylor, *Reinventing Shakespeare: A Cultural History from the Restoration to the Present* (London: Hogarth Press, 1989). In the mid-twentieth century, Bertolt Brecht rejected the post-Coleridgian view of Shakespeare as a psychological portraitist; see Margot Heinemann, "How Brecht read Shakespeare," in *Political Shakespeare: New Essays in Cultural Materialism*, ed. Jonathan Dollimore and Alan Sinfield (Manchester: Manchester University Press, 1985), 214–17.

4. Daniel Paul Schreber, *Memoirs of My Nervous Illness* (1903), trans. Ida Macalpine and Richard A. Hunter (Cambridge: Harvard University Press, 1988), 45. Quoted in Tom Lutz, *American Nervousness, 1903: An Anecdotal History* (Ithaca: Cornell University Press, 1991), 286.

5. F. G. Gosling, *Before Freud: Neurasthenia and the American Medical Community, 1870–1910* (Urbana: University of Illinois Press, 1987), traces the transformation of etiological concepts of "nervousness" from a somatic to a psychosomatic disorder.

6. Fairfield Porter, *Thomas Eakins* (New York: George Braziller, 1959), 26.

7. Albert Aurier, "The Symbolist Painters" (1892), quoted in Herschel B. Chipp, *Theories of Modern Art: A Source Book by Artists and Critics* (Berkeley and Los Angeles: University of California Press, 1971), 93–94.

8. For details on the creation of this painting, see Lloyd Goodrich, *Thomas Eakins,* 2 vols. (Cambridge: Harvard University Press for the National Gallery of Art, Washington, D.C., 1982), 2:137–44, and for an interpretive reading see Bryan Wolf's entry in *Thomas Eakins,* ed. John Wilmerding (Washington, D.C.: Smithsonian Institution Press, 1993), 128–33. Describing Eakins's 1897 visit to Maine to paint Rowland at the latter's Mount Desert summer residence, Stephen May, in "Two Geniuses and a Paintbrush," *Down East* 41 (Aug. 1994), 67, 86, writes: "With his predilection for mathematics and science, Eakins sought exactitude in his work as a means of achieving visual truth. This stubborn trait must have drawn him to Rowland, known for the precision of his inventions." My claim in this chapter is that by 1897 Eakins no longer considered exactitude the royal road to truth, and that portraits such as *Professor Henry A. Rowland* hint insistently that there are unseeable and unmeasurable dimensions to reality.

9. The best recent exploration of Copley's faux-psychological portraiture as a sophisticated form of public enunciation is Carrie Rebora, Paul Staiti, et al., *John Singleton Copley in America,* exhib. cat. (New York: Metropolitan Museum of Art, 1995).

10. Quoted in Lloyd Goodrich, *Thomas Eakins: His Life and Work* (New York: Whitney Museum of Art, 1933), 116.

11. Surely *The Anatomy Clinic of Dr. Samuel Gross* (1875), also known as *The Gross Clinic,* must be considered a psychological portrait, but as the titles imply, it is a genre scene, or depiction of modern everyday life, as well.

12. Contemporary criticisms of *The Artist's Wife* are quoted in Natalie Spassky et al., *American Paintings in the Metropolitan Museum of Art,* vol. 2 (New York: Metropolitan Museum of Art, 1985), 616. The illustration in question, a photogravure of the painting in M. G. Van Rensselaer, *The Book of American Figure Painters* (1886), is reproduced in Spassky on 614. William Dean Howells, *Criticism and Fiction* (New York: Harper & Brothers, 1891), 128, was originally published as a series of editorials in *Harper's Magazine* between 1886 and 1891.

13. For a historical account of the cultural process of middle-class interiorization as evidenced in selected art and fiction of the period, see Jean-Christophe Agnew, "A House of Fiction: Domestic Interiors and the Commodity Aesthetic," in *Consuming Visions,* ed. Simon J. Bronner (New York: Norton, 1989).

14. William James, *The Varieties of Religious Experience: A Study in Human Nature* (1902; rpt., New York: Mentor, 1964), 377–78. Further page references to this edition will be given in the text.

15. Henry James, "The Art of Fiction" (1888), in *Henry James: Selected Fiction,* ed. Leon Edel (New York: Dutton, 1953), 595.

16. Quotations from Caffin in Spassky et al., *American Paintings,* 624. As early as 1885 an unnamed reviewer for the *Philadelphia Evening Press* (October 31, 1885) wrote of Eakins, who showed *Portrait of J. Laurie Wallace* (c. 1885) and (probably) *The Veteran: Portrait of George Reynolds* (1885–86) at the annual Pennsylvania Academy exhibition: "He has manifestly a way of getting at the very psychology of his model through its external characteristics, which strikes me as almost uncanny. The portrait of Professor Wallace is remorseless in this respect. . . . [I]t is low in tone and a trifle moody in color, but the

'character' is all there. The sitter may have done his best; he has certainly been unable to circumvent Mr. Eakins' fatal penetration."

17. As the review quoted in the previous note continues: "If anyone fancies that he may look as he pleases, that his outward man does not really betray him, to preserve his illusions he must shun Mr. Eakins. [The portrait of Wallace] is extremely unlovely and gives to the whole canvas an air of what would be called indiscretion, if it did not justify itself by such extraordinary verity."

18. Note that James's therapeutic language implies that the "real wrongness in this world" is to be "squarely met and overcome" not so much by direct social or political action as by a privatized, apolitical "appeal to the soul's heroic resources" and "cleansed away" by personal, spiritual suffering.

19. This and the quotation in the following paragraph are from S. Weir Mitchell, *Wear and Tear, or Hints for the Overworked* (rev. 5th ed., Philadelphia: J. B. Lippincott, 1887; rpt., New York: Arno Press, 1973), 31–32. See Norma Lifton, "Thomas Eakins and S. Weir Mitchell: Images and Cures in the Late Nineteenth Century," in *Psychoanalytic Perspectives on American Art*, vol. 2, ed. Mary Mathews Gedo (Hillsdale, N.J.: Analytic Press, 1987), 247–74. See also Elizabeth Johns, *Thomas Eakins: The Heroism of Modern Life* (Princeton: Princeton University Press, 1983), 159–62, 167–68, and Lutz, *American Nervousness*, 280–83, 316–17, n. 6. For details on the rest cure itself, see Suzanne Poirier, "The Weir Mitchell Rest Cure: Doctors and Patients," *Women's Studies* 10 (1983): 15–40, and, for more general information about medicine and gender during this period, John S. Haller, Jr., and Robin Haller, *The Physician and Sexuality in Victorian America* (New York: Norton, 1974).

20. See Charlotte Perkins Gilman, "The Yellow Wallpaper" (1892) and "Why I Wrote 'The Yellow Wallpaper'" (1913), in *The Charlotte Perkins Gilman Reader*, ed. and intro. Ann J. Lane (New York: Pantheon, 1980), 3–20.

21. D. M. Bourneville and P. Regnard, *Iconographie photographique de la Salpêtrière*, 3 vols. (Paris: Delahaye, 1876–80). See Elaine Showalter, *The Female Malady: Women, Madness, and English Culture, 1830–1980* (New York: Penguin, 1987), 147–54, and George Frederick Drinka, *The Birth of Neurosis: Myth, Malady and The Victorians* (New York: Simon and Schuster, 1984), 74–84, 87–102. Joan Copjec, *"Flavit et Dissipati Sunt," October* 18 (Fall 1981): 21–40, provides a feminist Lacanian discussion of the Charcot photographs, understanding them to have participated in a conceptualization of hysteria as primarily and intrinsically a female disorder. Although men and women alike sat for Eakins's late portraits, a significantly greater number of the figures appearing melancholy or distressed are female.

22. Showalter, *Female Malady*, 86–96; *The Face of Madness: Hugh W. Diamond and the Origin of Psychiatric Photography*, ed. Sander L. Gilman (New York: Brunner/Mazel, 1976). Gilman's *Seeing the Insane* (New York: John Wiley, 1982) surveys a variety of representations of madness in Western art and culture. On Victorian conventions for showing *proper* melancholy in situations calling for grief, such as mourning rituals, see Karen Halttunen, *Confidence Men and Painted Ladies: A Study of Middle-Class Culture in America, 1830–1870* (New Haven: Yale University Press, 1982). The stoicism that Eakins's late portraits attribute to sitters who appear to be shouldering personal psychological suffering may have been his way of performing a masculine revision of the feminized, sentimentalized self-presentation of grief favored by Victorians during his childhood and early youth.

23. On Eakins's portrait of Tanner, see Martin A. Berger's entry on the painting in

Thomas Eakins, ed. Wilmerding, 150–53. On Tanner, see Albert Boime, "Henry Ossawa Tanner's Subversion of Genre," *Art Bulletin* 75:3 (Sept. 1993): 415–42, and Dewey Mosby, *Henry Ossawa Tanner* (Philadelphia: Philadelphia Museum of Art, 1991).

24. See Brian W. Dippie, "The Moving Finger Writes: Western Art and the Dynamics of Change," in Jules David Prown et al., *Discovered Lands, Invented Places: Transforming Visions of the American West* (New Haven: Yale University Press, 1992), 89–115, and Julie Schimmel, "Inventing 'the Indian,'" in *The West as America: Reinterpreting Images of the Frontier, 1820–1920,* ed. William H. Truettner (Washington, D.C.: Smithsonian Institution Press, 1991), 149–89; on *End of the Trail,* see 172–74.

25. On Cushing, see William H. Truettner, "Dressing the Part: Thomas Eakins's *Portrait of Frank Hamilton Cushing,*" *American Art Journal* 17 (Spring 1985): 49–72. As examples of popular magazine work by Curtis, see E. S. Curtis, "Vanishing Indian Types: The Tribes of the Southwest," *Scribner's Magazine* 39:5 (May 1906): 513–29, and idem., "Vanishing Indian Types: The Tribes of the Northwest Plains," *Scribner's Magazine* 39:6 (June 1906): 657–71.

26. Goodrich, *Thomas Eakins,* 1:76–79.

27. W. E. B. Du Bois, *The Philadelphia Negro: A Social Study* (1899; reprint with intro. by E. Digby Baltzell, New York: Schocken, 1967), Roger Lane, *Roots of Violence in Black Philadelphia, 1860–1900* (Cambridge: Harvard University Press, 1986), and idem., *William Dorsey's Philadelphia and Ours: On the Past and Future of the Black City in America* (New York: Oxford University Press, 1991), xii–xiii.

28. See Norman Mailer, "The White Negro" (1957) in *Advertisements for Myself* (New York: Putnam, 1959). Lippmann, *Drift and Mastery* (1914), intro and notes by William E. Leuchtenburg (Madison: University of Wisconsin Press, 1985), 118.

29. On the psychological suffering of William James and other well-bred male members of the New England upper classes, see George Cotkin, *William James, Public Philosopher* (Baltimore: Johns Hopkins University Press, 1990), chs. 1–5, and for James's female counterpart—his sister, Alice—see Jean Strouse, *Alice James* (Boston: Houghton Mifflin, 1980). Today the best-known fictional depictions of turn-of-the-century female *tedium vitae* include Kate Chopin, *The Awakening* (1899), and Gilman, "The Yellow Wallpaper." James uses the term *tedium vitae* in his essay "Vacations" (1873), in *Essays, Comments, and Reviews* (Cambridge: Harvard University Press, 1987), 3–4, quoted in Cotkin, *William James,* 74. See also Beard, *American Nervousness: Its Causes and Consequences* (1881; rpt., New York: Arno Press, 1972), Charles E. Rosenberg, "George M. Beard and American Nervousness," in *No Other Gods: On Science and American Social Thought* (Baltimore: Johns Hopkins University Press, 1978), 98–108, and all of Lutz, *American Nervousness.*

30. Roberta Pearson, *Eloquent Gestures: The Transformation of Performance Style in the Griffith Biograph Films* (Berkeley: University of California Press, 1992). Also on the transformation of film acting styles, see Charles Affron, *Star Acting: Gish, Garbo, Davis* (New York: Dutton, 1977), *Star Texts: Image and Performance in Film and Television,* ed. Jeremy G. Butler (Detroit: Wayne State University Press, 1991), and James Naremore, *Acting in the Cinema* (Berkeley: University of California Press, 1988).

31. Brooks, *The Wine of the Puritans* (1908); and idem., "On Creating a Usable Past," *The Dial* 64 (Apr. 11, 1918): 337–41. See *Van Wyck Brooks: The Early Years, A Selection from His Works, 1908–1921,* ed. and intro. Claire Sprague (rev. ed., Boston: Northeastern University Press, 1993).

32. Henri, *The Art Spirit*, notes, articles, and fragments of letters and talks to students compiled by Margery A. Ryerson (1923; rpt., Philadelphia: Lippincott, 1960), 91, 79, 115–17, 165, 88.

33. Gilbert Sunderland Parker, "Thomas Eakins, Realist," in *Memorial Exhibition of the Works of the Late Thomas Eakins* (Philadelphia: Pennsylvania Academy of the Fine Arts, 1917), 10. See also Frank Jewett Mather (1931) quoted in Spassky et al., *American Paintings*, 624: "No portrait painter of his age, whether in America or Europe, has left a more various and speaking gallery of thinking and feeling fellow mortals." In the same passage Mather points out that Eakins's contemporaries were unable to appreciate the psychological characteristics of his portraits because "In a generation that sorely overvalued brilliant handling, Eakins simply offered nothing that could be talked about, and was naturally neglected. Today, I trust, we are more interested in what is expressed than in the rhetoric of expression, and Eakins is coming into his own." Bourne, "The Puritan's Will to Power," can be found in *Randolph Bourne—The Radical Will: Selected Writings, 1911–1918,* ed. Olaf Hansen (rpt., Berkeley: University of California Press, 1992), 301–06.

34. McBride, "Modern Art," *The Dial* (Feb. 1922): 221.

35. Mumford, *Herman Melville* (New York: Harcourt, Brace, 1929), 361. For a critical account of the "positive thinking" tradition to which the "tragic sense of life" intellectuals were opposed, see Donald Meyer, *The Positive Thinkers: Religion as Pop Psychology from Mary Baker Eddy to Oral Roberts* (rev. ed.; New York: Pantheon, 1980).

36. Francis Henry Taylor, "Thomas Eakins—Positivist," *Parnassus* 2 (Mar. 1930).

37. Goodrich, *Thomas Eakins* (1933), 114.

38. Schendler, *Eakins* (Boston: Little, Brown, 1967), 134; Wilmerding, "Thomas Eakins' Late Portraits," *Arts* 53:9 (May 1979): 108.

39. Goodrich, *Thomas Eakins* (1982), Johns, *Thomas Eakins,* Lubin, *Act of Portrayal: Eakins, Sargent, James* (New Haven: Yale University Press, 1985), Fried, *Writing, Realism, Disfiguration: On Thomas Eakins and Stephen Crane* (Chicago: University of Chicago Press, 1987), and Johns, "An Avowal of Artistic Community: Nudity and Fantasy in Thomas Eakins's Photographs," in *Eakins and the Photograph: Works by Thomas Eakins and His Circle in the Collection of the Pennsylvania Academy of Fine Arts,* ed. Susan Danly and Cheryl Leibold (Washington, D.C.: Smithsonian Institution Press, 1994): 65–93. For brief surveys of changing attitudes toward Eakins's art, see "The Critical Reception of Thomas Eakins's Work, I: Lifetime," by Amy Werbel, and "II: Posthumous," by Jennifer Hardin, in *Thomas Eakins,* ed. Wilmerding, 192–94, 195–98.

CHAPTER SEVEN

Glamorizing the Psychological: The Politics of the Performances of Modern Psychological Identities

JOEL PFISTER

When did it become chic to be "neurotic"—or, more broadly, to survey and present oneself as "psychological"—and how and why did this happen? Probably by the 1910s and surely by the 1920s we can properly speak of the growing popularity and even the cachet of "psychological" identities partly produced by and made available through mass and high culture (psychological and pop psychological books, articles, and advertisements, therapy, literature, theater, films, art). One of my aims here is to explore what is at stake in the cultural fabrication and acceptance of the term *psychological identities,* but for now I shall define this as an identity conferred upon one who recognizes and refers to himself or herself as determined by, or sometimes beset by, distinct "psychological" processes, patterns, and problems. This mass-cultural and high-cultural "psychological" spin on the formation of subjectivities was in certain respects something new in American culture, a hallmark of the "modern." Its multifaceted social implications merit pondering, not least of all because many Americans today—inundated with "psychological," self-help, and recovery movement conceptions of the self—live out versions of these "psychological" identities.

I do not mean to imply that prior to the early decades of this century Americans never imagined themselves as psychological. Elsewhere I have argued that antebellum writing by Nathaniel Hawthorne, Edgar Allan Poe, Herman Melville, female authors of sentimental fiction, advice-book writers, and literary reviewers can be read as a nascent pop psychology that is engaged in making—and sometimes in dismantling—assumptions about middle-class selfhood. The emerging middle class was then experiencing and advancing

what Philippe Ariès termed the "emotional revolution"—involving the sentimentalization of the family and the gradual privatization of an "obsessive love"—
that accompanied the Industrial Revolution.[1] Some fiction by Hawthorne and his
contemporaries is hyperpsychological and takes for its subject what we would
now term obsession, ambivalence, incestuous desire, projection, denial, and
repression—in a word, psychological "depth"—often in the context of over-
heated marital or familial relations. In opposition to much criticism, I argued
against the psychoanalysis-inspired premise that Hawthorne and his contemporaries foreshadowed Sigmund Freud and were homegrown geniuses who boldly
peered into the darkest recesses of eternal "human nature." Instead I proposed
that this complex literature of the "emotional revolution," understood historically,
made Freud's own psychoanalytic imaginings of the self and of the family predictable in the sense that these fictions were, decades earlier, encoding and narrating—that is, helping to remake—the self and the family as fundamentally
"psychological." Freud doesn't "explain" Hawthorne; nineteenth-century middle-
class fiction like Hawthorne's, situated historically, helps to "explain" Freud.[2]

Notwithstanding the fertile flowering of nineteenth-century psychological
fiction, psychological models of the self tied to explicitly psychological language
would not become commonsensical for members of the urban white middle
class until the 1910s and 1920s. The field of psychology, particularly through
writings by William James, gained popularity only in the late nineteenth century. By the 1920s and 1930s, however, we find a full-fledged pop psychological essence-and-identity industry. The mind boggles when speculating how
Hawthorne, Poe, or Melville might have responded to Dr. Louis Bisch's *Be Glad
You're Neurotic* (1936), in which Bisch enjoins us to "submit to being called neurotic" because "all the greatest things we know have come to us from neu-
rotics."[3] Such sales pitches to imagine oneself in distinctively "psychological"
terms are based on the marketing knowledge that "psychological" identities
can now be hawked profitably as commodities.

In Hawthorne's era psychiatry was associated mainly with the custodial
treatment of the "insane" in asylums, and that brought patients a stigma
which decades later carried over to asylum physicians.[4] By the late nineteenth
and early twentieth centuries, the jurisdiction of psychology expanded to include the treatment of nervousness (neurasthenia), neurosis, and malaise. In
this key transitional era, psychiatrists more frequently established private practices and became affiliated with hospitals rather than asylums. This professional route, first established by prestigious neurologists, was usually more
lucrative and elite.[5] By the 1910s psychiatrists tended to jettison the category of
"insanity" for terms like mental illness, mental health, and mental hygiene.
During the 1910s and 1920s we see a movement to what historians often call
"therapy for the normal." The psychiatric treatment of soldiers who suffered shell

shock in World War I gave cultural legitimation and value to the notion of therapy as a process of psychic repair because, as Richard Fox explains, the war
"revealed that not only 'normal' but also 'heroic' individuals might be unexpectedly affected for a time." Increasingly popular concepts of mental health and
hygiene, observes Joel Kovel, also had the effect of reinventing the "mental" not
simply as an aspect of self but as a somewhat autonomous "existent thing" (analyzed by "experts"). Therapeutic counseling in Hawthorne's day, to the extent
that it existed, might have entailed a visit to a minister whose primary concern
would probably have been the salvation of his parishioner's "soul"—not his
parishioner's mental hygiene or malaise or stunted capacity for emotional
growth.[6] With this crucial shift in terminology, cultural authority, and jurisdiction—from caring for the insane to "therapizing" anyone (who could afford it)—
psychology expanded its cultural visibility and consumer base and instituted
itself as a scientific response to "needs" which it persuaded patients were "inner."

In this chapter I shall offer perspectives on how and why "the psychological" turned into a value, an identity, and a performance of the self during the
1910s and 1920s. Because this is a complex historical issue I shall limit my contribution here: in the first section I shall analyze the early glamorizing of "the
psychological" as an identity and a performance; in the following three sections
I shall examine some of the implications of the "psychological" re-signification
of the "inner" self as primitive (a source of subjective potency);[7] in the penul-
timate section I shall review the provocative work of two women who challenged notions of the "psychological" self by focusing on the cultural making
of categories of interiority; and in the coda I shall argue that the glamorizing of
"the psychological" makes sense as part of a larger cultural project to reinvigo-
rate discourses of "the individual."

When referring to the transformation of psychological discourse during
these two decades I have put "the psychological" in quotation marks for much
the same reason that Michel Foucault put "sexuality" in quotation marks when
referring to the reinvention of sex as "sexuality" (the nineteenth-century bourgeoisie's newly minted "truth" of the self).[8] During the 1910s and 1920s "the psychological" became a popular "truth" discourse freighted with meanings, values,
significances, and practices that were only beginning to develop in the mid-
ninctccnth century. Because many Americans see themselves as "psychological,"
it is vital to defamiliarize this term, and the quotation marks help in this regard.

Announcing, Glamorizing, and Performing
"the Psychological"

During the eighteenth and nineteenth centuries *glamour*—a Scottish cor-
ruption of *grammar*—was defined as an enchantment or charm that one cast

on others, like a magical net. During the Depression, glamour assumed sparkling new life in America as a verb. It was now understood that the media had the power to *glamorize* persons, frequently movie stars. The photography spreads, interviews, and gossip columns in Hollywood magazines might glamorize a star by artfully enhancing his or her sex appeal or "individual" mystique. To glamorize is to confer status by making someone or something seem fascinating (for example, movies are capable of glamorizing mass murderers and millionaires).[9] But glossy magazines like *Vanity Fair* (1913–1936) had specialized in glamorizing the lifestyles of the rich years before the word *glamorizing* became popular.

Numerous writers helped glamorize psychoanalysis during the 1910s and 1920s. They enticed readers by suggesting that the consumption of psychoanalysis would enrich one's subjective potency—one's "psychological" capital. Word spread through bohemia and beyond.[10] In his memoirs, Joseph Freeman, an editor of *The New Masses*, recalled his stint as a young, romantic, Ivy League bohemian intellectual in the early 1920s. Like others in this group he was enchanted with the language of psychoanalysis and the revelatory powers ascribed to it. However, he came to realize that the social interchange of psychoanalytic categories and narratives could operate as a script that *generated* public and private performances of ostensibly subtextual "psychological" selves: "We began to have alarming dreams, or perhaps, as the Freudians might say, we stopped repressing our dreams and became conscious of them. We talked all day long; we analyzed each other's dreams, fantasies and slips of the tongue. . . . New fears developed. . . . We suffered from various 'complexes.' We concluded in turn that we were extroverts, introverts, schizophrenics, paranoiacs and victims of dementia praecox."[11] Learning their lines they partly became their lines and so rehearsed the Freudian self into prominent everyday reality.

Freeman's youthful fascination is mixed with a degree of skepticism that recognizes the "psychological" reading of others as an exercise of power. The sense that psychologization can be a performance of cultural power is even more evident, perhaps unintentionally so, in A. A. Brill's somewhat similar reminiscence of his early training in symptom detection with Freud—a training in reading (encoding) the self and others that had begun to run amok within the avid cadre of Freud's disciples: "We had to keep ourselves well in hand, ever ready and alert, for there was no telling when and where there would be an attack." The statements of Freeman and Brill support Fredric Jameson's historical perception that "the Freudian typology of the mental functions may be seen as the return of a new type of allegorical vision."[12] I would emend this only by observing that the Freudian typology led to some culturally revealing *performances* of psycho-allegorical vision.

If Freeman views psychoanalysis as a discourse that conferred intellectual as well as "psychological" éclat on himself and his confrères, Floyd Dell, a socialist editor of *The Masses,* seemed explicitly to promote psychoanalytic language as a script for new everyday rituals of middle- and upper-class social interaction and identification. In "Speaking of Psycho-Analysis: The New Boon for Dinner Table Conversationalists" (1915)—published, appropriately, not in *The Masses* but in *Vanity Fair*—Dell at times appears to be writing a fashion advertisement for a cocktail-party psychoanalysis that will attire one in "the most charmingly recondite technical vocabulary ever invented." Its glamour resides in the scientific permission it gives one to be deliciously naughty and indulgently transgressive. Psychoanalytic conversationalists can engage in "new extremes of frankness in regard to [themselves]" and project "an air of pedantic importance."[13] Yet Dell's ad copy possesses a self-mocking quality ("pedantic importance") and hints more critically that "new extremes of frankness" are being dramatized for class-specific reasons. Dinner-table confession is framed, not as a display of character flaws or unseemly self-absorption, but as a recital of class sexiness, boldness, and elitism. Dell intimates that psychoanalysis is being used by members of the middle and upper classes to stage a "psychological" self and a therapeutic hierarchy of concerns especially formulated to nourish and insulate their sense of self-significance.

In the same year, Max Eastman, Dell's socialist co-editor of *The Masses,* published two articles in *Everybody's Magazine* that popularized psychoanalysis. In these curious pieces Eastman, like Dell, seems to endow psychoanalysis with an aura—associated with wealth, glamour, and hidden mystery—that should naturally fascinate "everybody" as a "deep" comprehension of the self. Yet Eastman, like Dell, sometimes implies that psychoanalysis is being fashioned by the rich to license a self-serving (class-serving) performance of "self": "[Psychoanalysis] is becoming so popular a form of treatment with those who can afford to make a business of being sick that they are paying from two to five hundred dollars a month to have their souls analyzed."[14]

A year after Dell's and Eastman's somewhat double-edged advertisements for psychoanalysis appeared, Aleister Crowley, in *Vanity Fair,* portrayed psychoanalysis as the inspiration for a high-society jabber that delighted in making the revelation of well-labeled "psychological" debilities seem enthralling and potent: "Just ask your pretty neighbor at dinner to-night whether she has introverted her Electra complex, because it will surely become one of the favorite conversational gambits of the coming season." Also noteworthy is Crowley's example of a woman eager to tell all. In various popularizations of psychoanalysis, women who styled themselves as neurotic and in need of therapy were regarded as charming and sexy. Thus Rachel Crother's popular play *Expressing Willie* (1924) features an ardent convert who seems to discover on her therapist's couch what 900-number callers today purchase in "phone sex": My

7.1. Actress Lynn Fontanne from *The Sketch Book* (c. April 1928), with the caption "Bright Star of the Theatre Guild: Lynn Fontanne, whose acting genius makes an absorbing study of Nina, the neurotic heroine of Eugene O'Neill's more than full length play, 'Strange Interlude.'" Yale Collection of American Literature Photographs, Beinecke Rare Book and Manuscript Library, Yale University.

analyst, she gushed, "probed the very depths of my being and *oh* the things we brought up out of my subconscious."[15]

Women—long signified by American culture as bearers of fashion—were deployed during the 1920s to help make psychoanalysis and the class identity and self-preoccupation it represented as "inner" seem chic. The Theatre Guild's celebrated Lynn Fontanne, who starred as the sexy, savage, and neurotic Nina Leeds in Eugene O'Neill's pop psychological smash hit *Strange Interlude* (1928), appeared in seemingly countless newspaper and magazine photos adorned in evening gowns and was sometimes explicitly billed as "neurotic" (fig. 7.1). Such photo spreads of neurotic femininity enthroned helped make a modern

7.2. Actress Judith Anderson, Angelus Lipstick advertisement, *New York Daily News,* **October 21, 1928. Yale Collection of American Literature Photographs, Beinecke Rare Book and Manuscript Library, Yale University.**

"psychological" brand of femininity seem alluring and sophisticated. By the time Judith Anderson took over Fontanne's part, the "neurotic" glamour of O'Neill's heroine had been so thoroughly publicized as romantically beguiling that Anderson was hired to appear in cosmetics advertisements (made more enchanting with the *couleur* of French copy), which of course made reference to her *Strange Interlude* stardom (fig. 7.2).[16]

O'Neill himself had amassed great quantities of the "psychological" currency that these actresses staged, advertised, and made enviable. Karl Menninger, the eminent psychoanalyst, estimated in 1938 that O'Neill had exposed more Americans to psychoanalytic notions "than all the scientific books put together."[17] As his dramas became more pop psychological during the 1920s, O'Neill identified his writing as "deep" (a key word also used by enthusiastic reviewers of his plays). Carl Van Vechten's intriguing 1933 photograph of O'Neill (fig. 7.3) was no doubt meant to evoke this much-rewarded quality of "depth." Van Vechten photographed O'Neill draped in black against a black backdrop to create the illusion—almost the apparition—of a floating head. This moody, cerebral effect is intensified by O'Neill's eyes—which are closed, turned inward no doubt, a sign of his "inner" vision. Van Vechten uses shadows to place the right half of O'Neill's face in darkness, thus associating the playwright's "psychological" and aesthetic "depth" with a romantic doubleness of character—and perhaps also with a romantic racial doubleness.

But a careful inspection of the photograph reveals its conventionality, its semiotics of "depth." The image is theatrical: O'Neill is willingly posing and performing "depth." His "makeup" might be likened to the "psychological" dividedness of Robert Louis Stevenson's Dr. Jekyll and Mr. Hyde (the not quite hidden half of the dramatist's face), but with a crucial difference. In Stevenson's novel of 1886, Dr. Jekyll-as-Hyde is described as "ugly," "ape-like," "savage," "primitive," as "the brute that slept within me." Several of these terms were used in the rhetoric of pop psychological "depth" (see below), but by 1933 they have been transfigured and revalued: the two-faced O'Neill-in-the-shadows has sex appeal, mystery, sophistication, class, *glamour*.[18]

The social, economic, and political causes of this middle- and upper-class pursuit of "depth" are complex, as I have endeavored to show in my recent work. America was entering a phase of advanced corporate or monopoly capitalism during the 1920s, and, as Jackson Lears and other historians have noted, confidence in the nineteenth-century ideology of self-making had eroded with the advent of corporate hierarchies.[19] Discourses of "depth"—packaged in various forms by O'Neill's plays, Sherwood Anderson's fiction, pop psychologists, therapists, and others—provided a class of white-collar professionals and managers with a compensatory belief in and often sexy fascination with its own "psychological" significance and individualism, a "depth" that corporate authority seemingly could not standardize, control, or own. Such discourses gave weight to the premise that there exists a deeper, truer, precultural self that is more essential than the social self.

If we aim to grasp the dimensions and implications of modern ideologies of subjectivity, I would contend that it is important to add this category of "depth" to the two key categories—"character" and "personality"—proposed by Warren Susman. Susman has studied the shift from the nineteenth century's producer and entrepreneurial culture of "character" (a molding of self that values morality, self-denial, self-sacrifice, the work ethic, respectability) to a modern consumer and corporate culture of "personality" (a design of self that promotes self-gratification, sex appeal, consumption, popularity). Although there is bountiful evidence that modern professionals and managers cultivated "personality" in order to succeed, there is also evidence that they were often keen to buy (and buy into) therapeutic discourses of "depth." Indeed, these

7.3. Playwright Eugene O'Neill in 1933, photographed by Carl Van Vechten. Yale Collection of American Literature Photographs, Beinecke Rare Book and Manuscript Library, Yale University. Reprinted with the permission of the Estate of Carl Van Vechten, Joseph Solomon, Executor.

genres often merged, as in Bisch's *Be Glad You're Neurotic,* which advised readers on how to "Turn Your Handicaps into Assets" and "Profit by Your Neurosis."[20]

I have traced the idea of "depth," as a psychological and aesthetic value, back to the 1840s and 1850s (Hawthorne's fiction, for instance, was praised as "an awful probing into the most forbidden regions of consciousness") and have argued that "character" does not wholly account for the ways in which the middle class was producing (and heating up) subjectivities.[21] But this antebellum version of "depth" was not yet assigned the scientific aura of "psychological" significance or the glow of transgressive glamour that is apparent in the reception of O'Neill's plays during the 1920s and early 1930s. The elaborate twentieth-century construction of "depth" had acquired some of the magnetism and charm of "personality" (as can be seen in Van Vechten's photo of O'Neill). In O'Neill's era, not yet in Hawthorne's, "depth" was fast becoming a commonsense category that supported the ideological proliferation of "psychological" *identities.*[22]

Unenchanted with these developments in 1926, Charlotte Perkins Gilman, a renowned socialist and feminist, deglamorized psychoanalytic therapy as a porcine preoccupation of former radicals who had become more prosperous: they are, she charged, "wallow[ing] in Freudian Psycho-analysis, which has the combined advantages of wide popular appeal in its subject matter, an imposing technology, and profitable use as a business."[23] Gilman's impression that psychoanalysis displaced bohemian and middle- and upper-class interest in socialism by the 1920s has some validity. During the 1910s psychoanalysis was often coupled with socialism, the birth control movement, and other radical causes, as the trendy writings of Dell and Eastman in *The Masses* and *The Liberator* make clear. But World War I, the Russian Revolution of 1917, various internal party disputes, and the relative prosperity of the twenties factionalized socialists. By the 1920s a divide was often in place between movements of "personal" and "political" emancipation. As Eli Zaretsky summarizes it, currents of personal radicalism fundamental to socialists and other leftists during the 1910s were increasingly dismissed by Communists (concerned mainly with economic and state issues) as "petty bourgeois" or "romantic." In turn, various ideologies of personal life spurned a Communism whose revolutionary interests neglected their notions of "liberation."[24]

Yet Susan Glaspell and George Cram Cook's play *Suppressed Desires* (1915) hinted provocatively that psychoanalysis had even in the early years of its American debut become attractive for the more bohemian members of the middle and upper class precisely because it offered them a conveniently narrow sexualized and individualized style of "radicalism" that filled up their mental space (and social space) with sexy anxieties about repression and taboos. Michel Foucault has made the case that psychoanalysis proved ideologically useful to the European bourgeoisie because it enabled them to link "truth" (Foucault does not believe in truth, only in suspicious games of truth) to "the challenging of taboos."[25] Glaspell and Cook's Provincetown Players' satire may well have piqued Foucault's historical curiosity, had he been aware of it, because it suggests that the new psychoanalytic encoding of the self, rather than unveiling a taboo-breaking "truth," authorized class-specific performances of "depth" in a game of "truth." Henrietta, the play's Greenwich Village acolyte of psychoanalysis, exhorts Steve, her amused and skeptical husband, and Mabel, her befuddled sister, to employ terms like "subconscious mind," "complex," and "inhibited." Glaspell and Cook (as did Joseph Freeman in his reminiscences of the 1920s) spotlight how psychoanalytic language can help script a psychologically determined self as fashionably "radical": "The forbidden impulse is there full of energy," Henrietta lectures Steve and Mabel. "It breaks into your consciousness in disguise, masks itself in dreams, makes all sorts of trouble." Henrietta attempts to give them a "psychological" identity that will serve as an announcement of individuality and of a stylishly "radical" class status. According to this class reinscription of common sense, you now qualify as a "sinner"—as Freeman put it—if "you suffer from suppressed desires."[26] By implication, salvation means being unsuppressed.

From the outset, Steve, an architect, tolerates his wife's Liberal Club enthusiasm for "Freud the New Messiah" as an inexplicable yet temporary game. When Steve accedes to Henrietta's entreaties and finally visits her analyst, only to report that the therapist recommended that they get divorced (based on a silly reading of Steve's dreams), Henrietta decides abruptly that psychoanalysis constitutes an interior decorating that they—in their flat overlooking Washington Square—can live without. But what the play leaves undeveloped is why Henrietta was drawn to psychoanalysis in the first place. One clue may be that she seems to be unemployed—the wife of a professional. What is certain is that the idea of a "depth" whose "truth" is disguised by repression enthralls her; Henrietta's "psyching" (rewriting) of others clearly empowers her and makes her feel fashionably radical (she loves to "wear 'radical' clothes").[27] *Suppressed Desires* barely intimates that there was an unarticulated imbalance of power, respect, or prestige built into Henrietta's marriage that motivated her to adopt psychoanalysis in order to assert her intellectual and social worth to herself, to her husband, and to others.

This unarticulated gender factor is somewhat more evident in the case of Mabel Dodge, the wealthy patron of the arts in Greenwich Village and Provincetown, who, like Henrietta, sought meaningfulness and fun in psychoanalysis during the 1910s. Between August 1917 and February 1918 Dodge wrote a column for the Hearst newspapers in which she popularized psychoanalysis with all the histrionic zeal and playfulness one finds in writings by

Dell, Eastman, and Bisch.[28] She aimed to enchant readers of all classes with the lure of a psychoanalytic "depth" that held within it truer truths about the self than did everyday "surface" behavior. "All that we will ever know we will . . . find buried deep within ourselves, below the surface of our unconscious." Like Joseph Freeman and Glaspell and Cook's heroine, Dodge was dazzled by a novel language that reconfigured "a world where things fitted into a set of definitions and terms I had never dreamt of."[29] Dodge pictured the shadowy unconscious, not as a nether region harboring unsightly pleasure-seeking Mr. Hydes, but more sentimentally as a submerged sleeping self (almost a Sleeping Beauty) who dreams of arousal by the intrepid (male) psychoanalyst: awaiting "the magical awakening touch of the scientist, that patient deep sea diver who in our day is bringing so much to our eyes. The Unconscious is the true fairy-land." In her memoirs she recalls how thoroughly she enjoyed "tattling" on her lover (whom she finally hauled into analysis). Psychoanalysis is self-seductive play: "It became an absorbing game to play with oneself, reading one's motives, and trying to understand the symbols by which the soul expressed itself."[30]

The therapy that equipped Dodge with a new, exquisitely transgressive subtextual sense of individual importance and with a name game she could play with herself and others (all of which she valued), gradually took on the aspect of a disagreeable contest between the sexes. Dodge's eminent analysts during the 1910s were, first, Dr. Smith Ely Jelliffe, and, later, Dr. A. A. Brill.[31] In both cases the performances of analyst and analysand became too rehearsed; their interactional scripts became too rigid and stale; the game became too much of a labor for Dodge. Thus Dodge's memoirs turn the tables on her patriarchal "deep divers," her prickly Pygmalions (no longer Prince Charmings), who are sketched condescendingly as childish, spoiled, needy players who, lacking her finesse, take the game much too seriously. "Unless one fits oneself into their systems so they can pigeon-hole one into a type or case, they grow puzzled or angry or sad."[32] The language, the psychic strip-tease sexiness, and the self-monitoring lost their fairy-tale glitter. Brill, whom she claims ordered her to dream, "became arbitrary and dogmatic. Anything 'religious' was anathema to him. He consistently tried to remove every vestige of my belief in an inner power, and when I haltingly endeavored to convince him of something that counseled me and impelled me from my depths, he said scathing things about a Jehovah complex! It was only later that I realized I should have referred to God and Nature as 'the Unconscious'—and then they would have gotten by!" And so her assessment of psychoanalysis shifted; she originally exalted it as a revelation and a game of "truth" but by the 1930s deglamorized it as a (patriarchal) power relation and a business set up to profit from the sale of "psychological" identities and vocabulary: "When I think of the time I spent assuaging analysts at twenty dollars an hour!"[33]

To focus on the glamorizing of the "psychological"—obvious in Dodge's account—is not to deny that some patients were helped by psychoanalysts (to cite just one famous case, O'Neill's brief analysis with Dr. G. V. Hamilton in 1926 helped cure him of his alcoholism). Psychoanalysis, other therapies, and pop psychology grew more popular along with the real strains on workers and families in corporate America (the divorce rate rose to one-sixth of all marriages during the 1920s, with higher rates in some urban areas). "Modern psychology, and psychoanalysis in particular," Kovel argues, "was born in that moment when men realized that they had lost control over their social existence; and having been so engendered, it both kept them further from this realization and played into their control and estrangement."[34] The historical point I have been emphasizing is that by the 1910s and 1920s "psychological" disturbances had for increasing numbers of people become more than emotional troubles; these troubles or anxieties, their representation in "psychological" language and narratives, and their treatment in therapy were now constitutive of a new ideology of self—the middle- and upper-class performance of a "psychological" identity.

Sentiment and the "Psychological" Resignification of Female Desire

It makes sense that Brill and Dodge would clash over her apostasy—her disobedient tendency to define her "inner" self in nineteenth-century sentimental and spiritual terms. His role was to demonstrate that these older sentimental and spiritual scripts of emotions and inner power were outmoded and shallow, and that she should narrate herself scientifically as a "psychological" subject. The nomenclature of "depth" through which psychoanalysts wanted clients to see and to experience themselves also ascribed to them rather dramatic inner forces, but in different terms. "There are levels, true all of them, and . . . truest at the lowest, or perhaps most primitive," wrote Dodge. "Jelliffe had taught me to use that word: primitive."[35] This is a key word, as I shall make clear.

In some of her mid-1910s popularizations of psychoanalysis Dodge, like so many psychoanalysts and pop psychologists of this era, stripped women of sentiment and spirituality in order to posit a "psychological" subtext—not just of pathology, but of power. The clinging mother "must not keep [her son] by her," Dodge admonished, or "she will turn into the terrible destroying mother in spite of all her love." Feminine love, now seen as "psychological," is a force to be reckoned with. Sentimentality can be a stranglehold, one that mothers exercise because their opportunities to wield power in other spheres of social life have been constricted. "In a good many cases, a perfect mother makes a detestable wife," asserted pop psychoanalyst André Tridon in *Psychoanalysis and*

Love (1922). "Unable to dominate her husband she craves children whom she can dominate with a minimum of bodily strength and mental effort, and she devotes all her time and care to them."[36] Psychoanalysis and pop psychology attributed to sentimental "angels" in the house underground emotional and sexual power, the capacity to be angry, and the will to dominate—powers typically disguised in the more sanitized and limited emotional repertoire of female sentimental discourse.[37] Notwithstanding its monitory tone, the new psychoanalytic common sense sent an intriguing *antisentimental* invitation to women: learn the subterranean dimensions of your own "psychological" strength.

For some feminists the idea of a psychologically determined woman was much more exciting and empowering than the "repressed," ostensibly normal nineteenth-century model of the feminine angel, whose power was usually contingent on her morality, purity, self-control, and ability to inspire self-control and action in men. In *Margaret Fuller: A Psychological Biography* (1920), Katharine Anthony, one of America's first psychobiographers, reimagined Fuller, the antebellum women's rights advocate, in "psychological" terms and narratives in order to recast 1920s feminists as "psychological" subjects and postsuffrage feminism as a "psychological" project: "[Fuller] wanted elbow room and scope,—claiming her emotional rights with the same conviction as her economic and political rights." As her case study develops, Anthony seems to locate Fuller's feminist significance more in her "stronger passions" (for her father, for other women), her "neurotic disposition," and her "painful repressions" ("secret recesses") than in her political writings and reform activities. Anthony implies, in the most positive terms, that to be a feminist probably means that—like Fuller—one is neurotic and conflicted because of one's indomitable sexual drives. The neurotic woman, exemplified by Fuller, is romanticized as the exceptional, supremely individual woman of "depth." The female assertion of passion is read as inherently political, the wellspring of a "broader kind of feminism" that can develop "now that suffrage is out of the way."[38] To modify Foucault's observation about the bourgeoisie's invention of psychoanalysis: now feminist "truth" has become endlessly fascinating to itself as "the challenging of taboos."

In creating this "psychological" portrait, Anthony expurgated many of Fuller's sentimental views of herself and of others which were inextricably woven into her published and unpublished writings about gender and reform. Anthony's effort to reclaim Fuller as "psychological" is an understandable sign of the times. The birth control movement of the 1910s had spurred women to reevaluate the role and significance of passion, of sentiment, and of a more varied range of emotions in their lives, and Anthony, like Dodge and so many other writers of the period, was captivated by the proposition that the "psychological" self had certain types of hidden levels. For this "psychological" subtextu-alization of self suggested that all along women had, if not consciously then unconsciously, rebelled against the emotional confinement of a sentimental socialization that could now be reappraised as the product of "puritanical" cul-ture. Thus Phyllis Blanchard and Carlyn Manasses's *New Girls for Old* (1930) blasted the double standard and identified "earlier works of fiction" as having disseminated "over-sentimentalized picture[s]" that "evaded" women's sexual and psychological "realities." Prince Charming became just one of the crowd: "Relationships are matters of sex attraction, propinquity and other prosaic fac-tors, and not the result of a pre-destined coming together of two individuals who could not possibly have found happiness with any one else."[39] And so the (hetero)sexualization of female emotions was increasingly hailed as a value, a source of identity, and an antidote to their sentimentalization.

Yet to view the sentimentalization and the sexualization of female desire as strictly opposite ideological developments is to overlook their close historical ties, a complex relationship whose history I can do little more than allude to here.[40] As Zaretsky points out, during the Industrial Revolution the decline of middle-class women's productive labor in the home gave rise to their emotional labor in such areas as childrearing and therapeutic spouse support—all ele-ments of what Ariès calls the "emotional revolution." Women were instructed to become what Arlie Hochschild calls "feeling individual[s]" whose domestic expertise was as "managers" of feeling.[41] Historians have documented how sentimental discourses helped privatize emotions and establish "home" more as an emotional than an economic site (the "hothouse family" John Demos sketches in "Oedipus and America" [chapter 3]). Not only were women encour-aged to forge their sense of identity in connection with their emotional labors, but also the sentimental feelings it was their job to cultivate and to manage helped to make domestic emotions all the more fascinating as the "real" core of the self. This sentimental "hothouse" significance gave the family an aura of meaningfulness as the psychological bedrock of the self. To the degree that sen-timental discourse stressed self-control (that the "angel" in the house had to inspire) and that this control focused on sex (as it often did in the 1830s and after), it participated in making sex seem like a hidden "inner" force that required domestication.[42]

The genesis of "the psychological," then, is indebted to sentimental dis-courses that assigned women emotional identities, that represented the emo-tions within the family as more determinative, truer, and more significant than behavior in the marketplace, and that envisioned sexuality as a transgressive "expression" of a "secret" self beneath the social self. "Psychological" dis-courses gave to the family and the sexuality, both of which sentimental dis-courses had already manufactured as engrossing, an unfathomed subtextual meaningfulness and dimensionality that could be read as disturbing, yet also as intriguing, and that could be interpreted as a source of conflict, yet also as the basis of individuality. If sentiment translated female pain and discontentment into a suffer-and-be-still gender value (the moral transcendence of feminine angels who won their wings through emotional caretaking and self-sacrifice), "psychological" discourse gave female emotional pain and discontentment a somewhat different cultural value—it became a sign of one's "complex" "psychological" specificity and individuality.[43] Historically, "psychological" identity is as much a hothouse offspring of the nineteenth-century sentimentalization of middle-class identity as it is—in its more modern manifestations—a corporate and consumer era break with this class sentimentalization.

That increasing numbers of modern middle- and upper-class women were defining their desire and identity in "psychological" terms seems clear. But in the early twentieth century, sentimental discourse was still the major force in women's popular culture. The historian Nathan Hale has noted that several articles on psychoanalysis appeared in *Good Housekeeping* and *Ladies' Home Journal* as early as the mid-1910s. However, my perusal of issues of these two magazines from the 1910s and 1920s, as well as of *Women's Home Companion,* uncovered relatively few articles on psychoanalysis. *Good Housekeeping* includes articles on female emotions such as "Overlove and Its Consequences" (1928). *Women's Home Companion* features articles like Dr. G. V. Hamilton and Kenneth Macgowan's "How I Would Make My Husband Over" (1928). I would guess that readers got hooked on the cultural authority of pop psychology mainly through articles on childrearing and mothering. Modern moms were encouraged to go beyond sentimental advice to acquire the vocabulary and "insights" of the psychologist. Yet overall, female emotions were still represented and marketed in the terms, narratives, and values established by sentimental discourse.[44]

Restyling the Primitive as Sexy, Adventurous, and "Psychological"

Bearing these important historical connections and caveats in mind, it must nevertheless be emphasized that sexuality, especially female sexuality, did indeed undergo a dramatic revaluing as a source of identity, meaningfulness, and empowerment in the increasingly "psychological" culture of the 1910s and 1920s. During the antebellum period female sexuality, menstruation, and pregnancy could be represented as destabilizing biological forces that could unleash desire or violence in "angels"—who would then be classified as "out of order." Two medical texts from this era recount the tale of a "pregnant wife who killed her husband and ate him." Clitoridectomies and ovariotomies were introduced to prevent women from being tempted by such appetitive "disorders." Anita

Levy's observation about the turn-of-the-century British representation of the middle-class sexual woman as potentially "savage" also holds for the United States: "To be female is to contain within the self uncivilized or degenerate desires perpetually in need of control, lest they deprive one of femaleness."[45] But by the 1920s female "libido" had become the subject of detailed case studies that demonstrated that women had engaged in and could enjoy premarital sex, extramarital sex, childhood and adult masturbation, homosexuality, bisexuality, oral sex, anal sex, clitoral stimulation, (extremely) frequent sex, and intercourse during menstruation. Beatrice Hinkle, a feminist psychoanalyst, applauded as liberatory the New Woman's insistence on experimenting with "forbidden experiences." Radical pop psychologists such as Samuel Schmalhausen sounded the battle cry "orgasms for women" (in 1929) and read female sexual activities as "a re-discovery of herself."[46] Pop psychologists did not always concur about what constituted a woman's true "depth" (some still partly sentimentalized it), but it was quite common for them to link female "depth" to sexuality, and to glamorize this as "primitive"—the word that Dr. Jelliffe had instructed Mabel Dodge to use.

The glamorizing of the primitive is a major ideological shift in the making of white middle- and upper-class identities during the 1910s and 1920s, especially when one considers that during the nineteenth century the word *primitive* was often deployed by the "rational" bourgeoisie to devalue less "rational" (i.e., subordinated) groups like the working class and racialized "others."[47] By the 1920s *primitive* had been transformed into a term that betokened sophisticated middle- and upper-class insight (facing one's primitive within). Thus in 1931 Eugene O'Neill explained that what he aimed to stage in his plays "is the struggle of the primitive to emerge in more complicated people, the drama of its thwarted, warped, revengeful, hidden emerging." Recovering the primitive became tantamount to restoring one's "deeper" humanity. Hence we find pop psychology books like William J. Fielding's *The Caveman Within Us: His Peculiarities and Powers; How We Can Enlist his Aid for Health and Efficiency* (1922). The appeal of the primitive was in its anxiety-producing dangerousness as well as its sexiness—an appeal that was a selling point for psychoanalysis and its popularizations (the precarious but irresistible adventure of stripping off "the veneer of civilization," to quote the stock phrase).[48]

Psychoanalysis was cashing in on a cultural curiosity about the primitive that had been well established (in ethnography, fiction, art) since the late nineteenth century. Although the actual text of André Tridon's *Psychoanalysis and Love* did not play up the caveman-subdues-cavewoman motif, the marketing department of Truth Publishing Company knew well that a cartoon ad depicting "primeval man" about to overpower "the object of his affections" club-in-hand (the primitive basis for the "modern honeymoon") (fig. 7.4) would tan-

Amazing New Discoveries About Love

The Mightiest of All Human Passions!

When love came to the cave man he hunted the object of his affections with a club, overpowered her by brute force and fled through the wilds with her, dragging her by the hair. Is the modern honeymoon the present-day version of primeval man's flight with his mate? Many of our customs in love and marriage can be traced back to equally curious beginnings.

DO you ever dream of your "ideal" mate? Have you ever been in love with two people at the same time? Have you ever loved a person much older than yourself? Why do certain people attract you and others repulse you? What is the chief cause of unhappiness in married life? Why does a small man fall in love with a large woman, or vice versa? Why does bitter hate sometimes masquerade under the guise of love? Why do some people fall in love with their own relatives? Just what happens to a person to bring about the state of being in love? Why do lovers kiss? How do our glands affect us? Are they responsible for our personalities and our actions?

Love has always been the baffling mystery of the ages. Every individual is touched by the flame of love; it shapes the whole course of his or her life, bringing happiness or misery, success or failure. So overwhelming is its power that it may lead a man or woman to any extremity — to murder, to social infamy. "Look for the woman," the French say when a man has committed some strange, inexplicable crime.

And yet this irresistible power of love, in many ways the biggest thing in life, has always been a complete mystery. Few have even attempted to explain it. We have regarded it simply as some blind, unreasoning force — a force that without warning enfolds a man or woman and holds her or her beneath its magic spell.

The Soul of Love Laid Bare

But now science has revealed the cause of it! In the searching light of that most curious and interesting new method, psychoanalysis, the soul of love is laid bare! Now we can see exactly what love is, just how it affects us.

This amazing dissection of the mightiest of all human passions has been made by the eminent psychoanalyst, Andre Tridon. By means of new scientific methods he has stripped the veil from the deep, hidden sources of love and has shown what is beneath all our love impulses. His disclosures furnish one of the most surprising and startling pictures of our innermost selves that could be imagined. Just as love itself is the most fascinating mystery of human nature so these revelations of its intimate secrets are absolutely spellbinding in their intense personal interest.

With utter frankness Mr. Tridon has uncovered the real reasons for all our emotions, our feelings and our desires, known as love. He shows just what love is, why there are many different kinds of love; just what characteristics about certain types of people attract others and why; why love sometimes expresses itself in abnormal ways; what is behind the mask of modesty; why love dies. He explains why love often drives people to the most extreme acts; why it sometimes leads to sensational crimes.

One of the most remarkable discoveries is that of the effect of our glands upon us. Mr. Tridon tells just how our glands are largely responsible for making us what we are. Different types of people have different types of glands, and our natures, our actions, our emotions are to a great extent the result of the condition of the different glands in our bodies.

A Startling New Book

The whole amazing explanation of love, as revealed by the piercing light of psychoanalysis, is contained in Mr. Tridon's remarkable new book entitled "Psychoanalysis and Love." It is a book that will startle every one who reads it; a book that will shock many. But most people will realise that this new understanding of love leads to a healthy normal expression of our instincts and enables us to avoid the many mistakes and false ideas that cause so much unhappiness.

But you must see this amazing book for yourself. If you act quickly a copy of the limited edition will be sent to you without obligation to keep it after full examination.

Send No Money

Send no money. Simply send your name and address on the coupon below or in a letter. "Psychoanalysis and Love" will be mailed to you in plain wrapper. When it arrives pay the postman only $2.50 (plus postage). Then if you do not think that this great book is worth many times its small price, return it in 5 days and your money will be refunded in full. Send the coupon now, before this special offer is withdrawn.

TRUTH PUBLISHING CO.,
1400 Broadway, Dept. A-349, New York

Andre Tridon, the eminent psychoanalyst, whose astonishing disclosures of how and why we love have created a tremendous sensation.

People wonder why a small, delicate man sometimes marries a large, physically developed woman, or vice versa. Yet there is a very definite and surprising reason for this curious attraction.

Probably most of us recall an instance of marriage between a young man and a woman considerably older. Psychoanalysis now explains this phenomenon.

Why does love die? What happens after a man and woman are married that sometimes turns love to active dislike, even to hate? Read what psychoanalysts say.

A gentle, mild-mannered woman kills her lover, or her husband. Then she declares she killed him because she loved him. What was her strange, overpowering instinct?

7.4. Advertisement for André Tridon, *Psychoanalysis and Love* (1922), published in *The Liberator*, September 1922, inside back cover. Yale Collection of American Literature Photographs, Beinecke Rare Book and Manuscript Library, Yale University.

talize consumers—especially when the "object" appeared more invitingly help-less than angry. This standard "primeval" domination scene contributed to mass-cultural constructions of the erotic in psychology, pop psychology, and sexology texts. Fielding's *Sex and the Love-Life* (1927), for instance, quotes Have-lock Ellis's *Little Essays of Love and Virtue* (1922), which holds that a male's "exhi-bition of force" in his pursuit of a woman provides "pleasurable stimulation" "for civilized as well as for savage women."[49] The romance of the primitive made such power relations not only acceptable but exciting.

Even in 1922 many readers of the Tridon ad would have identified the cave couple with Edgar Rice Burroughs's Tarzan and Jane (about two dozen Tarzan novels appeared between 1912 and the 1930s). Tarzan's draw was his "half-civilized" makeup: he had sex appeal but also good manners; he swung almost completely naked and was often surrounded by equally naked women, some-times illustrated for readers (fig. 7.5). Both subhuman and superhuman, he was in some ways a "jungle" fantasy of the autonomous, self-made capitalist who knew when to go for the jugular (literally, with his teeth); he was power-fully primitive but not "psychologically" self-absorbed. Burroughs assigned Tarzan two models of "depth" that were in push-pull tension: his Lord Grey-stoke "heredity" could restrain him from following his ape "training," while his "untamed" anger and sexuality could break through (yes) "the thin veneer of civilization."[50] This combination soothes Jane's "sick nerves" and turns her on to the sexy possibility of swinging as a primeval woman in this passage from 1915: "[Tarzan] kissed her not once, but a hundred times, until she lay there panting for breath; yet when he stopped she put her arms about his neck and drew his lips to hers once more." When Tarzan kisses, Jane's lips are "crushed to his." During Tarzan's fight with a lusty ape to "win" her (a scene rife with displaced fears connected to miscegenation, interracial warfare, and resistance to imperialism), Jane's primitive within is aroused by the sight of her savior's penetrating knife drinking "deep a dozen times of [the ape's] heart's blood."[51] With one impassioned plunge after another, the call of the primitive eroticizes female helplessness and spectatorship as sexually adven-turous.

But if Tarzan partially primitivizes Jane, she partly civilizes and psycholo-gizes her ape-man (his awareness of sexual difference and emotional depen-dency gives birth to shame, guilt, compassion, and ambivalence). Tarzan's lim-ited "psychological" re-entry into the "human" race (he is too primitive and healthy to be overly "psychological") is also part of his 1910s and 1920s charm. Lovesick for Jane and reflecting on the violence endemic to so-called civiliza-tion, Tarzan actually wonders if he will soon "develop a set of nerves." *Nerves* is the appropriate word because the Tarzan novels arrived at the end of the era of neurasthenia and at the beginning of the age of psychoanalysis (and behavior-

" He shall die!" croaked the harsh voice of the sorcerer

7.5. Edgar Rice Burroughs's Tarzan and his scantily clad captors, from the magazine *Argosy Weekly*, September 19, 1936, page 6. Illustration from *Tarzan and the Magic Men* ©1936 Edgar Rice Burroughs, Inc., reprinted with the permission of Edgar Rice Burroughs, Inc. Photograph courtesy of Yale Collection of American Literature, Beinecke Rare Book and Manuscript Library, Yale University.

ism). Tarzan's "jungle" adventures are analogous to the "strenuous life" tours that neurasthenic men were advised to take out West. However, the neurasthenic woman who was prescribed isolating rest cures is now replaced with a New Woman—Jane—who, though still sentimental, consciously revitalizes her emotions by getting in touch with her sexy primitive within.[52]

These neurasthenic and pop psychological aspects are more apparent in Burroughs's *Cave Girl* (serialized 1913 and 1915, published as a novel 1925). The hero, Waldo Emerson Smith-Jones (later renamed Thandar), is a neurasthenic Harvard weakling of Boston Brahmin stock who is shipwrecked on an island populated by primeval cave dwellers. Waldo meets Nadara, an uninhibited cave girl who initiates him into aggressive and sexual cavestyle virility. At first Burroughs seems coy about stating that the unembarrassed Nadara is topless, but, getting over this reserve, he soon has her eagerly discarding her "scanty" skirt

7.6. Edgar Rice Burroughs's cave girl (given extra clothes by the artist) to the rescue, from *The Cave Girl* (1925). Illustration from *The Cave Girl* ©1913 Frank A. Munsey Company, reprinted with the permission of Edgar Rice Burroughs, Inc. Photograph courtesy of Yale University Library.

and inviting the mortified Waldo to go skinny-dipping. As Waldo undergoes his Tarzanization he learns to look at her "unashamed" and in one bloody battle with a caveman seems encouraged by "her rapidly rising and falling breasts" (covered by Burroughs's artist: fig. 7.6). Later, at his reunion with Nadara, he "crushed her to him" and "did not ask if she loved him, for he was Thandar, the cave man." Nevertheless, his Brahmin upbringing (like Tarzan's Greystoke lineage) restrains him from having premarital cave sex with the terrifically disappointed Nadara, who is only acquainted with the "take them by the hair and drag them" custom.[53] They get married in Hawaii (after rescuing their rescuers) and discover that cave girl was herself shipwrecked as a babe and is really a French countess. Countess though she be, Burroughs takes a step beyond Jane to give us a red-blooded heroine who goes naked, grooves on watching her Harvard man sink his teeth into a competitor's neck, and is hot-to-trot. Enacting the "cave girl" within had come into vogue.

On the Gender, Racial, and Class Politics
of the Primitive Within

What are the political implications of recasting the sentimental angel in the house as the cave woman within? Isn't this simply progress? To understand the politics of the wide-ranging cultural production of "primitive" interiority during the 1910s and 1920s one would have to review in detail intersecting issues of class, racism, gender, sexuality, and imperialism—a project that is beyond the scope of this chapter. But I shall touch on some of these issues first by mentioning what must be obvious from my accounts of Burroughs's novels: Jane swings, but as a weightless doll in Tarzan's arms; and cave girl, for all of her eye-catching bare-breasted uninhibitedness, is more of a masculinity cheerleader than a player. Burroughs's heroines, fundamentally, are sexier makeovers of the nineteenth century's "angel" housewives who gave emotional support to husbands who did battle in the capitalist marketplace. As "therapeutic," as "psychologically" meaningful, and as sexy as sexuality became in its early twentieth-century challenging-of-taboos routine, we would probably do well to keep an eye on what else a mass-marketed sexier sex was used to make sexy. What sorts of power and social relations did sexualized identity make exciting and liberatory? How did the transgressive romance of unforbidden psychosexual identity repackage the very notion of the "power" that must be resisted?

Long before Foucault voiced skepticism about the emancipatory value of the bourgeoisie's psychoanalysis-inspired game of taboo-busting as "truth," the British Marxist Christopher Caudwell criticized "Freudianism" as a sly restyling of the bourgeois "individual." "Whether [psychoanalysts] study primitive man or lay down general laws of the soul," he maintained, "it is always with ideas formulated from a bourgeois psyche studying other bourgeois psyches, and so the instincts play always the part of splendid and free brutes, crippled by the repressions of a cruel culture." But Caudwell had another "crippling" on his mind during the 1930s. He went on to contend that the "Freudian 'libido' in bondage to 'repression'" that the bourgeoisie encouraged itself to worry about and to fascinate itself with was in fact "a pale subjective reflection" of a "system of production relations [that] is crippling man's splendid powers."[54] Caudwell was attacking the reduction of the notion of culture to a system of taboos that exists to restrain the instinctive cave-pleasures of the "individual." If "Freudianism" can persuade "individuals" to imagine power and liberation in this abstracted and individualized framework, it succeeds in deflecting attention from specific social groups who dominate other groups, thus making "culture" and not the capitalists' exploitation of the working class, for example, the compelling problem to be fretted over. Caudwell sees that psychoanalysis is effective as a bourgeois ideology because it recognizes a specific kind of conflict ("psychological") and controls the terms and field within which this type of conflict is made much more interesting and important to the (bourgeois) self than other forms of conflict and power struggles within society. Once this "psychological" model is adopted, a suspicious leveling takes place: now we all get to see ourselves as victims of culture—the rich and the starving, the oppressors and the oppressed. Now we are all "free brutes" who suffer from taboos.

Richard Dyer has pursued a related line of critique. Dyer's concern also is with how sexuality and the body have been represented and used by the bourgeoisie to cook up appetizing and relatively easy-to-swallow notions of power and emancipation for its consumption. He observes quite simply that for the "past few centuries" meanings have been inscribed on the body that have masked "the fact that its predominant use has been as the labour of the majority in the interests of the few. One way of doing this has been the idea of sexuality, an ever increasing focus on the genitals as a concentrate of physical need and desire."[55] Dyer suggests that the hypersexualization and exoticizing of the black-as-primitive during the 1920s reencoded—denied—the exploited black worker's body. Caudwell's and Dyer's arguments combined can help us reconstruct the intriguing shift I have been tracing in the tactics of bourgeois "self"-making: the modern bourgeoisie exhibits the tendency to encode some groups it exploits as sexy and primitive (and childish), and then it identifies with these newly encoded groups for therapeutic reasons, as the "primitive" within itself.

In the antebellum era the "primitive" was not usually imagined or prized as a source of middle-class emotional identity (although subdued Native Americans had been romanticized as "noble savages," especially during the 1820s and 1830s).[56] But even then the "primitive" was represented as a crude state of psychic health. "Insanity is rare in a savage state of society," wrote the trustees of Worcester Hospital. "Among the ignorant and uncultivated, the mental faculties lie dormant, and hence are less liable to derangement." Dr. Edward Jarvis and later in the century Dr. George Beard and others expressed a certain nervousness that the pressures and pace of American civilization made people too nervous.[57] Growing out of this ideological soil, the early twentieth-century category of the primitive was used in two ways. First, sophisticated persons (like O'Neill and Dodge) had to relearn how to connect with the primitive within— this promised an increase rather than a decrease in sophistication; second, the primitive referred to groups who were well-endowed with healthy primitiveness but who could never really acquire intellectual and cultural sophistication. Thus Burroughs, as much as he loves a romp through the "jungle" stereotypes of his imagination, makes Tarzan a lord and cave girl a countess because he is fundamentally uninterested in having them stay just primitive. To visit the primitive can be restorative and romantic (as O'Neill discovered in his youthful Jack Londonesque sailor days), but one doesn't want to get stuck there.

O'Neill, whose early reputation was built on his late 1910s plays about lowly sailors (in his hit *The Hairy Ape* [1922] they are depicted as "neanderthals"), viewed workers with an oddly sympathetic blend of envy and condescension: they are inherently dramatic (by implication, also inherently dumb) because they are not "steeped in the evasions" and are not "handicapped by [the] inhibitions" of the sophisticated. Magnanimously, so he thought, he put these "inarticulate" creatures on stage "to interpret for them."[58] O'Neill invokes the "psychological"—the "evasions" and "inhibitions" of his social group—to delineate class hierarchy even as he seems to be applauding workers.

The envying and discounting of the so-called primitive was even more palpable in the "psychological" resignification of racial hierarchies during the 1920s. For this reason, perhaps, Albert Barnes, a wealthy white art collector (of modern and "primitive" art) and contributor to Alain Locke's *The New Negro* (1925), was careful when rhapsodizing overmuch about the black's "psychological complexion," "emotional endowment," and "primitive nature" to value this as artistic capital. By contrast, the noted critic Joseph Wood Krutch expunged African American intellectual mastery and skill when he commended the black actor's "instinctive sense for participation in an emotion larger than his comprehension."[59]

Those who understood all too well the primitive not as depth but as performance—a stereotype of blackness contrived to erect white subjective potency—were those who were expected to perform primitivism in daily life.[60] Langston Hughes's satiric "Slave on the Block" (1934) tells the story of a fashionably bohemian white couple, Michael and Anne Carraway, who "went in for" the seemingly artless "Art of Negroes—the dancing that had jungle life about it, the songs, that were so simple and fervent, the poetry that was so direct, so real." These Greenwich Village pseudo artists fuel their romance with "primitive" transgressiveness by making uptown safaris to Harlem's Cotton Club and "the Hot Dime, where white folks couldn't get in—unless they knew the man. (And tipped heavily.)" When they meet their late cook's nephew, Luther, an "ebony boy," Anne gushes, "He is the jungle," and Michael ejaculates, "He's so utterly Negro." They hire this ebony status symbol as their gardener and have him pose for Anne's painting of a slave market, *The Boy on the Block*. Yet Luther is quickly bored with his role as slave-and-savage psychofurniture and, finally, after happily getting himself sacked, grins the grin that Anne misread joyously (and condescendingly) as jungle spontaneity (and simplemindedness). The Carraways remain blithely unaware that Luther possesses the independence, sense of irony, and self-respect to mock performances of the primitive that refashioned (but didn't eliminate) racial hierarchies in white "liberal-minded" bohemia.[61]

Henry Louis Gates has observed that the Harlem Renaissance's version of a "new negro" who was associated with aesthetic and instinctual primitivism was preceded by a militant late 1910s concept of the "new negro." Race riots in East St. Louis, Houston, Chicago, and elsewhere, the black soldiers who returned from World War I, and Marcus Garvey's black nationalist followers (who dressed in military-style uniforms) may well have been perceived by whites as threatening (the Ku Klux Klan thrived and spread to the North during the 1920s). Such militant developments may have helped set the scene for the Harlem Renaissance promotion of a less angry black "primitiveness" that stressed *sexuality* (a condition for greater black visibility in mainstream, white-dominated culture). Consequently Harlem became the locus for what historian Nathan Huggins terms a therapeutic "soft rebellion" for whites like the Carraways, who sought and paid for black performances of "primitiveness" that could provide them with entertaining emotional release, countercultural prestige, and artistic persons and creations that elicited not only their fascination but also—Huggins suggests—their condescension and dread.[62]

Women's suffrage and its aftermath also help clarify the politics of the mass-marketing of primitive and "psychological" identities. With the passage of the Nineteenth Amendment in 1920, women seemed to be on the march. The influx of women into workplaces and institutions of higher learning had unhitched them from solely domestic identities. In 1920 more than 40 percent of college and university students were female. The 1930 census listed 40 percent of all "professional and kindred workers" as female, but did not supply more telling details about the actual power these women held. The articulate feminism of the 1910s, which contributed to these advances, stood for equality between the sexes in the economic, legal, political, cultural, and, not least of all, sexual realms.[63] But writing about and for women during the 1920s frequently contracted the orbit of female concerns to the (hetero)sexual (centering on marriage as a goal) and often detached this heightened consciousness about sexual relations from feminist critique. Aspects of this shift drew fire from older feminists like Jane Addams (who worried that the emotional absorption with "sex taboos" distracted women from caring about the ways in which many women were still economically, legally, politically, and culturally bound) and Charlotte Perkins Gilman (who interpreted the sex fling as the reaction of "a servile class suddenly set free"). The twenties' ideal of "companionate marriage" lent support to premarital sexual arrangements, birth control, and the notion of lovers as intimate pals and equals, but it did not, as Nancy Cott points out, demand "sexual parity in the public world as well as the bedroom" (as did many feminists of the previous decade).[64]

The astronomical growth of the advertising industry and beauty industry (which were symbiotic) during the 1920s suggests not only that sex was being made commercially sexier (an attribute that could be attached to commodities and lifestyles) than ever before, but also that sex was being used to *refeminize* women. The glamorizing of the "psychological" and of the primitive were inextricably linked to a larger cultural and corporate campaign to glamorize both sex and sexualized femininity. This feminization of women is evident in numerous texts that champion the sexualization of women. Writing in 1930 about the "psychological" "new girl" of the twenties, Blanchard and Manasses touted her alluringly kissable transgressiveness: "Now she must be conversant, superficially, at least, with Freud and Havelock Ellis, and she can listen to a lecture on the pros and cons of birth control without the slightest paling beneath her rouge and lipstick." The unquestioned assumption is that sex (Freud, Ellis) and femininity (rouge, lipstick) go together; "new girls" are feminine taboo-breakers. Likewise, Robert Latou Dickenson and Lura Beam's *Thousand Marriages* (1931) makes a habit of pointing out that women with untabooed sexual appetites can still be good homemakers. One woman's "auto-erotism began at twelve; homosexuality at sixteen; heterosexuality at seventeen; marriage at twenty-one; adultery at twenty-two"; but all is well with the world because "in everything except sexuality she is the typical honest, hard-working, self-respecting, quiet-mannered domestic."[65] Angels with instincts can still be angels.

"Psychological" identities that helped eroticize, glamorize, and commodify femininity in new ways performed subtle ideological services for liberal corporate culture. They helped make women's me-Tarzan-you-Jane subordination in a variety of social relations seem sexy and acceptably feminine at a moment when more women than ever, particularly college graduates, had the potential to gain access to social, economic, institutional, and cultural power—and not just as cave/office-girl cheerleaders—in universities, corporate workplaces, and professional organizations.[66] To adapt Dyer's insight: the psychosexualization of female bodies (and notions of emancipation) in this context could obscure the female body's significance as a laboring body that was still largely being exploited (despite some gains). The "primitive within" gave femininity a "deeper" ideological lease on life and aided an advertising industry that relied on female consumers who could be made anxious about the potency of what they had been convinced were their most valuable "psychological" and "individual" assets—their femininity and their sex appeal.

The Disassembling and Uprooting of "Emotional Equipment"

I would never suggest that the concerns taken up in the feminist essays of Florence Guy Seabury and the feminist plays of Susan Glaspell were untouched by the let's-challenge-taboos spirit that animated writers like Katharine Anthony. But neither Seabury nor Glaspell—during the 1910s and 1920s—felt moved to rescript women's "nature" or "depth" within the terms of emerging "psychological" identities. Their strategies of empowering women developed out of different, more skeptical theoretical premises: both authors identified what Seabury called "emotional equipment" as the *invention* of culture. Only in the past few years have Glaspell's iconoclastic plays begun to receive the critical attention they deserve, while Seabury's humorous feminist writings have been almost completely forgotten.

Seabury wrote for magazines like the *New Republic* and the *Nation* and in 1926 published a collection of satiric sketches about gender and emotional roles: *The Delicatessen Husband and Other Essays* (with comical illustrations by Clarence Day, Jr.). Her interests were political: she had worked in settlement houses, campaigned for suffrage, was a socialist, and studied the conditions of female factory workers.[67] Although Seabury does not set out to identify the social causes of anxieties about gender during the 1920s, a recurrent theme is male nervousness about increasing numbers of women in the workplace and about "taking orders from women" (17–18). Seabury's critical emphasis is on how "standardized" "patterns" of gender assemble "emotional equipment" in men and women that is devised to perpetuate the illusion of sexual difference (264). She contests the naturalness of the categories of "man" and "woman": "We need a whole new gallery of mental pictures," she proposes, "if it is true that what we call man and woman are only rough-and-ready terms for the preponderance of masculine and feminine elements in the individual" (27). Seabury encourages her readers to wonder why the culture has made gender and emotional differentiation based on anatomy so important and to weigh the damage "caused by compulsory conformity to standardized sex characteristics" (19–20).

Although Seabury mentions in passing heredity and environment as factors that shape the self, her point is that, however human beings are influenced, we should not allow the culture to make the emotional outcome—be it labeled masculine or feminine or any mix of the two—into a matter of significance, anxiety, or stigma: "Maybe, when Nature shuffles the cards, and deals out human characteristics, it is not as ludicrous as we have supposed, when they fall, not according to sex, but by disposition and temperament" (224). Notwithstanding her theoretical stress on "stereotypes" of gender, Seabury occasionally posits a "real nature" (27) that underlies stereotypes; but she shows little interest in accounting for or elaborating on this in "psychological" language. "Real nature" or "depth," for her, is simply what the self seems inclined to be.

What makes Seabury's cultural—nonpsychological—take on subjectivity all the more intriguing is that in 1923 she had married David Seabury, a conventional pop psychologist (to whom her 1926 book is dedicated), who published a string of catchily titled pop psychology books starting with *Unmasking Our Minds* (1925) (dedicated to his wife). Like so many pop psychology texts of the twenties, David Seabury's book promises readers a "fascinating" "look below the surface at last" and offers them a golden opportunity to be "not the plaything of life, but the actual commander of [one's] destiny."[68] Not only did Florence Seabury not employ below-the-surface spatial rhetoric, she indirectly attacked the notion of the "primitive within"—what she labeled the "cave idea"—which so much popular "depth" rhetoric invoked to justify itself. It is hard not to think of Burroughs's creations of Tarzan and Waldo/Thandar ("cave manikens") when she charges: "[Man] wants to live up to the cave idea; he thinks he should strut or fume, take the initiative, be dominant." Seabury sees this as a performance, a "masquerade" men carry out because their masculinity act is "wobbly" (67–68).

Her satirical tactics of inversion include rescripting the "cave" identity for the modern independent, aggressive, and sexual cave woman. Citing a newspaper report, she tells the tale of four women on a deserted road who came across a man and dragged him into their car for purposes of sexual play. Dissatisfied with the man's "ardor," one stuck him with a hatpin and ejected him (136) (fig. 7.7). Another newspaper story she relates is an episode in which three women kidnapped a man and one of them tried to coerce him to marry her (fig. 7.8) ("The lengths to which modern cave women will go is beyond belief" [256]). Seabury's cave woman anecdotes have us consider instances of female aggression, not as expressions of unregulated biology or as naughty little transgressions against femininity, but as actions that shatter the very category—or stereotype—of femininity. After narrating the exploits of a pregnant bank-robber and of a female French Bolshevik terrorist she notes: "Hardly a day passes without record of some deeds of violence by women" (185). Seabury's defeminized cave women are the *me*-Jane-you-Tarzan variety.

Katharine Anthony would have appreciated the sexiness of these cave women; yet Seabury does not make sexuality the key to the female self. Indeed, she hints her skepticism about the liberatory newness of the "new morality" in her essay "Men Who Understand Women" (1924): "The angel picture . . . has had some rude blows. As portrayed by the vanguard of radicals and interpreters, however, the changing conventions have their roots in the old generalizations and phantasies."[69] By the depths of the Depression, however, Seabury was espousing her husband's style of pop psychology and billed herself as "Consultant in Human Relations." But that is another story.[70]

Glaspell's and Seabury's thinking during the 1910s and 1920s had much in common: both women belonged to Greenwich Village's feminist Heterodoxy club. Several of the plays that Glaspell wrote alone, after writing *Suppressed Desires* with her husband, were expressly feminist: *Trifles* (1916), *Woman's Honor*

ONE OF THE GIRLS, ENRAGED AT HIS LACK OF ARDOR,
STABBED HIM WITH A HATPIN.

7.7. Illustration by Clarence Day, Jr., of the unsatisfied women and the man frightened of
sexual play in Florence Guy Seabury's *The Delicatessen Husband and Other Essays* (1926).
Yale Collection of American Literature, Beinecke Rare Book and Manuscript Library, Yale
University.

(1917), and the drama I shall discuss here, *The Verge* (1921).[71] Like Dell, Eastman, and Dodge, whom she knew, Glaspell was attentive to the idea of suppression; but for her the more fundamental concern was to reconsider how and
why the culture created the very ("female") emotions that it then seemed to
"suppress."

When Hutchins Hapgood, a longtime member of Glaspell's circle, saw *The
Verge*, he recoiled from his friend's "half mad feminism." Yet his memoirs
recorded that members of the Heterodoxy club who attended the performance
responded as if they had been "in church."[72] The Heterodites were no doubt
stirred by Claire Archer, Glaspell's heroine, whose feminist discontents and
dreams drove her to convert her greenhouse into "a place for experiments"
(58). Claire's experiments to breed new plants like her Edge Vine are symbolic
of her wish to invent new "forms" of life and "otherness" for humans labeled

THE LENGTHS TO WHICH CAVE WOMEN WILL GO.

7.8. Illustration by Clarence Day, Jr., of a muscular marriage-minded woman kidnapping a man in Florence Guy Seabury's *The Delicatessen Husband and Other Essays* (1926). Yale Collection of American Literature, Beinecke Rare Book and Manuscript Library, Yale University.

women. She aims to disassemble common sense about what women and female emotions are "meant to be": "the old pattern, done again, again and again. So long it doesn't even know itself for a pattern" (79, 77). In response to her sister's charge that she is an unloving mother and an "unnatural woman," Claire retorts: "At least it saves me from being a natural one" (84). As Claire reflects on the difficulty of "get[ting] past . . . [o]ur own dead things," one can imagine Glaspell musing about the relationship of her own drama to previous representations of women's "natural" possibilities. Claire is empowered—like Seabury's cave women—by "breaking up what exists" (71). Thus she rips up her experimental Edge Vine by the roots when she discerns that "It's running back, back to—'all the girls'" (77).

Claire assails normative assumptions not only about the category of woman but about the category of sanity, which she derides (many decades before R. D. Laing romanticized madness) as the "life [that] can't break up and go outside what it was" (65). Her husband and sister diagnose Claire's undomestic creativity as a case of "nerves" and call in a neurologist (whom Claire dubs the "insanity man"). Having more faith in the neurologist than in Claire's antifeminine performances, some critics stereotyped *The Verge* as a play about a "neurotic" woman. But Glaspell is unwilling to encase Claire within what her contemporaries thought of as a "psychological" identity; she suggests instead that both neurology and psychoanalysis are inadequate to the task of comprehending the oppressive scope and subtlety of the gender relations and structures of feeling against which Claire rebels. The rejoinder of her friend Tom Edgeworth (and perhaps Glaspell) to the charge that she is "hysterical" is emphatic: "That was not hysterical" (71). Claire's sexual and emotional advances toward Tom make it plain that her "passion"—feared by Tom, who overidealizes Claire—is important. Nonetheless, she tries to explain to him that her passion is "sometimes more than I am. And yet—I am more than it is" (87). As with Seabury's cave women, the reality of female sexuality is acknowledged—as is the female capacity for aggression—but not as the key to a female "psychological" "depth."

In Act III Claire's frustration and anger break loose as she strangles Tom, exclaiming, "You are *too much*! You are *not enough*!" (99). Claire's violence seems even more directed against the feminized self she is afraid of returning to—her Edge Vine socialization that would run "back to—'all the girls.'" Shortly before strangling Tom, Claire is hit by a wave of Edge Vine resignation: "because we are tired—lonely—and afraid, we stop with you [men like Tom]. Don't get through—to what you're in the way of" (98). Tom's pledge to "keep" her "safe" ("safe?" she echoes) was surely not the thing to say to a woman committed to going over the edge into "what hasn't been" (61).

The most controversial moment in the drama for most auditors must have been Claire's throttling of Tom—an unsafe over-the-edge leap that set Claire, and Glaspell too, apart from a cuter, transgressively lipsticked, let's-not-blush-as-we-listen-to-lectures-on-Freud flapper feminism. Claire's annihilation of Tom prevents anyone from viewing her as adorably neurotic, naughty, and eccentric (like O'Neill's glamorously "neurotic" Nina Leeds). Her act is all the more controversial because the play is somewhat ambiguous, or inarticulate, about what Claire sees as the problem. Claire's language is often tentative, groping, fragmented—as if neither she nor anyone is yet capable of grasping the full extent and ramifications of the problem that both surrounds and seems to inhabit them.

Here the historical complexity and significance of *The Verge* might be partly illuminated by placing it in dialogue with a tradition of late nineteenth-century fictions written by women about women on the edge, fictions that also possess a creatively articulate and inarticulate power. In Kate Chopin's *The Awakening* (1899), Edna Pontellier increasingly wonders why she feels what she feels and is overwhelmed by an unfolding sense of her potential that "is necessarily vague, tangled, chaotic, and exceedingly disturbing."[73] Elizabeth Stuart Phelps Ward's *Story of Avis* (1877) and *Doctor Zay* (1882) are, like *The Awakening*, novels about women who do not quite succeed in resisting the programming of their culturally produced "emotional equipment." Both Avis, an artist, and Zay, a physician, after being chased and worn down by cocksure suitors for hundreds of pages, capitulate to Edge Vine marriages that threaten to restore them to a conventional domestic femininity that they finally experience as the call of female nature. Chopin's heroine surrenders neither to her husband nor to the lover who abandoned her but decides that she must drown herself (and hyper-romanticizes her soggy solution as the expression of her "inner" and consummately "individual" self). Glaspell's punchy heroine, by contrast, chokes her would-be lover, not herself, and refuses to submit to a "safe" relationship that would sink her. This ending is closer to that of Charlotte Perkins Gilman's "The Yellow Wallpaper" (1892), in which a victim of a neurasthenic rest cure, prescribed by her husband, literally and symbolically shreds the patterns of femininity and domesticity (children's wallpaper) that would wall her in and paper her over. The nineteenth-century novels of potential and of resignation I have mentioned—which fantasize about women of the future who will cultivate "nerve" (to quote Avis)—are like the forms of "our own dead things" that *The Verge* seeks to "break through."[74] The word Claire intones three times in her final lines is "out."

Glaspell's "hothouse" drama makes a provocative breakthrough in the imagination of "emotional equipment." While Glaspell recognizes that culture fabricates the forms and vocabularies of emotions, of meaningfulness, and of "problems" that constitute and preoccupy the self, she also sees that this ideological "equipment" seems to grow roots, to become organic, and to gestate in the self as it enacts "nature"—almost convincing us that it must have been "human" and deep inside us all along.

Coda: Glamorizing and Performing "the Individual"

Having offered perspectives on some key historical and ideological events, trends, and texts that pertain to the early popularizing of the "psychological," I shall propose more sweepingly that the "psychological" was glamorized successfully as a value, an identity, and a performance of the self in large part because it was so connected to related rewritings of the self during the 1910s and 1920s. I have suggested that psychoanalysis and pop psychology benefited from and contributed to a growing interest in the discourse of the primitive, and, even more significant, that it profited from and supported a consumer-era cultural vogue to sexualize femininity and concepts of female desire. A cultural "project" that was perhaps even more encompassing and foundational than the primitive and the feminine sexualization developments was the glamorizing and revitalizing of "the individual." Here I must again bring up historians' central point that there was in the early twentieth century a crisis of faith in self-making and individuality—an effect of the ascendancy of liberal corporate culture, or monopoly capitalism. Liberal corporate culture underwrote some revealing arrays of compensations for this crisis.

During the 1910s and 1920s we find multiple strategies of "individualization."[75] The ideological field of "the individual," as it developed during these years, is a capacious one and contains what at first glance may seem to be radically different or even contradictory constructions and performances of "individuality." Burroughs, for example, through Tarzan employs the discourse of primitivism to empower the reader's belief in individual agency and self-making. In another more middlebrow-highbrow sector of this ideological field, O'Neill—like pop psychologists—reinvigorates "individuality" by giving "psychological" conflict and weakness a sophisticated, "modern" subjective potency and by making "psychological" identity fascinating. Tarzan's muscular primitivism and O'Neill's "psychological" subtextuality, in different romantic ways, restore faith in the idea that the standardizing corporate order cannot strangle the significance of the "individual" self. In a different sector, sentimental discourse concentrates love and emotional care on individuals at home, where one is truly "individual."

Even Seabury and Glaspell occupy another portion of this ideological field. Their writing, which disassembles their culture's machinery of selfing, nevertheless conceives of agency and resistance mostly in the language of "the individual": feminists, Seabury asserts, "insist on being individuals first and not sex functions or social institutions" (268). The commonsensical dichotomy we find in Burroughs and O'Neill also reigns in Seabury's and Glaspell's writings: "the individual" versus society. Summing up the ideological trajectory of feminism during the 1920s, Elaine Showalter concludes, "From now on, progress, or lack of it, was to be measured in individual terms, not in the situation of the whole sex." As Nancy Cott has emphasized, the rhetoric of "the individual"—which many 1920s feminists adopted—was essential to the ideological stability of the liberal corporate state (thus Herbert Hoover was a vocal proponent of accelerated corporate growth—aided by the state—and what he called "the new individualism"—aided by the culture).[76]

The liberal corporate state could profit from having people "rebel" against standardization in individualized ways (e.g., by buying cars or by consuming literature that were styled as trademarks of individuality). Within the register of individualized "soft rebellions," specifically, therapeutic "rebellions" were desirable as approved liberal corporate order rebellions went (mounted by rebels who paid to unchain the instinctual "free brutes" or to arouse the Sleeping Beauties within them). The mass-cultural marketing of sex as the truth and expression of "individuality"—which was given some scientific legitimacy by the popularization of "psychological" identity and "psychological" common sense—helped to privatize "rebellion" by locating "emancipation" within the personal sphere (both the marriage rate and the divorce rate were sky-high in the twenties).[77]

What the liberal corporate order had accomplished was a way of ruling, not so much by dictatorial oppression or by using brute force to get Americans to go to work, but by creating "psychological" and "individual" significance and by allowing "freedom" to be popularized and enacted as the challenging of taboos (rather than the challenging of the liberal corporate order).[78] And even when some middle- and upper-class "individuals" were able to identify the liberal corporate order as the structural condition underlying manifold contradictions, inequalities, and injustices in America, well, gosh, challenging taboos could seem much more glamorous, meaningful, transgressive, performable—and *sexy*. "You could get only a handful of Village radicals to demand the liberation of Eugene Debs, Tom Mooney or Sacco and Vanzetti," Joseph Freeman reminisced about Greenwich Village in the late 1910s and 1920s. "But you could organize a one hundred per cent united front in protest against the suppression of Arthur Schnitzler's novelette about Casanova . . . . [who] symbolized the dream that everything is permitted."[79]

Notes

1. See Ariès, "The Family and the City in the Old World and the New," in *Changing Images of the Family,* ed. Virginia Tufte and Barbara Myerhoff (New Haven: Yale University Press, 1979), 32. Also see Ariès, *Centuries of Childhood: A Social History of Family Life,* trans. Robert Baldick (New York: Vintage, 1962), 413.

2. See Pfister, *The Production of Personal Life: Class, Gender, and the Psychological in Hawthorne's Fiction* (Stanford: Stanford University Press, 1991), especially 49–58.

3. Bisch, *Be Glad You're Neurotic* (New York: McGraw-Hill, 1946), 229.

4. See Gerald N. Grob, *The Mad Among Us: A History of the Care of America's Mentally Ill* (New York: Free Press, 1994), 60, 64, 76, 77, 142. Also see Robert Castel, Françoise Castel, Anne Lovell, *The Psychiatric Society,* trans. Arthur Goldhammer (New York: Columbia University Press, 1983), 19–20. On the stigma associated with those who entered nineteenth-century asylums see Richard Wightman Fox, *So Far Disordered in Mind: Insanity in California, 1870–1930* (Berkeley: University of California Press, 1978), 164.

5. For a discussion of the history of neurology and the expansion of psychology's jurisdiction consult Andrew Abbott, *The System of Professions: An Essay on the Division of Expert Labor* (Chicago: University of Chicago Press, 1988), 290–97. Also see Castel, Cas-

tel, and Lovell, *Psychiatric Society,* 25–26. On neurasthenia and its appeal for the white Protestant middle and upper classes, see Tom Lutz, *American Nervousness, 1903: An Anecdotal History* (Ithaca: Cornell University Press, 1991), 6–7.

6. Fox, *So Far Disordered,* 171. Kovel, "The American Mental Health Industry," in *Critical Psychiatry: The Politics of Mental Health,* ed. David Ingleby (New York: Pantheon, 1980), 80. On the somewhat displaced clergy and the way they adapted to the rise of therapeutic culture see Abbott, *System of Professions,* 309, 285–86. Abbott writes: "The nervous diseases had become a fixture of American experience by 1910" (284). On the shift from the asylum to "therapy for the normal" also see Elizabeth Lunbeck, *The Psychiatric Persuasion: Knowledge, Gender, and Power in Modern America* (Princeton: Princeton University Press, 1994), 11–77. For an example of the transformation of "sin" into "psychological" discourse see Karl Menninger, M.D., *Whatever Became of Sin?* (New York: Hawthorn Books, 1973), especially 74–93.

7. I am grateful to Indira Karamcheti for introducing me to the term *subjective potency,* which she concocted to describe what I was arguing in another project.

8. Foucault, *The History of Sexuality, Volume I: An Introduction,* trans. Robert Hurley (New York: Vintage, 1980), 56, 66, 70, 72, 157, 159. I thank Henry Abelove for describing my historical project (developed in several of my publications) in these terms to a colleague; I agree with Abelove's illuminating characterization.

9. I thank Rishona Zimring for suggesting that I look up *glamour* (whose history she recalled) in the *Oxford English Dictionary* and then refer to the brief discussion of *glamour* and *grammar* in Walter J. Ong, S.J., *The Presence of the Word: Some Prolegomena for Cultural and Religious History* (New Haven: Yale University Press, 1967), 209.

10. See John C. Burnham, "The New Psychology" (117–27), Sanford Gifford, "The American Reception of Psychoanalysis, 1908–1922" (128–45), and Fred Matthews, "The New Psychology and American Drama" (146–56), all in *1915, The Cultural Moment: The New Politics, the New Woman, the New Psychology, the New Art and the New Theatre in America,* ed. Adele Heller and Lois Rudnick (New Brunswick, N.J.: Rutgers University Press, 1991). Also Nathan Hale, Jr., *Freud and the Americans: The Beginnings of Psychoanalysis in the United States, 1876–1917* (1971; rprt. New York: Oxford University Press, 1995), 369–96.

11. Freeman, *An American Testament: A Narrative of Rebels and Romantics* (New York: Farrar & Rinehart, 1936), 158. Sherwood Anderson, like Freeman, had a critical response to the "'Freudian games' of 'psyching' oneself and friends" in Chicago during the 1910s. See F. H. Matthews, "The Americanization of Sigmund Freud: Adaptations of Psychoanalysis before 1917," *Journal of American Studies* 1 (April 1967): 54.

12. Brill is quoted in Philip Rieff, introduction to Sigmund Freud, *Dora: An Analysis of a Case of Hysteria* (New York: Collier, 1963), 19. Rieff reads this not as an indication of how modes of encoding the self can alter the self, but as yet another example of how "aggression appears even among professional students of aggression" (19). Jameson, *Marxism and Form: Twentieth-Century Dialectical Theories of Literature* (Princeton: Princeton University Press, 1974), 27.

13. Dell, "Speaking of Psycho-Analysis: The New Boon for Dinner Table Conversationalists," *Vanity Fair* 5 (Dec. 1915): 53.

14. Eastman, "Exploring the Soul and Healing the Body," *Everybody's Magazine* 23 (June 1915): 743. For a discussion of Dell, Eastman, and their respective interests in psychoanalysis see Nathan Hale, Jr., *The Rise and Crisis of Psychoanalysis in the United States:*

Freud and the Americans, 1917–1985 (New York: Oxford University Press, 1995), 64–66, 68–69.

15. Crowley, "An Improvement of Psycho-Analysis," *Vanity Fair* 7 (Dec. 1916): 60. Crothers, *Expressing Willie, Nice People, 39 East* (New York: Brentano's, 1924), 30.

16. See Theatre Guild Press Books, Beinecke Rare Book and Manuscript Library, Yale University, scrapbooks 80 (Fontanne) and 81 (Anderson).

17. Menninger wrote this in an essay on psychiatry in America ("Psychiatry") that was published in *America Now: An Inquiry into Civilization in the United States*, ed. Harold E. Stearns (New York: Scribner's, 1938), 425–55; he is quoted in Hale, *Rise and Crisis of Psychoanalysis*, 77. I thank Sarah Winter for bringing this quotation to my attention.

18. For a somewhat different discussion of this photograph in the context of related photographs of O'Neill (looking "deep" while he is ostensibly writing his plays in managerial pinstripes) see Joel Pfister, *Staging Depth: Eugene O'Neill and the Politics of Psychological Discourse* (Chapel Hill: University of North Carolina Press, 1995), 1–11. Stevenson, "The Strange Case of Dr. Jekyll and Mr. Hyde," in *The Works of Robert Louis Stevenson*, vol. 5, ed. Charles Curtis Bigelow and Temple Scott (New York: National Library, 1906), 240, 247, 254, 275, 291, 304. I would not have identified the possibility of there being a racial dimension in Van Vechten's photograph if not for a provocative lecture given by Eric Lott on postwar film noir and racial anxieties, entitled "Filling in the Blanc: Whiteness and Upheaval in Post-war America" (Wesleyan University Center for the Humanities, March 4, 1996). Both Van Vechten and O'Neill romanticized African American psychological "primitiveness" and made pilgrimages to Harlem's nightclubs (O'Neill accompanied by Paul Robeson) in the 1920s. I shall have more to say below about this white romanticism (which Van Vechten, who wrote the novel *Nigger Heaven* [1926], took to extremes).

19. See Lears, "From Salvation to Self-Realization: Advertising and the Therapeutic Roots of the Consumer Culture, 1880–1930," in *The Culture of Consumption: Critical Essays in American History, 1880–1980*, ed. Richard Wightman Fox and T. J. Jackson Lears (New York: Pantheon, 1983), 1–38, and Olivier Zunz, *Making America Corporate, 1879–1920* (Chicago: University of Chicago Press, 1990), esp. his chapter "Lost Autonomy," 11–36. Also see David Brion Davis's 1968 essay, "Stress-Seeking and the Self-Made Man in American Literature, 1894–1914," reprinted in his *From Homicide to Slavery: Studies in American Culture* (New York: Oxford University Press, 1986), 52–72, John G. Cawelti, *Apostles of the Self-Made Man* (Chicago: University of Chicago Press, 1965), and Irvin G. Wyllie, *The Self-Made Man in America: The Myth of Rags to Riches* (New York: Free Press, 1954). For recent critical (mainly anthropological) perspectives on the significance of ideologies of self-making in America see *Rhetorics of Self-Making*, ed. Debbora Battaglia (Berkeley: University of California Press, 1995).

20. Susman, "'Personality' and the Making of Twentieth-Century Culture," in his *Culture as History: The Transformation of Society in the Twentieth Century* (New York: Pantheon, 1984), 271–85. Also see Pierre Bourdieu's discussion of this transformation and his critique of the twentieth-century consumer culture's therapeutic ethos in "From Duty to the Fun Ethic" in his *Distinction: A Social Critique of the Judgement of Taste* (Cambridge: Harvard University Press, 1984), 365–71: "The fear of not getting enough pleasure, is combined with the search for self-expression and 'bodily expression' and for communication with others . . . even immersion in others . . . and the old personal ethic is thus rejected for a cult of personal health and psychological therapy. At the opposite pole from the

'politicization' which depersonalizes personal experiences by presenting them as particular cases of generic experiences common to a class, 'moralization' and 'psychologization' personalize experiences, and are thus perfectly consistent with the more or less secular forms of the search for religious salvation" (367). Bisch, *Be Glad You're Neurotic,* 230.

21. Pfister, *Production of Personal Life,* 27, 55–56, and *Staging Depth,* 7–8, 286.

22. See Christopher Herbert, *Culture and Anomie: Ethnographic Imagination in the Nineteenth Century* (Chicago: University of Chicago Press, 1991). Herbert reflects upon a "metaphorics of 'depth'" that *produces* identities. "Depth" rears its head in England in the nineteenth century, linking "such diverse fields of discourse and practice as Methodist theology, ethnographic fieldwork, psychoanalysis, and popular fiction: all institute mechanisms through which one sheds or pierces social conventionality in order to reach knowledge of deeper-lying truths and thus some version of what Wesley called 'justification.' In all these contexts, 'deep' is a radically metaphorical value word, a *rhetorical intensifier,* rather than the descriptive one which it claims to be. . . . To grant a royal privilege to this category of invisibility as we automatically do, to define as most authentic that which is least accessible to direct observation, signals . . . a huge investment of prestige in various methods of investigation—essential truth must be deeply hidden, otherwise what function can be performed by strenuous technologies of discovery like psychoanalysis?" (emphasis supplied, 255). The novel participates in popularizing and laying the groundwork for such prestigious "technologies" (exemplified by psychoanalysis): "the novelistic effect known as 'depth' has always been closely correlated with the narrative of solitary individual character, particularly at moments of crisis or even of breakdown . . . that bring secret facets of the mind into view and create with this device the wonderful novelistic illusion of individuality generating itself before our eyes. . . . Individuality is effectively defined within the rhetorical system of nineteenth-century novels as one's capacity for resisting pressures of conformity. To incorporate into fiction in any concerted, explicit way the ethnographic thesis that individuality is parasitic upon standardized or stereotyped cultural patterns, that emotions are not the antithesis of social institutions but *are* social institutions themselves, and that events spring not from personal will but from the 'subtle and complex [causation] which runs,' as [Herbert] Spencer said, 'through the actions of incorporated men' . . . would undo at its root the vital principle of novelistic imagination" (258–59). As Herbert notes, "depth" is "a trope [that has been] endowed with . . . much rhetorical power" (256): its historical causes and ideological operations must be clarified if we are to conceptualize an American history of psychological life. An exemplary book that contributes to this clarification by focusing on the categories of "the unconscious" and "the primitive" and the politics of "Modern Man discourse" is Michael Leja's *Reframing Abstract Expressionism: Subjectivity and Painting in the 1940s* (New Haven: Yale University Press, 1993).

23. Gilman is quoted in "Where Are the Pre-War Radicals?" *Survey Graphic* 55 (Feb. 1926): 564.

24. See Zaretsky, *Capitalism, the Family, and Personal Life* (New York: Harper Colophon, 1979), 91–96, Mari Jo Buhle, *Women and American Socialism, 1870–1920* (Urbana: University of Illinois Press, 1981), 254, 257, 268, 272, 284, and Pfister, *Staging Depth,* 139–42.

25. Foucault, *History of Sexuality,* 130.

26. Glaspell, *Plays* (Boston: Small, Maynard, 1920), 241. Freeman, *American Testament,* 159.

27. Glaspell, *Plays,* 235.

28. For background on this see Winifred L. Frazer, *Mabel Dodge Luhan* (Boston: Twayne, 1984), 61–64. Also see Hale's discussion of Dodge and psychoanalysis in *Rise and Crisis of Psychoanalysis,* 66–68.

29. The first quotation comes from Dodge, "Mabel Dodge Tells About the Unconscious: From Error Comes Wisdom. Watch Yourself," in Mabel Dodge Luhan Scrapbooks, vol. 17, Beinecke Rare Book and Manuscript Library, Yale University. The second is from Dodge, *Movers and Shakers* (Albuquerque: University of New Mexico Press, 1985), 440.

30. The first quotation is from Dodge, "Mabel Dodge Tells About the Unconscious"; the second is from her *Movers and Shakers,* 439.

31. See Lois Palken Rudnick, *Mabel Dodge Luhan: New Woman, New Worlds* (Albuquerque: University of New Mexico Press, 1984), 131, 137.

32. Dodge, *Lorenzo in Taos* (New York: Knopf, 1932), 71. Also see Christopher Lasch, *The New Radicalism in America [1889–1963]: The Intellectual as Social Type* (New York: Knopf, 1965), 139.

33. The first quotation is from Dodge, *Movers and Shakers,* 511, and the second is from Dodge, *Lorenzo in Taos,* 71. However, her curiosity with psychoanalytic fads didn't end.

34. For a sketch of contemporary notions about the relationship between therapy and creativity as well as a brief discussion of O'Neill's experience with analysis see Pfister, *Staging Depth,* 55–58. On the rising divorce rate see Elaine Tyler May, *Great Expectations: Marriage and Divorce in Post-Victorian America* (Chicago: University of Chicago Press, 1980), and Steven Mintz and Susan Kellogg, *Domestic Revolutions: A Social History of Family Life* (New York: Free Press, 1988), 109. Kovel, *The Age of Desire: Reflections of a Radical Psychoanalyst* (New York: Pantheon, 1981), 52.

35. Dodge, *Movers and Shakers,* 455.

36. Dodge, "Mabel Dodge Talks on Mothers of Men," in Mabel Dodge Luhan Scrapbooks, vol. 15, Beinecke Rare Book and Manuscript Library, Yale University. Tridon, *Psychoanalysis and Love* (New York: Brentano's, 1922), 246.

37. On how the "moral superiority" of middle-class "angels" both prohibited them from showing anger openly and permitted them to manifest it in other ways (e.g., crying, making an antagonist feel guilty) see Carol Zisowitz Stearns and Peter N. Stearns, *Anger: The Struggle for Emotional Control in American History* (Chicago: University of Chicago Press, 1986), 61.

38. Anthony, *Margaret Fuller: A Psychological Biography* (New York: Harcourt, Brace and Howe, 1920), 19, 81, 79, 17, 25, v.

39. See Bell Gale Chevigny, *The Woman and the Myth: Margaret Fuller's Life and Writings* (Boston: Northeastern University Press, 1994). For example, see Fuller's self-abasing, extravagantly mushy, and touching dependence fantasy about Beethoven—"To Beethoven, November 25, 1843" (61–62)—and Fuller's remark: "The Woman in me kneels and weeps in tender rapture; the Man in me rushes forth but only to be baffled" (216). On birth control, feminism, and romance see Margaret Sanger's *Woman and the New Race* (New York: Brentano's, 1920) and *Happiness in Marriage* (Fairview Park, N.Y.: Maxwell Reprint Co., 1969). Blanchard and Manasses, *New Girls for Old* (New York: Macaulay, 1930), 233–34. On sexology and femininity in the 1920s see Nina Miller, "The Bonds of Free Love: Constructing the Female Bohemian Self," *Genders* 11 (Fall 1991): 38–41.

40. Historians and critics are finding out how complex it is to generalize about the

sorts of subjectivities that nineteenth-century sentimental cultures helped produce. On the intensity of sexual and emotional bonds in the nineteenth-century middle-class home see Karen Lystra, *Searching the Heart: Women, Men, and Romantic Love in Nineteenth-Century America* (New York: Oxford University Press, 1989). But Nina Baym points out that sentimental culture also fostered public concerns in women that extended beyond the walls of the home in *American Women Writers and the Work of History, 1790–1860* (New Brunswick, N.J.: Rutgers University Press, 1995). And on sentimental culture and women reformers see Barbara Berg, *The Remembered Gate: Origins of American Feminism: The Woman and the City, 1800–1860* (New York: Oxford University Press, 1978). Some of the ways in which seemingly "private" sentiment was complicit in racial and class ideologies are explored in a volume that contains excellent samples of work in this field: *The Culture of Sentiment: Race, Gender, and Sentimentality in Nineteenth-Century America*, ed. Shirley Samuels (New York: Oxford University Press, 1992).

41. Zaretsky, *Capitalism, the Family, and Personal Life*, 113. Hochschild, *The Managed Heart: Commercialization of Human Feeling* (Berkeley: University of California Press, 1983), 2.

42. See Carroll Smith-Rosenberg, "Sex as Symbol in Victorian Purity: An Ethnohistorical Analysis of Jacksonian America," *American Journal of Sociology* 84 (Special Summer Supplement, 1978): 212–47; Stephen Nissenbaum, *Sex, Diet, and Debility in Jacksonian America: Sylvester Graham and Health Reform* (Westport, Conn.: Greenwood Press, 1980); and G. J. Barker-Benfield, *The Horrors of the Half-Known Life: Male Attitudes Toward Women and Sexuality in Nineteenth-Century America* (New York: Harper Colophon, 1976).

43. I thank Franny Nudelman for making her term—*psychological specificity*—available to me.

44. Hale, *Freud and the Americans*, 397–408. On the growing importance of psychology as a discourse that defined the identity, goals, and problems of family life in the 1920s see Paula Fass, *The Damned and the Beautiful: American Youth in the 1920s* (New York: Oxford University Press, 1977). Some pieces both defended the authority of psychological science (against sentiment) and criticized Freud's sexualization of women. See Edward Spencer Cowles, M.D., "The Soul and Body Clinic," *Women's Home Companion* 50 (Oct. 1923): 16, 146–47, and Cowles's "Dangerous Currents: A Candid Talk about Amateur Self-Analysis and Its Effect on the Youth of To-day," *Women's Home Companion* 51 (Nov. 1924): 4, 148.

45. On the tale of the man-eating woman see Michael Paul Rogin, *Fathers and Children: Andrew Jackson and the Subjugation of the American Indian* (New York: Vintage, 1975), 71. For an analysis of the social anxieties underlying clitoridectomies and ovariotomies see Barker-Benfield, *Horrors*. Levy, *Other Women: The Writing of Class, Race, and Gender, 1832–1898* (Princeton: Princeton University Press, 1991), 119.

46. Case studies that bring up these sexual acts are discussed in Robert Latou Dickenson and Lura Beam, *A Thousand Marriages: A Medical Study of Sexual Adjustment* (1931; rpt., Westport, Conn.: Greenwood Press, 1970), Katherine Bement Davis, *Factors in the Sex Life of Twenty-Two Hundred Women* (New York: Arno Press, 1972, originally published in 1929). For advice on intercourse during menstruation see William J. Robinson, M.D., *Woman: Her Sex and Love Life* (New York: Eugenics Publishing, 1925), 280–81. On clitoral stimulation see William J. Fielding, *Sex and the Love-Life* (New York: Dodd Mead, 1927), 139. Hinkle, "Woman and the New Morality," in *Our Changing Morality*, ed. Freda Kirchwey (1930; rpt., New York: Arno Press, 1972), 247. Schmalhausen, *Our Changing Human Nature* (New York: Macaulay, 1929), 117.

47. See George W. Stocking, Jr., *Victorian Anthropology* (New York: Free Press, 1987), Henrika Kulick, *The Savage Within: The Social History of British Anthropology, 1885–1945* (Cambridge: Cambridge University Press, 1991), Adam Kuper, *The Invention of Primitive Society: Transformations of an Illusion* (New York: Routledge, 1988). See Richard Slotkin's analysis of the representation of workers as savages in the Great Strike of 1877 in *The Fatal Environment: The Myth of the Frontier in the Age of Industrialization, 1800–1890* (Middletown, Conn.: Wesleyan University Press, 1986), 477–98.

48. See Michael Leja's work on American abstract artists of the 1940s who deployed the category of "the primitive" to construct an ideological discourse of "Modern Man" in *Reframing Abstract Expressionism*, 49–120. O'Neill, *Selected Letters of Eugene O'Neill*, ed. Travis Bogard and Jackson R. Bryer (New Haven: Yale University Press, 1988), 391. On "the veneer of civilization" see Morton W. Peck, M.D., "Psychoanalysis and Humankind," *The Survey* 64 (May 1, 1930): 127.

49. The ad for Tridon's *Psychoanalysis and Love* is on the inside back cover of *The Liberator*, Sept. 1922. Fielding, *Sex and the Love-Life*, 138.

50. Burroughs, *The Return of Tarzan* (New York: Grosset & Dunlap, 1915), 18. For an excellent discussion of some of the Tarzan novels see Marianna Torgovnick, *Gone Primitive: Savage Intellects, Modern Lives* (Chicago: University of Chicago Press, 1990), 42–72 (Torgovnick mentions the enormous output of Tarzan novels on 42). Eric Cheyfitz offers perceptive insights into *Tarzan* and early twentieth-century ideologies of imperialism and individualism in *The Poetics of Imperialism: Translation and Colonization from* The Tempest *to* Tarzan (New York: Oxford University Press, 1991), 3–21. And for another astute analysis of the ideological uses of "the primitive" in this century see Catherine A. Lutz and Jane L. Collins, *Reading National Geographic* (Chicago: University of Chicago Press, 1993).

51. Burroughs, *Return of Tarzan*, 351. Burroughs, *Tarzan of the Apes* (1912; rpt., Racine, Wisc.: Whitman, n.d.), 253, 182. See Torgovnick on the miscegenation anxieties (*Gone Primitive*, 52–53).

52. Burroughs, *Return of Tarzan*, 152. See Lutz, *American Nervousness*.

53. Burroughs, *Cave Girl* (New York: Grosset & Dunlap, 1925), 95, 140, 162.

54. Some of Caudwell's writings from the 1930s are reprinted as *Studies and Further Studies in a Dying Culture* (New York: Monthly Review Press, 1971), 187–88.

55. Dyer, *Heavenly Bodies: Film Stars and Society* (New York: St. Martin's Press, 1986), 138.

56. See Robert F. Berkhoffer, Jr., *The White Man's Indian: Images of the American Indian from Columbus to the Present* (New York: Vintage, 1979), 86–96, and for a discussion of the earlier European uses of the Indian as noble savage see 72–80. American authors of the 1820s and 1830s, like James Fenimore Cooper, Henry Wadsworth Longfellow, and Lydia Maria Child "romanticize[d] the safely dead Indian" (90). On the American cultural and literary history of the noble savage in the first half of the nineteenth century, also see Roy Harvey Pearce, *The Savages of America: A Study of the Indian and the Idea of Civilization* (Baltimore: Johns Hopkins Press, 1953), 136–50, 169–95, 197–98.

57. See Grob, *Mad Among Us*, 61. Edward Jarvis, M.D., "On the Supposed Increase in Insanity," *American Journal of Insanity* 8 (1851–52): 333–64. Jarvis had a pretty clear idea about what was driving mid-nineteenth-century male Americans crazy. For example: "There are many new trades and new employments; there are new schemes of increasing wealth, new articles of merchandise, and speculations in many things of new and

multiplying kinds. All these increase the activity of the commercial world. . . . [The] inflation or expansion of prices . . . makes many kinds of business more uncertain, and many men's fortunes more precarious. This increases the doubts and perplexities of business, the necessity of more labor and watchfulness, greater fear and anxiety, and the end is more frequently in loss, and failure of plans, and mental disturbance" (361–62). Jarvis does not label this process capitalism. He uses another word, which carries connotations of inevitable progress: "Insanity is then a part of the price which we pay for civilization. The causes of the one increase with the developments and results of the other. This is not necessarily the case, but it is so now" (363). On Beard see Lutz, *American Nervousness,* 3–7.

58. O'Neill, *Conversations with Eugene O'Neill,* ed. Mark W. Estrin (Jackson: University Press of Mississippi, 1990), 53.

59. See Barnes, "Negro Art in America," in *The New Negro,* ed. Alain Locke (New York: Atheneum, 1980), 19, 20. Krutch is quoted in Martin Bauml Duberman, *Paul Robeson* (New York: Knopf, 1988), 65.

60. On the Harlem Renaissance and some of the "performative" strategies that preoccupied its artists see Houston A. Baker, Jr., *Modernism and the Harlem Renaissance* (Chicago: University of Chicago Press, 1987). In writing this chapter I have kept in mind Judith Butler's notion of "performativity" as a scripting of gender subjectivity (or, more broadly, social identity) that is "compulsory" and not often obvious to the performer as a scripting of self. See the following works by Butler: "Performative Acts and Gender Constitution: An Essay in Phenomenology and Feminist Theory," in *Performing Feminisms: Feminist Critical Theory and Theatre,* ed. Sue-Ellen Case (Baltimore: Johns Hopkins University Press, 1990), 210–82, *Gender Trouble: Feminism and the Subversion of Identity* (New York: Routledge, 1990), 128–41, and "Critically Queer," *GLQ: A Journal of Lesbian and Gay Studies* 1 (1993): 17–32 (I thank my colleague Henry Abelove for directing me to the latter article). My own broad sense of performance in this chapter is that it can indeed be compulsory and not evident to the performer, but the scripting can at times be quite conscious and enacted willingly. That is, this boundary is permeable. I have also been influenced by Ken Plummer's discussion of the social interactionist concept of scripting in "Symbolic Interactionism and Sexual Conduct: An Emergent Perspective," in *Human Sexual Relations: Towards a Redefinition of Sexual Politics,* ed. Mike Brake (New York: Pantheon, 1982), 223–41, and Stephen Greenblatt's reflections on performance in *Renaissance Self-Fashioning: From More to Shakespeare* (Chicago: University of Chicago Press, 1980). Also see *Performativity and Performance,* ed. Andrew Parker and Eve Kosofsky Sedgwick (New York: Routledge, 1995), *Cruising the Performative: Interventions into the Representation of Ethnicity, Nationality, and Sexuality,* ed. Sue-Ellen Case, Philip Brett, and Susan Leigh Foster (Bloomington: Indiana University Press, 1995), Richard Schechner, *The Future of Ritual: Writings on Culture and Performance* (New York: Routledge, 1993), and Victor Turner, *From Ritual to Theatre: The Human Seriousness of Play* (New York: Performing Arts Journal Publications, 1982).

61. Hughes, *The Ways of White Folks* (New York: Knopf, 1969), 19, 20, 21, 22, 27.

62. Gates, "The Trope of a New Negro and the Reconstruction of the Black," *Representations* 24 (Fall 1988): 129–55. On the race riots see a perceptive article written by the (unspecified) editors of a provocative black socialist monthly, "The Causes and Remedy of Race Riots," *The Messenger* (Sept. 1919): 19–21. For a discussion of the race riots and

white and black attitudes toward returning soldiers see David Levering Lewis, *When Harlem Was in Vogue* (New York: Knopf, 1981), 9–15. On Garvey see James Weldon Johnson, *Black Manhattan* (New York: Arno Press, 1968), 254–56, and Tony Martin, *Literary Garveyism: Garvey, Black Arts and the Harlem Renaissance* (Dover, Mass.: The Majority Press, 1983). On the Ku Klux Klan see Howard Zinn, *A People's History of the United States* (New York: Harper Perennial, 1990), 373. Huggins, *Harlem Renaissance* (New York: Oxford University Press, 1971), 91, 254.

63. See Nancy Cott, *The Grounding of Modern Feminism* (New Haven: Yale University Press, 1987), 7, 217, 156. Also see Dorothy M. Brown, *Setting a Course: American Women in the 1920s* (Boston: G. K. Hall, 1987), 248.

64. Cott, *Grounding*, 148, 150, 157. Also see Rayna Rapp and Ellen Ross, "The Twenties Backlash: Compulsory Heterosexuality, the Consumer Family, and the Waning of Feminism," in *Class, Race, and Sex: The Dynamics of Control*, ed. Amy Swerdlow and Hanna Lessinger (Boston: G. K. Hall, 1983), 93, 103–104.

65. Frederick Lewis Allen estimates that there were few beauticians in the United States in the mid-1910s but that by 1927 there were 18,000 (*Only Yesterday: An Informal History of the Nineteen-Twenties* [New York: Harper, 1931], 107). On the 1920s beauty industry see Lois W. Banner, *American Beauty* (New York: Knopf, 1983), 271–80. Also see Banner's discussion of the first Miss America pageants in the 1920s: the American "beauty" could be sexually attractive (she did parade in a bathing suit—albeit an unrevealing one), but she absolutely had to seem *feminine* (265–70). Blanchard and Manasses, *New Girls for Old*, 2. Dickenson and Beam, *A Thousand Marriages*, 150.

66. See Peter G. Filene, *Him/Her/Self* (Baltimore: Johns Hopkins University Press, 1986), 120–35.

67. Florence Guy Seabury, *The Delicatessen Husband and Other Essays* (New York: Harcourt, Brace, 1926): henceforth all quotations from this book will be followed by page numbers in parenthesis in the text. On Seabury see Zita Dresner, "Heterodite Humor: Alice Duer Miller and Florence Guy Seabury," *Journal of American Culture* 10 (Fall 1987): 36–38, and Nancy A. Walker, *A Very Serious Thing: Women's Humor and American Culture* (Minnesota: University of Minnesota Press, 1988), 50–51, 136. My information about Seabury's political activism comes from Gail S. Agronick, "Feminist Psychologists, 1915–1930: Personal, Political, and Professional Constraints," B.A. honors thesis (Wesleyan University, 1988), 69–71. Agronick got much of her information from *Woman's Who's Who of America*, ed. John William Leonard (New York: American Commonwealth, 1914). Leonard indicates that Florence Guy married Howard B. Woolston (her entry is under the name Florence Guy Woolston) in 1904 (when she was twenty-three). Leonard lists numerous feminist and socialist organizations to which she belonged and notes that she has published articles in magazines including *The Survey, Women's Era, Intercollegiate Socialist Society, Woman's Suffrage Party*, and *Redbook*.

68. David Seabury, *Unmasking Our Minds* (New York: Boni & Liverwright, 1925), xxii, xvi, xxiv. *Who's Who in America*, ed. Albert Nelson Marquis, vol. 17, 1932–33 (Chicago: Marquis, 1932), does not include an entry on Florence Seabury, but the entry on David Seabury lists their date of marriage as May 13, 1923.

69. Florence Guy Seabury, "Men Who Understand Women," *Nation* 119 (Nov. 12, 1924): 516–18, see 518. This essay was reprinted in a slightly revised version in 1929 entitled "Stereotypes" in *Our Changing Morality*, 219–31. One 1929 revision, though small, is sig-

nificant, perhaps, when one considers that Florence Seabury would increasingly come under the sway of David Seabury's brand of pop psychology. In 1924 Florence Seabury contends that the stereotyped "picture" of women, "even in the interpretations of those who claim to understand the modern woman, is chiefly one of sex, not character" (518). This is clearly a jab at the pictures of women painted by sexologists and some pop psychologists: "sex" became a dominant discourse within which femaleness was "discovered" (perhaps constructed) in the 1920s. But in the 1929 revision she substitutes "function" for "sex" ("chiefly of function, not character" [231]), thus making the target of her criticism less specific. By 1929 she had been married to David Seabury for six years. Other articles dating from Seabury's *Delicatessen Husband* phase exhibit her feminist satire, humor, and strategies of inversion—reminiscent of Fanny Fern's comical, yet biting women's rights journalism during the 1850s and 1860s, and in harmony with Katha Pollitt's feminist wit during the 1980s and 1990s. Florence Seabury's "A White, White Rose for Mother," *New Republic* 42 (May 6, 1925): 228–29, satirizes how mass culture structures male emotions to be dependent on "mother-stuff" stereotypes; "The Dodder," *New Republic* 42 (March 11, 1925), 67–69, is about the new class of emotionally independent professional women who help support male lover-parasites ("dodders") so that their careers remain unsnagged by wedlock; and "By Any Other Name," *New Republic* 46 (May 5, 1926), 325–27, concerns the ideological power of naming (women assuming the name of their mate) and suggests (tongue-in-cheek, I infer) that increasing numbers of enlightened men are refusing to rename their wives: "As feminism sweeps forward, some Patrick Henry will surely arise in the masculine revolution and waving his name in the air, cry out again 'Give me my name or give me death!'" (327). Yet Florence Guy consented to be renamed by David Seabury (and before that by her first husband, Howard B. Woolston).

70. I have been able to reconstruct only bits of this story. Florence Guy Seabury's second and final book was *Love Is a Challenge* (New York: Whittlesey House, 1936). In its blending of pop psychology, quotable maxims, and fictional anecdotes/case studies it resembles the easy-going style of David Seabury's books of that period, such as *The Art of Selfishness* (New York: Julian Messner, 1937). Her book has residues of the feisty feminist satire and humor so evident in her earlier book (some of which I will quote), but her 1930s tone often has a preachy quality. Florence Seabury's 1920s critical emphasis on the cultural production of gender stereotypes is largely replaced in 1936 with her stress on childhood training and conflicts, "primitive instincts" (68), and the unconscious as explanations for what hampers the efforts of men and women to establish a loving "intimacy." Intimacy rather than "the reorganization of society" (28) is her utopian goal (the former, she hopes vaguely, will lay the foundation of the latter). If she saw individuality in 1926 as being constituted by narrow gender definitions, in 1936 she conceptualizes individuality as a psychological developmental project or goal (evolving beyond one's "primitive" within and reeducating one's emotions to adjust to basic realities). In other words, psychological analysis partly replaces her former feminist analysis (centering on roles) of conjugal relations. Thus she leans toward invoking Freud's death drive (which she claims is not necessarily a permanent instinct) to explain marital discord: "The enjoyment of hostility is one of the paradoxes of marriage" (230). Her long list of attitudes and problems that may jeopardize connubial bliss include "*Radicalism*": "Skepticism about marriage, home, family. A declared belief that free relations are better than accepted forms of marriage. Rebellion against adjustments in intimacy" (20). In lieu of

advocating the dismantling of an "emotional machinery" installed by the culture within the family and within the self, her foe is "neurosis" (60) and her solution is "emotional education" and "emotional expansion" (111). The "cave woman" who forces her economic will on her man is in 1936 cast as a psychological loser: "a man does not live in economic servitude without protest. If he has been captured by the machinations of some powerful cave woman against his inherent desires, he is at heart rebellious, and after a while he breaks his chains, to the joy of the tabloids" (131).

Yet the Florence Seabury of 1926 who seemed skeptical of "primitive depth" as the explanation for behavior is not entirely absent in 1936. Seabury—like Joseph Freeman— recognized psychoanalysis as a cultural mode of reading the self and others that could get out of hand: "Inspired by [Freud's] followers, telling the truth about one's relatives, which had never been done, except in a last extremity of exasperation to some intimate, became the fashion; and mothers and fathers . . . were execrated with alacrity" (255). The Seabury of 1936 continues to refuse to make sexuality the key to the self and sometimes imagines desire in more encompassing terms (terms which, however, do not extend much into the realm beyond "intimacy"): "An individual who is focused in an extreme way upon sex may not be searching for physical release but may be unconsciously pursuing a satisfaction he cannot define" (328). Notwithstanding her basic David Seabury pop psychological orientation, she occasionally observes that love is a challenge because "it has been buried under a mass of stereotypes and enshrouded by economic pressures" (71). Her sharp feminist sting also sometimes penetrates the layers of psychological padding packed with advice about readjustment: "Each new generation has its way of proving the happiest love relations are those in which the little lady has her master's voice and knows her place" (23).

In "Mental Hygiene for Mothers" (*Parents' Magazine* 13 [May 1938]: 22–23, 66–67) Seabury adopted the title "Consultant in Human Relations." Her counsel to mothers is conventional: because unconscious childhood emotional conflicts often determine one's adult disposition (psychologically, we are all child-adults), mothers must not reproduce in their children the same conflicts that shaped them. Her four-column article offers mothers "simple methods of self-help" (67). Florence Seabury's brief obituary (*New York Times*, October 8, 1951, 21) identifies her as a feminist and a teacher of "applied psychology at Briarcliff Junior College." David Seabury is not brought up. His fairly long obituary (*New York Times*, April 3, 1960, 86) notes that he was a consulting psychologist since 1921 (although he only received his Ph.D. in 1950—at age 64), the author of fifteen books, and something of an entrepreneur—the "founder and president of the David Seabury School of Psychology and . . . president of Seabury University Adult Education." It also portrays him as "an articulate lecturer who often spoke on marital problems." *Who's Who in America*, ed. Albert Nelson Marquis, vol. 24, 1946–1947 (Chicago: Marquis, 1946), notes that David Seabury (there is no entry for Florence) remarried in 1945 (the previous volume still lists his date of marriage to Florence Seabury). It seems likely then that Florence and David Seabury were divorced in the early or mid-1940s. Florence Seabury's *Love Is a Challenge* was dedicated to her mother; a cursory two-paragraph foreword by her husband follows this. There is no acknowledgment of Florence in David Seabury's *Art of Selfishness* (1937). He dedicated this book to two friends "who took such good care of me while I was writing this book." One might conjecture: could it be that by 1936 Florence had "intimate" as well as intellectual reasons for writing *Love Is a Challenge*? One might also wonder how during the late 1930s and early 1940s she might have reflected on the theoretical change in direction her writing had taken since the mid-1920s.

71. For a discussion of these plays (with a somewhat different slant on *The Verge*) and for citations of recent criticism on Glaspell see Pfister, *Staging Depth*, 187–203, 214–15.

72. Quoted in Judith Schwarz, *The Radical Feminists of Heterodoxy* (Lebanon, N.H.: New Victoria Publishers, 1982), 3. Glaspell, *Plays by Susan Glaspell*, ed. C. W. E. Bigsby (Cambridge: Cambridge University Press, 1991): henceforth all quotations from this play will be followed by page numbers in parenthesis in the text.

73. Chopin, *The Awakening*, ed. Nancy A. Walker (Boston: St. Martin's, 1993), 32. For critical perspectives on *The Awakening*, the ideological production of feminine subjectivity, and Edna Pontellier's assertion of "bourgeois individualist desires" see Dale Bauer, *Feminist Dialogics: A Theory of Failed Community* (Albany: State University of New York Press, 1988), 129–58.

74. Ward, *The Story of Avis*, ed. Elizabeth Hardwick (New Brunswick, N.J.: Rutgers University Press, 1985), 246. Also see Elizabeth Stuart Phelps Ward, *Doctor Zay* (Boston: Houghton Mifflin, 1882).

75. On "individualization" as an ideological process see Foucault, "The Subject and Power," in *Beyond Structuralism and Hermeneutics*, ed. Hubert L. Dreyfus and Paul Rabinow (Chicago: University of Chicago Press, 1983), 213. For insights into abstract artists' involvement in such strategies of "individualization" in the 1940s see Leja, *Reframing Abstract Expressionism*. Two useful early twentieth-century critiques of individualization are DeLeon's argument in Daniel DeLeon and Thomas E. Carmody, "DeLeon-Carmody Debate: Individualism vs. Socialism" (Troy, N.Y.: n.p., 1912), and John Dewey's 1929–30 analysis in *Individualism Old and New* (New York: Capricorn, 1962). More recent useful work on the history and politics of individualization are Nancy Armstrong and Leonard Tennenhouse, *The Imaginary Puritan: Literature, Intellectual Labor, and the Origins of Personal Life* (Berkeley: University of California Press, 1992), 17–18, 161–62, 171–72, *Reconstructing Individualism: Autonomy, Individuality, and the Self in Western Thought*, ed. Thomas C. Heller, Morton Sosna, and David Wellbery, with Arnold I. Davidson, Ann Swidler, and Ian Watt (Stanford: Stanford University Press, 1986), Louis Dumont, *Essays on Individualism: Modern Ideology in Anthropological Perspective* (Chicago: University of Chicago Press, 1986), *The Category of the Person: Anthropology, Philosophy, History*, ed. Michael Carrithers, Steven Collins, and Steven Lukes (Cambridge: Cambridge University Press, 1985), D. F. B. Tucker, *Marxism and Individualism* (Oxford: Basil Blackwell, 1980), Ian Forbes, *Marx and the New Individual* (London: Unwin Hyman, 1990), and Robert N. Bellah, Richard Madsen, William M. Sullivan, Ann Swidler, and Steven M. Tipton, *Habits of the Heart: Individualism and Commitment in American Life* (New York: Harper & Row, 1985). See Raymond Williams's essay on "individual" in his *Keywords: A Vocabulary of Culture and Society* (New York: Oxford University Press, 1976), 133–36, and Gillian Brown's discussion of "individualism" in *A Companion to American Thought*, ed. Richard Wightman Fox and James Kloppenberg (Oxford: Blackwell, 1995), 337–40.

76. Illuminating some of the implications of the misleading ideological dichotomy society (or history) versus the "individual," Fredric Jameson writes: "To imagine that, sheltered from the omnipresence of history and the implacable influence of the social, there already exists a realm of freedom . . . is only to strengthen the grip of Necessity over all such blind zones in which the individual subject seeks refuge, in pursuit of a

purely individual, a merely psychological, project of salvation" (*The Political Unconscious: Narrative As a Socially Symbolic Act* [Ithaca: Cornell University Press, 1980], 20). Showalter, introduction to *These Modern Women: Autobiographical Essays from the Twenties*, ed. Elaine Showalter (Old Westbury, N.Y.: Feminist Press, 1978), 10. Cott, *Grounding*, 280–82, 365. See Herbert Hoover, *American Individualism* (Garden City, N.Y.: Doubleday, Page, 1922).

77. Elaine Tyler May observes: "Between 1867 and 1929 the population of the United States grew 300 percent, the number of marriages increased 400 percent, and the divorce rate rose by 2,000 percent. By the end of the 1920s more than one in every six marriages terminated in court, and the United States had achieved the dubious distinction of having the highest divorce rate in the world." See May, "Myths and Realities of the American Family," in *Riddles of Identity in Modern Times*, ed. Antoine Prost and Gerard Vincent, vol. 5 of *A History of Private Life*, ed. Philippe Ariès and Georges Duby, trans. Arthur Goldhammer (Cambridge: Harvard University Press, 1991), 553.

78. What I am describing is a modern establishment of hegemony, which Antonio Gramsci theorized as rule by consent (the cultural production of consent), not overt coercion. As Alan Sinfield put it, " 'Hegemony' is the term elaborated by Gramsci to address the way a class may achieve domination in a particular socio-political situation, not so much by exercising manifest and direct control, but by gaining acceptance for its way of looking at the world" (*Alfred Tennyson* [Oxford: Basil Blackwell, 1986], 14).

79. Freeman, *American Testament*, 267. Malcolm Cowley offered two provocative criticisms that, placed in conjunction with Freeman's observation, further develop its implications. In a review of Floyd Dell's *Love in the Machine Age* (1930) Cowley suggested that the production of psychological subjects who are guided by a nonjudgmental, permissive therapeutic ethos (that celebrates a "laissez-faire of the instincts") is also the making of political subjects. The psychological stress on acceptance, he claimed, functioned to refashion middle-class evasiveness as emotional health: "We are increasingly tolerant toward evils—sexual, economic, political—which we have not the strength to correct. . . . Our psychologists and sociologists . . . . reflect that it is easier to adapt the individual to his environment than to adapt the environment to the individual" ("Happiness Made Easy," *New Republic* 62 [Apr. 30, 1930]: 304). And in his *Exile's Return* (1934), not only did Cowley underscore that many of Greenwich Village's ostensibly antibourgeois psychosexual "bohemians" were consummately bourgeois (quite interested in growing rich from exploiting Village real estate and the Village image), he argued that their pseudo-radical repackaging of bourgeois identity was essential to the glamorizing and stylizing of consumer "individualities" based on a consumer ethos. After World War I the industrial complex that had been enlarged rapidly to support the war required "new domestic market[s]" and "a *consumption* ethic" (62): "The [consumer culture] revolution would have occurred if the Village had never existed, but—the point is important—it would not have followed the same course. The Village, older in revolt, gave form to the movement, created its fashions, and supplied writers and illustrators who would render them popular." Corporate America came to recognize that "sex appeal"—as "self-expression"—made glossy in its "advertising pages," animated in its "movie palaces," and given "philosophical justification" by "Freudian psychology"—would help fuel its machines, expand its markets, and swell its profits (62). And so the Greenwich Village that promoted psychosexual individualism as both chic and therapeutic turned out to be commercially useful after all. Rather than recycling the conventional reading of the Vil-

lage as a haven of "individuals" who opposed "society," Cowley realized that the Village's glamorous sexiness, permissiveness, and uniforms of individuality were being main-streamed and incorporated into the American Consumer Way: "American business and the whole of middle-class America had been going Greenwich Village" (63). This was America's twentieth-century revolution—the revolution that rocked and still rocks the "free world." See Cowley, *Exile's Return: A Literary Odyssey of the 1920s* (1934), ed. Donald W. Faulkner (New York: Penguin, 1994).

PART IV

The Twentieth-Century Institutionalization of the Psychological

Educating the Emotions: Academic Psychology, Textbooks, and the Psychology Industry, 1890–1940

JILL G. MORAWSKI

In this chapter I shall recover an important yet relatively neglected dimension of the history—and education—of "the psychological." While historians have explored the early history of the mental health industry, with its novel language, technologies, and institutions, there exists hardly any analysis of the work that took place in the academy. The oversight of the work performed within colleges and universities may suggest the reluctance of scholars to question certain analytic distinctions between knowledge (science) and culture. Historians and psychologists, nevertheless, can only benefit from traversing more freely across the presumed boundaries of the scientific and the cultural, the professional and the popular, in order to better understand how psychological knowledges about social and personal life were manufactured, disseminated, and made meaningful. Here my focus is on psychology textbooks published between 1890 and 1940, a literary genre generally regarded as neither wholly scientific nor simply popular. These textbooks offer an opportunity to assess more comprehensively the relationship between the academy and the mass circulation of psychological ideas and ideologies, and have much to say about the politics of the early twentieth-century "higher education" of emotions.

In his 1890 introductory psychology textbook, William James presented a new theory of emotions as internal, physical happenings which are afterward felt as mental experiences. James reversed what he called the "natural way of thinking" about emotions that assumes that "mental perception of some fact excites the mental affection called the emotion." In contrast to the view that emotions were the result of mental processes, James proposed that they actually preceded the thought process: *"the bodily changes follow directly the perceptions of the exciting fact, and our feeling of the same changes as they occur IS the emotion."*[1] James's theory, informed by the research of physiologist Carl Lange, was to guide emotion research for half a century, bestowing upon the new scientific psychology an organic, natural, yet fundamentally mechanistic explanation of human emotions.

The new scientific psychology, heavily influenced by James, and disseminated in textbooks and experimental reports, signals an apparent lacuna if not contradiction in the conventional histories of psychological life at the turn of the century. On the one hand, cultural historians have garnered considerable evidence of the "modern" psychological beings who, freed from nineteenth-century moralism and nourished by a culture of consumption, were conceiving themselves as self-gratifying, yearning "individuals." On the other hand, historians of science have reported how the new academic psychology was positing the idea of psychological beings as determined, biomechanical, and limited in their power to alter themselves. The first representation depicts agents who are seemingly able to make themselves into whatever they desired, while the second portrays beings whose lives are determined by invisible yet forceful laws of nature. I shall examine the emerging scientific or determinist view of emotions as a means to consider the extent and dynamics of the apparent contradiction in historical accounts.[2] Representations of emotions in psychology textbooks—representations that are also evident in scientific practice and popular cultural understandings of emotion—are not simply determinant ones and, in fact, reveal that this contradiction is intriguingly multivalent. What was at stake in the mixed and multivalent signals sent by the "new psychology" must be grasped as more than an effort to establish the scientific status of psychology. With a subtle infusion of dynamic notions of personhood, the determinist model of emotions offered solace to a culture in which rationality, self-sufficiency, and social order were at once championed and doubted: on the surface they certified the certainty and stability of scientific laws while acknowledging a place for motivation, desire, and change. However, these conflicting notions of human capacities cannot be comprehended in terms of an ultimate dominance or victory of one over the other model but, rather, in terms of their co-existence.

Mark Seltzer has argued that during the early twentieth century two divergent cultural beliefs, emphasizing the natural and the made, respectively, resulted in a double discourse that blurred divides between natural and constructed, between the agentic and determined, and that recast "nature in terms of the *naturalist machine* . . . and individuals as *statistical persons.*"[3] The work of scientific psychology as it was published in the textbooks I shall discuss exhibits a similar boundary-blurring language.[4] I shall suggest that these mixed signals and blurred boundaries buttressed psychologists' larger scientific and ideological project. The centrality of scientific determinism in psychological theories provided the discipline with authority and legitimacy, while attention to the desires and interests of middle-class individuals helped to make psychology a commercial success—a sought-after commodity that apparently served their personal and occupational aspirations. The success of this project depended not simply on a mixed rhetoric but also on an assumption that emotional experiences and expressions vary according to a social hierarchy: emotions are distributed, experienced, and managed differently by different persons and *classes* of persons. I will show that this social distribution of emotions, together with the strategic use of a double discourse, gave psychologists effective resources with which to proffer determinist theories of emotional life.

Psychology Versus Culture?

There exists in accounts of the culture of consumption and of the reception of psychoanalysis, a picture of middle-class individuals becoming caught up in the magnification and glorification of self—via self-interest, self-realization, self-control, self-presentation—and placing less significance on nineteenth-century ideals of self-sacrifice, strenuousness, and the control if not repression of desire.[5] Psychoanalysis, through the translations, adaptations, and popularization of Freud's work, provided an imagery and language that described this new self and a technology for treating it. This increasingly influential therapeutic ethos fixated on social life, primarily the family and intimate others.[6] Yet, while Freud was developing psychoanalysis, the modern human sciences were generating a different rendition of persons, one that purportedly was more methodical in casting human action in biomechanical, rationalist, determinist forms.[7] In its purist form, this scientific perspective set limits to self-realization.

As exemplified in the James-Lange theory of emotion, scientific psychology appeared to be declaring the primacy of the body, not the mind; psychological research sought to locate the control of psychological life, not in desires or will or social life more generally, but in fixed, often physiological, mechanisms. While both perspectives on human action addressed the growing uncertainties about the source and form of reality, and proposed that the real mechanisms of human action lie in internal processes—either in the physiological or psychic interior—they offered strikingly discrepant procedures for analysis and control of these governing mechanisms. Although the scientific psychology that dominated work in the academy seemingly rejected a therapeutic ethos of self-discovery and cure, and also selectively discarded conceits of rational beings, it relied on a laboratory ethos of objective observation, calculation, and dissection that was linked with professional interests in producing social control technologies that used asocial, scientific-technical practices. Scientific psychologists' aspirations for social control extended beyond the management of experimental variables in the laboratory to beliefs that an orderly and rational social life required control and regulation and that their knowledge could be applied to these ends.[8]

The tensions between these two opposed conceptions of "the psychological," then, comprised not a simple clash of scientific versus the popular everyday explanations. Rather, the contradictions represented in these two discourses are visible *within* scientific psychology itself in at least two forms. First, based on the notion that body determines conduct, one inspired by a Darwinism that undercut conceptions of human rationality, scientific psychology nevertheless took itself to be a rational practice that assumed the possibility that passions, desires, and emotions—irrational processes—could be controlled in order to produce a rationally functioning human world.[9] Although the late nineteenth century had yielded doubts about the rational, autonomous individual, such uncertainties did not seriously compromise the maturing ideals of rational science; thus, the very mission of scientific psychology juxtaposed conflicting ideas about rationality. Second, scientific psychologists themselves often experienced the push and pull of these competing conceptions of the psychological. Just as James introduced a biomechanical explanation of emotions, he also wrote about self-discovery and self-realization, became engaged with spiritualism, and suffered the agonies and therapies associated with neurasthenia. Other scientific psychologists of the period struggled to find a place for will in a deterministic world, wrestled with their "feminine" or nonanalytic characteristics, and sometimes contributed popular articles on self-determination and self-discovery at the same time that they were promulgating a deterministic and mechanistic psychology.[10]

Introductory psychology textbooks published during this period exemplify some of the strategies developed to handle these apparent contradictions. In the texts middle-class readers, particularly undergraduate students, were presented with sophisticated and persuasive accounts of persons as biomechanical, mainly determined beings. At first sight, these accounts give little support to the popular notions of self-gratification and the centrality of social life to the maintenance and enhancement of psychological functioning. However, the texts also conveyed an alternative conceptualization of persons, one that worked through and around scientific and mechanistic terms to signal ways out of the period's uncertainties and anxieties about rationality, self-determination, and improvement. What the texts offered, in the end, was a double discourse of the natural and the made, of persons as at once organic forms and social entities. Just as they describe the determined, biomechanical body, so they present readers as social agents who could will and ultimately determine the direction of their lives. Whereas nineteenth-century psychologists defined sociality in terms of interacting individuals, twentieth-century American psychologists perceived sociality in terms of causal influences such that "the individual ended up either at the receiving end of these influences or as the manipulator." By fitting social events to lawful causal models, the "social" had been submitted to determinism. With the use of this sometimes subtle double accounting, psychology textbooks traversed lines of several binary notions: between the body and the machine, between the natural and the artificial (or the natural and some version of the social), and between determinism and willed action.[11]

Psychology textbooks reflected emerging contradictions in notions of selfhood and social life. What was being enacted in them was the tension between cultural understandings of nature and technology at the turn of the century. In his study of double discourse, Seltzer documents how mass-produced cultural forms including literature, visual representations, and technology variously coupled the natural body and the fabricated machine. Technologies of the industrial age consisted of practices that at once changed human experience and offered new ways of imaging the natural; thus control technologies like "the electric switch, ready at hand, promises to reconnect the interrupted links between conception and execution, agency and expression."[12] During the first two decades of the twentieth century, scientific psychology established itself as a technology, one that by virtue of its subject matter—human mental life— was especially concerned with the relays between the natural and the technological. What has been neglected in many cultural histories of the psychological is precisely the play of these two cultural forms and its consequences for twentieth-century conceptions of personhood and social relations. While psychologists did not always successfully engage these forms or resolve the attendant contradictions, they were able to strengthen their accounts by subtle appeals to cultural norms, particularly to the status quo social order of personhood that attributed psychological qualities according to persons' social positions and identities. As we shall see, this social order is presumed in the very dialogue established between authors and readers.

Readers, Authors, and Texts in American Psychology

In his 1894 introductory textbook, William Krohn asserted that "with a clean, well-trained eye and the mind's 'retinal field' cleared of all floating specks, the student of Psychology may ever seek the truth, the truth alone, if he would not be handicapped."[13] Another author, in a textbook published the same year, informed student readers that "Real knowledge and power" requires that the pupil "observe and analyze the actual processes of his own mind and those of others instead of taking what the author tells him about imaginary mental processes."[14] Readers of psychology textbooks were frequently identified as a special class of "educated men" who seek knowledge about reality and who stand apart from the class of "lazy readers."[15] "Self-control," one textbook author posited in 1898, is "the greatest end of all education."[16] Robert Yerkes expanded on this theme of a privileged and enlightened knowledge by noting that those who had not acquired the skills of psychology were "poverty stricken," adding, "Millions of human beings—unfortunate but all unconscious of what they are missing—go through life blind to the psychological world."[17] Psychology, another author concluded, benefits "all individuals interested in studying or controlling human nature."[18] These and other textbook authors identified psychological knowledge both with mastery in the world and with professional aspirations and, in turn, advertised these features to readers, thus enabling them to set themselves apart from ordinary citizens.

A distinct portrait of students was taking form in psychology's textbooks during the last decade of the nineteenth century. Readers were presented as ambitious and ahead of the pack, striving to know—and control—reality, including the reality of their own selves. Their images in these texts contrasted with the mid-nineteenth-century portrayal of the gentleman reader who read moral philosophy for introspective and spiritual insight.[19] This shift in representation from the gentlemen of high moral fiber to ambitious, yearning youth parallels changes in higher education and academic psychology alike. The numbers of students seeking undergraduate degrees increased fourfold between 1870 and 1890, and the number of institutions of higher education increased by more than 70 percent. The dramatic rise in college attendance reflected social structural changes: in the early nineteenth century most college students were affluent, and a lesser number were middle- or lower-class individuals who sought preparation for teaching or ministerial careers, whereas by the late nineteenth century, college life attracted large numbers from the middle class, including an increasing number of women.[20] These new students sought not so much genteel company or speculative inquiry as opportunities for vocational advancement in the new professions and corporate organizations. They sought positions as white-collar workers and experts in a world of technological change, growing urban populations, and greater wealth. As such, they were also seeking a place in a dramatically mobile social world where individuals were to experience social relations as ever shifting, proliferating, and sometimes alienating.[21]

The audience for the "new" psychology textbooks, then, was largely white, American-born, middle-class youth who were about to enter an adult world of new social arrangements and who saw higher education as an opportunity to improve their social and economic standing. Education came to be equated with professionalization—the standardization of middle-class work. In Burton Bledstein's words, education established "a formal context for the competitive spirit of individual egos." Professionalism constituted not simply a legitimization of certain skills and organization of work, but a culture which engendered the mentalities of its producers and consumers alike, a culture "by which middle-class individuals sharpened their emotional needs and measured their powers of intelligence."[22] Not surprisingly, psychology textbooks also were engaged in educating the emotions, not just dissecting, analyzing, and labeling them.

Participants in this culture confronted a new field of tensions. One set of tensions emerged as the possibilities for vertical mobility coincided with the formation, in all institutions, of corporate hierarchies or broad pyramids where only few were to reach the peak. On another level the nineteenth-century "producer culture" emphasis on ambition, dedication, and self-control—or plain old hard work—existed alongside newer sanctions for leisure, sport, and the permissive consumption of new mass-marketed products. In colleges, study was not supposed to interfere with good times; collective entertainment, whether it be football or fraternities, occupied a significant portion of students' time.[23] Popular literature offered accounts of frolic and adventure, and magazines promoted new products, not to mention new identities. Identity came to be less about character with the sublimation of individual desires to moral ends, and more about personality realized through self-fulfillment, confidence, and a desirable presentation of self.[24] Finally, the middle-class culture of professionalism encouraged awareness of the experience of "reality" in both work and play.

Experience and reality, however, were becoming increasingly difficult to locate. The buzz—and expansion—of experience suggested excitement and possibilities, but there was another side: the dynamic complexity, multiplicity, and obscurity of experience were daunting. The growing trust in the veracity of scientific knowledge, the faith axiomatic to professionalism, promised ultimate access to reality, yet at the same time the proliferation of new expert knowledge sometimes looked like life was multiple realities, if not *un*reality. Social science in particular challenged the very idea of reality in its repeated assaults on common sense (notably in proclamations about the inaccuracy and subjectivity of ordinary perceptions) and on the notion of autonomous action. The sense of unreality (or of the plurality of realities) did not originate with the social sciences but coincided with massive changes in social life and technology. Thus, for example, mass communication and transportation, along with growing diversity of reading experiences and the fantasies if not acts of consumption, increased the "complexity and varieties of voices represented in conversations with the self" during the late nineteenth and early twentieth centuries. Contending with these widening experiences, people confronted not only multiple realities but the possibility of multiple selves. The perceived unrealness of experience and the elusiveness of reality were addressed in the new psychotherapeutic sciences, including psychology, which claimed the ultimate ability to chart reality. In turn, these promises provided the psychotherapeutic sciences with a new opportunity to assert their importance in human affairs.[25]

By the 1890s, academic psychology too had entered a period of expansion. Prior to 1878 no American university had a doctoral program in psychology. By 1904 psychology had produced more than one hundred Ph.D.s and ranked fourth among the sciences in the number of such degrees conferred. That year at least sixty-two institutions had three or more psychology courses and some required a psychology course for completion of a B.A. The establishment of psychological laboratories, a symbol of psychology's independence from philosophy and of its status as science, also increased. In 1892 there were eighteen laboratories situated in institutions of higher education, just eight years later that number had increased to forty-two, and by 1926 there were approximately one hundred and seventeen.[26]

Psychology textbooks mark both the growth and orientation of American psychology. Few undergraduate students actually entered the new psychological laboratories that symbolized the scientific legitimacy of the discipline, but many students were to discover that science through introductory textbooks. In the 1870s only six first-edition introductory psychology texts were published in the United States, in the 1890s there were thirty-three, and in the first decade of the twentieth century there were thirty-eight. After 1890, most of these texts were authored by individuals with graduate training in psychology, including many of the discipline's leading scientists. By 1910 these books had become a standardized commodity; although occasionally the texts proffered an author's favorite theory or school, most contained a standard compendium of topics—sensation, physiology, learning, and emotion—and staunchly advocated a scientific orientation to psychological inquiry. In their uniformity they stand as but one example of a burgeoning textbook industry, earning authors profit and sometimes professional status. In their language of esoteric methods, they helped introduce and buttress a professional psychological culture. In their representation of human psychic forces as biomechanical and calculable, they both constituted and contributed to a rationalist science/technology of personhood.

How did these scientific treatises expounding deterministic axioms of psychological processes respond to or accommodate the discourses of self-realization, the culture of self-gratification and consumption, and the anxieties about rationality that were dramatically expressed in both popular and psychoanalytic thought? How did the texts reconcile the bio-politics inherent in their scientific vision with an emerging psychic account (however confusing in its entirety) of personal fulfillment and growth? In other words, how did they (if they did at all) address the cultural and personal experiences of this new breed of readers who appeared to be self-conscious about their selves?

One plausible resolution of the conflicting visions—the biomechanical and the self-enabling—was offered by William James in "The Gospel of Relaxation" (1898). In that essay James applied the James-Lange deterministic theory of emotions to a practicable therapeutic of the self. James first extended the theory to prescribe that, because feelings follow from bodily activities, we should pay more attention to what we *do* than what we *feel*. Then by arguing that Americans' pathological "bottled lightning" of anxieties and tensions is the result of bad habits of action, he suggested that Americans change their actions in order to relieve their tense minds.[27] While resembling the behaviorist platform that was to emerge within the next twenty years, James's psychotherapeutic diverged from that program in important respects. His apparently contradictory advice was that we manage not only our actions but our entire selves by "freeing" our ideation and volition "from the inhibitive influences of reflection upon them, of egoistic preoccupation about their results."[28] Repeatedly deploying mechanical metaphors and a play between freedom and control, James urged his readers to "*Unclamp,* in a word, your intellectual and practical machinery, and let it run free: and the service it will do you will be twice as good." His advice was aimed at students, "especially to girl-students," reminding them that "Just as a bicycle-chain may be too tight, so may one's carefulness and conscientiousness be so tense as to hinder the running of one's mind."[29] James concluded by designating God as a helpmate for female readers who tended to become "strenuously relaxed" rather than freely discharging their tensions.[30]

Unlike James's didactic psychology, standardized introductory textbooks typically make no place for will or God. However, like James's account, the texts juxtapose a rhetoric of mechanics with that of freedom. Nikolas Rose has discussed these features of psychology in terms of their contribution to "technologies of the self," to a science that offers not unhuman technology but potentials: it is "the promise of personhood, of being adequate to the real nature of the persons to be governed, that underlies the power that psychology seeks and finds with such technologies."[31] In this regard psychology can be viewed as a "generous" discipline readily accessible to various agents of social authority: "the key to the social penetration of psychology lies in its capacity to lend itself freely to others, who will 'borrow' it because of what it offers them in the way of a justification and guide to action."[32] Scientific psychology, as illustrated in its textbooks, did not so much propose a model of personhood that conflicted with other cultural productions and conceptions as it generated

a new field of possibilities for personhood, a grid upon which often contradictory conceptions were mapped and aligned, superimposed and coordinated.

James's essay on relaxation illustrates the multiple versions of personhood
constituting the emerging technologies of the self. Introductory textbook
authors also mapped and coordinated discordant images of the self in their
treatment of emotions: they charted a biomechanical model but often inter-
jected notions of self-management and change that belied a determinant view
of emotions. Their combined talk of determinism and voluntary action, the natural and the social, was sustained through an implicit system of human relations which distributed the nature and intensity of emotions according to social
classes and identities. Figuring prominently in the rhetoric of the psychology
textbooks is a dependence on a hierarchy of social agents—specifically on an
order of authority (expertise) and regulation that locates and organizes emotional experiences.

The Biomechanics of Emotions

By the mid-nineteenth century, the subject of emotion had gained a permanent place in the proto-textbooks of psychology; at that time the texts were
usually designated as "moral" or "mental" philosophy. However, even by the
final decade of that century the terms and processes used to describe and constitute emotions had been transformed. In early texts emotions were described
as physical, aesthetic, *and* volitional and were appreciated for their multitudinous, nuanced, and both culturally and cognitively diverse forms. Later texts
represented emotions as distinctly affective (composed of feeling rather than
thinking). In the earlier texts, emotion was the compounding or culmination
of various elementary mental states. Sentiment, passion, and morality were
directly tied up with emotion, and it was not uncommon for these textbook
accounts to be illustrated with complex cultural artifacts, for example, Old Testament parables, Socratic claims, poetry for children, and passages from great
literature. Frequent attempts were made to enumerate the different emotions,
often resulting in elaborate taxonomies and lists (including such affections as
conjugal love, piety, patriotism, and the love of home and such aesthetic emotions as novelty, fashion, harmony, and variety in unity).[33] Dispensing with the
tasks of enumeration and extension, along with culturally complex literary and
historical exemplars, the "new" psychology textbooks focused on identifying
essential mechanisms of emotion.

There are at least four dimensions that distinguish the more modern
accounts of emotion that followed from the James-Lange theory. Representations shifted from conveying the multifaceted variations and artifices of emotions to describing them as *natural* and *biological* mechanisms. The location of

emotions simultaneously was moved from volition—in the head—to the *phys-iological* and *visceral*—in the *body*. Thus, their regulation for the most part went from being associated with mechanisms of moral or inner control to those of external, sometimes *social controls,* and their phenomenal qualities were moved from being identified with sentiment, private, and subjective experience to physical experiences that were most accurately located through the *objective observation* of scientists.

Naturalization and Biological Representation

The James-Lange theory of emotions, along with several variations of that theory, dominate the textbooks after 1890. Informed by Darwinian thought as well as physiological research, these theories naturalize emotions by represent-ing them as basic processes that function to guide adaptive action. Emotions are nothing more than the product of biomechanics. Emotions are a modifica-tion, often seen as an "interruption" of normal conscious processes that can be stated in biomechanical terms as "derived from the afferent nervous impulses originating in muscular disturbances of the digestive, circulatory, and respira-tory tracts."[34] According to James Angell, emotion is a "general monitor" of friction within the organism that directs active adjustment of the organism to the external stimuli which gave rise to the bodily changes. Heeding Darwin, Angell goes on to say that expressions of emotion "are simply acts which are, or once were, useful under the circumstances calling forth the activity."[35] In these texts emotions were thus naturalized in two ways: as organic, bodily processes (or products of those processes) and as functional activities in the natural order of evolution.

Bodily Location

The James-Lange theory established a new locus of origin for emotions, removing them from their previous habitat in volitional processes, in the head, to more visceral, bodily locations. Adopting this new site, textbook authors sit-uated the origin (or accompaniment) of emotions in the circulatory system, nerves, muscles, digestive tract, respiratory system, neural mechanisms, sen-sory organs, and adrenal glands. Although many of these authors did not endorse the James-Lange theory in toto, they nevertheless conceded the cen-trality of organic states. Yerkes argued that the initial feeling in an emotion-arousing situation is not a product of bodily sensation but conceded that it "immediately is supplanted by the sensations arising from our bodily condi-tions."[36] Similarly skeptical about the veracity of the James-Lange theory because it abstracts the emotional event from our experiences of it, Harvey Carr

nevertheless accepted much of the theory, thus joining his colleagues in match-
ing emotions with specific anatomical parts. He defined disgust, noting that "it
is the alimentary mechanism that is primarily involved in the emotional reaction" and that joy consists "of a rather widespread and exhilarative organic
reaction involving especially the vaso-motor mechanisms and accompanied by
a great variety of motor manifestations."[37] Even Mary Whiton Calkins, one of
the last remaining researchers committed to a psychology of consciousness
(rather than one of behavior or physiology), incorporated biological mechanisms into her 1905 definition, citing the activity of specific cerebral locations
like the Rolandic cells and frontal lobes.[38] One author made literal the metaphoric loss of head, claiming that unruly undesired emotions replace reasoned
activity when the individual loses his head: "If he completely loses his head, his
sensations become a diffuse mass of feeling and his set for overt activity
becomes a blind struggle."[39] The most reticent authors relocated emotions from
the mind to internal organs and processes.

Experience and Control

How do individuals imagine and experience emotions once they are
defined less as private events of consciousness and more as organic occurrences? The notion of emotions as determined, biological events has two
notable implications: first, authority to know and name the emotions is shifted
to the expert observer (scientist), and, second, emotional experiences and
expressions cannot be controlled or altered by the persons who have them. The
classic example, appearing in James's text and reproduced in many others, is
that an individual experiences fear only when he begins running from its
object, the running being an action caused by organic activities. If emotions are
constituted as physiological events, then the experience and control of those
emotions, logically speaking, are dependent on those events and not on the person's volition. It is at this juncture that the textbooks abandon or at least refor-
mulate the biomechanical person being represented in their pages. Experiences
of emotion *do* vary and *can* be varied; (self-)control of emotions is often presented as a possibility, although the mechanisms of control differ from text to
text. In these modifications of the biomechanical model, the self-searching,
self-gratifying, and autonomous individual gains a presence, becoming a force
that occasionally overrules the sometimes fatalist determinism of biomechanical processes.

As we shall see from the following textbook examples, creating a feasible
double language of educating the emotions yielded neither parsimonious nor
consensual views. But the need for a double discourse was considerable. Determinist, mechanical explanations of emotions established authority (for nam-

ing and regulating them) with the scientist. This line of authority helped bolster psychology's professional status and utility. It also reinforced the image of the largely white male scientists who posed as rational outsiders gazing on the chaos of everyday life. Psychologists saw as their mission the use of their superior rationality to create knowledge to control the "half-educated man" or "the other one"—the masses of ignorant, untrained beings.[40] However, the self-proclaimed epistemic security of the psychological scientist was being challenged, not only by social critics, like Walter Lippmann or Stephen Leacock (who lampooned the new psychology), but also from within the discipline. Many psychologists wondered aloud about the cognitive frailties of psychologists. Thus, Raymond Dodge worried about the "perils" of the psychologist who "may get lost in the chaos of details and never emerge. I have known such lost souls." The researcher "may find himself in conflict with his colleagues or with the native inhabitants of the dark continent of ignorance, who voluntarily choose darkness rather than light and prefer prejudice to information. Not all of them live in Tennessee," where anti-evolutionists were criticizing scientific knowledge.[41] Even John B. Watson, who was notoriously arrogant in his scientific claims, confessed privately to occasional feelings of helplessness in his quest to understand himself and others.[42]

Equipped with the masculine scientific stance of superiority and distance, and invested in the imminent success of psychology as a commodity, psychologists benefited from seeing emotions as a deep structure that existed outside of the understanding or control of the individuals who experienced them. However, without any identifiable means to control emotions, including those of psychologists, the professional project could not succeed. Ascribing to emotions some possibilities for control provided psychologists with a job, a skill to be marketed. Perhaps just as important, this view furnished a conception of personhood that would appeal to middle-class consumers of psychology: its promises of management and growth accorded with their self-images. With this double view of emotions as determined yet fabricated and socially malleable, mechanistic yet natural, readers could be educated both about the necessity of psychological science and their own possibilities for knowing and changing themselves as well as managing subordinates. Psychology was useful and it was desirable.

The texts are consistent in the effort to biologize emotions, but they differ both in the extent to which control of emotions was deemed possible and in the forms of control they delineate. To a few authors who most consistently maintained a deterministic, mechanical model, the control of emotions by the individual seemed impossible. Yerkes, for instance, asserted the limits of control by quoting from another textbook, that of Edward Titchener: emotions cannot be regulated as "we do not master them and use them at will for intellectual and practical ends as we do our ideas and judgments; rather they master us. For the time being one *is* the emotion."[43] Presenting the emotions as natural, akin to instincts, some authors viewed them as taking the individual "beyond the pale of social restraint."[44]

Despite classifying emotions as organic, bodily states, most authors nevertheless introduced mechanisms for modifying emotions or emotional expressions. The ability to control emotions successfully was variously associated with a number of factors, including self, experience, learning, individual differences, and society. Describing a case where an individual, while writing out a check for a purchase, learns that his bank has failed and his fortune is lost, Angell stated, "Such an event may or may not produce an emotion. It depends on the individual, not the emotion."[45] Other authors elaborated on how individual differences predispose individuals to certain emotional experiences. Some authors provided taxonomies of such differences, lists that sometimes resembled the ancient theory of humors—choleric, sanguine, melancholic, and phlegmatic personalities.[46] These individual types were occasionally linked to psychopathologies.[47]

For readers, mainly middle-class students seeking an education for the economic opportunities it promised at the time, the notion of controlling emotions was significant. Without such a notion the biomechanical theories of emotion offered no benefits: not only did such theories suggest the essential sameness of all people, of all classes and social groupings, but they afforded no knowledge that could be deployed to improve the self. The idea that strategies of control existed, and that they could be acquired and implemented by readers, intimated a means to personal improvement and advancement. In the textbook examples of emotional control, certain classes of people were exemplified as having symptoms of certain emotions which were often associated with professional middle-class life (such as the loss of control following the loss of one's savings). These symptoms required masking or reduction in order to conduct successfully the daily business of that life.

Even theoretical perspectives that focused on fixed predispositions, like individual differences, frequently incorporated other more voluntaristic mechanisms of control. Here again James set a pattern: his organic theory of emotions was surrounded by suggestions for control, including but extending well beyond the modest notion of individual differences. After claiming that "many of the manifestations [of emotions] are in organs over which we have no control," James instructed the reader on how to manage emotion.[48] His recommended controls include rehearsing contrary outward expressions, repressing emotional talk and display, and dissociating self from or suppressing the visceral manifestations of emotions. The first technique is illustrated by the adage of whistling to maintain one's courage (and reduce one's fear): "if we wish to conquer undesirable emotional tendencies in ourselves, we must assiduously, and in the first instance cold-bloodedly, go through the *outward* movements of those contrary dispositions which we prefer to cultivate."[49] Repression of emotions works similarly when one attempts to teach children to repress emotional display so "that they may *think* more; for, to a certain extent, whatever currents are diverted from the regions below, must swell the activity of the thought-tracts of the brain."[50] Other authors reported these techniques, writing about the repression, concealment, and substitution of emotional acts. Even authors like Yerkes, who claimed that emotions master us and that individuals cannot wholly suppress bodily conditions and expressions of emotion, proposed that individuals can control those expressions "to a limited extent." He claimed, "Indeed, if, in the face of a situation which is wholly calculated to call forth anger, I merely laugh and make light of the circumstances I do not express anger to any marked extent: I may even experience another kind of emotion."[51] Here, as in other examples, the quelling or management of emotional symptoms is considered to be crucial: such examples are driven by the idea of self-mastery and the associated social costs of losing that control. To name and describe these symptoms, emotional expressions, in biomechanical terms is insufficient; their control and maintenance is especially desired.

Another commonly named mechanism for modifying emotions entailed experience and learning, with experience being more idiosyncratic and diffuse and learning being more general and calculable. Experiences for the most part simply happen to an individual, a consequence of living, and these experiences can modify emotional occurrences and expressions. Thus, for instance, Robert Woodworth wrote that love and hate along with "the higher emotions, esthetic, social, religious, are sentiments towards certain types of objects and are built up in the individual's experience, with much assistance from the social environment."[52] As Woodworth described it, "social pressure trains" an individual to hide his feelings while "other people are always trying to discover how he feels." Consequently, "There is a race between concealment of the emotions on one side and detection of emotions on the other, like the race in warships between defensive armor and penetrating projectiles."[53] Carr similarly wrote that experience modifies what stimuli will evoke the emotion, suggesting that "Society intentionally instills certain fears and eliminates others. Parents attempt to eradicate the irrational and imaginary types of fear by the development of some sort of rational inhibition. Fear is often regarded as a childish weakness that should be repressed in order to develop courage."[54]

The textbook reviews of means for altering emotions added new dimensions to the simple biomechanical grid upon which they were charted. Carr's account of the modification of fear blurs the lines between experience and learning, and between the incidental and intentional; through its inclusion of parental and societal forces it names specific regulatory mechanisms, albeit fairly amorphous and complicated ones. Many textbooks, especially the later ones, cite scientific techniques of learning and conditioning as a certain means for modifying and controlling emotions. While some authors stated that social agencies "such as the church, state, and home" instill emotions as a means of establishing desired conduct,[55] others described these procedures in technical, scientific terms. To do so they typically either employed the language of behaviorism or recited experimental findings. Thus, the famous "Little Albert" experiment, where an infant is conditioned to fear furry objects, was used to illustrate the conditioning of emotional responses.[56] Writing in 1921, for instance, John Dashiell adopted such a behaviorist stance and with it the belief that emotional patterns are acquired; he also anticipated future experimental studies that would aid in the accurate detection and modification of emotions. The behaviorist position implied that "the popular conception of a person that attributes so many of his characteristics to his 'natural' propensities must be revised to make way for a view that is at the same time more practically useful, more fundamentally optimistic, and more ethically sound."[57] By 1935, textbook authors Edwin Boring, Herbert Langfeld, and Harry Weld confidently asserted, "Both anger and fear responses are easily attached to a new or different stimulus. These quickly established conditioned emotional responses may be altered by appropriate training or may persist over long periods of time."[58] They concluded their chapter with similar confidence: "In this process of conditioning, reconditioning and unconditioning we have a great deal of social facilitation and inhibition."[59] In these versions, behaviorism provided a response for middle-class needs for self-control.

Given the predominant stance of defining emotions as either constituted by or manifested through bodily surges, recipes for modifying and regulating emotions supply optimistic relief. Once fear is described as an event where "rational conduct has fled, and consciousness has become almost extinct, or else a mere riot of impulses," and embarrassment is taken as a condition where "we have been suddenly reduced to the mental condition of a vegetable,"[60] then who would not desire alternatives? It is at these moments that psychology could, and did, offer what Rose called "the promise of personhood" through its technologies. If psychology located such human problems, then it also created solutions. One such technology of personhood was simply *descriptive:* the language of psychological theories themselves enabled talk about changing either the emotion or its expression. For instance, when a theory introduced the function of a stimulus—a specific trigger for emotion—then one could talk about changing the stimulus or even altering the response to the stimulus. Thus Walter Pillsbury defined emotional expression as dependent upon the individual's attitude toward the stimulus, noting, "The attitude is in large measure under one's control" since stimuli can be reclassified to elicit a different emotion.[61]

The promise of personhood tendered by the new psychology, however, took primary form in a scientific account that cast people and their actions in an abstracted, decontextualized, and ahistorical manner. That scientific view presumed that the particularities of individuals were irrelevant to explaining and predicting their actions; all individuals behaved according to universal natural laws. The optimism afforded by strategies for self-control of emotions (or for the control of other people's emotions) was shadowed by this mechanistic rendition of human nature. In proposing this vision of human nature, psychology was capitalizing on the authority granted to modern science, an ideology that had apparently proven itself during the Industrial Revolution, surpassed the potentials of religious belief, and organized the entire world into an intelligible if complex scheme. If this rendition of humans threatened to erase significant social and class differences or undermine beliefs in personal improvement, then the ideas that emotions and their symptoms were indeed different between members of different social groups, and could be controlled, by *some* people, were ideologically comforting.

The special relation established between authors and readers—the notions that they shared a privileged stance and subjectivity apart from ordinary persons—provided common ground for controlling their inner selves as well as managing others.

Object

With the increase in experimentation on emotions, textbook authors had yet another technology at their service. While experiments ostensibly tested the veracity of one theory or another, they also *inscribed* emotions by giving them discrete, calculable form with identifiable and modifiable parts. That is, as a *technical* practice, experiments could actually modify natural emotions: by controlling or even creating one feature of emotional expression they produced particular events. In these technical productions, emotions were rendered artifice and, therefore, became modifiable. And, as a *scientific* practice, experiments were engaged to calculate, classify, and regulate what was irrational. This experimental logic is not delineated in the texts but rather is clearly conveyed by the power of the experiments themselves.[62] Persuasion is accomplished simply by describing how the administration of hormones could induce emotional moods or how dramatic mechanical devices (such as a chair that unexpectedly tilts the subject to a horizontal position) when used repeatedly eventually could elicit less organic and subjective traces of fear.[63] The persuasive power of the experiments inhered in several of their unique operations, notably instruments that measured phenomena undetectable to the ordinary observer and devices that stimulated, modified, or otherwise influenced subjects' responses. Illustrations of these experiments serve as powerful persuasive devices, for they show the reader how the world works; seeing is believing.[64] In addition, a fundamental feature of experiments is the condition of "assessment control," whereby through the particular social arrangement of the laboratory the experimenter directs the generation, evaluation, and reporting of the psychological experience.[65] Through this kind of control the subjects' reports may be deemed irrelevant and misleading; the final interpretation of the events is the jurisdiction of the experimenters alone.

Through psychology's technical devices of description and inscription, then, emotions were represented as natural, organic states *and* as artificial, malleable, and indeed correctable ones. Humans were rendered both natural and artificial simultaneously, and the textbooks could espouse a scientific naturalism (and thereby also reassert the authority of scientific knowledge) while making way for and promising a therapeutic means for improvement, growth, and attention to personal change. Further, explications of regulatory mechanisms provided an economy of emotions that both implied the necessary management of emotions and—like advice books—suggested when and where spontaneous emotional expression was appropriate and useful.[66] These explications, which balanced control and expression, contain a double discourse that meshes discordant visions of human nature.[67]

A Social Order of Emotions

Psychological accounts of emotions utilized an additional system of support, one that is intimated in the experimental technologies that were introduced. The rhetoric of the introductory texts, including their illustrative cases drawn from everyday life and from experiments, relies on a particular hierarchy of actors according to which human types were differentially accorded rationality and potential. Control was not equally available to everyone, nor did all individuals have comparable authority to name, explain, or assess emotional experiences and expressions. To the extent that readers resisted the idea of emotions as determined, irrational, and essentially biological happenings, psychologists' claims about mechanisms for control (such as learning and repressing) only partially alleviated such anxieties. A hierarchy of persons, or, more precisely, a particular order of social relations, not only rendered the biomechanical theories more believable but also lent additional reassurance about the regulation of emotional life.[68]

In the introductory texts, the relational order makes one appearance as a relatively standard relation between author and reader: readers, it was noted earlier, were given a special status as ambitious and successful and, therefore, were readily distinguishable from the "subjects" who were in the same class as the typical objects of the texts' psychological analyses. Although readers were not accorded the reason, control, or gaze of the authors (who double as experimental scientists), they often were invited to become like these experts, to see the world through the objective lens of psychologists, thereby enhancing their social-cognitive status.[69] These author-reader relations are one of three distinguishable social orders represented in introductory texts: analogous hierarchies also take form in the relations of characters in the case examples and in the relations of laboratory experiments. In keeping with the portrayal of emotions as natural, and with the concordant claims of their evolutionary and biological functions, the texts contained plentiful examples of diverse subjects, including children, animals, adults, witnesses, mental patients, actors, pilots, textbook readers, textbook authors, fictional characters, and even scientists. Yet, just as these examples may have demonstrated the ubiquity and, more important, the universality of emotions, they also mapped (albeit sometimes subtly) a *social order* of emotional expression.

Animals and children were most often used to illustrate raw emotions or their conditioning and learning, whereas normal adults (including the writers and readers of the introductory textbooks) displayed more circumspect, milder emotional expressions. Likewise, the emotions of unbalanced persons, those with personality abnormalities, were portrayed as more intense, prolonged, and less modified by experience or training than are those of "normal" individuals. The child, the cat, and the unstable adult alike were prone to screams and snarls, whereas the adult's expressions were less animated. The individual who lost his fortune, the researcher whose mother died, and the person who is watching a "sexy" motion picture displayed more moderate emotional expressions often modified by their personal experiences, training, and attitude. Different construals of personhood were implicit in the texts, and they depended on the readers' shared sense that adults were different from children, men from women, and the educated from the uneducated. According to this logic it followed that emotions, like IQ, varied (and not randomly) across different groups of humans. One author even conjectured about designing a "scale for emotional age, after the analogy of the Binet scale for mental age."[70]

These different controls of personhood often relied implicitly on shared understandings of types of persons (age, social class, gender). That is, in the textbook examples readers did not learn new information about different types of people as much as they used common knowledge to glean further differences explicated in these examples. The texts offer new class distinctions in associating certain aspects of emotion with certain classes: biology is emphasized in the emotional experiences of nonhumans and children; "primitive" emotions are associated with the uneducated.

The social arrangements of author-reader and of the hierarchical classifications in case studies have a parallel in the relations of the experiment. Although several texts discuss emotions in scientists, these experiences never transpire when the scientist is in the laboratory: during experiments, emotion is present only in the subjects. Given the ethics of experimentation (codes derived largely from cultural conventions about human rights), different kinds of subjects are treated differently. The utilization of laboratory devices, procedures, and stimuli is dependent on the kind of subject under scrutiny, as are the type and degree of emotion being elicited. Cats and dogs were submitted to manipulations of their bodies—to brain surgery, muscle removal, permanent anesthetizing. Even humans were differentially exposed to particular investigative techniques and were evaluated accordingly. Experimenters were exempt from observation of their "inner selves," whereas subjects, depending on their kind and social status, were scrutinized and through that interrogation were differentially treated.

Experimenters, however, were not always exempt from emotional images and symptomologies. Over the first three decades of the twentieth century, they expressed troublesome concerns about their colleagues and their own emotions, and noted the dangers that such emotionality posed for the conduct and management of rational scientific work. In one case, an experimental psychologist, Clark Hull, was so distraught over the emotionality of psychologists that he developed an elaborate system for the management of scientific work itself. In other instances, psychologists posited less concrete means to regulate scientists' mental lives.[71] The presumptions made by the authors of textbooks—that readers desired to control themselves and function as calculating, rational actors—mirrored their own preoccupations with self-regulation.

These social arrangements yielded compelling power in part because they were derived from hegemonic understandings about the world and agents in that world. As common sense, these relations helped smooth inconsistencies in the conflicting discourses of determinism and autonomous action, of the natural and the made. Humans (and nonhumans) at once were rendered biomechanical, but not all persons were just that. Some groups of people were opportunistically represented and situated such that even as biological beings they could change *or* be changed; they were differently endowed with potential and were differentially suited to governance through scientific technologies.[72]

Coda

The modern history of emotions is complicated once we begin to assess scientific productions and consolidate them with our understandings of related representations of emotion in popular culture, art, literature, and everyday life. By the close of the nineteenth century, psychology textbooks were generating conceptions that seemed to contradict increasingly dominant cultural manifestations of emotions and of personhood. The apparent contradictions between a determinist, biomechanical model of emotional expression and a self-gratifying, masterful, and profitably desirous one were reconfigured in these texts. Introductory psychology textbook authors never directly confronted these inconsistencies and contradictions; rather, they employed a double discourse that rearranged and ultimately celebrated both accounts of emotions (and of humanity). Simultaneously engaging in rhetorics of science and of common sense, these texts participated in educating the modern college-trained self as at once natural *and* artificial, biological *and* social. Psychology, in such texts and in its other practices, thus promulgated both the promise of self-gratification and the necessity of scientific technologies of regulation. College textbooks contributed to reinforcing cultural conceptions, and expectations, about the possibilities and the limits, the enablements and the constraints, of "human nature." They offered a template with which individuals could talk about, act, and modify their own (and others') emotional experiences and yet at the same time acknowledge their biomechanical essence. They provided an ideologically comfortable place for and grounded a dependence on the expertise of scientific technology. The legacy of such academic contributions lives on in our contemporary vacillations between self-mastery and therapeutic dependence. That legacy likewise continues in our ever-changing strategies (and our ambivalence about these strategies) of concealing, shaping, suppressing, and realizing— inventing—our emotions.[73]

Notes

Wendy Blumenthal, Sarah Carney, and April Weinberg assisted in the analyses of introductory psychology textbooks; I thank them for their substantial contributions. I thank Santina Scalia for her patient attention to preparation of the manuscript. My appreciation also goes to Joel Pfister and Nancy Schnog for their caring and helpful readings of earlier versions of this chapter.

1. William James, *The Principles of Psychology* (New York: Henry Holt, 1890), vol. 2, 450. James insisted that bodily states are emotions: *"If we fancy some strong emotion, and then try to abstract from our consciousness of it all the feelings of its bodily symptoms, we find we have nothing left behind, no 'mind-stuff' out of which the emotion can be constituted, and that a cold and neutral state of intellectual perception is all that remains"* (451).

2. We must examine the extent to which we continue to separate, juxtapose, and naturalize notions of the cultural and the scientific; we need to investigate the historical interdependence of those oppositions as well as their consequences for social life. Janice Radway, "Mail-Order Culture and Its Critics: The Book-of-the-Month Club, Commodification and Consumption, and the Problem of Cultural Authority," in *Cultural Studies*, ed.

Lawrence Grossberg, Cory Nelson, and Paula A. Treichler (New York: Routledge, 1992), 512–30. Studies attempting to reconfigure the science-culture divides include Frank M. Turner, "Public Science in Britain, 1880–1919," *Isis* 71 (1980): 589–608; *Expository Science: Forms and Functions of Popularization*, ed. Terry Shinn and Richard Whitely (Boston: D. Reidel, 1985); Steven Schlossman, "Perils of Popularization: The Founding of *Parents' Magazine*," in *History and Research in Child Development*, ed. A. Smuts and J. Hagen, *Monographs of the Society for Research in Child Development* 50 (1985): 65–77.

3. Mark Seltzer introduced the term *double discourse* in *Bodies and Machines* (New York: Routledge, 1992). On the function of psychological sciences to produce both technologies of personhood and new experiences of persons and on the complexities of the science as a reflection as well as producer of cultural forms see Nikolas Rose, "Engineering the Human Soul: Analyzing Psychological Expertise," *Science in Context* 5 (1992): 351–72; John H. Gagnon, "The Self, Its Voices, and Their Discord," in *Investigating Subjectivity: Research on Lived Experience*, ed. C. Ellis and M. G. Flaherty (Newbury Park, Calif.: Sage, 1992), 221–43; Philip Cushman, "Why the Self Is Empty: Toward a Historically Situated Psychology," *American Psychologist* 45 (1990): 599–611; Kurt Danziger, *Constructing the Subject: Historical Origins of Psychological Research* (Cambridge: Cambridge University Press, 1990).

4. Psychologists' estimate of introductory textbooks changed significantly during the period 1890–1940. Textbooks initially were taken as serious intellectual documents that considered and conveyed central scientific problems. Eventually texts lost their primary function as a forum for interrogating key issues and became more homogenized, their authors unabashedly writing them primarily for profit. Nevertheless, textbooks continued to present the dominant psychological perspectives on human nature. See Ned Levine, Colin Worboys, and Martin Taylor, "Psychology and the 'Psychology' Textbook: A Social Demographic Study," *Human Relations* 26 (1973): 467–78; Wayne Weiten and Randall D. Wight, "Portraits of a Discipline: An Examination of Introductory Psychology Textbooks in America," in *Teaching Psychology in America: A History*, ed. Antonio E. Puente, Janet R. Matthews, and Charles L. Brewer (Washington, D.C.: American Psychological Association, 1992), 453–504. On nineteenth-century moral philosophy textbooks, the precursors of psychology texts, see D. H. Meyer, *The Instructed Conscience: The Shaping of the American National Ethic* (Philadelphia: University of Pennsylvania Press, 1972).

5. On the emergence of notions of self-transformation, mastery, expression, and fulfillment see Warren Susman, *Culture as History: The Transformation of American Society in the Twentieth Century* (New York: Pantheon, 1985), 271–85; T. J. Jackson Lears, *No Place of Grace: Antimodernism and the Transformation of American Culture, 1880–1920* (New York: Pantheon, 1981); Tom Lutz, *American Nervousness, 1903: An Anecdotal History* (Ithaca: Cornell University Press, 1991); John Higham, *Writing American History: Essays on Modern Scholarship* (Bloomington: Indiana University Press, 1965), 73–104; T. J. Jackson Lears, "From Salvation to Self-Realization: Advertising and the Therapeutic Roots of Consumer Culture, 1880–1930," in *The Culture of Consumption: Critical Essays in American History, 1880–1980*, ed. Richard W. Fox and T. J. Jackson Lears (New York: Pantheon, 1983), 3–38.

6. John Burnham, "The New Psychology," in *1915, The Cultural Moment: The New Politics, the New Woman, the New Psychology, the New Art and the New Theatre in America*, ed. Adele Heller and Lois Rudnick (New Brunswick, N.J.: Rutgers University Press, 1991), 117–27.

7. John M. O'Donnell, *The Origins of Behaviorism: American Psychology, 1870–1920* (New

York: New York University Press, 1985); Roger Smith, *Inhibition: History and Meaning in the Sciences of Mind and Brain* (Berkeley: University of California Press, 1992); Philip J. Pauly, *Controlling Life: Jacques Loeb and the Engineering Ideal in Biology* (New York: Oxford University Press, 1987); Lorraine J. Daston, "The Theory of the Will Versus the Science of the Mind," in *The Problematic Science: Psychology in Nineteenth-Century Thought*, ed. W. R. Woodward and M. G. Ash (New York: Praeger, 1982), 88–115.

8. Danziger, *Constructing the Subject; Psychological Testing and American Society, 1890–1930*, ed. Michael M. Sokal (New Brunswick, N.J.: Rutgers University Press, 1987); *The Rise of Experimentation in American Psychology*, ed. Jill G. Morawski (New Haven: Yale University Press, 1987).

9. Psychologists' interest in social control, specifically in techniques for producing rational beings, is well documented. However, they struggled not only toward making a rationally functioning social world but also with reconciling contradictions between their conceptions of humankind as nonrational and their self-conceptions of science and scientists as rational. On social control see Ben Harris, "'Give me a Dozen Healthy Infants': John B. Watson's Popular Advice on Childrearing, Women, and the Family," in *In the Shadow of the Past: Psychology Portrays the Sexes*, ed. M. Lewin (New York: Columbia University Press, 1984), 126–54; Nikolas Rose, *Governing the Soul: The Shaping of the Private Self* (London: Routledge, 1990); John Burnham, "The New Psychology: From Narcissism to Social Control," in *Change and Continuity in Twentieth-Century America: The Nineteen-Twenties*, ed. J. Braemen, R. H. Bremmer, and D. Brody (Columbus: Ohio State University Press, 1968). On the construction of the rational psychological scientist and its special advantages, see Karl Scheibe, "Metamorphoses in the Psychologist's Advantage," in *Rise of Experimentation*, ed. Morawski, 53–71; Jill G. Morawski, "Self-Regard and Other Regard: Reflexive Practices in American Psychology, 1890–1940," *Science in Context* 5 (1992): 281–309. On the moral virtues critical to the scientist and the scientific attitude see David A. Hollinger, "Inquiry and Uplift: Late Nineteenth-Century American Academics and the Moral Efficacy of Scientific Practice," in *The Authority of Experts: Studies in History and Theory*, ed. Thomas L. Haskell (Bloomington: Indiana University Press, 1989), 142–56. On the rise and problems of scientific naturalism in American social science see Edward A. Purcell, Jr., *The Crisis of Democratic Theory: Scientific Naturalism and the Problem of Value* (Lexington: University of Kentucky, 1973).

10. On James's life see Daniel W. Bjork, *William James: The Center of His Vision* (New York: Columbia University Press, 1988). On the varied projects and life circumstances of this first generation of scientific psychologists see Kerry W. Buckley, *Mechanical Man: John Broadus Watson and the Beginnings of Behaviorism* (New York: Guilford Press, 1989); Matthew Hale, Jr., *Human Sciences and Social Order: Hugo Munsterberg and the Origins of Applied Psychology* (Philadelphia: Temple University Press, 1980); J. G. Morawski, "Assessing Psychology's Moral Heritage through Our Neglected Utopias," *American Psychologist* 37 (1982): 1082–95; E. Anthony Rotundo, *American Manhood: Transformations in Masculinity from the Revolution to the Modern Era* (New York: Basic Books, 1993); Elizabeth Scarborough and Laurel Furumoto, *Untold Lives: The First Generation of American Women Psychologists* (New York: Columbia University Press, 1988).

11. On changes in psychological conceptions of the social set see Kurt Danziger, "The Social Origins of Modern Psychology," in *Psychology in Social Context*, ed. Allan R. Buss (New York: Irvington, 1979), 40. Late nineteenth-century doubts about rationality and

autonomous individuals took varied forms, from disenchantment with the rational structures of society to anxieties about the authenticity of the self, from crises of representation (appearance versus reality) to fears about individual control. See Lears's *No Place of Grace* and his essay "Beyond Veblen: Rethinking Consumer Culture in America," in *Consuming Visions: Accumulation and Display of Goods in America, 1880–1920,* ed. S. J. Bronner (New York: Norton, 1989), 73–97; Jay Mechling, "The Collecting Self and American Youth Movements," in *Accumulation and Display: Mass-Marketing Household Goods in America, 1880–1920,* ed. Deborah Federhan (Winterthur, Del.: Winterthur Museum, 1986), 255–85; Higham, *Writing American History*; Burnham, "New Psychology: Narcissism to Social Control."

12. Seltzer, *Bodies and Machines,* 3, 11. Taking a somewhat different (although not necessarily incompatible) purchase on the effects of psychology textbooks, Graham Richards has suggested that James's introductory textbook, while containing such a mixed discourse, succeeded at engaging readers in a self-oriented, introspective survey of consciousness but failed in convincing them to resist determinism (and related biomechanical explanations). "James and Freud: Two Masters of Metaphor," *British Journal of Psychology* 82 (1991): 205–15.

13. W. O. Krohn, *Practical Lessons in Psychology* (Chicago: Werner, 1894), 20.

14. E. A. Kirkpatrick, *Introductory Psychology* (Wininanm, Minn.: Jones and Kroger, 1894), 3–4.

15. James Drever, *The Psychology of Everyday Life* (London: Methuen, 1921), v; William James in Edward L. Thorndike, *The Elements of Psychology* (New York: Sieler, 1905), vii.

16. B. P. Buell, *Essentials of Psychology* (Boston: Ginn, 1898), 4.

17. Robert M. Yerkes, *Introduction to Psychology* (New York: Henry Holt, 1911), 13.

18. F. H. C. Perrin and D. B. Klein, *Psychology: Its Methods and Principles* (New York: Henry Holt, 1926), 17–18.

19. For an extended discussion of the late nineteenth-century changes in the representation of readers in introductory psychology textbooks, see Jill G. Morawski, "There Is More to Our History of Giving: The Place of Introductory Textbooks in American Psychology," *American Psychologist* 47 (1992): 161–69.

20. Burton Bledstein, *The Culture of Professionalism: The Middle Class and the Development of Higher Education in America* (New York: Harper & Row, 1976); Lawrence R. Veysey, *The Emergence of the American University* (Chicago: University of Chicago Press, 1965).

21. Daniel J. Boorstin, *The Americans: The Democratic Experience* (New York: Random House, 1973); Bailey B. Burritt, *Professional Distribution of College and University Graduates* (Washington, D.C.: Government Printing Office, 1912); Christian Gauss, *Life in College* (New York: Scribner's, 1930); Helen L. Horowitz, *Campus Life: Undergraduate Culture from the End of the Eighteenth Century to the Present* (New York: Knopf, 1987); Henry D. Sheldon, *Student Life and Customs* (New York: Arno, 1969).

22. Bledstein, *Culture of Professionalism,* 31, x.

23. Daniel Boorstin suggested that American colleges became "less a place of instruction than a place of worship—worship of the growing individual" (*Americans,* 480). Cf. note 19.

24. Susman, *Culture as History*; *Culture of Consumption,* ed. Fox and Lears; *Consuming Visions,* ed. Bronner.

25. For instance, see Lutz, *American Nervousness*; Gagnon, "The Self, Its Voices," 231.

26. Boorstin, *Americans*; J. F. Fay, *American Psychology Before William James* (New Brunswick, N.J.: Rutgers University Press, 1939); Thomas Camfield, "Psychologists at War: The History of American Psychology" (Ph.D. diss., University of Texas at Austin, 1969); Veysey, *Emergence of the University*.

27. William James, "The Gospel of Relaxation," in *Talks to Teachers on Psychology* (Cambridge: Harvard University Press, 1983), 123.

28. Ibid., 127.

29. Ibid., 127–28.

30. Ibid., 131.

31. Rose's proposal for reconsidering the history of psychology resists the common bifurcations of technical, scientific psychology, and humanist psychologies and of academic psychology and popular psychology. He opens a way for exploring how the double discourse of the natural and the social, the discovered and the made, was assisted by ideas about potentials and possibilities, especially given the cultural confusion about what constituted self and the real. "Engineering the Human Soul," 357.

32. Ibid., 356.

33. For example, A. Schulyer, *Empirical and Rational Psychology* (New York: Van Antwerp, Brag, 1882).

34. James Angell, *Psychology* (New York: Henry Holt, 1904), 325.

35. Ibid., 324.

36. Yerkes, *Introduction to Psychology*, 184.

37. Harvey A. Carr, *Psychology: A Study of Mental Activity* (New York: Longmans, Green, 1926), 276.

38. Mary Whiton Calkins, *An Introduction to Psychology* (New York: Macmillan, 1905), 298.

39. Robert S. Woodworth, *Psychology*, 3rd ed. (New York: Hart, 1934), 358.

40. Edward L. Thorndike, "The Psychology of the Half-Educated Man," *Harper's* 140 (1920): 666–70; Max Meyer, *The Psychology of the Other One* (Columbia: Missouri Book, 1921).

41. Raymond Dodge, "Excursions in Experiential Psychology," *Scientific Monthly* 23 (1926): 129. On psychologists' reflexive thinking about their own inadequacies see Jill G. Morawski, "Organizing Knowledge and Behavior at Yale's Institute of Human Relations," *Isis* 77 (1986): 219–42. See n. 9.

42. Letter of John B. Watson to Robert M. Yerkes, Feb. 7, 1916, Yerkes Papers, Sterling Library, Yale University.

43. Yerkes, *Introduction to Psychology*, 81–82.

44. Walter S. Hunter, *General Psychology* (Chicago: University of Chicago Press, 1919), 179.

45. Angell, *Psychology*, 322.

46. Edward Titchener, *A Beginner's Psychology* (New York: Macmillan, 1916), 227; Yerkes, *Introduction to Psychology*, 183.

47. John F. Dashiell, *Fundamentals of Objective Psychology* (Boston: Houghton Mifflin, 1928); Floyd C. Dockeray, *Psychology* (New York: Prentice-Hall, 1946); Edwin G. Boring, Herbert S. Langfeld, and Harry P. Weld, *Psychology—A Factual Textbook* (New York: John Wiley, 1935).

48. James, *Principles of Psychology*, 2:462.

49. Ibid., 463.

50. Ibid., 466. The idea that the blocking (repressing) of an event or action results in rechanneling energies to another, usually higher-order event or action is not James's but is central to the concept of inhibition. Roger Smith has shown how inhibition provided not only a persuasive model with which the brain sciences could advance their claims to explain human conduct but also a metaphor that asserted social as well as biological hierarchies of control and regulation. Smith, *Inhibition*.

51. James, *Principles of Psychology,* 2:185.

52. Woodworth, *Psychology,* 354; Carr, *Psychology,* 270.

53. Woodworth, *Psychology,* 340.

54. Carr, *Psychology,* 273.

55. Ibid., 275.

56. The sensationalism of the Little Albert experiment led textbook authors to use it to demonstrate a wide range of psychological constructs. See Ben Harris, "What Ever Happened to Little Albert?" *American Psychologist* 34 (1979): 151–60.

57. Dashiell, *Objective Psychology,* 224–25.

58. Boring, Langfeld, and Weld, *Psychology*, 408, 413.

59. Ibid., 419.

60. Angell, *Psychology,* 320.

61. W. B. Pillsbury, *The Essentials of Psychology* (New York: Macmillan, 1911), 280.

62. This abbreviated comment merely intimates how experiments function as a practice and as a tool for persuasion. Experiments could locate and change emotions; reference to experiments could also serve rhetorical goals in textual accounts. Further, the reporting of experiments established new relations in reading between the firsthand observers who saw the event and the "virtual witnesses" who read the observers' accounts. On the powers of the experiment see Bruno Latour, *Science in Action: How to Follow Scientists and Engineers through Society* (Cambridge: Harvard University Press, 1987). On the relations of witnessing experiments see Steven Shapin, "Pump and Circumstance: Robert Boyle's Literary Technology," *Social Studies of Science* 14 (1984): 481–520.

63. Woodworth, *Psychology,* 357.

64. Latour, *Science in Action,* 45–48.

65. The development of psychological experimentation in the early twentieth century included methodological innovations that vested the experimenter with increasing control of the experimental situation, and participants, the subjects, with restricted options for action. These changes were based on two arguments: they increased objectivity in observations and they reduced the subjective components brought to the experiment by the untrained participants. Danziger, *Constructing the Subject*; Morawski, *Rise of Experimentation*.

66. In their history of childrearing and marriage manuals, Carol Z. Stearns and Peter N. Stearns have documented the rise of a management approach to emotions that encouraged consumption and eased tensions in the family. Similar measures to manage anger in the workplace helped workers adjust to changing labor conditions. *Anger: The Struggle for Emotional Control in America's History* (Chicago: University of Chicago Press, 1986), 69–156.

67. Peter N. Stearns has noted how the new strategies for controlling emotions com-

plicates any simple distinctions between nineteenth-century patterns of repression and self-control and twentieth-century ideals of expressivity. *Jealousy: The Evolution of an Emotion in American History* (New York: New York University Press, 1989).

68. The multiple axes of social relations located in these scientific accounts of emotion raise two theoretical questions: one concerning the analysis of author, text, and audience, and the other concerning the structure of emotions. The first question, one central to cultural studies, is finally a question about audience experiences—what they believed and how they made sense of what they read. The complexity of relations I have traced underscores a theoretical stance that does not privilege the text but rather sees audience and text in mutual relations of influence. This stance departs from the positivist assumptions in many studies of the popularization of science whereby readers are thought to believe and reflect scientific texts. A second theoretical question addresses the structure of emotions. The multiple dynamics of social relations located in the scientific texts suggest the need to consider how emotions can be defined only in relation to someone and/or to some event, whether that event be practical, moral, or economic. That is, the structure of emotions represented in the psychology texts belies the adequacy of viewing them as simply events or actions of individuals: these textbook accounts of emotions actually contradict the purported conception of emotions as individual experiences that are solely internal and in the head. See John Fiske, "Audiencing: Cultural Practice and Cultural Studies," in *Handbook of Qualitative Research*, ed. Norman K. Denzin and Yvonna S. Lincoln (Thousand Oaks, Calif.: Sage, 1994), 196; Gianna Pomata, "History, Particular and Universal: On Reading Some Recent Women's History Textbooks," *Feminist Studies* 19 (1993): 28. For an alternative (a dialogic, relational) perspective on emotions see Judith T. Irvine, "Registering Affect: Heteroglossia in the Linguistic Expression of Emotions," in *Language and the Politics of Emotion*, ed. Catherine A. Lutz and Lila Abu-Lughod (Cambridge: Cambridge University Press, 1990), 126–61.

69. Readers were often distinguished as a class apart from (and above) the ordinary persons to whom psychological analyses were applied. The psychologist's standpoint then became a motive for reading (and believing); the psychology textbooks' readers were invited to work toward the elevated position of the scientist. Morawski, "There Is More to Our History," 166–67.

70. Woodworth, *Psychology*, 353.

71. See Morawski, "Organizing Knowledge and Behavior."

72. Both feminist studies and social studies of science have indicated how formal knowledge systems have generated and proceeded only through distinct categorizations of the world—into the animate and inanimate, active and passive, moral and amoral. These categories have formed the basis of modern epistemology and politics. Donna J. Haraway, "A Game of Cats' Cradle: Science Studies, Feminist Theory, Cultural Studies," *Configurations* 1 (1994): 59–71; Bruno Latour, "The Impact of Science Studies on Political Philosophy," *Science, Technology and Human Values* 16 (1991): 3–19; Steve Woolgar, *Science: The Very Idea* (New York: Tavistock, 1988). Critical analyses of categories of agents in psychological research include Sharon Lamb, "Acts without Agents: An Analysis of Linguistic Avoidance in Journal Articles on Men Who Batter Women," *American Journal of Orthopsychiatry* 61 (1991): 250–57; Lola L. Lopes, "The Rhetoric of Rationality," *Theory and Psychology* 1 (1991): 65–82.

73. The historical and dynamic feedback between knowledge produced by scientific psychology and the activities of persons in everyday life is explored in Kenneth J. Gergen, "Social Psychology as History," *Journal of Personality and Social Psychology* 26 (1973): 309–20; Ian Hacking, "Making Up People," in *Reconstructing Individualism*, ed. T. C. Heller, M. Sosha, and D. Wellbery, with Arnold I. Davidson, Ann Swidler, and Ian Watt (Stanford: Stanford University Press, 1986), 222–36.

CHAPTER NINE

Epistemology of the Bunker: The Brainwashed and Other New Subjects of Permanent War

CATHERINE LUTZ

While psychology has had a history of collaboration with the military that extends back to the mass IQ testing of World War I army recruits, one can argue that professional and popular psychological discourses have bloomed with the emergence of the national security state around the time of World War II. As part of a larger project to trace the militarization of the psychological through the twentieth century, this chapter discusses some aspects of how the political economy and culture of permanent war used and shaped psychological science. Taken on to the project of covert warfare and deterrence, the discipline helped construct a new more vigilant self, a self not so much explicitly disciplined as suspicious of itself. There were now public and secret psychologies, governments, and selves. What I will call an "epistemology of the bunker" developed, solidifying certain widespread notions about subjectivity, danger, and authenticity. How this played out in debates about the "brainwashing" of prisoners of war during the Korean War gives a concrete example of its shaping of public discourse.

The Doubled State and the Subversive Self

In speaking of the national security state, I am drawing on Sidney Lens's persuasive thesis that 1945 marks the beginning of "permanent war." This comes about through the institution of a second, secret government via the National Security Act and a variety of executive orders.[1] Institutionally, it was constituted by the National Security Council, National Security Agency, the

Central Intelligence Agency, and a newly imperial presidency. But in late 1945 there was some strong popular revulsion at the use of the atomic bomb and resistance to a global U.S. military role in peacetime, both in the populace and in sectoral interests (such as the small entrepreneurial) not served by orientation toward overseas markets.[2] The international investment banking interests represented in the Truman administration won out, however, promoting a sharp reversal of the initial post–World War II demobilization. Not the Soviet A-bomb or Chinese military operations in Korea but the domestic political victors' ability to redefine "the national interest" prompted the growth of the military and, with it, military psychology.[3] Within two years of the end of the war, discursive legitimacy as well as institutional and financial support had gone to a military definition of the situation, and a large peacetime standing army had been normalized.[4] This unending state of emergency would require new forms of mental preparedness.

As many theorists of the postwar era have noted, nuclear weapons massively unmade the already fragile boundary between military and civilian targets and risks. As a technological secret, they provided ideological justification for the establishment of the national security state. This state was distinguished by radical erosion of the rule of law. National security interests, secretly defined, took precedence, and helped substitute the government of acts with the government of beliefs.[5] Nothing had more impact on cultural definitions of the person and citizenship than this growing sense that it was disloyal *feelings* rather than seditious *acts* that required direct state monitoring.[6] Government public opinion campaigns argued that the goal of "the underground operating directorate of world communism" was to weaken American civil society rather than to attack directly and militarily; officially generated fears consequently centered on spies, double agents, and internal subversion.[7] It became imperative but more difficult to know if a neighbor was a real American or a duplicitous fake, a defense asset or a security risk. In the process, boundaries between "us" and "them" were both made and washed away.[8]

A liberal consensus emerged that made dissent highly suspect or even outlawed, and that made individual change seem to offer, even more than in previous periods, the only solution to social crisis. Much anti-Communist rhetoric hinged on the newly politicized "individual"—positing him/her as perhaps the key marker of difference between U.S. and Soviet societies. The American favored psychological analysis, popular discourse had it, while the Reds used a debased social analysis. So the judge who sentenced the Rosenbergs could say they had committed a crime "worse than murder [which is] denial of the sanctity of the individual."[9] In this context, psychology could only ascend to a more hegemonic position.

Cleaning the Psyche Politic with Laundered Money

This ethos did not arise spontaneously. Help came from social science, especially psychological and communication studies, with substantial military funding. Although the latter did not grow as rapidly as health, education, and welfare funding, by one estimate it doubled during the six-year period from 1953 to 1958.[10] By another, 5 percent of the American Psychological Association worked full-time for the military in 1957, a similar percentage for the Veterans Administration, and many more on contract research at universities and in private defense industry.[11] Another doubling of funds for psychology occurred in the early 1960s with the strategic policy turn to counterinsurgency warfare.[12] These and other published figures, however, represent only publicly avowed funding.

Psychological research occurred under several auspices after the war: "in-house" with the Department of Defense or one of the services (e.g., the Human Factors Division of the Naval Electronics Lab); in military industrial firms (e.g., the Missile Systems Division at Lockheed Aircraft Corporation); on contracts to individual professors and university centers (e.g., Hadley Cantril, Princeton's Institute for International Social Research); and at a variety of psychological and social contract research centers established by the military at this time, including the very influential RAND Corporation and the Human Resources Research Office (HUMMRO), founded in 1951 by the future APA treasurer Meredith Crawford. Much of this work was hidden from both public and professional review. Research money from military agencies was sometimes laundered through foundations, an example being CIA funding at the University of Maryland on the psychology of prisoner "interrogation" in the 1950s. That produced numerous studies of psychological and other forms of coercion, including Louis Gottschalk's *Use of Drugs in Information-Seeking Interviews* (1958) and Albert Biderman's "Social-psychological needs and 'involuntary' behavior as illustrated by compliance in interrogation" (1960).[13] Another two cases that appear to have involved CIA money and research goals were $1 million through the Rockefeller Foundation to Princeton's Cantril for research into foreign and domestic public opinion, and $875,000 that, laundered through the Ford Foundation, went to set up the Center for International Studies (CENIS) at the Massachusetts Institute of Technology, from which a number of psychologists were to work on brainwashing and propaganda issues.[14] Extensive graduate student training in psychology came through research contracts from the Office of Naval Research; in 1952, the Group Psychology Branch alone had contracts funding 158 graduate students (135 men and 23 women) and directing their work, sometimes permanently, toward areas of interest to the military.[15]

This money, and the culture and political economy of permanent war more generally, shaped scientific and popular psychology in at least three ways—the matters defined as worthy of study, the epistemology of the subject that it strengthened, and its normalization of a militarized civilian subjectivity. I take up the first two aspects in overview, and the third in relationship the controversy over brainwashing of the Korean War POWs.

The Militarization of Psychology's Subject Matter

Psychologists did not just discover psychic processes for use by the military; they were also "tasked" with contributing to particular military goals that could require or obviate certain research questions or answers. Psychological thought experienced effects both specific (for example, an efflorescence of work on hypnosis and social isolation) and general (for example, an emphasis on mechanistic and top-down models of learning, an increasing conflation of education with training to pass competency tests). Whether or not research was explicitly done in service to the military, discourse on a certain psychological topic was often started in that context, legitimated as general or scientific psychology through publication in academic journals, and joined by nonmilitary psychologists' subsequent experimentation.

Psychological discourse responded to President Harry Truman's decision to focus on nuclear deterrence and technological superiority rather than on diplomacy or a continued mass-industrial army model.[16] These policy decisions prompted early and heavy defense use of emerging computer technologies that generated many analogically mechanistic metaphors for human thought. Truman's policy also created concerns with both secrecy (to prevent loss of technological, including psychological warfare, information to enemies foreign or domestic) and the soldier's limited cognitive capacity to run sophisticated equipment (which might instead be thought of as the lower education levels of those recruited to soldiering during this period). "Engineering psychology" and artificial intelligence developed continually as the perceived need to make humans more "machine-friendly" grew.[17] This paradigm was "an effort to theorize humans as component parts of weapons systems. Cognitive science may be read both metaphorically and literally as a theory of technological worker-soldiers."[18] While obviously facilitated by technological developments outside the military, this paradigm would not have developed its degree of importance had these military policies not been pursued.

The post–World War II army was basically nonprofessional, with large numbers of nearly illiterate soldiers and high turnover rates. This, combined with the rapid technological change that placed a premium on training soldiers for constantly changing tasks, boosted the stock of learning theory. Military training emphasized efficient (time-limited) problem solving and self-disciplined learners who were able to relieve the chain of command of moment-to-moment monitoring of their subordinates. It featured "task-specific performance, avoiding both 'undertraining' and 'overtraining'; . . . and instructional systems design, to ensure the compatibility of training to ongoing changes in mission and in weapons systems technology."[19] Resulting educational technologies and accompanying learning models conceived of the human as a complex information-processing system, and aimed for what one military psychologist described as "new methods of programming the learning experience" based on "precise derivation of objectives."[20]

Managing a permanent work force of millions, the army also had the problem of marketing its jobs to young civilians, and of personnel management and retention. It also set to work retaining its budget. The psychology of propaganda and public opinion was fertilized by the desire to mobilize a reluctant public to higher levels of military spending and international involvement and to protect expanding American markets overseas during the late 1940s. Such research could construct public opinion (through the researchers' question frames, for example) rather than simply discover it. Public opinion research, in fact, helped create a new definition of law and democratic process, as when study of public attitudes toward various kinds of wartime events was conducted in order to anticipate public resistance to a range of extreme measures. Alongside this project of control, the person was constituted as an autonomous "opinion generator."

Guarding what were posed as new fronts within civil society and at the boundaries of the mind, the military funded studies of hypnosis, interpersonal influence, and communication modes and impacts. Christopher Simpson's recent study shows how communication studies was virtually constituted by defense interests and funding.[21] Drawing on psychology and social psychology, the field's leading practitioners developed an especially quantified, coercive view of interpersonal communication. They studied "communication" between prisoners and captors, the characteristics of those best at keeping secrets, and projected community information flow after nuclear weapons use.

Counterinsurgency doctrine made the shaping of civilian populations a more central military goal. Newly relevant social psychology was mechanically placed within a cultural engineering frame: "unstable" societies needed "the military (social) mechanic [who] simply gets out his psychological tool-kit and tightens up a few nuts and bolts here and there."[22] The many Department of Defense-funded "psychological profiles" of individual countries, some conducted by psychological anthropologists like Margaret Mead and Clyde Kluckhohn, helped create a compendium of information on vulnerabilities and cultural patterns for use in counterinsurgency, a kind of cultural Bomber's Encyclopedia.[23] Some of the more striking examples during the 1950s include studies of culture-specific aversions for use in developing "smell bombs"; propitious days for bombing in each society for maximum effect; and cultural information that could be used to manufacture social dissension when needed.[24]

Psychology's subject matter has also been turned toward the face of battle itself, coming to focus on stress, vigilance, and other battle-relevant capacities more than a psychology that developed in a less militarized society would have.[25] Researchers looked, for example, at the psychology of men at the ends versus the center of a firing line, with an eye to reducing the "wild" ammunition use by the more vulnerable end men; the development of behavior modification techniques to make soldiers less averse to killing; and a spate of work on sensory deprivation and social isolation to train those who could be prisoners of war or captors.[26] So, too, psychiatry's focus on the repair of damage caused by trauma was the outcome of dealing with the large number of neuropsychiatric patients after World War II, as was the VA clinical training program that brought many young psychologists into contact with a militarily defined and damaged psyche.

Epistemology of the Nuclear Bunker

If ignorance is not—as it evidently is not—a single Manichaean, aboriginal maw of darkness from which the heroics of human cognition can occasionally wrestle facts, insights, freedoms, progress, perhaps there exists instead a plethora of *ignorances,* and we may begin to ask questions about the labor, erotics, and economics of their human production and distribution. Insofar as ignorance is ignorance *of* a knowledge—a knowledge that may itself, it goes without saying, be seen as either true or false under some other regime of truth—these ignorances, far from being pieces of the originary dark, are produced by and correspond to particular knowledges and circulate as part of particular regimes of truth.[27]

In *Epistemology of the Closet,* Eve Sedgwick weaves a stunning narrative of the relationship between sexuality, knowledge, ignorance, and speech. In it, the closet becomes not simply a location of hidden identities, but a historically specific, invented image that has remade the relation between the known and the unknown. The shibboleth that knowledge is power wilts before the complex ways that ignorance or performances of ignorance both make and unmake forms of knowledge and pursue power. So she can argue that there are "ignorance effects" that are often "harnessed, licensed, and regulated on a mass scale for striking enforcements."[28]

At mid-century, Strategic Air Command headquarters were dug deep under the Nebraska soil, nuclear bomb shelters bloomed beneath suburban yards, and journalists were excluded from the secret councils of the National Security Agency. The bunker, and the culture of secrecy prompted by the national security state, came to constitute a unique new form of ignorance, where the state's regulation of death more than of sexuality (though along with it) is central prompt. The ways this has played out and been amplified by the national security state are many. Deterrence theory in particular provided people with an incentive to rethink the relations between appearance, representation, and the unseen or unspeakable, as did new forms of disinformation, noninformation, and antidisinformation. By 1966, these had developed into language use of the kind an Air Force Information Officer performed after four nuclear weapons were accidentally scattered near the Spanish coast. When asked, "Where can we get information [about the risk of radiation], Colonel?" he responded, "From me. I have no comment to make about anything, and I cannot comment on why I have to say no comment." The question whether ignorance is feigned in this and innumerable other instances becomes irrelevant; its power exists, as Sedgwick shows of sexuality, in its performance. Moreover, there are, as we will see, *kinds* of ignorance in these matters, the most important being those of civilians versus military and security elites. Ignorance becomes a virtue here, as much or more than in the realm of sexuality. Antifoundational epistemologies can become more convincing.[29] Even more important, antidemocratic and thanatocratic knowledges are the better constructed through them.[30]

In discussing the historically recent closeting of homosexuality, Judith Butler argues further that it has helped create the very idea that people have gendered, internal identities; "invisibility," she says, produces "the effect of a structuring inner space."[31] The secrecy imperative of the national security state can be said to have done something similar, with the psychological becoming not just a discourse around war but a mode of warfare itself. The Cold War's distinction was that everyone, not simply the enemy, went into hiding, and so significant social relations became invisible. As they did, ghostly inner spaces were hypothesized to take their place, and the psyche was remade as a newly significant structuring principle.

The connection between epistemologies of the closet and the bunker are more than theoretical and more than uncanny, given that experts and politicians drew the categories "Communist" and "homosexual" together during the 1950s. Both figures were painted primarily as psychological defectives more than as ideologues or criminals or, of course, simply different ways of being in the world. As D'Emilio has eloquently pointed out, both "bore no identifying physical characteristics [and could] disguise their true selves."[32] Suspected homosexuals in government were fired as security risks at dramatically higher rates in the later 1940s and 1950s, something many observers relate to the 1948 Kinsey report, which gave the sense that gay men were more common and less detectable than had been thought. But the bunker, in hegemonic thought, contains the hero, the closet the pervert. And so the psychoanalytic "insights" used in Senate hearings to suggest that a closeted homosexual was as much a security risk as an out and obvious one were not applied to the dangers posed by the bunkering of the generals and the only pseudo protection of civilians sent hunkering down in school hallways and subway tunnels.[33]

The policy documents NSC 4 and NSC 4-A, approved by the National Security Council on December 7, 1947, provide a central starting point. Together, they claim to establish the state's right to conduct covert warfare. NSC 4 established a coordinated and overt propaganda campaign, described as a truth campaign to combat anti-American propaganda, and its contents were coded "confidential." This classification (lower than "top secret") allowed documents to be discussed but not shown to the public and was applied so that NSC 4's contents could be leaked to the press. NSC 4-A, approving covert psychological warfare, was passed moments later. This top secret document's existence could not be revealed; it was "deniable." With deep resonances of Freud, NSC 4-A contained the repressed content of NSC 4, which it contradicted, and produced layers of hidden work within the government. And, like Freud, the national security state saw "denial" as a defense mechanism in service to a higher state. Conscious/public democratic ideals overlaid the preconscious/"confidential" artifacts, which mediated relations between the conscious/public and the unconscious/"top secret" documents and actions.

The national security apparatus created "inside" spaces where security experts generated both knowledge and national safety. Civilians became "outsiders," defined as "naive" to the inverse extent that military-political elites claimed the secret space of knowledge and the doctrinal position of "realism."[34] The civilian was both critiqued and valorized for his/her ignorance, however, because no one but the authorized should know what or even if something was happening behind the curtain of secrecy. Certain dilemmas of the oxymoronic "secret knowledge" were evident in the mutual interest of the CIA and academic psychologists from prestigious universities in each other.[35] Scholars who would be spies could acquire knowledge made more valuable by definition of its secrecy and its association with the highest goals and powers of the state; spies who would be scholars could acquire the symbolic capital associated with the arena of public knowledge forbidden to those sworn to underground work. Neither public nor private knowledge was sufficient.

Ignorance effects reverberated further as time went on. The possibility was soon raised that a person might be unaware of his or her own indoctrination by Communist agents. This was particularly so because key points of Communist infiltration were thought to be ordinary organizations like the PTA, the National Council of Churches, and labor unions, "which are nothing less than the manifold voluntary associations that constitute a liberal democratic society."[36] While these groups were considered most American because they were most volun-taristic and democratic, they were now all potentially suspect as most un-American.[37] The new psychological ethic of militarized antisubversiveness cre-ated the discursive need to prove one's depths were American, to self-critique national neuroses, where an earlier century's was to prove spiritual election. Having become a permanent front, the mind was now a dangerous thing; knowing secrets, it could reveal them; it might turn against itself, against its own will; in short, it might be colonized.

Both secrecy and the exponential growth of militarized technological complexity drove an intensified search for certainty. They each contributed to an ideology of total defense that "assumes the possibility . . . of complete and consistent surveillance and comprehension of inherently unstable and danger-ous situations."[38] And the era did in fact give additional impetus to new forms of testing. The CIA began to make extensive use of polygraph tests to ferret out double agents and security risks. The invention of a noninvasive lie detector test (a voice stress analyzer) was prompted in the counterinsurgency environ-ment of Vietnam, where two military officers, Charles McQuiston and Allan Bell, found they needed a more portable means for interrogating prisoners.

Tests could also create an inner space for militarized vocational desire, that is, for coming to see oneself as in need of a career identity and, in the process, acquiring loyalty to the social institution that provides it.[39] The military's Armed Services Vocational Aptitude Battery (ASVAB) became the most widely given vocational test in American schools (because provided free by the Depart-ment of Defense). This testing promised to reveal the person's inherent inter-ests and capabilities. It also opens the individual both to recruiters, who offer to interpret the test and suggest an appropriate career, and to the notion of the individual as a stable bundle of traits, vocational desires, and abilities. Here again, psychology did more than simply offer its technical expertise in a social context that helped determine its uses; rather, the psychotechnical knowledge reflected that social context in its very form.

The doubled security state could prompt contradictory motives, then—not only the will to ignorance, but to further scientific digging, particularly into the mind, where the new subjectivism implied that truth and freedom lay. A dis-course emerged in which plumbing psychological depths—the search for either the mother's unhealthy effect or the secret Communist self—was heroic or patriotic. Unearthing psychological problems became a matter of national secu-rity, with Free World spies as well as military and industrial psychology work-ing to extend their ability to identify and eliminate troubled(troublemaking) individuals. So a contemporary trade magazine article, "Psychology Sifts Out Misfits" (1955), touted psychology as "a technique that lifts the 'iron curtain' that humans often hide behind."[40] The patriot had a transparent self, and psychology had the tools to identify that self accurately. Using them, it rooted out undesirable categories of people—the Communist, the misfit, the homosexual, the egghead, the dupe.[41]

Public concern with lobotomies and the impact of advertising was also heightened during this period. Anxiety about corporate manipulation of the mind was neither new nor a fantasy on the order of the Communist scare. But where the turn-of-the-century version of this discussion had focused on the problems of materialism and inauthenticity, all undergirded with a faith in "unified selfhood," the new bunkered atmosphere amplified and shaped these concerns in new ways.[42] Materialism was now both the sign of the superiority of the American system over the Soviets and potentially the slippery slope to its softness and downfall.[43] The urgent question was now not just whether but *how* the mind was affected by advertisements.

In his gossipy best-selling book *The Hidden Persuaders* (1957), Vance Packard took advertisers to task for using mass psychoanalysis to dip into the unconscious for "our hidden weaknesses and frailties." Referring to Madison Avenuers as the "depth boys" and glowering at their "subterranean operations," Packard could have been warning his readers about generals in nuclear bunkers, Russian double agents, or Chinese brainwashers. An emerging cultural common sense had it that those who go beneath "the surface" of American life are legitimately an object of public concern. But more than privacy was at stake in this popular view. It was the very future of the individual's "long struggle to become a rational and self-guiding being," the status of "will" or psychological freedom.[44] What can be called a "hypodermic model of influence" was at work in understanding all forms of indoctrination, exemplified most literally by the truth serums slipped to people in the spy stories ubiquitous to the era. This model's automatic quality was Janus-faced—it promised innocence of responsibility for those caught in its snare, but it also threatened a sudden and terrifying lack of self-control and authenticity.[45]

The spy, the psychoanalyst, and their marriage came up against two cultural problems, however. Their professional practice eroded widespread belief in the value of personal transparency as it blurred the surface-depth and truth-lie distinctions through the assumption that secret agents and civilian psyches were always potentially double. Spying and psychoanalysis also blurred the sense of where responsibility should be located, as when democratic organizations might be dupes of the Communists and adults likely be the damaged products of their mothers' upbringing. Moreover, the underground world that both spy and analyst entered put dirt on their hands and obscured their view of the horizons of truth and responsibility that they, in an earlier but still operative discourse, dipped "below."

Brainwashing and the Invasion of the Enemy Self

Popular media and scientific debates about the Communist brainwashing of American POWs during and after the Korean War provide a key illustration of this psychological discourse of subversive knowledges and patriotic denial, this new entangling of selves and militaries. That war destroyed more than four million lives, devastated rice fields and cities, and left in its wake the world's most militarized peninsula. By the end of the war in 1953, however, the horrors of napalm, millions of refugees, and physically maimed veterans receded before another question. As the POWs were released, twenty-three American men refused repatriation, and the prison camp behavior of many more came under intense scrutiny.[46] They had been submitted to "brainwashing," a term invented and launched in the American media two years earlier by CIA employee-under-journalist-cover Edward Hunter. Ostensibly describing a new Chinese Communist psychological weapon, the term appeared in a flood of media pieces to account for the POWs' actions: confessing to war crimes, signing peace petitions, and otherwise collaborating with the enemy. And many articulated the dilemma as did Air Force intelligence officer Stephen Pease: "We were very unprepared for an enemy that would take our sons and use them against us so easily."[47]

The central questions were psychological: had the Communists used an advanced psychological science? Did brainwashing simply use the techniques of Pavlovian psychology (already discredited in the media and science journals as a materialist psychology, debasing man by treating him as a conditioned animal)?[48] Had it been psychologically possible to resist the brainwashing? Some preferred or mixed in moral language: did the soldiers have their will and thus their personal responsibility dissolved by this technique? Those who answered no often made sharp distinctions between body and mind, seeing physical torture as necessary for loss of will. Their consequent criticism was often biting and accompanied by visual reproach as well; one widely circulated magazine photograph showed the released POW collaborators together in bathrobed slouchy leisure, while next to it, another picture showed the resisters in their military uniforms, smoking and looking tough.[49]

Most accounts focused on some combination of Communist savagery and American nonvigilance. Their debates hinged on the paradox of evil and power and thus of the nature of the Communist other's threat: was his evil brilliant or more primitive? Did the Russians have a kind of neuron bomb or was it a dud? But given the view of Communism as evil antithesis, the Soviets' behavior needed less explanatory work than did that of "turncoat" Americans. Nonrepatriating North Korean POWs were simply freedom-seeking, and the brutal behavior of the Communist captors was essential to their barbarism.[50] More elaborate accounts were made of American misbehavior: the POWs had been "mentally softened up" first by their own country and then by brainwashing. The American cultural degeneration argument was often made by contrasting the survival and defection rates of the small group of Turks and the U.S. POWs. Soldiers' "softness" was often attributed to women's influence, both in the home and in Korea, where United Nations broadcast propagandists used female voices for their "extra psychological impact."[51] One psychologist with much exposure in the popular press argued that indoctrination in American homes mirrored that behind the Iron Curtain, where "dominating parents can prepare their children at an early age for continual mental submission by imprinting on them the pattern of conformity."[52]

Although other commentators were more sympathetic to the soldiers, several POWs were tried for their camp behavior.[53] And in August 1955, President Eisenhower signed a new code of conduct for the armed forces that set the limits of POW behavior very narrowly, requiring that the soldier "never surrender of [his] own free will . . . never forget [he is] responsible for [his] actions" and that he is bound to give only name, rank, service number, and birthdate.[54] This code, distributed to all service members in pamphlet form, included photos of POWs engaged in derelict behavior in Korean prison camps (fig. 9.1). The black bars over their eyes suggest that the reader and the soldier both engaged in prurient, illicit looking. The bars also make an ambivalent judgment of criminality (the convicted and guilty criminal must look the public in the eye). That ambivalence is perhaps produced by the fact that psychologists had been at work with the military on this issue, and that work was only partially buried by the code's use of the characterological (and nonpsychological) language of military discipline. The attempt is to cover not only their identities, but their gaze at the forbidden word.

Brainwashing was a sometimes different kind of concern to the military, the populace, and the professional psychologists, and negotiations over its meaning were intense both within and across these categories of actors. Interservice rivalries and ideological differences over proper military discipline, for example, made the brainwashing case a key test of the validity of postwar changes in the military's disciplinary practices.[55] Veterans and other groups had made efforts to reduce the power of officers to enforce discipline capriciously, with the goal of democratizing the services and "improving morale." These efforts led to the passage of a new Uniform Code of Military Justice in 1946 (some provisions of which were not in place until mid-1950). This hotly contested code emerged at the same time that the services were engaged in both extensive rivalry with one another and disputes over the changing social composition of the services. After World War II, recruits were poorer, younger, less schooled, and racially more diverse. The behavior of the POWs and the proposals

9.1. The seen and the unseen: prisoners of war read Communist propaganda in the Department of the Army's indoctrination pamphlet "Communist Interrogation, Indoctrination, and Exploitation of Prisoners of War." Pamphlet 30–101. 15 May 1956.

for training soldiers to cope psychologically with new enemy tactics implicated all of these issues. Was collaboration the result of the power of the enemy's psychological weaponry, of relaxed discipline, of the class and race background of the soldiers, of the weakness of the Army in comparison with the Air Force?

A debate in psychological terms had the advantage of seeming to depoliticize the issue, making it a matter of individual psychological makeup rather than of social relations of class, race, or sexuality. It also depoliticized the matter of brainwashing by turning the question over from political debate between social segments to seemingly technical debate among experts. Each service, however, hired its own experts: access to the POWs or their dossiers went to Julius Segal (with the Army's HUMMRO, previously with the Air Force's Human Relations Research Laboratory), Edgar H. Schein (Walter Reed Army Institute, and then to MIT), Albert Biderman (Air University, Maxwell Air Force Base), Harry Harlow (with I. E. Farber and Louis Jolyon West for the Air Force), and Raymond Bauer (Harvard, MIT, including its CIA-connected CENIS).[56] And their positions and findings ranged from A to D.

Major William Mayer, an Army psychiatrist who studied one thousand POWs, concluded in a *U.S. News and World Report* article that the U.S. soldier was deficient in "character and self-discipline" and in general education, particularly about democracy.[57] Equally hard-hitting and even more widely read was a *New Yorker* piece by Eugene Kinkead, based on select Army informants. The Dutch émigré psychologist Joost Meerloo, on the other hand, claimed that "no man could resist" brainwashing's combination of Pavlovian conditioning and its exploitation of the "fear of freedom," and he dramatized brainwashing further as "menticide." Bauer argued that it was group conformity, not simple Pavlovian conditioning at work, while Segal found more psychological similarities between those POWs who actively resisted and those who collaborated: both resisters and collaborators were more outgoing and "deviant" than the largest group of more passive "Middle Men." Segal saw these results as demonstrating that "most men behaved primarily out of emotion and self-interest."[58]

When Biderman took the strongest stance against unreasonable expectations of POW resistance to brainwashing, his position reflected that of the Air Force. That service had split from the Army, Navy, and Marine Corps in seeking to allow airmen to give more information to the enemy.[59] Biderman drew on the widely shared psychologists' faith in the perfectibility of humans through their science, and saw his work as a criticism of "the traditional view" that men are motivated only by fear of punishment.[60] He explicitly criticized the strict code of conduct, which he thought was destined to produce guilt in soldiers who would all predictably fail to some degree to live up to its unrealistic psychological expectations. So, too, James Miller argued that the code did not face up to the technological advances in such areas as the psychology of interrogation, all of which would put the code in "the T.N.T. age of brainwashing rather than a future possible atomic age" of psychological warfare.[61] One proposed solution was intensified security and document classification procedures to further limit the secrets any person possesses: all GIs and citizens "know too much," an admiral-columnist observed in the *Saturday Evening Post*, but secrets one does not know cannot be betrayed.[62]

These conflicts between service branches affected the questions psychologists were tasked with: were there higher rates of collaboration in infantry or pilot POWs, for example? Was psychological torture equivalent to physical torture, meriting POW post-service benefits or not? The military was also interested in preventing propaganda coups by the enemy or loss of morale within the military ranks. They had to worry about the impact of disciplinary action or censure of POW "weakness" on the psychology of service members and on future recruiting in services already experiencing manpower "quality" decline, and on public support of high postwar military budgets.

The POWs presented psychologists with other dilemmas. Debates over licensing and other aspects of professionalization in the immediate postwar period were heated, particularly given the meteoric rise in the demand for psy-

chological services together with insufficient training opportunities and certi-
fication procedures. The public debate about brainwashing provided an opportunity for asserting professional claims. Evoking earlier struggles with spiritualism, they made it clear that brainwashing could be uncovered and controlled
by their expertise.[63] The widely circulating notion that the POWs simply needed
more "will" to resist successfully was obliquely or directly attacked: as one psychologist noted in a professional journal, "it is questionable whether it is wise
for scientists in serious discourse to oppose spiritual power and conditioned
reflexes [to psychological torture]."[64] Psychologists' legitimacy required, however, that they provide authoritative answers to the question of brainwashing
within the bounds of a moral, that is, appropriately anti-Communist science.

Popular commentators took a variety of more flamboyant tacks. Two of the
most widely read were Edward Hunter's *Brainwashing* (1956) and Virginia
Pasley's *Twenty-One Stayed* (1955), as well as a host of articles in major newspapers and magazines.[65] Hunter opened his book with an evocation of common
social evolutionary thinking; he distinguished brainwashing from education
or persuasion, the former being "more like witchcraft, with its incantations,
trances, poisons, and potions, with a strange flair of science about it all, like a
devil dancer in a tuxedo, carrying his magic brew in a test tube."[66] The Russian
or Chinese psychologist occupied the space between primitivity and civilization,
which is barbarism, the space between the irrational and the rational, which
is efficacious evil. The proof could be found in the fact that were it a truly scientific psychology, the psychological abnormality of Communist investigators
would become self-evident, resulting in their "de-Communiz[ing] themselves
in the very act of seeking better psychological weapons for Communism."[67]
With a mix of moral and psychological language, Hunter posits a deterioration
of character, loss of American stamina and discipline, and the emergence of a
"moral gap" between us and them.[68]

Pasley's Pulitzer Prize-winning book, *Twenty-One Stayed*, was lavishly praised
for revealing "one of the greatest mysteries of our time—the problems of 21
families hit by tragedy harder to bear and understand than death itself."[69] A
journalist, Pasley searched the childhoods of the unrepatriated soldiers for the
source of their otherwise inexplicable behavior. A common thread of their boyhoods, she found, was that many of them "felt unloved or unwanted by fathers
or stepfathers," were beaten by them, and/or lost them through death or
divorce. Their mothers had in many cases died or were separated from them
early on, had drinking problems, worked away from home, or were "unusually
strict." The men's IQ is consistently noted, and, although by her figures they fall
exactly around the mean, Pasley summarizes thus: "16 [of the twenty-one]
were average or below in I.Q." Most grew up in poverty, were socially "with-
drawn, lone wolves," and virtually all "had never heard of Communism except

as a dirty word" and did not know why they were fighting in Korea. Newspaper reports of the "secret Army study" of these men also refer to them as "'lone wolves' who took little part in group activities at home" and as coming in many cases from "broken or unhappy homes."[70]

So, too, a major piece in the *New York Times*, "The War for the POW's Mind" (1953), described susceptibility to Communism as the result of personality alone; the collaborator is "the man with no strong focus in his life. He is likely to be a late adolescent, with no career started, no knowledge of world affairs, no real knowledge of his own country and its ways, no great convictions or at least no articulate support for them. Maybe he has a background of family instability or poor school experience. He is likely to be heavily reliant on others for leadership in thought and action. [The resistor has] strong religion, success in life and a happy family figuring in his make-up (any single one of these may be enough; it doesn't take all of them)."[71]

In both popular and professional discussions of the POWs, the diagnosis was *psychological*, and the psychologist was hailed to provide both cures and prophylactic measures as an ally of the state.[72] If the diagnosis was poor childrearing, the cure was developmental and educational. The imminent physicality of the combat soldier's danger, on the other hand, had been leading psychiatrists to treat combat "mental disorder" as a matter of "any man's breaking point"; much discussion of the POW remained less universalizing and more purely psychological than psychophysiological, focusing on the changeable disposition of a few.[73] Battlefield "cowardice," it seems, could be remade as stress disorder more readily than prison camp "collaboration" to the extent that a physical instinct would be drawn into the former's explanation: the psychological was not completely triumphant. And from the perspective of some in the military, moral language retained its value and fervor. So when the Defense Department committee that developed the code of conduct summarized their assessment of the twenty-one men who stayed, it was in purely moral terms. "Few of these twenty-one were 'sincere' converts to communism. Expediencey [sic], opportunism, and fear of reprisal" were main influences.[74]

In the shadow of the psychological, moreover, was a class-based conflict over character and social background. At the trial of one of the collaborators, Corporal Edward Dickenson, the defense psychiatrist testified that Dickenson was "emotionally unstable" and so "might be an easy prey for Communist bullies," that he had a "passive-aggressive personality," with a background of "insecurity, deprivation, and a feeling that nobody really cared for him." These personality factors made capitulation more likely. When further described in the *New York Times* as a mountain boy, readers could add regional and class stereotyping to family-based notions of where weak minds and weak links in national security were likely to be found. There was much concern through the early Cold War with manipulation of the dull by the Communist, something presumably more likely in the undereducated. On the other hand, Biderman attacks the "soft living," "tut-tutting" readers of Kinkead's criticism of the POWs, flanked as it was by the "effetely materialistic advertising" in the *New Yorker*.[75] Similarly, the more middlebrow *Saturday Evening Post* editorialized that working-class GIs outshone the professional eggheads in universities and government, who had already demonstrated themselves liable to serve as dupes of the Communists. Playing the middle against the ends, the editor argues that the highly educated, who have never experienced torture, should not expect "Private Zilch" of "no particular background" to do so.[76]

Public discussion of brainwashing declined by the late 1950s but emerged again during the 1960 Moscow trial of Francis Gary Powers. Reissuing *Brainwashing* with a new final chapter of psychological diagnosis of the American international dilemma, Edward Hunter cited neuropsychiatrist Leon Freedom, who had identified a "national neurosis" created "by communism for purposes of subversion and conquest."[77] The primary symptom of this neurosis was loss of the sense of indignation over outrages foreign (the Communist invasion of Hungary) and domestic ("teenage murders on city streets"). Signaling the psychological's further entrenchment, as well as the continuing sense of the need for a bunkered mind, was the popular film *The Manchurian Candidate* (1962). Unlike the traditional western, whose male lead's violent acts are sufficient to right wrongs and establish his character, this film focused on the inner life of its American hero and showed "what can go wrong with [American] ideals when the inner life is made unsound or is invaded by political virus."[78]

After the Korean War, the term *brainwashing* migrated widely, most strikingly to segregationist discourses about the rising civil rights movement. Two examples: a University of Alabama student's father accused a psychology professor of "brainwashing" his daughter to believe in integration, and Governor Orval Faubus charged that antisegregationist Presbyterian ministers had been brainwashed by "left-wingers and Communists."[79] By the 1960s, the term frequently described the techniques of expanding religious sects, or any instance where undue or inexplicable persuasions on the once and ideally unitary American mind were seen at work.

With the coming of the national security state, psychological discourse was already widely available to help construct and further colonize new areas of concern. Permanent war's focus on the dangers of indirect homefront attack and cultural erosion was easily mapped onto psychological discourses of emotional and mental vulnerability. Psychologists themselves—most dramatically in the brainwashing scandal—helped invent mass concerns with hidden politically subversive interiorities, mental weakness, and suggestibility to Communist blandishments. And, less dramatically because made secretly, weaponry defined as psychological was made to seem both modern and humane through association with this most "human" science. The needs of the self and the state were produced or redefined—in ways that this chapter has just begun to suggest—in a society now teeming with soldiers, psychologists, and militarized subjects.

Notes

I thank Victor Braitberg, Kurt Danziger, Marilyn Ivy, James Peacock, Joel Pfister, Rayna Rapp, and Nancy Schnog for insightful comments on previous drafts, and Victor Braitberg for expert bibliographic assistance. Conversations with Micaela diLeonardo and Britt Harville have also helped clarify my thinking.

1. Sidney Lens, *Permanent War: The Militarization of America* (New York: Schocken, 1987). The radical shifts in military-society relationships after 1945 have been theorized in a variety of ways, but Lens's "depth" model of the postwar sociopolitical formation clearly relates to the cultures of both secrecy and Freudianism. For other explorations of the implications for the "psychological" of permanent war's remaking of cultural geography, see John D'Emilio, *Sexual Politics, Sexual Communities: The Making of a Homosexual Minority in the United States, 1940–1970* (Chicago: University of Chicago Press, 1983), 49; Sam Marullo, *Ending the Cold War at Home: From Militarism to a More Peaceful World Order* (New York: Lexington Books, 1993); Anne Markusen et al., *The Rise of the Gun Belt: The Military Remapping of Industrial America* (New York: Oxford University Press, 1991); Elaine Tyler May, *Homeward Bound: American Families in the Cold War Era* (New York: Basic Books, 1988); Ellen Herman, *The Romance of Psychology: Political Culture in the Age of Experts* (Berkeley: University of California, 1995).

2. Paul Boyer, *By the Bomb's Early Light: American Thought and Culture at the Dawn of the Atomic Age* (Chapel Hill: University of North Carolina Press, 1985); Benjamin Fordham, *Building the Cold War Consensus: The Political Economy of U.S. National Security Policy, 1949–51* (Ann Arbor, Mich.: University Microfilms International, 1994).

3. Fordham, *Building the Cold War Consensus*. See also Alan Wolfe, *America's Impasse: The Rise and Fall of the Politics of Growth* (New York: Pantheon Books, 1981) on "the growth consensus," and Mary Kaldor, *The Imaginary War: Understanding the East-West Conflict* (Oxford: Blackwell, 1990), for her argument that the Cold War was primarily fueled by domestic politics in both the United States and the USSR, with social divisions created and managed through its discourse.

4. C. Wright Mills, *The Power Elite* (New York: Oxford University Press, 1956).

5. Lens, *Permanent War*, 133.

6. A longer-standing U.S. nationalism has done something similar by creating an indivisible "we" of the state and the person ("we invaded Iraq"), which itself allows the construction of political difference from the state as nefarious or pathological secret self.

7. The quoted phrase is Kennan's, cited in Frederick M. Dolan, *Allegories of America: Narratives, Metaphysics, Politics* (Ithaca: Cornell University Press, 1994), 72.

8. Dolan, *Allegories*.

9. Cited in Stephen J. Whitfield, *The Culture of the Cold War* (Baltimore: Johns Hopkins University Press, 1991), 31.

10. Marguerite L. Young and Henry S. Odbert, "Government Support of Psychological Research—Fiscal Year 1958," *American Psychologist* 14 (1959): 497–500.

11. Arthur W. Melton, "Military Psychology in the United States of America," *American Psychologist* 12 (1957): 740–46.

12. Charles Windle and T. R. Vallance, "The Future of Military Psychology: Paramilitary Psychology," *American Psychologist* 19 (1964): 119–29.

13. The former was published as BSSR report 322, December 1958, the latter in *Sociometry* 23, no. 2 (June 1960): 120–47. See John Marks, *The Search for the "Manchurian Candidate": The CIA and Mind Control* (New York: Times Books, 1979), on the related secret military work of University of Rochester psychology department chair G. Richard Wendt, whose grant covers claimed that he was working on motion sickness. Racial dimensions in this work included the frequent use of black prisoners in the United States to test, for example, the effects of various drugs on interrogation.

14. Christopher Simpson, *Science of Coercion: Communication Research and Psychological Warfare, 1945–1960* (New York: Oxford University Press, 1994), 82. The national security interests in the struggle to establish CENIS, which funded several prominent academic psychologists' work, have been researched in Allan A. Needell, " 'Truth Is Our Weapon': Project TROY, Political Warfare, and Government-Academic Relations in the National Security State," *Diplomatic History* 17 (3): 399–420.

15. John Darley, "Psychology and the Office of Naval Research: A decade of development," *American Psychologist* 12 (1957): 317–18.

16. Marullo, *Ending the Cold War.*

17. Chris Hables Gray, *Computers as Weapons and Metaphors: The U.S. Military, 1940–1990, and Postmodern War.* Working Paper no. 1, Cultural Studies of Science and Technology Research Group (University of California at Santa Cruz, 1991); David Noble, *The Classroom Arsenal: Military Research, Information Technology, and Public Education* (London: Falmer Press, 1991), 23; Nikolas Rose, *Governing the Soul: The Shaping of the Private Self* (London: Routledge, 1990).

18. Edwards in Noble, *Classroom Arsenal,* 43.

19. Noble, *Classroom Arsenal,* 17.

20. Meredith P. Crawford, "Military Psychology and General Psychology," *American Psychologist* 25 (1970): 329.

21. Simpson, *Science of Coercion.*

22. P. Watson, *War on the Mind* (London: Hutchinson, 1978), 40.

23. See Denise Riley, *War in the Nursery: Theories of the Child and Mother* (London: Virago, 1983); Simpson, *Science of Coercion.* This kind of work, of course, has deeper origins in the rise of Freudian thinking in interwar anthropology and was used significantly during the Second World War. An impulse for Japanese national character studies, for example, was the hope that postwar psychoanalytically influenced education could modify totalitarian patterns.

24. Watson, *War on the Mind.*

25. Robert Kugelmann, *Stress: The Nature and History of Engineered Grief* (Westport, Conn.: Praeger, 1992).

26. See Marks, *The Search for the "Manchurian Candidate."*

27. Eve Kosofsky Sedgwick, *Epistemology of the Closet* (Berkeley: University of California Press, 1990), 8.

28. Sedgwick, *Epistemology of the Closet,* 5.

29. Dolan, *Allegories*.

30. Peter Linebaugh, "Gruesome Gertie at the Buckle of the Bible Belt," *New Left Review* 209 (1995): 15–30.

31. Judith Butler, "Gender Trouble, Feminist Theory, and Psychoanalytic Discourse," in *Feminism/Postmodernism*, ed. Linda Nicholson (New York: Routledge, 1990); Judith Butler, "Imitation and Gender Insubordination," in *Inside/Out: Lesbian Theories, Gay Theories*, ed. Diana Fuss (New York: Routledge, 1991).

32. D'Emilio, *Sexual Politics*, 49.

33. Those Senate Appropriation Committee hearings helped establish that "if the government could not expel 'passing' lesbians and gay men on the basis of their behavior, it could on the basis of their psychological profile. Indeed, their very 'normalcy' was a sign that they were disturbed." See Robert J. Corber, *In the Name of National Security: Hitchcock, Homophobia, and the Political Construction of Gender in Postwar America* (Durham, N.C.: Duke University Press, 1993), 63.

34. Hugh Gusterson, "Realism and the International Order after the Cold War," *Social Research* 60 (Summer 1993): 279–301.

35. They are also evident in a psychological warfare treatise that raised the possibility of changing U.S. laws to allow "pro-American secret activities to be launched" by private citizens "without permitting anti-American activities of the same kind" (Paul M. A. Linebarger, *Psychological Warfare* [Washington, D.C.: Combat Forces Press, 1954], 298). This raises the conundrum of a government that tries to keep secrets from itself while remaining efficacious.

36. Dolan, *Allegories*, 72.

37. Dolan, *Allegories*.

38. Edwards cited in Noble, *Classroom Arsenal*, 33.

39. See F. Allan Hanson, *Testing Testing: Social Consequences of the Examined Life* (Berkeley: University of California Press, 1993), on this process, which he calls "vocationalization."

40. Cited in Vance Packard, *The Hidden Persuaders* (New York: David McKay, 1957), 206.

41. The egghead joins this group because, as noted above, knowledge becomes suspect in the culture of secrecy, especially outside the national security establishment.

42. Jackson Lears, "The Ad Man and the Grand Inquisitor: Intimacy, Publicity and the Managed Self in America, 1880–1940," in *Constructions of the Self*, ed. George Levine (New Brunswick, N.J.: Rutgers University Press, 1992), 111.

43. May, *Homeward Bound*.

44. Packard, *Hidden Persuaders*, 6. The effects could be automatic. As one marketing professor said of the psychology of advertising in 1925, once the consumer's attention is captured, "his will is dead" (in Lears, "Ad Man," 118). The effects of television, also discussed in psychological idiom, raised this same fear: John Steinbeck lamented the packaging of Republican politicians in 1956 television campaign spots, for example, which found "millions of people in a will-less, helpless state, unable to resist any suggestion offered" (cited in Packard, 194).

45. This is Victor Braitberg's discerning insight.

46. Only twenty-one eventually stayed in North Korea. The other two men changed their minds and were court-martialed on their return. Of the 7,000 Americans captured, approximately one-third died in captivity. A commonly cited estimate was that one in

three survivors collaborated in some way. Media coverage of North Korean and Chinese POWs in UN camps was quite different. Starvation, overcrowding, and officially sanctioned intragroup violence at the Koje Island camp and elsewhere, which had resulted in at least 6,600 POW deaths, were only alluded to in an official military history; moreover, these were described as problems "aggravated by . . . the difficulties of approach to prisoners who were both communists and Orientals" (*Logistics in the Korean Operations,* 4 vols., HQ U.S. Army Forces, Far East and 8th U.S. Army [rear], Military History Section, LKO, Camp Zama, Japan, Dec. 1955, vol. I, chapter 3, 58). This same history notes that when "mass rioting increased on Koje-do, the need increased for greater quantities of chemical irritants" (58); hundreds of POWs were killed in those incidents. See also Jon Haliday and Bruce Cumings, *Korea: The Unknown War* (New York: Viking, 1988). There was also a sense that the nonrepatriation of these POWs did not require explanation.

47. Stephen E. Pease, *Psywar: Psychological Warfare in Korea, 1950–1953* (Harrisburg, Pa.: Stackpole Books, 1992), xiii.

48. The psychologist Raymond Bauer, working at Harvard's Russian Research Project—jointly funded by Carnegie Corporation, the air force, and the CIA—wrote frequently about the flaws and social uses of Pavlovianism during this period. One of his most influential works was a 1954 psychological warfare study for the air force, "Strategic Psychological and Sociological Strengths and Vulnerabilities of the Soviet Social System," which—minus four pages of suggestions and with a laundered title (*How the Soviet System Works: Cultural, Psychological, and Social Themes,* 1956)—became a widely used university text (Simpson, *Science of Coercion,* 186).

49. "The GIs Who Fell for the Reds," *Saturday Evening Post,* Mar. 6, 1954, 17–19.

50. Although their freedom to choose sides was manifestly absent, it was nonetheless assumed in these documents and the press. In this context, it is important to note that by 1952, U.S. desertions were five times higher than earlier in the war, and that self-inflicted wounds accounted for 90 percent of all hospitalized British soldiers (Haliday and Cumings, *Korea*).

51. See Edward Hunter, *Brainwashing: From Pavlov to Powers* (New York: The Bookmailer, 1956 [1960]), 314; Michael Rogin, *"Ronald Reagan," The Movie and Other Episodes in Political Demonology* (Berkeley: University of California Press, 1987). The observation about female voices in propaganda is from Pease, *Psywar,* 114.

52. Psychologist Joost Meerloo, once head of the Netherlands Forces psychology department, had become an American citizen by 1950; *New York Times,* May 9, 1954, 33. In a related vein, the *Times* reported on April 10 of that same year on the psychological research of Dr. Helen Beier of the Russian Research Center, who found Russians less introspective than Americans.

53. According to Albert Biderman, in *March to Calumny: The Story of American POW's in the Korean War* (New York: Macmillan, 1963), of the hundreds of soldiers who were initially placed under suspicion, only eleven were convicted. But concern was so high that, as the trials were pending, the Defense Department withdrew its once lavish support of the just released fictional film *Prisoners of War.* Department lawyers apparently worried about its plot: a soldier is intentionally captured and falsely confesses to war crimes in order to report on conditions in the camps, suggesting there were circumstances that warranted surrender and collaboration (*New York Times,* Mar. 20, 1954).

54. Department of Army pamphlet no. 30–101, *Communist Interrogation, Indoctrination, and Exploitation of Prisoners of War* (Washington, D.C., May 15, 1956), 2.

55. The code was seen as a victory for the army's vision of proper conduct; *New York Times*, Aug. 18, 1955.

56. Julius Segal, "Correlates of Collaboration and Resistance Behavior among U.S. Army POWs in Korea," *Journal of Social Issues* 13 (September 1957): 31–40. Like several others, Segal's writing on this topic took three forms: an initial, often confidential military report, an academic journal article, and a popular magazine article (Julius Segal, "Were They Really Brainwashed?" *Look* 20, June 1956). Biderman's later related work was funded by the CIA through its conduit, the Society for the Investigation of Human Ecology (later the Human Ecology Fund). This work was conducted with Ecology Fund members Lawrence E. Hinkle and Harold G. Wolff, who wrote "Communist Interrogation and Indoctrination of 'Enemies of the State,'" *Archives of Neurology and Psychiatry* 76 (1956): 115–74. Prior to being hired to study the POWs at John Foster Dulles's invitation, Cornell neurologist Wolff had been treating Dulles's son, who, in bitter irony, had been shot in the head during the Korean War (Marks, *The Search for the "Manchurian Candidate,"* 127).

57. William Mayer, "Why Did So Many GI Captives Cave In?" *U.S. News and World Report*, Feb. 24, 1956, 56–62; Kinkead's article was eventually published as a book, *In Every War But One* (New York: Norton, 1959).

58. Segal, "Correlates of Collaboration," 37.

59. *New York Times*, Aug. 18, 1955.

60. Biderman, *March to Calumny*, 67.

61. James G. Miller, "Brainwashing: Present and Future," *Journal of Social Issues* 13 (1957): 48–55, 52.

62. Rear Admiral D.V. Gallery, "We Can Baffle the Brainwashers," *Saturday Evening Post*, Jan. 22, 1955.

63. See Deborah J. Coon, "Testing the Limits of Sense and Science: American Experimental Psychologists Combat Spiritualism, 1880–1920," *American Psychologist* 47 (1992): 143–51.

64. Miller, "Brainwashing," 50.

65. Virginia Pasley, *Twenty-One Stayed: The Story of the American GI's Who Chose Communist China—Who They Were and Why They Stayed* (New York: Farrar, Straus and Cuhady, 1955).

66. Hunter, *Brainwashing*, 3–4.

67. Linebarger, *Psychological Warfare*, 296.

68. Hunter, *Brainwashing*, 324, obviously from the book's second edition, playing as it does on "the missile gap" debate of the 1960 presidential elections.

69. *Chicago Sunday Tribune*, June 26, 1955.

70. *New York Times*, Jan. 29, 1954.

71. *New York Times Magazine*, Sept. 13, 1953, 39.

72. The mass media picked up other research circling around this explanatory problem as well: research, for example, linked psychological health with the ability to survive disasters (*New York Times*, Sept. 8, 1955) and with political moderation (*New York Times*, Sept. 3, 1955), quoting one Yale social scientist on his findings that "an unsatisfactory private life is a necessary basis for intense political interests."

73. Herman, *Romance of Psychology*.

74. *New York Times,* Aug. 18, 1955.

75. Biderman, *March to Calumny,* 153, 154. So, too, Tennessee Senator Estes Kefauver complained of the code that its principles "are excellent and highly beneficial for club conditions. . . . But what I would like to know is whether we as a nation are playing square with some of the boys . . . from rural communities . . . who had but a few years of education." *New York Times,* Aug. 21, 1955.

76. "G.I.s Outshine Eggheads in Resisting Reds," *Saturday Evening Post,* Oct. 31, 1953, 10–12.

77. Hunter, *Brainwashing,* 324.

78. Fred Inglis, *The Cruel Peace: Everyday Life in the Cold War* (New York: Basic Books, 1991), 99; Richard Slotkin, *Gunfighter Nation: The Myth of the Frontier in Twentieth-Century America* (New York: Harper Perennial, 1992).

79. *New York Times,* May 30, 1955; *New York Times,* Sept. 17, 1958.

PART V

Race, Gender, and the Psychological in Twentieth-Century Mass Culture

CHAPTER TEN

Deep Jazz: Notes on Interiority, Race, and Criticism

ROBERT WALSER

Interiority is anything but private. When country singer Randy Travis wrote and recorded "The Box," a top-ten hit on the country-western charts in the spring of 1995, he extended a Western tradition (dating back to the sixteenth century) of using music to produce socially grounded experiences of inner, personal "depth." In Travis's song, the narrator's father has just died, and as his family glumly sorts through the things he left behind, they find a wooden box on the top shelf of his workshop. Inside it, they discover evidence of feelings that the man never displayed: a picture of his wife from their courting years, a pocketknife given by the narrator for Father's Day and long thought lost, a worn Bible, and, most startling of all, a poem in which he expresses love for his wife and children with an intensity they had never suspected.

The music makes us feel what they feel. Like most country singers, Travis cultivates a voice that will project sincerity; he artfully offers artless truth, while the intricate finger-picking of the acoustic guitar and the fiddle's slow swoops back him up with the semiotics of rural honesty. Only the fancy swelling and fading of the pedal steel, its fluid pitches stirring desire and resolving perfectly, give us a glimpse of the stakes of interiority. The narrator muses on how difficult it is for some men to show their feelings as the box forces his father's whole life to be reevaluated, his patriarchal gruffness explained away. The family posthumously excuses Dad's behavior on the basis of an interiority that was never manifested in a way that touched those around him. "We all thought his heart was made of solid rock. But that was long before we found the Box."[1]

Such evocations of an inner emotional realm seem natural to us because they have so powerfully shaped our lives. They produce an individualized image of the self, an "inside" not only defined against the outside, but imagined as somehow autonomous from it. They ask us to accept an intangible inner life as the essence of a person: truer than behavior, deeper than one's closest relationships. They offer psychological explanations of an identity which is often made to seem free-floating, detached from social experiences of class, race, ethnicity, and gender. They paint the social world as a shallow backdrop to the mysterious wellsprings of subjectivity.

Music has long been central to such cultural constructions of private experience. Because it operates through shared conventions that are invisible and nonverbal, music is often taken to stand outside the very social contexts that make it possible and meaningful. Yet this asocial way of understanding music is relatively uncommon in world culture, and even in European history. It was developed by Enlightenment, Romantic, and modernist philosophers and musicians during the expansion of industrial capitalism, as part of a set of strategies for coping with the breakdown of patronage structures and the resulting changes in art's status as a commodity. Audiences came to understand art as a refuge from a dynamic, volatile social world, with its unstable processes of identity formation. There is thus a resistive aspect to this sensibility, a refusal to accept the idea that all experiences can be contained or accounted for by social structures that have been increasingly dominated by commercial transaction. Yet it is also a strategy of disengagement that depends on naturalizing the values and desires of some people as "deeper" and thus more prestigious than others.

Scholars have just begun to reread the past in terms of how communities have used music to produce, alter, and maintain forms of subjectivity at various historical moments.[2] Because jazz, and popular music more generally, have largely escaped this kind of analysis, despite an enormous critical literature, this chapter investigates the idea of "interiority" as a set of assumptions that enables certain ways of thinking about jazz and obscures others.[3] First, I shall quickly survey the development of commentary on jazz with an eye to how conceptions of interiority have circulated throughout the twentieth century. This has involved, among other things, the basic problem of what sort of self or experience jazz was thought to articulate or represent: whether it was to be understood as embodying primitive license or modern vigor. Second, from this perspective, I shall take a closer look at the rise of musical analysis in jazz scholarship of the 1950s, which founded a tradition that has become increasingly influential with the growth of jazz studies in the academy. As in classical music, analysts have presented the interrelationships of musical details—which are understood to be "inside" the piece "itself"—as an objective alternative to messy debates over meaning. Yet I shall argue that such analysis is also predicated on ideas of psychological interiority that disguise the social grounding of musical practices and experiences.

Although I do not attempt here a history of interiority—a survey of when and where such ways of thinking have circulated—jazz emerged and jazz criticism developed during a period when notions of a specifically psychological interiority were becoming increasingly popular throughout American culture. For example, Joel Pfister has traced the cultural significance of the dramas of Eugene O'Neill for his audience of the 1920s and 1930s, a group that historians have described as the American professional-managerial class: "O'Neill's plays fortified their faith in the existence of a complex, contradictory, and dramatic psychological individuality whose depth never could be fully scripted or fathomed by corporate America."[4] Pfister points to the growing influence of psychoanalysis as another factor that helped to produce the atomized subject of capitalism, distrustful of social relations that seem to boil down to dollars, heavily invested in the family as a separate sphere of intimacy, and increasingly fascinated by the new idea that the familial training of childhood, rather than the social negotiations of adult life, might best account for one's interior richness.

Many early reactions to jazz echoed the logic of Freud's ideas about repression. In 1917, an article in *The Literary Digest* quoted a certain Professor William Morrison Patterson: "The music of contemporary savages taunts us with a lost art of rhythm. Modern sophistication has inhibited many native instincts, and the mere fact that our conventional dignity usually forbids us to sway our bodies or to tap our feet when we hear effective music has deprived us of unsuspected pleasures."[5] From this perspective, jazz liberated an instinctual vital essence, with results that were variously understood as dangerous, exhilarating, or both.

Others who praised jazz, such as the conductor Leopold Stokowski, related the success of jazz to the excitement of modernity, attributing the creativity of African American culture not to the richness of its inherited resources and conventions, but to their nonexistence: " 'Jazz' has come to stay," Stokowski wrote in 1924: "It is an expression of the times, of the breathless, energetic, superactive times in which we are living, and it is useless to fight against it. Already its vigor, its new vitality, is beginning to manifest itself. The Negro musicians of America are playing a great part in this change. They have an open mind, and unbiased outlook. They are not hampered by traditions or conventions, and with their new ideas, their constant experiments, they are causing new blood to flow in the veins of music. In America, I think, there lies perhaps the greatest hope in the whole musical world."[6] When he argues that African American musicians are unhampered by traditions or conventions, Stokowski is speaking, of course, of *his* traditions and conventions. This allows him to celebrate their fresh perspective as suitable, even therapeutic, for rapidly changing times.

The author of the first British book about jazz, R. W. S. Mendl, hedged his bets, vacillating between instinctual and social explanations for the music's controversial success in the years following World War I:

This syncopated dance music of to-day strikes a chord of which we civilised beings were, previously, but dimly conscious—something elemental, something crude, if you like, but something which once felt, cannot be ignored. It makes our blood tingle, and there is nothing surprising in the fact that some people find it makes their blood boil. Jazz music has permeated through all "strata" of society. It shows, so to speak, no respect of persons or classes, but exercises its stimulating or disturbing influence over rich and poor alike. . . .

Jazz is the product of a restless age: an age in which the fever of war is only now beginning to abate its fury; when men and women, after their efforts in the great struggle, are still too much disturbed to be content with a tranquil existence; when freaks and stunts and sensations are the order— or disorder—of the day; when painters delight in portraying that which is not, and sculptors in twisting the human limbs into strange, fantastic shapes; when America is turning out her merchandise at an unprecedented speed and motor cars are racing along the roads; when aeroplanes are beating successive records and ladies are in so great a hurry that they wear short skirts which enable them to move faster and cut off their hair to save a few precious moments of the day. . . . Amid this seething, bubbling turmoil, jazz hurries along its course, riding exultantly on the eddying stream.[7]

That jazz had "permeated through all 'strata' of society" was often interpreted as evidence that it wrought its effects at a level of human experience lower and more fundamental—"deeper," in one sense—than culture. Yet Mendl, to his credit, insisted elsewhere that the meanings of jazz must vary significantly among the residents of different countries, because of their differing experiences of war and racism.

The Swiss conductor Ernest Ansermet is often invoked by jazz historians because he was one of the first "serious" musicians to express approval of jazz. His famous praise of 1919, however, was tinged by uncertainty; he admired what he heard, but was troubled by his inability to gauge the musicians' interiority: "The first thing that strikes one about the Southern Syncopated Orchestra is the astonishing perfection, the superb taste, and the fervor of its playing. I couldn't tell whether these artists feel it is their duty to be sincere, or whether they are driven by the idea that they have a 'mission' to fulfill, or whether they are convinced of the 'nobility' of their task, or have that holy 'audacity' and that sacred 'valor' which the musical code requires of our European musicians, nor indeed whether they are animated by any 'idea' whatsoever." Ansermet did perceive the complexity of the social experience of performing jazz:

But I can see they have a very keen sense of the music they love, and a pleasure in making it which they communicate to the hearer with irresistible force—a pleasure which pushes them to outdo themselves all the time, to constantly enrich and refine their medium. They play generally without written music, and even when they have it, the score only serves to indicate the general line, for there are very few numbers I have heard them execute twice with exactly the same effects. I imagine that, knowing the voice attributed to them in the harmonic ensemble and conscious of the role their instrument is to play, they can let themselves go, in a certain direction and within certain limits, as their hearts desire.

Yet Ansermet remained uncertain about whether these black musicians had interior "depth," and by the end of his article he had recast the musicians' creative interactions as the symptoms of ritual possession. And while possession has always been important in African American culture, here it is placed within a European dichotomy that strictly separates it from reason, allowing the "depth" of these musicians to become associated with the power of nature and the thrill of barbarism: "They are so entirely possessed by the music they play that they can't stop themselves from dancing inwardly to it in such a way that their playing is a real show. When they indulge in one of their favorite effects, which is to take up the refrain of a dance in a tempo suddenly twice as slow and with redoubled intensity and figuration, a truly gripping thing takes place: it seems as if a great wind is passing over a forest or as if a door is suddenly opened on a wild orgy."[8]

Primitivism worked both ways. While some critics celebrated their liberating contact with what they imagined was someone else's unrepressed "depth," others condemned jazz for corrupting white interiority: "If jazz originated in the dance rhythms of the negro, it was at least interesting as the self-expression of a primitive race. When jazz was adopted by the 'highly civilized' white race, it tended to degenerate it towards primitivity. When a savage distorts his features and paints his face so as to produce startling effects, we smile at his childishness; but when a civilized man imitates him, not as a joke but in all seriousness, we turn away in disgust." Such racist denunciations of jazz were common in the United States during the 1920s.[9]

In contrast, praise of jazz primitivism was particularly common in France, in part because it participated in a broader movement in the arts, but also because it opposed American exceptionalism, allowing French critics and fans to participate equally in jazz. During World War II, Charles Delaunay wrote to *Down Beat* from "somewhere in France," where "man seems to have lost all relation to civilized life and appears to be slowly sinking into the primeval ooze." Even while he testified to the lawless horrors of war, Delaunay used the idea that jazz "had the instinct to abandon the tics, conventions, and all the draperies of an Art mummified by scholastic routine" to justify his pleasure in it: "Jazz is much more than an American music—it is the first universal music. It may be termed international because, instead of addressing itself solely *to the mind* (which is dependent on national tradition and culture), it speaks directly *to the hearts* of men (who, when the fictions of 'education,' 'tradition,' and 'nation' are ignored, are very similar, just as the Lord intended them to be)."[10] Unlike earlier critics who had placed jazz on the devalued side of the Cartesian mind/body split, Delaunay's dichotomy is between the mind, which he understands to be shaped by culture, and the emotions, which he sees as universal, unconstructed, and natural. Like so many subsequent commentators, he valorizes jazz by dehistoricizing it, validating his own pleasures not by accounting for them, but rather by suggesting that all such experiences are deeper than the reach of cultural accountability and hence ineffable.

This discourse of interiority, however—this "deep jazz" thinking—had little to do with the ways in which jazz musicians talked about their music. The autobiographies of Jelly Roll Morton and Louis Armstrong, for example, presented jazz as a shared public discourse that requires skill and discipline—as the fulfillment of traditions rather than escape from them. Neither musician talks about expressing some inner essence or feelings; instead, both acknowledge the cultural sources of the music and offer lessons in how to be good performers, how to impress and affect an audience, how to organize a band or an arrangement.[11]

No one has explained more eloquently than the clarinetist and soprano saxophonist Sidney Bechet how jazz developed out of historical experience rather than a pre-civilized essence: "My story goes a long way back. It goes further back than I had anything to do with. My music is like that. . . . I got it from something inherited, just like the stories my father gave down to me. And those stories are all I know about some of the things bringing me to where I am. And all my life I've been trying to explain about something, something I understand—the part of me that was there before I was. It was there waiting to be me. It was there waiting to be the music. It's that part I've been trying to explain to myself all my life." Bechet makes his story vivid and evocative by personifying the musical tradition to which he belonged, enabling him to present jazz as something that is experienced as deeply personal, yet that is shared socially and rooted historically.[12] Similarly, poet Langston Hughes used the word "inherent" to describe jazz, but only as a defense of the cultural specificity of African American experience: "Jazz to me is one of the inherent expressions of Negro life in America: the eternal tom-tom beating in the Negro soul—the tom-tom of revolt against weariness in a white world, a world of subway trains, and work, work, work; the tom-tom of joy and laughter, and pain swallowed in a smile."[13]

In contrast, admirers of "inherent" qualities sometimes bury culture even when they praise it. A white critic insisted in 1946: "Only Negroes can play jazz. . . . I may say that *authentic* jazz can be created only by Negroes; any other jazz by white men, whether they played in New Orleans in 1910 or Chicago in 1926, is not authentic. They cannot emulate the feeling or expression of their Negro contemporaries because they are alien to the mystical and profound inspirations which motivate the Negro musician. Therefore what they play is inferior, in the light of pure jazz music, and even (to my ears) not jazz at all."[14] Compare this romantic projection of a primitive, however admirable, interiority, to Max Roach's matter-of-fact historicism: "White musicians have not contributed for the same reason that no blacks have come to the stature of Debussy and Schoenberg and others in Western European music. For, society has forbidden either musician to be fully engaged in the other's culture. And, all of our art forms grow out of culture."[15]

Thus far, these examples show a tendency for white critics to explain jazz in terms of precultural, racial, instinctual interiority, which fails to square with the ways in which black musicians and critics made sense of the music. To be sure, neither of these traditions is monolithic—there is, for instance, white pianist and critic Ben Sidran's sensitive cultural analysis of black orality, published in 1971, as well as a number of subsequent studies—yet this split does describe two large streams of writing about jazz.[16] Musicians such as Miles Davis have continued to emphasize cultural experience in their accounts, and LeRoi Jones devoted the first book about jazz written by an African American to the thesis that jazz comes out of a coherent philosophy based in shared experience. Although he has often been unfairly typed as "anti-white," Jones went so far as to celebrate white jazz musicians like Bix Beiderbecke as proof that jazz could be learned, demonstrating that it was not founded in some mysterious racial essence.[17]

Critic and novelist Albert Murray, one of the preeminent African American intellectuals of his generation, has even directly repudiated the idea that musicians are engaged in "expression" of anything "interior":

When working musicians (whether they execute by ear or by score) announce that they are about to play the blues, what they most often mean is either that the next number on the program is composed in the traditional twelve-bar blues-chorus form, or that they are about to use the traditional twelve-bar chorus or stanza as the basis for improvisation. They do not mean that they are about to display their own raw emotions. They are not really going to be crying, grieving, groaning, moaning, or shouting and screaming. They mean that they are about to proceed in terms of a very specific technology of stylization. . . .

After all, no matter how deeply moved a musician may be, whether by personal, social, or even aesthetic circumstances, he [sic] must always play notes that fulfill the requirements of the context, a feat which presupposes far more skill and taste than raw emotion.[18]

To be sure, not all black musicians and critics have taken this position on the question of interiority. Harlem Renaissance intellectual Alain Locke tried to defend jazz against charges of immorality by distinguishing between folk and commercial versions, "the original peasant paganism" versus "its hectic, artificial and sometimes morally vicious counterpart." "The one is primitively erotic," he argued; "the other, decadently neurotic."[19] Locke's defense is best understood against the early twentieth-century culture of neurasthenia that Tom Lutz has analyzed so well—the "American nervousness" afflicting that privileged elite who felt most civilized and most affected by modernity. Unlike W. E. B. Du Bois, who had tried to enfranchise blacks culturally by claiming that they, too, were sensitive enough to suffer from neurasthenia, Locke rejected this kind of psychologized interiority, preferring (in his words) the primitive to the decadent, the erotic to the neurotic, the pagan to the commercial, folksy people to the sophisticates, music's function as a safety valve to its embodiment of hysteria, healthy experiences to morbid ones.[20] In effect, Locke was carefully valorizing a version of "primitive" depth, betraying perhaps some influence of psychoanalytic thinking, but differing from the new idea of psychologized depth as the measure of human complexity.

In 1986 Billy Taylor, in an article explicitly concerned with elevating jazz within the terms of European concert music, argued that "Americans of African descent, in producing music which expressed themselves, not only developed a new musical vocabulary, they created a *classical* music—an authentic *American* music which articulated uniquely American feelings and thoughts."[21] For Taylor, jazz expresses a selfhood that is already there, rather than producing subjectivity through the cultural work it does. Moreover, the self that jazz expresses is "American"—not "black," which would be more specific, but also not "Western" or "human," which would be less specific. Somehow, the essence of jazz is circumscribed by the imagined community of the nation-state—but once interiority is evoked, no precise explanations of this coincidence seem necessary.[22] Taylor's theorization of jazz works to position the music within a classicizing discourse that has stripped away historical specificity from a great variety of musics as a condition of bestowing prestige upon them.[23] Moreover, it shows how the idea of interiority continues to be deployed to blur the social construction of identities.

In a thoughtful afterword to his magisterial collection of essays, *The Jazz Tradition* (1993), Martin Williams wrestled with a final problem: the "deeper meaning" of jazz and, in particular, his dissatisfaction with what he identified as the two main approaches to analyzing the music's meaning: the "impressionist" and the "Marxist." Williams objected to the first for allowing the writer's own experiences to displace all others, and to the second for turning art into "a reductive 'nothing but' proposition, robbed of its complexities and its humanity." Marxist interpretations of jazz are too obsessed with protest, Williams argued, and they "see the complexities of man [*sic*] and his art as merely the transient tools of 'social forces.'"[24] Here and throughout his criticism, Williams argued for the depth of individuals and the shallowness of social relations. They are corollary: only once the complexity of the social world is dissipated can it seem inadequate to the world of art. Only when the world's contradictions are made to seem remote can the tensions within the artwork seem to confirm the depth of the self.

To be fair to Williams, I should acknowledge that he was reacting against a Marxist tradition which has included some critics who make individuals shallow and social relations complex. However, I am arguing that individual complexity cannot be separated from social complexity, whereas Williams made explicit the strict separation of "inner" and "outer" worlds upon which his criticism depended: "It is easy enough to say that the conflicts with the outer world experienced by Negroes gave the music its birth and have kept it alive. But I believe that if those outer conflicts were somehow resolved, the conflicts that are fundamental within each human being would then keep jazz alive and developing, for jazz has been deeply in touch with those fundamental conflicts all along. And it is from these inner conflicts that comes the true impetus of art."[25] Autonomous art requires a deep self, and vice versa, both notions depending on the fantasy that the "outer" world could somehow undergo radical change without affecting the people who live in that world or the art that they make. Aesthetic depth and psychological depth are thus ideologically linked.

Such a critical approach has the effect of effacing historical conflicts and tensions, and for jazz, chief among these is racism. Williams's closing summary of the significance of jazz for African Americans is rich and poignant: "Jazz is the music of a people who have been told that they are unworthy. And in jazz, these people discover their own worthiness." But, he went on to say, "the music involves discovery of one's worthiness from within. And thus it is an experience that men [*sic*] of many races and many circumstances have responded to." Williams, like so many other critics, used depth to solve the problem of accounting for the different meanings jazz has for various people. If, "down deep," we are all the same, culturally specific meanings disappear. Once invoked, depth made it possible for Williams to disclaim responsibility for certain types of meaning that one might assume should be important for historical criticism: "I do not, and would not, presume to say what jazz means at its

origins and in the immediate context of the lives of Negro Americans."
Williams seems content to deepen what is surely a scandalous gap in jazz history—the lack of interest most historians have shown in the reception of jazz
among African Americans. The interested reader is simply referred to Albert
Murray, which frees Williams to invoke Carl Jung's mystical universalism and
the idea that only "innerness" can mediate differences among people.

Whether found by white Americans in early jazz, or in the even earlier
spectacles of the minstrel show, the pleasures of primitivism have always
depended on an imaginary depth—that is, a repository of illicit desires and
fantasies—that was justified and controlled by being ascribed to others.[26] But
once critics began to identify themselves with jazz, developing an attitude of
intimate involvement rather than distanced spectatorship, different forms of
depth emerged. Scott DeVeaux has brilliantly analyzed one of these, the production of depth through the construction of a jazz tradition: "Without the
sense of depth that only a narrative can provide, jazz would be literally rootless,
indistinguishable from a variety of other 'popular' genres that combine virtuosity and craftsmanship with dance rhythms."[27] DeVeaux shows that critics and
historians began deploying metaphors of growth and evolution during the
1930s, firming up the boundaries of a genre, jazz, which then came to seem to
have its own "inner logic." Through the continuing efforts of the critics of the
1940s and 1950s, jazz itself came to have a "self"—it acquired an essence, a
"transcendent principle of continuity."[28] Most important, DeVeaux points to
how narratives of jazz history are most tendentious when they seem most
objective: critics periodically rewrite the narrative of jazz to suit their purposes,
but jazz "itself" is supposed to be the agent of this history.

Besides tradition, I want to argue that scholars and critics invented for jazz
yet another type of depth: once the jazz tradition as a whole was understood to
have internal properties that reflected an integral essence, individual compositions could be seen in the same light. In particular, as jazz began to attract the
attention and admiration of classically trained musicians, the premises of modernist aesthetics supported jazz's climb up the ladder of cultural prestige.
Again, we now take this perspective for granted, but the idea that a piece of
music could have "internal" qualities is closely related not only to the notion
that a tradition can have an inner logic, but also to the belief that a person can
have an inner essence. It requires that the piece be seen as an autonomous
entity, rather than as a result of historically enabled human labor and interaction. It shifts attention toward a composer who can appear as an independent
point of origin, and away from the dialogue of musicians. Thus it supports
other forms of interiority and opposes the view that art and the social world
mediate the differences that individuals may experience as unique and private.

Foreshadowed in critical writings of the late 1930s, this sort of musical analysis was established for jazz in the 1950s and has continued to the present day. For the remainder of this chapter, I shall explore this version of interiority, taking as my texts what are probably the two most famous musical analyses in jazz scholarship: André Hodeir's treatment of Duke Ellington's "Concerto for Cootie" (1940), the centerpiece of his influential book, *Jazz: Its Evolution and Essence* (1956); and Gunther Schuller's (1958) analysis of Sonny Rollins's recording of "Blue 7" (1956).[29] This reappraisal is particularly important because of the ongoing influence of the tradition founded by Hodeir and Schuller; as it has come to seem a natural, objective, intellectual approach, its premises have rarely been examined.[30]

Hodeir's agenda is clearly signaled by his chapter title: "A Masterpiece: Concerto for Cootie." Like many who have loved jazz, he rose to its defense in the face of racism and prejudicial assumptions about the superiority of European traditions. Because he was a composer, Hodeir was able to bring to bear an array of technical terms from the European analytical tradition, which made his discussions of jazz much more musically specific than those of earlier writers. While his excitement is plain, so is his methodological rigor; in fact, he hoped that his book would become "the *Discourse on Method* of jazz."[31]

Hodeir's analysis covered several aspects of the piece. He first produced a formal diagram, divided into an exposition, a middle section, and a "re-exposition and coda"; an introduction precedes the exposition, which is made up of a statement of "theme A," a slightly varied restatement, the presentation of theme B, another repetition of A, and a brief transition; the middle section moves to a different key to introduce theme C, after which a short modulation leads back to the final statement of A and some closing material. Hodeir commented on the complexity of Ellington's harmony, and on the daring and skill with which he was able to make phrases of irregular length sound smooth and natural. Hodeir used musical notation to show subtle variations among presentations of the main theme, and he praised Ellington's handling of the concerto format, comparing him to Mozart because the orchestra supports the soloist so elegantly and economically. Hodeir favorably assessed the performances of individual musicians, especially the soloist, trumpeter Cootie Williams. In the end, he suggested that the lack of improvisation in this piece was the inevitable price that had to be paid for the overall control that allowed Ellington to make it "a real *composition* as European musicians understand this word."[32] Hodeir summed up his argument:

"Concerto For Cootie" is a masterpiece because everything in it is pure; because it doesn't have that slight touch of softness which is enough to make so many other deserving records insipid. "Concerto For Cootie" is a masterpiece because the arranger and the soloist have refused in it any temptation to achieve an easy effect, and because the musical substance of it is so rich that not for one instant does the listener have an impression of monotony. "Concerto For Cootie" is a masterpiece because it shows the game being played for all it is worth, without anything's being held back, and because the game is won. We have here a real concerto in which the orchestra is not a simple background, in which the soloist doesn't waste his time in technical acrobatics or in gratuitous effects. Both have something to say, they say it well, and what they say is beautiful. Finally, "Concerto For Cootie" is a masterpiece because what the orchestra says is the indispensable complement to what the soloist says; because nothing is out of place or superfluous in it; and because the composition thus attains unity.[33]

Despite the formal diagram and the musical notation, there is an odd lack of precision when Hodeir attempts to convince us that "Concerto for Cootie" deserves to be called a "masterpiece." But perhaps this is not so strange, since the very notion of a masterpiece is itself rather vague and mystical. Such a goal may make it impossible to avoid begging basic questions: what is the piece's "musical substance," which Hodeir invokes but does not explain? He speaks of "what the orchestra says" and "what the soloist says," but he never tells us what they are saying. How do we know that "the listener" (whoever that is) never experiences "an impression of monotony"? Why would "technical acrobatics" be a waste of time, and why would effects be "gratuitous"? What exactly does it mean to say that every aspect of the piece can be considered "pure"?

Despite the importance of Hodeir's achievement—he launched technical analysis of jazz, the precise consideration of the musical details of a style that many people didn't think *had* musical details—his rigor did not help him escape the limitations of "deep jazz" thinking. In Randy Travis's terms, Hodeir found and measured the box, and he itemized its wonderful contents—purity, unity, and so on—for the benefit of those who could not see beneath jazz's exterior and so judged it too harshly. But Hodeir managed to construct only the most tenuous of links between those inner qualities and the piece's observable behavior—what we can actually hear. We have to take his correlations of internal qualities and experiential value on faith, since the piece has been analyzed in a social vacuum. Could a musical analysis move beyond this disabling split?

In the case of "Concerto for Cootie," this seems a daunting challenge. It is, after all, slightly over three minutes of smooth, tasteful, ballroom dance music—in many respects not unlike thousands of other recordings in this genre. In fact, perhaps the masterpiece idea has led us astray; is it really possible to lift these three minutes out of Ellington's oeuvre, out of a typical night's performance, out of the whole huge phenomenon of the swing era, and look for meaningful bits to analyze? I think so, as long as those bits are not decontextualized: *something* made Hodeir and others hail this as an extraordinary piece, and it ought to be possible to illuminate the features and meanings that have distinguished this recording for critics and audiences.[34]

First, we will need to convert Hodeir's static formal plan into a narrative, moving from a synchronic vision of balance to a sense that the listener is actually led through a progression of events. From this perspective, the piece is made up of a series of similar statements of the A theme, broken up by two contrasting sections. Hodeir called these theme B and theme C; I shall call them the growl chorus and the flat-six envelope.

These interruptions differ markedly from the main theme, a sinuous but stable melody that is always played with a mute—a device that makes the trumpet, often an aggressive-sounding instrument, seem cooler. As Hodeir pointed out, Ellington pulls off a marvelous sleight of hand with the primary theme, which sounds complete but is oddly constructed: instead of the usual eight-measure phrase, this one cadences on bar six and is elongated to ten measures by an answering tag. This irregular phrase structure might be considered the harmonic equivalent of the mute, since it elides what would ordinarily be the pushiest part of the progression. As with every other aspect of the performance, Ellington avoids any sense of urgency or tension. There is no need to drive toward a resolution on the tonic chord; suddenly, we are already there.[35]

The growl chorus is a deviation from the polish and restraint of the rest of the performance, but not a random one; this rough sound, produced through subtle manipulations of the trumpeter's throat and tongue, has its own history. Ever since his days leading the house band at the Cotton Club—where he had to compose accompaniments to skits featuring white women saved from the clutches of African "savages," for the delectation of wealthy white patrons— Ellington had used the growling trumpet of Cootie Williams to evoke what even he called "jungle music."[36] In "Concerto for Cootie," this timbre is particularly revealing, since it is during this growl chorus that the blues basis of the entire composition becomes plain: throughout the piece, the trumpet states a motive, states it again over a different chord, and plays an answering phrase that resolves the melodic and harmonic tension. This is the basic procedure of the blues, but Ellington disguises his use of it in two ways: he defuses the harmonic drive and regularity of the form by resolving immediately on the answering phrase (instead of moving to the dominant), and he alters the second chord, retaining most of its functional effect but creating some ambiguity. In the growl chorus, though, the earthiness of the blues—a genre that was disliked by many African Americans who preferred the sort of elegance that Ellington projected through his appearance and bearing—is emphasized by the deliberate primitivism of the growl, until both are swept away and recontained by the return of the main theme. Outside of the Cotton Club and similar venues,

long after Ellington had achieved critical respect and increasing cultural legitimacy, growling trumpets and trombones could still evoke a kind of thrill that
had once been linked directly to racist spectacles.

The flat-six envelope is a different sort of deviation. First, Ellington
changes the key, moving to what musicians call the flat-six degree of the scale.
This is significant, for composers from Franz Schubert to George Michael have
used precisely this key area to construct a kind of utopian refuge, illogically
related to the main key and fated not to last, since the original key will eventually take over again.[37] As is customary, the flat-six section is marked by other
changes: Cootie Williams ascends to the high register that has gone unused in
this piece, plays for the first time without a mute, and pulls yearningly against
the beat in a soaring, rhapsodic style. Williams is expansive, strong, and sweet
(sounding like his hero, Louis Armstrong) until the blue notes at the end of the
section, which recall the growl chorus and lead back to the main theme, in the
original key.

More details could be discussed: how Williams uses an alternate fingering
to enable a discrete trill on the main theme, how he playfully varies the melody
on its last appearance. The essential point, though, is that Ellington constructed
a narrative where both primitivity and intense subjective desire are evoked yet
contained within an overall mood of upper-class elegance and restraint. He did
this by taking advantage of the special strengths of Cootie Williams: growl and
lead playing. "Those were my two ways of being," Williams once said. "Both
expressed the truth" (a statement which illustrates how musicians increasingly
came to think in terms of depth as a means of explaining their rhetorical skills
and their feelings in performance).[38] It is after the growl chorus that Williams
offers the most placid (no lip trills), most muted version of the main theme.
And it is after the flat-six section that the original key and theme are reasserted
and the piece can end on a note of effortless balance.

It is this narrative that justifies the title "Concerto." The eighteenth-
century concerto had enacted the reconciliation of social harmony and individual freedom, with the exciting excesses of the soloist both enabled and
bounded by the group.[39] Hodeir never explained why this piece qualifies as a
concerto, beyond the simple contrast of soloist and group. But if we take Ellington's term seriously, we can hear him staging, among other things, a sophisticated evocation and reconciliation of racial imagery in 1940. Together Williams
and Ellington offer the thrill of the "jungle"—as it was imagined and performed by Americans—and the glory of individual freedom, supported by the
literal social harmony of ensemble parts that are warm and intricate. Ellington's scoring and the skill of his musicians create the illusion of perfect balance,
no matter how irregular the phrases.

Williams, Hodeir, Ellington's dancing crowds in 1940, critics of later generations—we could not all experience this music in precisely the same way. But that is not an argument against interpretation; it is rather a call for socially complex interpretations. Musical material is always already part of a social fabric that is rich enough to offer a variety of identifications and experiences, and the conflicted dynamics of race—central to early criticism and much later commentary, but erased by strictly formal analysis—are important to the "political unconscious" of the music, the import it had for those who made and heard it. Such social analysis does not read "into" the text (as though the text has an "inside" that must be protected) but rather reconstructs meanings that people have experienced through their involvements with texts.

Once we start paying attention to past cultural competencies, we can begin to examine how and why jazz produces particular kinds of meanings for us. This is not a "reduction" of the music in the terms feared by Martin Williams. On the contrary, nothing could be more reductive than the bottom line he offers for "Concerto for Cootie": "It is dedicated to the variety of sounds that [Cootie] Williams resourcefully evokes from his open horn and from the use of several mutes in several ways: manipulated plunger on open horn, plunger over the small 'pixie' version of the straight-mute, plunger in tight, and so on."[40] We have a choice: we can conclude either that "Concerto for Cootie" participated in the most consequential social currents of its time and continues to resonate for us for complex reasons, or that it is simply about using lots of mutes.

Even more than Hodeir, Gunther Schuller saw jazz history as an evolution, and his musical analysis of Sonny Rollins's "Blue 7" was meant to mark and celebrate a new level in the progress of jazz.[41] Schuller began by pointing out that many improvised solos, however fine, have been assembled out of strings of unrelated ideas. This prepared the way for him to hail Sonny Rollins for having achieved in his improvisations what musicians like the Modern Jazz Quartet were developing through written composition: structural unity. With a brief apology for applying technical analysis to jazz—necessary since most jazz critics had little or no experience as musicians and were sometimes resentful of notation and musicological terminology—Schuller explained how Rollins created a thematically unified solo in "Blue 7." He began with the theme of the piece, a disjunct, fragmentary set of utterances built around the notes D, A flat, and E. These notes Schuller found exciting in themselves, since they could be related to more than one key, and he compared their bitonal ambiguity to a famous spot in Stravinsky's *Petrushka*.[42] But his main point was to show how these notes and the pattern which contains them is developed and varied throughout the piece, lending coherence and demonstrating an "intellectuality" that exceeds "*purely* intuitive emotional outpouring."[43]

For Schuller, Rollins's organic unity represented progress, and "Blue 7" was a sign that jazz had evolved, surpassing "humble beginnings that were sometimes hardly more than sociological manifestations of a particular American milieu" to acquire greater expressive capacities and "intellectual properties."[44] Schuller cautioned that the lack of such unity does not forestall artistic success, any more than its presence guarantees it. But he clearly approved of these "forward strides," and he even invoked the history of Western music since the Middle Ages—which, he argued, has chiefly been a history of thematic development—as another sign that Rollins's solo extended a trajectory that may have been predestined for jazz.

"Concerto for Cootie" and "Blue 7" do not have much in common, other than their shared debts to the blues. One is swing, the other hard bop; one was recorded by a big band, the other by a small combo; one is wholly scored, the other almost wholly improvised. Yet it is striking how similar Hodeir and Schuller make them seem. Both studied in an analytical tradition that emphasized organic unity as the sine qua non of any respectable piece of music, and they found what they had been trained to look for. Both arguably reinscribe their loyalty to certain critical conventions more than they illuminate the objects of their analyses, for in each case, the objective rigor of formal analysis substitutes for a contextual discussion of history and rhetoric.

The latter surfaces only once, parenthetically and awkwardly, in Schuller's article: "At the same time, speaking strictly melodically, the intervals D to A flat (tritone) and A flat to E (major third) are among the most beautiful and most potent intervals in the Western musical scale. (That Rollins, whose music I find both beautiful and potent, chose these intervals could be interpreted as an unconscious expression of affinity for these attributes, but this brings us into the realm of the psychological and subconscious nature of inspiration and thus quite beyond the intent of this article.)"[45] Schuller erased culture in order to protect the linked priorities of demonstrable formal unity and ineffable subjective depth (signaled by his use of terms like *psychological* and *unconscious*). Indeed, we can see that this type of analysis depends upon displacing specific social meanings, but it is nonetheless always motivated by the desire to establish others. As Fredric Jameson puts it, "the working theoretical framework or presuppositions of a given method are in general the ideology which that method seeks to perpetuate."[46] To prove organic unity is to guarantee the worth of the music and the defensibility of the pleasures it offers; it is to validate the organic integrity of the subjectivities of both the artist and the analyst. Moreover, it conflates these subjectivities; by thinking in terms of interiority, critics (nearly all of whom have been white and middle-class) have thought they could transcend the social differences that separate them from musicians, substituting an inner connection that is unaccountable.

In his own comments on "Blue 7" (which were otherwise largely cribbed from Schuller), Martin Williams attempted to situate the recording, if not in history, at least in Rollins's personal history: "Inevitably the growing musical maturity of the Sonny Rollins of mid-1956 is not without its basis in the facts of Sonny Rollins's personal life. The LP was made when Rollins was a member of the Clifford Brown–Max Roach quintet. He had joined the group a few months earlier in Chicago at the climax of a period of rigorous self-assessment and personal and musical discipline, reflection, and study."[47]

But if this period of self-assessment is relevant to our understanding of this music, surely it would be appropriate to consider Rollins's contemporary involvement with the bohemian intellectuals around the Five Spot in New York—a crowd that included Allen Ginsberg, Bob Kaufman, Jack Kerouac, and Willem de Kooning as well as Charles Mingus, Thelonious Monk, Ornette Coleman, and Cecil Taylor. Although Rollins was somewhat solitary, he shared in this bohemian sense of rebellion against conventional values; in fact, the period of "self-assessment" of which Williams writes was the period during which Rollins kicked his heroin habit. Moreover, the assessment was not only of his "self"; Rollins was becoming increasingly outspoken about American racism as well. In an interview in 1971, he approvingly cited Frank Kofsky's Marxist book on modern jazz, pleased that Kofsky had credited him with being "one of the first guys in the modern era to bring the political thing into music. My composition 'Airegin' (Nigeria spelled backward), also the *Freedom Suite*."[48] One of those compositions dates from two years before "Blue 7," and the other was recorded two years after it. When this sort of contextual information is no longer ignored, it is clear enough that the piece does not express some essential self but rather is a performance framed by a complex political history.

Schuller scarcely mentioned that "Blue 7" follows a blues progression, presumably because that conventional base seems to offer little purchase for analytical commentary. Yet it is only up against the rich but predictable framework of the blues that Rollins can construct his solo. Moreover, the blues itself does not have monolithic significance in jazz. Walter Bishop, Jr., who played piano with Jackie McLean and Charlie Parker, recalls that his generation of musicians rebelled against the blues: "I couldn't even play the blues till later years. I didn't want to know about the blues because to me the generation of the blues was representative of the subservient black. We'd graduated from that."[49] It was not until the late 1950s—around the time of "Blue 7"—that rising black militancy converted blues and soul into symbols of racial pride.

Similarly, Schuller's discussion of the melody seems partial and forced. After all, Rollins does not state his odd theme until the bass player has already thoroughly established the key of B flat (playing two whole choruses as an introduction), so that the motive's D, A flat, and E appear very clearly as the third, seventh, and flatted fifth of the key. Instead of explaining away the E by imagining it as part of an abstract "bitonal complex," we might try to assess its rhetorical significance. For the flatted fifth was not merely a technical detail—initially, it was a startling challenge to harmony-as-usual, shocking and delighting both musicians and audiences. In his autobiography, Dizzy Gillespie tells of his joy when he "discovered" it in 1938, explains how it spread rapidly among the most hip musicians, and jokes about how such players would greet each other with raised open hands, "the sign of the flatted fifth." In "Blue 7," this sedimented history of nonconformism is evoked, even if—especially if—it has by then become a generic norm.[50]

Rollins's virtuosic performance, then, can be seen as a creative negotiation with conventions: when he accentuated the flatted fifth and other dissonant notes, alternated fast complex passages with willful, bluesy coolness, and superimposed thematic development upon the repeated twelve-bar choruses, Rollins carved out a distinct identity by pushing against norms. It was this that drew like-minded audiences to come hear him play, not some general devotion to the abstract qualities that so impressed Schuller. This is not to say that Rollins himself was not interested in such qualities—when he composed his *Freedom Suite,* he used a single melodic figure as the basis for development and improvisation, and something of the same cohesion and economy of means clearly is present in "Blue 7." But I differ from Schuller in thinking that this is by no means the most significant aspect of the piece, and, more important, in insisting that a *description* of such features does not constitute an analysis of their significance.

Constructions of interiority serve social purposes, and when Schuller attempts to legitimate Rollins's work by demonstrating that it fulfills some of the cherished ideals of a prestigious tradition, his move "into" the piece disguises the historical basis of those ideals and evades questions of their relevance. On the one hand, thematic development has always been involved with performances of identity, however much our contemporary analytical vocabulary sometimes obscures that history in the case of European concert music. Schuller was delighted to find organic unity and thematic development in jazz because he considered them objective signs of musical excellence, rather than historically specific features, bound to the narrative procedures and subject formations of the eighteenth and nineteenth centuries. Despite the fact that analysts of classical music have tended to produce abstract descriptions of pitch relationships, paving the way for Schuller to do the same with jazz, Rollins's engagement with a host of conventions belongs to a cultural moment which made his choices particularly meaningful for particular listeners. If we had evidence that many listeners (besides Schuller) seized upon thematic development as the most powerful aspect of Rollins's solo, we would need to investigate further the social meanings of that technique in this twentieth-century context.

On the other hand, many aspects of Rollins's performance suggest parallels with the convention-resisting virtuosi whose exploits have since been classicized. Around Franz Liszt as much as Rollins, the members of a bohemian subculture explored, expressed, and confirmed their resistive identities by consolidating themselves as an audience. Bohemianism and racism in Eisenhower's America are part of the context within which Rollins's audience would have made sense of his performances, however much these aspects of the music are erased by discourses of formalism and psychological interiority. Where Schuller found orderly, logical development, confirming the universality of developmental structures, their participation in the Five Spot scene suggests that they were much more likely to have heard conventions evoked as a backdrop for creative, idiosyncratic, and rebellious signifying. Among jazz scholars and fans, Schuller's article helps construct a different context for Rollins's work, foregrounding certain musical details and social values so as to enhance appreciation by an audience with priorities that may differ significantly from those of Rollins's original audience. Like André Hodeir and Martin Williams, Schuller evacuated the social in order to mystify the personal and elevate the tradition.[51]

Later scholars have followed suit. To take only a single example, Frank Tirro's "Constructive Elements in Jazz Improvisation" (1974) was widely hailed as a great step forward for the academic study of jazz because it appeared in the leading journal in the field of musicology (a discipline which had been, and to a great extent remains, hostile toward popular musics). But in his discussion of more than a dozen improvised solos from the 1940s and 1950s, Tirro furnishes the date of only one; for the purposes of this kind of analysis, they could have been performed anytime, anywhere. Tirro argues that like classical music, jazz has "a coherent syntax and a hierarchical structure which provides a means for deferred gratification through a perception of the music's embodied meaning," but he never tells us anything specific about such meanings for particular people or groups of people.[52] Pieces of music have by now come to seem analyzable "on their own terms," but infusing jazz with such depth only disguises the agency of musicians, audiences, and critics, distracting us from the processes whereby people make and experience meanings.

This duality of technical features and feeling, the specifiable and the ineffable, runs through the entire history of jazz criticism and analysis, shaping debates, assumptions, and evaluations. Whether jazz is being attacked or defended, the same separation between musical techniques and personal interiority is typically maintained. James Dugan and John Hammond had already put it succinctly in their program notes to a 1938 concert: "Good jazz has outlived its highbrow detractors of the twenties and will continue to refute their petty charges. Look to it for the same qualities you expect in the classics: expert instrumentation, a musical structure (even in *ad lib* jazz), and a quality that we must call sincerity. The best hot musicians are men of profound feeling, even if this feeling is inarticulate."[53] Precisely specifiable technical features, on the one hand, and ineffable, inarticulate interiority, on the other, guarantee the value of the experiences jazz offers. But as the foregoing discussion indicates, this sense of romanticized inarticulateness, which supports the idea that emotional experiences are inherently ineffable, requires that we ignore what musicians such as Roach, Bechet, Morton, Davis, Armstrong, and others have actually said about their craft. It forces analysis away from cultural history and musical rhetoric, toward celebration of organic unity and lots of mutes.

The discourse of interiority we can trace in jazz criticism is part of a much larger pattern of thinking: "deep jazz" is related to "The Box." Millions of people have found Randy Travis's song powerfully moving because it spoke to their desires and fears. In general, it affirmed the existence of an inner essence that somehow defines a person more accurately than behavior, carving out a comforting sense of autonomy in an uncertain world. More specifically, it also reassured them that men who show no tender feelings nonetheless feel; it articulated the hope that uncaring men, deep down, care. The lyrics at once defend and make bearable a certain tradition of masculine conduct, and Travis's skillful music seems to provide direct access to the interiority that he presents in his lyrics.[54]

Many people have found the ways of thinking that I have labeled "deep jazz" similarly meaningful and illuminating. Accordingly, my purpose has been less to challenge the validity of such thinking and feeling than to argue that their existence is itself informative, revealing of larger social patterns, and deserving of analysis. However, while all perspectives are partial, the modes of thought I have described have been particularly disabling of historical understanding. I have tried to acknowledge why some listeners, musicians, and critics have found such ways of relating to music attractive, at the same time that I have shown how others, from Louis Armstrong to Albert Murray, have understood their involvement with jazz very differently. Ultimately, though, deep jazz thinking is a polemical mode that is selfish and misleading when it opposes interiority to social complexity, as selves are the product of experiences, social interactions, education, and institutions, and ideas about interiority are thus socially motivated, enabled, and valued. If jazz is to be the subject of serious historical inquiry, its role in the social production of interiorities must come under scrutiny. As listeners, we might treasure the "private" experiences music offers us, but as historians, we must seek to understand how such experiences are produced and why they are valued.

It could be argued that the discourses of interiority in jazz have had respectable effects, insofar as they have sometimes been invoked to combat racist essentialism by positing a substratum of humanity shared by all. But erasing differences, even with the best of intentions, is a tricky business. On the one hand, it can help bring people together by creating a sense of shared culture; and when cultural boundaries are drawn by racism, those who oppose racism may be the first to resent and deny cultural boundaries. On the other hand, it tends to accomplish this unity by relying on misleading, even damaging, assumptions about just what it is that is being shared.

If primitivism projects a certain kind of depth onto others, deep jazz thinking bestows depth upon the self; in both cases, some people's cultural values are validated by being universalized, through means that circumvent evidence and forestall challenge. Arguments that some music is "deeper" than other music are useful in the social negotiation of value precisely because they blur the social construction of both subjectivities and aesthetic values. They amount to claims of special privilege, and it is because they are rarely recognized as such that they warrant criticism. To locate value "inside" something—whether a person, a tradition, or a recording—is to attempt to evade what is "outside": history, culture, politics, contingency, contestation. Yet to evoke interiority is inevitably to argue about society, and it is precisely because the stakes of personal identity, historical memory, and artistic experience are so high that interiority is so public.

Notes

I am grateful for the advice of George Lipsitz, Susan McClary, and Jennifer Rycenga, who read and commented on a draft of this chapter, and Joel Pfister and Nancy Schnog, who conjured it into existence through their initiative, encouragement, inspiration, insistence, and most tactful prodding. For invitations to present earlier versions of this work, I thank Timothy Taylor of the Ethnic Studies Department at the University of California at Berkeley, Bettie Jo Hoffman and Andrew Maz, coordinators of the musicology lecture series at UCLA, and Dion Scott-Kakures, Director of the Scripps College Humanities Institute. The challenging questions and lively discussions which followed these presentations helped me considerably.

1. Randy Travis and Buck Moore, "The Box," recorded on Randy Travis, *This Is Me* (Warner Bros., 1994).

2. I am thinking especially of recent work such as the following: Susan McClary, "Narrative Agendas in 'Absolute' Music: Identity and Difference in Brahms's Third Symphony," in *Musicology and Difference: Gender and Sexuality in Music Scholarship*, ed. Ruth A. Solie (Berkeley: University of California Press, 1993), 326–44, and "Narratives of Bourgeois Subjectivity in Mozart's *Prague* Symphony," in *Understanding Narrative*, ed. James Phelan and Peter J. Rabinowitz (Columbus: Ohio State University Press, 1994), 65–98; Richard Leppert, *The Sight of Sound: Music, Representation, and the History of the Body* (Berkeley: University of California Press, 1993); Lawrence Kramer, *Music as Cultural Practice, 1800–1900* (Berkeley: University of California Press, 1990); and *Queering the Pitch: The New*

Gay and Lesbian Musicology, ed. Philip Brett, Elizabeth Wood, and Gary C. Thomas (New York: Routledge, 1994). An exception is the much earlier work of Theodor W. Adorno, who had always been concerned with the articulations of subjectivity in European music from Bach to Schoenberg.

3. The closest we have come to such a project is John Gennari's excellent analysis of the ideologies of jazz criticism; see his "Jazz Criticism: Its Development and Ideologies," *Black American Literature Forum* 25 (Fall 1991): 449–523. Other critical studies of this literature that I have found helpful include Krin Gabbard, "The Jazz Canon and Its Consequences," *Annual Review of Jazz Studies* 6 (1993): 65–98, reprinted in *Jazz Among the Discourses*, ed. Krin Gabbard (Durham, N.C.: Duke University Press, 1995), 1–28; Bernard Gendron, "Moldy Figs and Modernists: Jazz at War (1942–1946)," *Discourse* 15 (Spring 1993): 130–57, also reprinted in *Jazz Among the Discourses*, 31–56; Ron Welburn, "Jazz Magazines of the 1930s: An Overview of Their Provocative Journalism," *American Music* 5 (Fall 1987): 255–70; Ron Welburn, "American Jazz Criticism, 1914–1940" (Ph.D. diss., New York University, 1983); Mary Herron DuPree, "'Jazz,' the Critics, and American Art Music in the 1920s," *American Music* 4 (Fall 1986): 187–301; Roger Pryor Dodge, "Consider the Critics," in *Jazzmen*, ed. Frederic Ramsey, Jr., and Charles Edward Smith (New York: Harcourt, Brace, 1939), 301–42; and Ingrid Monson, "The Problem with White Hipness: Race, Gender, and Cultural Conceptions in Jazz Historical Discourse," *Journal of the American Musicological Society* 48 (1995): 396–422. The last of these reached me only after this chapter was completed, so I have not been able to draw upon or engage Monson's important evidence and argumentation.

4. Pfister, *Staging Depth: Eugene O'Neill and the Politics of Psychological Discourse* (Chapel Hill: University of North Carolina Press, 1995), 80.

5. "The Appeal of the Primitive Jazz," *The Literary Digest* (Aug. 25, 1917): 28.

6. Leopold Stokowski, quoted in "Where Is Jazz Leading America? Part II," *The Etude* (Sept. 1924): 595.

7. R. W. S. Mendl, *The Appeal of Jazz* (London: Philip Allan, 1927), 80–85, 92–108, 186–87.

8. E. Ansermet, "On a Negro Orchestra," trans. Walter E. Schaap, in *Jazz Hot* (Nov.-Dec. 1938), 4–9. Originally published as "Sur un Orchestre Nègre," *Revue Romande* (Oct. 1919).

9. Dr. Frank Damrosch, quoted in "Where Is Jazz Leading America?" *The Etude* (Aug. 1924): 518. For discussions of primitivism in jazz, see Gennari, "Jazz Criticism," 466–67, Kathy J. Ogren, *The Jazz Revolution: Twenties America and the Meaning of Jazz* (New York: Oxford University Press, 1989), and Ted Gioia, "Jazz and the Primitivist Myth," in his *The Imperfect Art: Reflections on Jazz and Modern Culture* (New York: Oxford University Press, 1988), 19–49. The problem with Gioia's argument, as I see it, is that he defends jazz against the primitivists by stressing the fact that many jazz musicians have been familiar with European music and music theory. In other words, he accepts the idea that there are such things as "primitive" musics, but insists that jazz is not among them. See the insightful critique by David Horn, "Review of *The Imperfect Art: Essays on Jazz and Modern Culture*, by Ted Gioia," *Popular Music* 10 (1991): 103–07.

10. Charles Delaunay, "Delaunay in Trenches, Writes 'Jazz Not American,'" *Down Beat* (May 1, 1940): 6.

11. See Louis Armstrong, *Swing That Music* (New York: Da Capo, 1993 [1936]), and

Alan Lomax, *Mister Jelly Roll* (New York: Pantheon, 1993 [1950]). I should also mention here that in criticizing versions of interiority that I have labeled "deep jazz," I intend no disrespect to Robert Palmer, who uses the metaphor of depth in ways that are explicitly historical and cultural; see his excellent book *Deep Blues* (New York: Penguin, 1982).

12. Sidney Bechet, *Treat It Gentle: An Autobiography* (New York: Da Capo, 1978 [1960]), 4. But compare Martin Williams's misconstrual of this explanation in *The Jazz Tradition*, 2d rev. ed. (New York: Oxford University Press, 1993), 266. Earlier editions were published in 1970 and 1983.

13. Langston Hughes, "The Negro Artist and the Racial Mountain," *The Nation* (June 23, 1926): 694.

14. R. E. Stearns, "A Purist Looks at Jazz," *Jazz Music* (1946): 9.

15. Max Roach, "What 'Jazz' Means to Me," *The Black Scholar* (Summer 1972): 6.

16. Ben Sidran, *Black Talk* (New York: Harper & Row, 1971). Lewis Porter has usefully compared some stereotypes found in white critics' writings with corresponding attitudes in black musicians' oral histories, in "Some Problems in Jazz Research," *Black Music Research Journal* 8 (Fall 1988): 195–206. Porter's emphasis is on different ways of understanding pedagogical and technical norms of the music; his examples are consistent with my exploration of interiority and social explanations, though he does not pursue his analysis in those terms.

17. LeRoi Jones, *Blues People* (New York: William Morrow, 1963), 154–55. Miles Davis with Quincy Troupe, *Miles: The Autobiography* (New York: Simon and Schuster, 1989).

18. Albert Murray, *Stomping the Blues* (New York: Vintage, 1982 [1976]), 87–90, 98.

19. Alain Locke, *The Negro and His Music* (Washington, D.C.: Associates in Negro Folk Education, 1936), 87.

20. See Tom Lutz, *American Nervousness, 1903: An Anecdotal History* (Ithaca: Cornell University Press, 1991), especially 261–75.

21. William "Billy" Taylor, "Jazz: America's Classical Music," *The Black Perspective in Music* 14 (Winter 1986): 21.

22. See Benedict Anderson, *Imagined Communities: Reflections on the Origin and Spread of Nationalism* (London: Verso, 1983).

23. On the development and consequences of "classical music," see Lawrence W. Levine, *Highbrow/Lowbrow: The Emergence of Cultural Hierarchy in America* (Cambridge: Harvard University Press, 1988), Christopher Small, *Music-Society-Education* (London: John Calder, 1977), Lydia Goehr, *The Imaginary Museum of Musical Works: An Essay in the Philosophy of Music* (New York: Oxford University Press, 1992), and Joseph Horowitz, *Understanding Toscanini: How He Became an American Culture-God and Helped Create a New Audience for Old Music* (Minneapolis: University of Minnesota Press, 1987). On related issues, see also Stephanie Sieburth, *Inventing High and Low: Literature, Mass Culture, and Uneven Modernity in Spain* (Durham, N.C.: Duke University Press, 1994).

24. Williams, *Jazz Tradition*, 261–62.

25. Ibid., 267.

26. On minstrelsy, see the last chapter of Nathan Irvin Huggins, *Harlem Renaissance* (New York: Oxford University Press, 1971).

27. Scott DeVeaux, "Constructing the Jazz Tradition. Jazz Historiography," *Black American Literature Forum* 25 (Fall 1991): 530.

28. Ibid., 540.

29. Duke Ellington and His Famous Orchestra, "Concerto for Cootie," recorded Mar. 15, 1940, first issued on Victor 26598. Sonny Rollins Quartet, "Blue 7," recorded June 22, 1956, first issued on Prestige LP 7079.

30. For an early adumbration of this sort of analysis, see Winthrop Sargeant, *Jazz, Hot and Hybrid* (Arrow Editions, 1938; reprint of the third, enlarged edition, New York: Da Capo, 1975). Another influential analysis of a single piece of jazz is Lewis Porter's "John Coltrane's *A Love Supreme*: Jazz Improvisation as Composition," *Journal of the American Musicological Society* 38 (Fall 1985): 593–621. I have chosen to limit my discussion to Hodeir and Schuller because of their importance as founders of this analytical tradition in the 1950s. Moreover, Porter was able to sketch some of the social meanings of Coltrane's performance to the extent that they appear to be revealed by the presence of a poetic text. To work toward explanations of the social meanings of completely instrumental works seems a more difficult and urgent task, since such pieces dominate jazz history; see my "'Out of Notes': Signification, Interpretation, and the Problem of Miles Davis," *The Musical Quarterly* 77 (Summer 1993): 343–65, reprinted in *Jazz Among the Discourses*, 165–88. For an overview of recent examples of jazz analysis, including approaches which variously emphasize melodic formulas, harmonic schemas, Schenkerian narratives, pitch class set theory, and syntactical conventions, see Gary Potter, "Analyzing Improvised Jazz," *College Music Symposium* 30 (Spring 1990): 64–74. For examples of such analysis, see also Barry Kernfeld, "Two Coltranes," *Annual Review of Jazz Studies* 2 (1983): 7–66; Lawrence Gushee, "Lester Young's 'Shoeshine Boy,'" in International Musicological Society, *Report of the Twelfth International Congress, Berkeley, 1977*, ed. Daniel Heartz and Bonnie Wade (Kassel: Barenreiter, 1981), 151–69, reprinted in *A Lester Young Reader*, ed. Lewis Porter (Washington, D.C.: Smithsonian Institution Press, 1991), 224–54; Lawrence O. Koch, "Thelonious Monk: Compositional Techniques," *Annual Review of Jazz Studies* 2 (1983): 66–80; Paul Rinzler, "McCoy Tyner: Style and Syntax," *Annual Review of Jazz Studies* 2 (1983): 109–49. All of these examples reflect acceptance of most of the central premises of Hodeir and Schuller as they are discussed below.

31. André Hodeir, *Jazz: Its Evolution and Essence*, revised edition (New York: Grove Press, 1980), 19. First published as *Hommes et Problèmes du Jazz* (Paris, 1954); first English translation, Grove Press, 1956.

32. Ibid., 91.

33. Ibid., 79–80.

34. I am taking the piece, the performance, and the recording to be basically the same thing in this case, because there is no improvisation and Ellington both composed the piece and conducted the recording.

35. When he converted "Concerto for Cootie" into a popular song, "Do Nothin' Till You Hear from Me" (recorded in 1947, but dating from 1943), Ellington rewrote this section with more conventional harmonic progression and phrasing.

36. Before Williams, trumpeter Bubber Miley had been the Ellington band's growler, along with trombonist Joe "Tricky Sam" Nanton, from whom Williams learned the growling style. See Stanley Dance, *The World of Duke Ellington* (New York: Scribner's, 1970), 105–06.

37. See Susan McClary, "Pitches, Expression, Ideology: An Exercise in Mediation," *Enclitic* 7:1 (Spring 1983): 76–86. The term *flat-six envelope* is McClary's; she developed this concept in order to account for signification in early nineteenth-century German

music. The George Michael example is mine; I am thinking of "Hand to Mouth," where music and lyrics evoke a brief utopian vision collapsing back into struggle; see his album *Faith* (1987). A great many other examples could be cited.

38. Quoted in Dance, *World of Duke Ellington,* 106. The interview which produced this statement appears to have been conducted in 1967.

39. See Susan McClary, "The Blasphemy of Talking Politics during Bach Year," in *Music and Society: The Politics of Composition, Performance, and Reception,* ed. Richard Leppert and Susan McClary (Cambridge: Cambridge University Press, 1987), 13–62. My argument is not that certain meanings inhere forever within particular musical procedures, but rather that in this case, similar means were used to articulate comparable models of social relationship.

40. Martin Williams, "Notes for *The Smithsonian Collection of Classic Jazz,*" revised edition (Washington, D.C.: Smithsonian Institution, 1987), 67.

41. Gunther Schuller, "Sonny Rollins and the Challenge of Thematic Improvisation," *The Jazz Review* 1 (Nov. 1958): 6–11, 21. Reprinted in Schuller's *Musings: The Musical Worlds of Gunther Schuller* (New York: Oxford University Press, 1986), 86–97.

42. "The primary notes of the theme (D, A flat, E) which, taken by themselves, make up the essential notes of an E-seventh chord thus reveal themselves as performing a double function: the D is the third of B flat and at the same time the seventh of E; the A flat is the seventh of B flat and also (enharmonically as G sharp) the third of E; the E is the flatted fifth of B flat and the tonic of E. The result is that the three tones create a bitonal complex of notes in which the 'blue notes' predominate. . . . Bitonality implies the simultaneous presence of two tonal centers or keys. This particular combination of keys (E and B flat—a tritone relationship), although used occasionally by earlier composers, notably Franz Liszt in his *Malediction Concerto,* did not become prominent as a distinct musical device until Stravinsky's famous '*Petrushka* chord' (F sharp and C) in 1911." Schuller, "Sonny Rollins," 7.

43. Ibid., 8.

44. Ibid., 8–9. John Gennari has ably criticized Schuller for stripping away contextual significance in order to legitimate jazz as "art" ("Jazz Criticism," 452–53); in what follows, I shall restore some context in order to sketch what else might have been said about the music of "Blue 7."

45. Schuller, "Sonny Rollins," 7.

46. Fredric Jameson, *The Political Unconscious: Narrative as a Socially Symbolic Act* (Ithaca: Cornell University Press, 1981), 58. Musicologist Joseph Kerman had made essentially this point with respect to music theory in "How We Got into Analysis, and How to Get Out," *Critical Inquiry* 7 (1980): 311–31.

47. Williams, "Notes for *Smithsonian Collection of Classic Jazz,*" p. 84.

48. Arthur Taylor, *Notes and Tones: Musician-to-Musician Interviews,* expanded edition (New York: Da Capo, 1993), 171. See Frank Kofsky, *Black Nationalism and the Revolution in Music* (New York: Pathfinder Press, 1970).

49. David H. Rosenthal, *Hard Bop: Jazz and Black Music, 1955–1965* (New York: Oxford University Press, 1992), 72. Parker, whose playing is filled with blues influences and who based a number of his compositions on blues progressions, is certainly an exception to this tendency.

50. Dizzy Gillespie with Al Fraser, *To Be or Not To Bop* (New York: Da Capo, 1979), 92,

343. On the idea of sedimented memory in popular culture, see George Lipsitz, *Time Passages: Collective Memory and American Popular Culture* (Minneapolis: University of Minnesota Press, 1990).

51. On identity construction in classical music, see the sources listed in note 2. A thorough reading of the Rollins example would wrestle more fully with cultural differences in significance among black and white audiences, and within them. My main point here is to show how these issues have been effaced altogether. For more detailed readings of the meanings of popular music for specific audiences, see my *Running with the Devil: Power, Gender, and Madness in Heavy Metal Music* (Hanover, N.H.: University Press of New England, 1993), and "Rhythm, Rhyme, and Rhetoric in the Music of Public Enemy," *Ethnomusicology* 39 (Spring–Summer 1995): 193–217.

52. Frank Tirro, "Constructive Elements in Jazz Improvisation," *Journal of the American Musicological Society* 27 (1974): 302.

53. James Dugan and John Hammond, "An Early Black-Music Concert From Spirituals to Swing," *The Black Perspective in Music* 2 (Fall 1974): 194. This is a reprint of the concert program notes of 1938.

54. This is similar, in some respects, to the workings of the romance novel as analyzed by Janice A. Radway in *Reading the Romance: Women, Patriarchy, and Popular Literature* (Chapel Hill: University of North Carolina Press, 1984).

CHAPTER ELEVEN

Beyond the Talking Cure: Listening to Female Testimony on *The Oprah Winfrey Show*

FRANNY NUDELMAN

On January 13, 1995, Oprah Winfrey confessed, on the air, to having used crack cocaine.[1] Responding to a young woman's account of her crack addiction, Winfrey revealed, "In my twenties I have done this drug. I know exactly what you're talking about." Struggling to hold back her tears, she admitted her "life's great secret." Unlike other talk show hosts, Winfrey's private life has consistently informed her public appearance, painful confessions such as this one punctuating her television career.[2] She has discussed the sexual abuse she suffered as a child, her subsequent mistreatment by men, her struggle to lose weight, her on-again off-again romance with Stedman Graham. Winfrey's own autobiographical disclosures provide a context for the daily revelations made by women on her show. Over the years, *The Oprah Winfrey Show* has featured guests, typically women, who speak to a studio audience, most of whom are also women, about their personal trials. While the program, by necessity, treats diverse topics, it has returned with regularity to the subject of sexual abuse and domestic violence.

Since the mid-1980s we have seen a diffusion of popular forms which publicize the abuse, and consequent suffering, of women. Survivor discourse, self-help manuals, and television talk shows all feature women talking about their victimization.[3] This form of public speech has confirmed and elaborated a certain construction of female subjectivity. Women, we have come to believe, are prone to psychic pain.[4] Bound to feel pain, they are bound, as well, to articulate it: the pained female psyche has its counterpart in the inevitable and intense expression of that pain. Popular renditions of female pain tend to essentialize and objectify not only female suffering but also female self-expression. And yet, if talk functions as a symptom of an essentialized female duress, it also holds out the promise of relief. Traversing the border between private and public by introducing personal troubles into the public sphere, these disclosures initiate the process of recovery. In the context of therapy and reform, talk is taken to free women from the very trials talk describes. The psychologization of the female subject goes hand in hand with the notion of progress, construed as recovery or as liberation, that gives social urgency to her public speech.[5]

Thus the public appeal of the female sufferer reliably raises the question: are the circumstances of the private woman transformed by her public appearance or is her affinity with suffering, and the emotional outcry such suffering provokes, simply reasserted? Reproducing the paradox embedded in the confession itself, scholars debate whether the female complaint intensifies or alleviates the suffering of women.[6] These analyses, which attempt to discern the efficacy of female speech by focusing solely on its attributes, threaten to recapitulate an emphasis on female expressiveness that establishes the pained woman as an object of interest. In order to unsettle the terms—repression and expression, illness and cure—which govern narratives of recovery, we must ask how the articulation of female suffering calls certain audiences into being, audiences which inevitably influence the meaning and the consequences of public testimony.

Talk show viewers, for instance, frequently respond to female testimony with skepticism and derision. Winfrey's recent confession was dismissed by the press as a desperate attempt to boost ratings in the face of competition from the *Ricki Lake Show*. More broadly, media commentators often denigrate talk show speech. One journalist describes women who appear on talk shows as "life's losers . . . the ones who, for the chance to be on TV, will confess to virtually anything, including sleeping with their husband's mortician."[7] When I talk to people about *The Oprah Winfrey Show* their responses, while less vicious, are similarly incredulous. They inevitably ask, "Why in the world would anyone go on the show?" Women's motivations for appearing on television are construed as, at best, unfathomable. Even as we embrace the notion that women feel and express intense pain, we tend to regard women's problems as unseemly and their disclosures as unreliable.

In her book on "self-help fashion," *I'm Dysfunctional, You're Dysfunctional* (1992), Wendy Kaminer takes a similarly dim view of talk show speech. Kaminer regards the preoccupation with individual transformation that characterizes the recovery movement of the 1980s as the consequence of mass culture's misappropriation of a feminist emphasis on the personal. Echoing the work of Richard Sennett and Christopher Lasch, Kaminer takes therapeutic culture as a sign of the demise of public life. More specifically, Kaminer argues that when women testify on television talk shows they degrade a feminist tradition of consciousness-raising that encouraged women to speak out as a means of politicizing their private experience. Noting that women have traditionally been taught to listen, attentively, to men, Kaminer claims that "Feminism is women talking." But it does not follow, she insists, that broadcasting female self-absorption is political. While consciousness-raising was conceptualized as a means to activism and institutional reform, women on talk shows treat self-revelation as an end in itself: "Feminism is women talking, but it is not women only talking and not women talking only about themselves." Lamenting that "what might once have been called whining is now exalted as a process of asserting selfhood," Kaminer objects to popular forms that try to pass off tales of personal pain and rehabilitation as political speech.[8]

Kaminer associates the talk show with the world of pop psychology and poses both against a feminist tradition. In doing so, she underestimates the similarities between feminist and therapeutic understandings of female self-expression. Whether female trauma is understood as psychological or social in origin, both feminist and therapeutic constructions of talk rely on the pained female subject as their point of origin and construe her self-expression as a means to progress. Consciousness-raising and recovery discourse, in particular, regard talk as a means of overcoming isolation and establishing solidarity: in both contexts, testimony creates identifications between the speaker and her audience, thus providing a basis for the development of actual or imagined communities of women. The talk show, by contrast, constructs talk as indeterminate, even incoherent, thus undermining the possibility of a listening audience and dismantling the alliance of talk and progress.

Opposing feminist and therapeutic discourse, and associating talk shows with the latter, Kaminer misreads the talk show. By investigating the similarities between consciousness-raising and recovery discourse, I do not mean to equate their purposes but to complicate our understanding of the current craze for talk. In this chapter, I will consider what consciousness-raising (a feminist project) and self-help (a therapeutic project) have in common, not in order to assert the feminist content of therapeutic discourse, but to examine how the talk show revises both feminist and therapeutic constructions of traumatized feminine speech.

Kathie Sarachild, a member of New York Radical Women, the first women's liberation group to practice consciousness-raising, would have found Kaminer's objections to television talk shows familiar, if disturbing. Writing in 1973, she remembers the response of the male establishment, left and right, to consciousness-raising: when talking about issues like "housework, child care and sex," their discussion was dismissed as "not political"; when attempting to figure out why women don't get equal pay for equal work, "what we were doing wasn't politics, economics or even study at all, but 'therapy'"; when discussing male chauvinism, "we were just women who complained all the time, who stayed in the personal realm and never took any action."[9] Kaminer's indictment of television testimony echoes the criticism leveled against consciousness-raising, and feminism more generally, by the left establishment. In the context of early feminism, as today, the label "therapy" works to deny the political implications of women's speech.

Without conflating therapy and consciousness-raising, it is important to consider their historical interrelationship: consciousness-raising was powerfully influenced by psychotherapeutic theory and practice. According to Ellen Herman, early second-wave feminists were engaged in a complex negotiation with psychotherapy. Herman argues that feminists repudiated "the authority of psychological experts" to define female nature, even as they embraced a psychological emphasis on "the nuances of subjectivity and identity." Feminists wanted to narrate their own experience in order to contest a thriving psychotherapeutic establishment that essentialized and pathologized women's troubles. By claiming that "experience—not expertise—imparted deserved authority," feminists challenged the power of professionals while leaving a therapeutic emphasis on female experience itself uncontested.[10] In consciousness-raising groups, women embraced the imperative to confess subjective experience while claiming the role of expert interpreter for themselves.[11]

Analyzing their own experience in a collective setting, feminists employed therapeutic methods while reformulating the tendency of therapeutic diagnoses to figure the pained woman as undone by feeling, eccentric, and alone. Early feminists saw talk as an analytical tool, a means of arriving at a theoretical position. Consciousness-raising would "develop 'generalizations' about women's lives from which theory could be made and power challenged."[12] Theory would, in turn, provide the guidelines for effective action. The testimonial was a means to analysis and community; talking about one's feelings would not reactivate them but rather attenuate their emotional immediacy, opening the space for reflection and solidarity. According to Robin Morgan, consciousness-raising showed women that "personal experiences" were not the same as "private hang-ups" but were "shared by every woman, and . . . therefore political."[13] Ann Forer wrote, "just recognizing that what we thought was an individual problem that we are suffering from alone is instead a class problem and all women suffer from it tends to lift the problem off your shoulders. It is no longer so personal."[14]

Feminists who claimed "the personal is political" attempted to give women a foothold in the public sphere, specifically the power to analyze and improve it, by virtue of their distinctive claim to traumatic personal experience.

Recent descriptions of consciousness-raising have overemphasized the importance of self-expression in the overall process. Consciousness-raising, according to Sarachild, had everything to do with listening: "The purpose of hearing
people's feelings and experience was not . . . to give someone a chance to get
something off her chest. . . . It was to hear what she had to say. The importance
of listening to a woman's feelings was collectively to analyze the situation of
women not to analyze her."[15] Consciousness-raising was not intended to benefit the speaker so much as to provide the basis for a community of listeners who
would gather information from what they heard, information which would
help them describe and redress problems common to women.[16]

Similarly, recovery discourse charts an individual's progress in relation to
a generic model of traumatized experience that is derived from and reinforced
by the articulation of discrete personal testimonies.[17] Self-help programs, for
example, transform individual "dysfunction" by way of mass-produced manuals. These manuals, like twelve-step programs, convert the problems people
experience as singular into common problems that can be redressed by standardized solutions. While they do not aspire to social reform, self-help programs replicate the structure of consciousness-raising—accumulating personal
narratives in order to produce useful generalizations.[18] Survivor discourse also
collects stories of abuse—in edited volumes, at speak-outs or Take Back the
Night marches—in order to show survivors of incest and sexual assault that
their experience is not unusual and that they need not be ashamed. As in consciousness-raising groups, narration elaborates a common model of experience.

Robin Norwood's influential *Women Who Love Too Much* (1985) is a case in
point.[19] The bulk of Norwood's book recounts the narratives of women she has
counseled. The book alternates between women's stories, told in their own
words, and Norwood's analysis of them. While these women have all suffered
in abusive relationships, each recounts a particular history and pattern of
abuse. It is not until the end of the book that Norwood offers a detailed program that draws conclusions from these narratives and tells readers how to
solve their problems. In concluding, Norwood synthesizes these disparate stories into a coherent, replicable regime for the reading public; individual trauma
is transformed into a widely applicable program for women.[20]

This generic model implies a degree of solidarity with other women who
share similar concerns.[21] In her study of self-help culture, Wendy Simonds
argues that women who read self-help literature are seeking companionship
rather than advice. On the basis of her interviews of self-help readers and her
reading of letters written by readers to authors Betty Friedan and Robin Norwood, Simonds observes that women feel great satisfaction when they recognize themselves in an author's account of her own experience or of another
woman's. As in consciousness-raising, listening to the stories of other women

and discovering that they are familiar helps "women realize that they [are] not abnormal and alone." Robin Norwood had this sense of community in mind when she decided to publish the letters written to her by her readers; in the preface of this collection she remarks, "Now, hopefully through the vehicle of this book, you will be sharing with each other."[22] Listening—as a participant in the semi-public scene of consciousness-raising, as a witness at a speak-out, or as a self-help reader in the privacy of one's own home—is the means of discovering solidarity with other women who have similar problems.

Airing her own troubles, Winfrey clearly provides encouragement for women who appear on the show and for those who watch: if she has succeeded in the face of dire difficulties, and succeeded on such a grand scale, perhaps they can too. The show's theme song—"I'm Every Woman"—promises that Winfrey's personal history, and her methods for overcoming it, are applicable to women generally.[23] Marking, repeatedly, a series of transitions in her own life—from poverty to wealth, insecurity to self-confidence, obscurity to superstardom—Winfrey's confessions, and the narrative of development they imply, suggest that talk is a vehicle of personal transformation.[24] In this sense, the program participates in the mass media's popularization and dissemination of therapeutic precepts.

And yet, while promoting the transformative potential of public confession, the talk show, in a variety of ways, refuses generalizations and thus denies its audience a standpoint from which to hear, understand, and interpret female talk. Kaminer's characterization of female testimony as "whining" is ultimately a comment not on what women who appear on talk shows have to say but on how we, their audiences, are taught to listen. The problems aired on *The Oprah Winfrey Show* are hardly insignificant. Women on the program discuss sexual harassment in the workplace, domestic violence, judicial bias against single mothers. Our hostility toward television testimony, our inability to hear what these women have to say is, in large part, the product of the program's formal traits: insisting on the indeterminacy of subjective experience, *The Oprah Winfrey Show* circumscribes the meanings of female speech; staging the proliferation of narrated trauma, the program makes it difficult to discover continuities between these stories. The talk show differs from the consciousness-raising group not because the subject matter it presents is insignificant but because the program's structure makes it difficult for viewers to construct generalizations from what they hear. While what women say on *The Oprah Winfrey Show* is often explicitly political, the structure of the show works to scramble their testimony. The talk show, in its thoroughgoing celebration of female speech and accompanying refusal of interpretive structures, minimizes the possibility of a feminist audience.

Winfrey herself valorizes the nuances of subjective experience at the expense of consensus. One afternoon, for example, the show featured mothers whose daughters refused to live with them. Winfrey introduced Debbie, whose teenaged daughter, Missy, chose to live with her father. Debbie and Missy argued over what had happened between them while a psychologist attempted to mediate. At one point the psychologist praised Debbie, the mother, for her willingness to admit her mistakes. Winfrey intervened, claiming that she did not hear Debbie apologize to Missy. She agreed, however, that such an apology was in order, explaining that "everyone who feels that they've been wronged wants to be heard . . . to be validated and to know that what they felt was legitimate." Missy, Winfrey insisted, needs to hear her mother's apology so that she can feel acknowledged. The psychologist backed down in the face of Winfrey's outburst, conceding, "I guess I heard it differently," and Winfrey replied that, of course, "we all hear differently." Having claimed that we all need to be heard, Winfrey turned around and said that we all hear differently—an assertion illustrated by the fact that the psychologist heard Debbie apologize while Winfrey heard her fail to apologize. The question arises: how can a victim find "validation" in being heard if everyone who listens to her hears something different?

The structure of the show reinforces Winfrey's point of view by rendering consensus difficult, if not impossible, to achieve. The program tries to satisfy a wronged woman's need to be heard by giving her an opportunity to tell her story. But these accounts are invariably followed by a competing narrative: the supposed wrongdoer—boyfriend, daughter, doctor—gets a chance to tell his or her side of the story, one that inevitably contradicts the victim's narrative. *The Oprah Winfrey Show* constructs a viewing audience that, while eager to hear stories of female victimization, is ultimately unable to credit them. While imitating a courtroom setting in which a jury listens to the testimony of a variety of witnesses in an effort to discern the truth, the program ultimately exalts personal experience as the only measure of veracity, thus obviating consensus. The show publicizes female pain while qualifying the generalizations or conclusions we can make on the basis of these revelations.

Not only do the stories on a given day fail to add up, but it is also impossible to see the show, day to day, year to year, as a coherent object. The show differs dramatically from one day to the next. A show on the sexual abuse of infants might be followed by an hour-long interview with actress Julia Roberts and then by a show on doing kind things for strangers. To argue, as I have, that *The Oprah Winfrey Show* takes up important issues is to watch only on certain days. The program has also undergone radical transformations over time. For instance, the format I have just described is less and less characteristic of today's show. In recent months, as other talk shows have become increasingly confrontational, Winfrey has made the decision to move away from sensational topics. During the first week of the 1995 season, Winfrey aired shows on people who were disappointed over the holidays, people who have found ways to get things for free, the twenty-fifth anniversary of the soap opera *All My Children,* and mothers who are addicted to drugs and alcohol. This last show, reminiscent of *The Oprah Winfrey Show* of years past, is now something of an anomaly in the context of Winfrey's new format, which stresses uplift and play.[25] Indeed, any generalizations I make about the show should be taken with a grain of salt: through its celebration of irreconcilable narratives and the determined inconsistency of its own format, the program institutes incoherence and frustrates analysis. In a variety of ways, *The Oprah Winfrey Show* obstructs theory.

Making it difficult for audience members to listen, the program encourages them to speak. The diverse testimony offered, day in and day out, provides a model for speaking out. As the show progresses, speakers and narratives multiply wildly. While it might seem an imitation of the "talking cure," this proliferation of voices effectively dismantles therapeutic structures and assumptions. The show often begins with between one and four guests seated on stage. Winfrey summarizes their dilemma and then focuses on a single person, or a couple, soliciting her/their story in some detail. But as the show progresses, it becomes increasingly hard for Winfrey or her home audience to focus their attention. Throughout the hour, new guests appear. One has the impression that they have been sitting onstage the whole time and that the camera angle has simply widened, offering them to view. (In fact, additional chairs have been brought on stage during the commercial break.) We realize that there is always a heterogeneous group on the scene of communication, multiple speakers and listeners, infinite (minor) variations on every story. For seasoned viewers, this technique creates a distracting anticipation as we wonder, "what next?" As the show progresses, this building sense of narrative chaos is accentuated by more and more frequent commercial breaks. By the end of the hour commercials come so thick and fast that it is difficult to follow the train of conversation. The show then ends abruptly, cutting Winfrey, or one of her guests, off in mid-sentence.

The program also stages diversity of opinion and perspective visually. Winfrey stands amid her studio audience. As a result, when the camera turns, as it often does, to document her facial response, it captures, incidentally, the reaction of someone sitting behind her. Similarly, those sitting near someone in the audience who has stood to speak often offer pointed visual commentary— shaking their heads, rolling their eyes, moving their lips soundlessly. Again, we realize that each time someone speaks she invites someone else's comment or disagreement: every utterance calls forth an array of competing reactions. As the hour proceeds, Winfrey begins to solicit the participation of audience members. They respond with advice, criticism, or sympathy. Frequently, however, rather than commenting on what they have heard, audience members stand up to tell their own stories. The reactions of the studio audience, a central feature of the program's drama, and Winfrey's occasional testimonial, construct responsiveness not as listening, but as speaking.

Establishing a therapeutic dyad—an individual in need, speaking, and a sympathetic audience, listening—and then dismantling it in favor of the articulation of more and more irresolvable distress, the program suggests the irrelevance of therapeutic assumptions. In this context, the voice of the expert loses its authority. Midway through the show, Winfrey introduces an expert, often a psychologist, whom we expect to resolve the problem at hand. But the expert is treated much like any other speaker—she is interrupted, challenged, and frequently silenced. Rather than offering an analysis which generalizes on the basis of these disparate accounts, the expert voice, deprived of its authority, contributes yet another point of view. As it is not grounded in personal experience, expert testimony is particularly expendable.

The show consistently promotes therapeutic formulations, while short-circuiting therapeutic solutions. In an interview with Forrest Sawyer on the ABC newsmagazine *Day One* (originally aired January 5, 1995), Winfrey suggested that a therapeutic understanding of her show is, at best, peripheral. Pressing for a succinct formulation of the program's aims, Sawyer asked, "So this is about more than your fixing the places in you that feel broken?" Winfrey agreed, emphatically, that it was not about "that cliched therapy stuff." Instead, Sawyer offered that it was about "the struggle for our souls." Winfrey lit up. "You've got it, Forrest . . . it really is about the struggle for our very souls. You got it." In Winfrey's accounts of her own life and of the show, narratives of recovery compete with narratives of faith, divine will, and salvation as ways of figuring personal progress. The routine appeal to a higher power in twelve-step programs suggests pop psychology's debt to religion. Indeed, many participants understand twelve-step programs as, first and foremost, part of a spiritual quest. Whether one understands the audience for religious speech as God or as one's local religious community, speaking in a religious context is an act of devotion in which content, often prescribed, is less important than the act of speaking itself. Rejecting a therapeutic interpretation of the show in favor of a religious one, Winfrey suggests that the transformations that occur on the show are swift and radical: her guests may be converted by simply appearing, and speaking, before the community.

In light of the program's rejection of therapeutic solutions, Winfrey's public revelations take on a slightly different cast. On one hand, her confessions make it clear that she has not always been a rich, influential celebrity. Charting the distance between her past and her present, these confessions suggest Winfrey's tremendous powers of self-transformation. On the other, to the extent that her public confessions involve ongoing uncertainty—Winfrey's weight continues to fluctuate and it is unclear whether or not she and Graham will ever marry—her biographical narrative reads much differently. Winfrey's revelations, and the media's preoccupation with them, depict her life as an ongoing struggle with men and with her body, a struggle that has its narrative origins in the abuse she suffered as a child but has no narrative resolution. Despite her wealth and fame, Winfrey's life is depicted as forever poised at a moment of transition. Only in the context of Winfrey's repeated trials, triumphs, and upsets could *TV Guide* announce 1994, almost ten years into her career as a national icon, as the year that "Oprah grows up."[26] An element of suspense nourishes the curiosity of *Oprah* fans; subject to reversals and breakthroughs, Winfrey's personal life remains of interest.

Winfrey demonstrated her unwillingness to offer a conclusive account of her life when, in June 1993, she canceled the publication of her autobiography only months before its scheduled and much anticipated release. Winfrey's decision draws our attention to an important difference between spoken and written accounts of experience: talking about her life, Winfrey leaves room for additions, retractions, and clarifications that are themselves a source of ongoing interest; a written text would establish Winfrey's life as something, to date, complete, thus putting speculation to rest. Announcing her decision to delay publication indefinitely, Winfrey describes her experience as open-ended, explaining, "I am in the heart of the learning curve. . . . I feel there are important discoveries yet to be made."[27]

While foregrounding women talking about their problems, *The Oprah Winfrey Show* rejects both a therapeutic commitment to a talking cure that refers female speech to the process of recovery and the more radical account of female testimony as consciousness-raising in which the revelation of personal experience founds a community with common grievances and aims. Consciousness-raising groups, interested in alleviating oppression, tried to strike a delicate balance between speaking and reception in order to produce working generalizations. But *The Oprah Winfrey Show* has no way of generating analysis; the program cannot fulfill a model of personal testimony which accrues, culminating in politically useful generalizations. If we are willing to accept a feminist construction of the progressive alliance of experience and theory, the trouble with talk shows is that their presentation of women's problems makes analysis impossible.

Nor does *The Oprah Winfrey Show* fulfill a model of personal development, or recovery, that underwrites the therapeutic tradition. Unlike psychotherapy or self-help, the television talk show has little interest in transformation of any

sort. Rather than walking the troubled individual through the process of confession, toward self-discovery and a cure, talk shows stage the proliferation of
irreconcilable and inconclusive accounts of traumatic experience. Rather than
engaging a complex problem and tailoring it toward a generic solution, talk
shows take a relatively simple situation and complicate it by introducing its
many, seemingly infinite, variants. As audience members are cast as actual or
potential speakers, as experts are reduced to audience status and narratives
multiply, it becomes increasingly difficult to narrate individual or social
progress.

Media critics who have analyzed the television talk show celebrate it for
disrupting the conventions of public speech. Two fascinating essays argue that
television talk shows, by collapsing familiar oppositions between speaker and
audience, victim and expert, private and public, use the female voice to decon-
struct the hierarchies that typically order public discourse. Paolo Carpignano,
Robin Andersen, Stanley Aronowitz, and William DiFazio, the authors of
"Chatter in the Age of Electronic Reproduction" (1993), argue that by conflating performance and audience, the talk show constructs a mass audience distinguished not by mindless vulnerability but by expressive agency. Reacting to
scholarship that blames the mass media for undermining rational public
debate, they argue that this critique of media culture assumes a strict schism
between viewer and spectacle, consumption and production. This split defines
the public, both as media viewers and as political participants, as an "undiffer-
entiated mass" of essentially passive "recipients of political messages."[28] Talk
shows, they argue, suggest the inadequacy of this model. Because they feature
the media public, in the form of the studio audience, as a protagonist, television talk shows redefine watching as a form of participation and thus call into
question a distinction between performing and viewing, producing and consuming. The talk show literalizes the presence of an active viewing public
whose reactions are indispensable to the construction of media events.

In her essay on *The Oprah Winfrey Show,* Gloria-Jean Masciarotte also argues
that the audience's participation complicates the dichotomies that typically
structure public discourse. Because the talk show asks each listener to speak in
turn, the "talk show's storytelling results in a series of I's and not an exchange
between I/You." Rather than designating a representative speaker or offering a
definitive narrative, the program stages the proliferation of subjectivities. This
multiplicity, in turn, denies the subject depth or, as we understand it, individuality. Because there are so many voices speaking, the individual subject is
denied psychological specificity. *The Oprah Winfrey Show* creates a scene of democratic participation in which identity, or representation, plays no part. In Masciarotte's view, "talk," rather than expressing or defining individuality, disman-

tles it: "the individual hailed or fixed by the television talk show format is disseminated, collated, fragmented, even simulated and represented as it recognizes itself in the mass/public act of telling its own story."[29]

Stressing the conflictual, multiplicitous, static nature of the talk show,
both essays describe how the form derails conventional models of talk that rely
on a coherent (if traumatized) subject and the problem of that subject's integration into collective life. Distinctions between speaker and audience, individual and mass, production and consumption, are indispensable to the public
sphere conceived as the scene of either individual distinction or rational consensus. These critics welcome the talk show's revision of public debate as multiple, biased, and open-ended. And they identify much of what is potentially
progressive about the talk show: an expanded sense of what is worth talking
about; the possibility of airing conflict and difference in a public setting; the
visibility of the audience, its undeniable participation in the public scene.[30]

While I find these characterizations of talk shows accurate and illuminating, I am disquieted by a tendency to conflate these "new discursive practices"
with the women who use them. Carpignano et al. assert that "women's struggles have redefined the relationship between the public and the private. The
result of the politicization of the private is a transformation in the nature of the
political." They proceed to describe this transformed "political" as relying "more
on the circulation of discursive practices than on formal political agendas."[31]
Strict divisions between audience and performance, consumption and production, private and public are transformed into a discourse characterized not by
rational debate, aimed at resolution, that characterizes "formal politics," but by
"circulation." This account runs the risk of essentialism: in a variety of contexts,
most notably French feminism, "circulation," taken to figure female physicality, is projected as a characteristic of female speech. Using the concept of circulation to describe the relationship between women and public discourse, these
authors avoid accounting for a speaker's agency or purpose. It is as if once
women voice their personal concerns in public, the public sphere, as represented by the talk show, begins to take on "feminine" and, implicitly, progressive characteristics.

While these critics are correct to draw our attention to the way the female
voice is used to collapse the distinction between public and private, and while
I am drawn to the utopian possibilities of this conflation, a brief look at the dissemination of the female complaint into the culture at large suggests a more
sobering account of the cultural influence of the television talk show. From
television newsmagazines (*Dateline, 20/20, Day One*), which feature the complaints of disgruntled consumers and violated citizens, to talk radio, a forum in
which similar complaints have garnered terrific electoral clout, to the town hall
meetings of the 1992 presidential campaign in which Bill Clinton's congenial

manner shone to advantage, talk has become an increasingly important feature of our cultural and political landscape.[32] How are we to understand the increasing popularity and visibility of talk as a medium which bridges popular and political culture?

Anita Hill's testimony before the Senate Judiciary Committee allows us to consider this question. While I would hesitate to assert that we watched the Senate confirmation hearings as if we were watching *The Oprah Winfrey Show*, Hill's public testimony brought the confession of sexual victimization, a convention of female speech most energetically popularized by the talk show in recent years, into an explicitly political forum. Rather than treating Hill's testimony as an occasion for the adjudication of public policy (specifically, Clarence Thomas's appointment to the Supreme Court, more broadly, the handling of sexual harassment complaints), media coverage construed it as an instance of national humiliation. Hill's victimization, ostensibly the object of inquiry, curiously provided a model for Thomas's victimization and for the victimization of the viewing public.

Both Hill and Thomas were described as reluctant witnesses mistreated by an amorphous "process." Consistently their similarities were emphasized and their differences minimized. One commentator went so far as to make the bizarre claim that "If Clarence Thomas had been a woman he might have been Anita Hill."[33] The spectating nation was figured as similarly victimized: "transfixed by testimony that seeped into every conversation . . . the actual spectacle left the watcher feeling demeaned and terribly sad. . . . In the end, of course, there would be no winners, only scars."[34] Construed as a form of victimization, public debate was pathologized. Asserting that public hearings are no way to "conduct our national soul-searching," *Newsweek* concluded that "Politics has become a pathology."[35] Columnist Russell Baker wrote, "Washington is having a nervous breakdown." He continued, "The hysteria about the Thomas nomination is not the cause of it, just the final bursting of the dam when all restraints collapse and howling replaces civil discourse."[36]

Pathology, nervous breakdown, hysteria—these are terms that have long been associated with the discontent of middle-class women. The juxtaposition of "howling" and "civil discourse" evokes a distinction between emotional speech, the product of inarticulate pain, and rational speech, the source of social order. But even as Baker seems to be protesting the breakdown of the public/private divide, he is, at least rhetorically, enacting it. There is no reason not to understand Anita Hill's disclosures as the substance of and occasion for "civil discourse." Instead, the concept of psychological malaise, typically the vehicle for the victimized woman's public complaint, is extended to absorb and virtually nullify both Hill's disclosure and the ensuing public discussion. Heralding the public disclosure of sexual information as indicative of the collapse of public and private, and casting this collapse in lurid, psychological terms, the media pathologized public debate, figuring the nation itself as a troubled subject.[37]

The public confession of private pain, a form which historically has marked the difference between public and private and commented on the effect of that difference on women, increasingly dominates public speech. Psychological discourses take the victim as their site of inquiry, asking after the effects of traumatic experience on the individual. Likewise, discourses of liberation take the victim of oppression as their subject. In both contexts, suffering is a problem which must be solved. *The Oprah Winfrey Show,* I have suggested, is less interested in analyzing and resolving pain, using either political or psychological tools, than it is in reproducing it. Similarly, public expressions of suffering and misfortune are increasingly generalized as the means by which one participates in public debate and claims citizenship. The media's metaphorization of the public-as-victim concurs with the dissemination of the citizen's complaint as a vehicle for political culture. Even as public policies seeking to redress victimization are increasingly under attack, the language of victimization proliferates. The National Rifle Association, for example, constructs its gun-toting clients as potential victims who need to defend their homes and families, and the militia movement has gone some distance toward defining victimization by the federal government as the standard for patriotism. This trend, however, seems to have no positive bearing on the complaints that women most frequently bring to *The Oprah Winfrey Show.*

To the extent that the disclosure of traumatic female experience provides a model for talk show speech, these programs participate in a tradition that has taken the public expression of private trauma as the means by which women enter the public sphere. While foregrounding the public expression of female experience, the television talk show significantly revises this tradition. Whether the emphasis is on selfhood, as in the recovery movement, or on collectivity, as in consciousness-raising, a distinction between private and public works, in both instances, to maintain the possibility of movement between the two; this division invites the transformation of the individual and her society.[38] This distinction also creates a public that, although silent, is far from inactive, an audience that is responsible for reacting to female testimony.

Rather than figuring the relationship between private and public, between individuality and collectivity, talk show testimony conflates private experience and public debate. I would maintain that as long as women are, in practice, oppressed, the language of "public" and "private," which provides for the articulation of marginalization, is useful, if not indispensable. The television talk show, effectively dismantling this distinction, threatens to obscure the fact that, while everyone may be talking the way women usually do, no one is necessarily listening. Cast as representative speakers, women do not necessarily effect change or gain power.

The split between private and public organizes the way we conceptualize oppression—as exclusion, dependence, marginalization—as well as its articulation and transformation. This division gives women, specifically, a structure for thinking and talking about what they might do in public, how they might influence and alter collective life. "The personal is political" represents a watershed in how we think about the suffering of women, not because it equates the personal and the political but because it calls attention to, and in time institutionalizes, the public/private split as an idea that organizes both the oppression of women and their activism. In reaction to this utopian claim, we begin to debate the political meaning of women's experiences and their public revelation. When public and private are conflated, however, women can only *be* in public, or be *the* public: on *The Oprah Winfrey Show*, and, more broadly, in today's tremendously popular mass forums for talk, female subjectivity, as it is expressed by the confession of traumatic private experience, is generalized. The injured woman becomes the representative speaker, while women, deprived of a listening audience, find their ability to influence public life radically curtailed.

Notes

My deepest thanks to Carolyn Porter for her encouragement, Joel Pfister and Nancy Schnog for their attentive and rigorous editing, Laura King, Barbara Leckie, and Steven Meyer for their willingness to talk, and listen.

1. Critics have used the terms *confession* and *testimony* to refer to the practice of speaking about traumatic experience in public and semi-public settings. For example, Michel Foucault uses *confession*, emphasizing the influence of religious practice on medicine and jurisprudence, while Shoshana Felman and Dori Laub use the term *testimony* in order to emphasize the process of bearing witness. Quite simply, I take *confession* to foreground the intimate content of speech and the potential for individual redemption or conversion, whereas *testimony* implies a public capable of judging speech and of being transformed by it. Evoking the strictures of a juridical setting, testimony also suggests the conventions that govern public address. I have used both terms throughout, as it is precisely the question of how we regard the public speech of women—as testimony or as confession—that is at stake here. Foucault, *The History of Sexuality*, vol. I, *An Introduction* (New York: Vintage, 1978), 58–73. Shoshana Felman and Dori Laub, M.D., *Testimony: Crises of Witnessing in Literature, Psychoanalysis, and History* (New York: Routledge, 1992).

2. Winfrey first surprised viewers and distinguished herself from other talk show hosts in 1985, when, responding to a woman who was speaking about sexual abuse, she confessed, "The same thing happened to me." Winfrey, like her audience, was surprised by this revelation; she later remarked, "I hadn't planned to say it. It just came out." Nellie Bly, *Oprah! Up Close and Down Home* (New York: Zebra, 1993), 53.

3. The recent boom in talk about women's problems participates in a long-standing

tradition of women appearing in public by virtue of their painful, private experience. The distinction between public and private has organized the oppression of middle-class women since the early nineteenth century. The valorization of privacy has never meant, however, that women were not heard in public. To the contrary, the disclosure of female suffering—the subject of sentimental, reformist, and psychiatric discourses, among others—has been vital to any number of public debates. The separation of spheres has determined scandal as the appropriate occasion for female speech, and, by extension, for public debates over the status of women.

4. In this chapter I do not take up the important question: how do class and race influence the formulations "women in pain" and "women talking"? While critics have generally understood the psychologized subject that I discuss here as white and middle-class, it is not yet clear to me how the current phase in the dissemination and commodification of therapeutic precepts and practices qualifies this profile. While self-help readership, for example, is largely white and middle-class, the talk show draws a more diverse audience. For a discussion of the revelation of female pain in the context of anti-slavery discourse see Franny Nudelman, "Harriet Jacobs and the Sentimental Politics of Female Suffering," *English Literary History* 59 (1992): 939–64; on *The Oprah Winfrey Show*'s treatment of race see Janice Peck, "Talk About Racism: Framing a Popular Discourse of Race on *Oprah Winfrey*," *Cultural Critique* 27 (Spring 1994): 89–126; on the politics of race and class on newer, increasingly popular talk shows see Jill Nelson, "Talk Is Cheap," *Nation* (June 5, 1995): 800–02.

5. Foucault has asked us to scrutinize the assumption that speech is liberatory. Refuting the truism that talk about sex has been repressed, he challenges the corresponding claim that such talk is emancipating. Instead, he argues that talk about sex has proliferated over the past two centuries, fueling the development, codification, and policing of a plethora of sexual identities and behaviors. "The obligation to confess," far from being a "truth, lodged in our most secret nature, [that] 'demands' only to surface," is a form of speech "incited" by a society eager to construe and organize it (*History of Sexuality,* 60).

6. For important discussions of this problem see Ann Cvetkovich, *Mixed Feelings: Feminism, Mass Culture, and Victorian Sensationalism* (New Brunswick, N.J.: Rutgers University Press, 1992), and Linda Alcoff and Laura Gray, "Survivor Discourse: Transgression or Recuperation?" *Signs: A Journal of Women in Culture and Society* 18 (Winter 1993): 260–90.

7. Mike Littwin, *Baltimore Sun,* January 16, 1995, 1D.

8. Kaminer, *I'm Dysfunctional, You're Dysfunctional: The Recovery Movement and Other Self-Help Fashions* (Reading, Mass.: Addison-Wesley, 1992), 29–43.

9. Sarachild, "Consciousness-Raising: A Radical Weapon," in *Feminist Revolution,* ed. Redstockings (New York: Random House, 1975), 146–47.

10. Herman, *The Romance of American Psychology: Political Culture in the Age of Experts* (Berkeley: University of California Press, 1995), 280, 286–87.

11. In their essay on survivor discourse, Linda Alcoff and Laura Gray argue that if women are to determine the social and political consequences of their public speech, they must seize the role of interpreter and analyze their own experience. If women have been consistently "constructed as 'naive transmitters of raw experience,'" thus reproducing coarse distinctions between experience and theory, affect and knowledge, they must now "transform arrangements of speaking to create spaces where survivors are

authorized to be both witnesses and experts, both reporters of experience and theorists of experience" ("Survivor Discourse," 280, 282).

12. Alice Echols, *Daring To Be Bad: Radical Feminism in America, 1967–1975* (Minneapolis: University of Minnesota Press, 1989), 88.

13. Morgan, "Introduction: The Women's Revolution," in *Sisterhood Is Powerful,* ed. Robin Morgan (New York: Random House, 1970), xvii.

14. Forer, "Thoughts on Consciousness-Raising," in *Feminist Revolution,* 151.

15. Sarachild, "Consciousness-Raising," 148.

16. Robin Morgan recalls efforts in consciousness-raising groups to organize speaking and listening to a productive end. As feminist groups were prompted in part by the discrimination women encountered when attempting to organize with men, many women were dismayed to find their own organizations reproducing hierarchies of race and class. When the Feminists, a New York-based group, found that women with more education were doing more of the talking in their group, they improvised the Disc System in an attempt to remedy this discrepancy. Each woman received an allotment of discs, and each time she spoke she spent one disc. Morgan remembers that the "first time this system was tried, the apocryphal story goes, no one in the room had any discs left after fifteen minutes." The next meeting was "slow almost to silence because everyone was hoarding her discs." With time, however, "the device worked its way into everyone's consciousness as a symbol for the need to listen to each other, and not interrupt or monopolize the conversation" (*Sisterhood Is Powerful,* xxvii).

17. I use the term *recovery discourse* to refer to self-help programs, twelve-step programs, and survivor discourse. I take these practices to be a subset of the larger "therapeutic culture." Recovery discourse is of particular interest here because it encourages the recovering individual's engagement with a public through the consumption of mass-produced manuals and through the public and semi-public settings—such as speak-outs and twelve-step meetings—in which she talks to others about her problems.

18. Perhaps the most significant difference between feminism and self-help is that while feminism encourages female agency, self-help programs tend to counsel submission and resignation. In her discussion of pop psychology, Susan Faludi stresses the degree to which the self-help movement encourages women to surrender their will in order to make peace with difficult situations. See Faludi, *Backlash: The Undeclared War Against American Women* (New York: Anchor, 1991), 335–62.

19. Norwood, *Women Who Love Too Much: When You Keep Wishing and Hoping He'll Change* (New York: Pocket Books, 1985).

20. According to Faludi, some of the case studies in *Women Who Love Too Much* are fabricated: many of the patients are fictionalized representations of Norwood's own experience. While seeming to extrapolate a common model from diverse experiences, Norwood may have projected her own experience, under the guise of different voices, as the basis for her therapeutic model (*Backlash,* 355).

21. The book's popularity gave rise to Women Who Love Too Much support groups. On the face of it, these groups, in which each woman has an opportunity to tell the story of her abusive relationship, resemble consciousness-raising groups. But in such support groups no one is allowed to interrupt or comment on another woman's story. Similarly, no "cross talk" is permitted in twelve-step meetings. Conversation, central to the collaborative process of developing theory in consciousness-raising groups, is forbidden in

self-help settings, which proceed from generic models rather than working to formulate them.

22. Simonds, *Women and Self-Help Culture: Reading Between the Lines* (New Brunswick, N.J.: Rutgers University Press, 1992), 85, 81.

23. While Winfrey's public disclosure of sexual abuse suggests a racialized history of the black female body's real and represented subjection, it also suggests a tradition of taking the abuse of black women as an occasion for discussing the victimization of women generally. Just as the generalization of the model of woman-as-victim by media culture obscures the oppression of women as a class, the effort to present Winfrey as "everywoman" obscures the racial history that underwrites her public meanings.

24. The show has literalized the rhetoric of confession by staging Winfrey's entrance onto the public scene at the beginning of each day's program. *The Oprah Winfrey Show* now begins with the camera following Winfrey, from behind, as she walks on stage to meet her audience. Beginning backstage, with a private moment, and rehearsing, daily, Winfrey's entrance onto the public stage, the program performs the transition from privacy to publicity and, implicitly, Winfrey's own passage from obscurity to superstardom. Once onstage, Winfrey spends a few moments chatting with the audience before she announces the beginning of the day's "real" show. Again, this introduction constructs the difference between Winfrey onstage and off, between Winfrey the person and Oprah the celebrity, while also implying a certain continuity between the two.

25. See two articles by John Kiesewetter, "Sticking with Oprah," *Cincinnati Enquirer,* Oct. 20, 1994, C1, C5, and "Oprah Executive Pleased with Reaction to Positive Topics," *Cincinnati Enquirer,* Oct. 21, 1994, D5. These articles are distributed by Harpo Productions as part of their effort to promote the new *Oprah Winfrey Show.*

26. Gretchen Reynolds, "A Year to Remember: Oprah Grows Up," *TV Guide,* Jan. 7–13, 1995, 14–20.

27. Bly, *Oprah!* 350.

28. Carpignano, Andersen, Aronowitz, and DiFazio, "Chatter in the Age of Electronic Reproduction: Talk Television and the 'Public Mind,'" in *The Phantom Public Sphere,* ed. Bruce Robbins (Minneapolis: University of Minnesota Press, 1993), 95.

29. Masciarotte, "C'Mon Girl: Oprah Winfrey and the Discourse of Feminine Talk," *Genders* 11 (Fall 1991): 86, 82.

30. In his book-length study of the talk show, Wayne Munson also emphasizes its "inclusive, contingent, postmodern logic." And yet he is cautious in his assessment of these qualities. He asks, "Has the medium loosely known as the talkshow become another source of harmful effects for a degraded 'public life.' . . . Or is it a harbinger of a new, revitalized public and political life in which the citizenry is finally heard through interactivity?" Refusing to valorize or vilify talk, Munson offers a rich analysis of talk formats as well as a detailed account of their evolution over the course of the twentieth century. See *All Talk: The Talkshow in Media Culture* (Philadelphia: Temple University Press, 1993), 5, 3.

31. Carpignano et al., "Chatter," 116.

32. To pursue this line of argument one would have to consider the influence of the Internet, where conversation, occasional and unsupervised, flourishes. How is this technology changing the way we consume talk in forums that are more rigidly structured?

33. Richard Lacayo, "A Question of Character," *Time,* Oct. 21, 1991, 44.

34. Nancy Gibbs, "An Ugly Circus," *Time*, Oct. 21, 1991, 35.

35. "Anatomy of a Debacle," *Newsweek*, Oct. 21, 1991, 32.

36. Russell Baker, "Potomac Breakdown," *New York Times*, Oct. 12, 1991, A19.

37. On October 13, 1992, one year after the Senate confirmation hearings, the PBS documentary series *Frontline* aired a program entitled "Clarence Thomas and Anita Hill: Public Hearing, Private Pain" that examined the reaction of the African American community to the confirmation hearings. While writer and narrator Ofra Bikel emphasized the distress of the African American community, she concluded the program by observing that every group that watched the hearings felt, for different reasons, victimized and indignant: "The hearings, someone said, were like an inkblot test, you looked at it and saw your own fears and frustrations reflected back at you. White women saw an abused woman. Men saw a beleaguered man. Liberals saw conservatives run amok, while conservatives saw a liberal plot. And the black community saw themselves used by a smug and insensitive white society, oblivious to their feelings and their traumatic memories."

The inkblot test invites the psychological subject to see herself in the mark of ink on paper, a mark which itself has no representational content. Bikel's comparison suggests that, like the inkblot test, this public event can accommodate a variety of diverse and contradictory grievances. When Bikel chooses this image, with its connotation of individuated psychological perceptions, to figure an emphatically public event, we see just how capacious the notion of private pain has become: Anita Hill's and Clarence Thomas's testimony means what we hear in it, and we all, as Winfrey has noted, hear something different.

38. When bell hooks considers the fate of consciousness-raising, she criticizes "the personal is political" for positing identity as an end in itself. Describing politics as a process of becoming, hooks claims that, if "the personal and the political are one and the same, then there is no politicization, no way to become the radical feminist subject." Equating the personal and the political fosters complacency, whereas distinguishing between them (while placing them on the same continuum) encourages the individual's transformation, her movement beyond personal concerns, and the consequent transformation of the community. While I think hooks misconstrues the aspirations of consciousness-raising, she powerfully articulates how the public/private distinction can be used to structure an individual's politicization. See "feminist politicization: a comment," in hooks's *Talking Back: Thinking feminist, thinking black* (Boston: South End Press, 1989), 106.

Index